# THE BOBBIO MISSAL

*Liturgy and Religious Culture in Merovingian Gaul*

The Bobbio Missal is one of the most intriguing manuscripts to have been produced in Merovingian Francia. It was copied in south-eastern Gaul around the end of the seventh and beginning of the eighth century and it contains a unique combination of a lectionary and a sacramentary, to which a plethora of canonical and non-canonical material was added. The Missal is therefore highly regarded by liturgists; but, additionally, medieval historians welcome the information to be derived from material attached to the codex which provides valuable data about the role and education of priests in Francia at that time, and indeed on their cultural and ideological background. The breadth of specialist knowledge provided by the team of scholars writing for this book enables the manuscript to be viewed as a whole, and not as a narrow liturgical study. Collectively, the essays view the manuscript as physical object: they discuss the contents, they examine the language, and they look at the cultural context in which the codex was written. The entire volume is a major re-evaluation of the Bobbio Missal, its content and purpose.

YITZHAK HEN teaches Medieval History at Ben-Gurion University of the Negev. His recent publications include *Culture and Religion in Merovingian Gaul* (1995); *The Sacramentary of Echternach* (1997); *The Uses of the Past in the Early Middle Ages*, co-edited with Matthew Innes (2000); and *The Royal Patronage of Liturgy in Frankish Gaul* (2001). He is the General Editor of the series Cultural Encounters in Late Antiquity and the Middle Ages.

ROB MEENS teaches Medieval History at the University of Utrecht. He is leading the research project 'Building a Christian society. Penitentials of the tenth and eleventh centuries: Text and Context'. His recent publications include *Het tripartite boeteboek. Overlevering en betekenis van vroegmiddeleeuwse biechtvoorschriften* (1994). He is also the editor of the journal *Millennium*.

## Cambridge Studies in Palaeography and Codicology

FOUNDING EDITORS

Albinia de la Mare
Rosamond McKitterick *Newnham College, University of Cambridge*

GENERAL EDITORS

David Ganz *King's College London*
Teresa Webber *Trinity College, University of Cambridge*

This series has been established to further the study of manuscripts from the Middle
Ages to the Renaissance. It includes books devoted to particular types of manuscripts,
their production and circulation, to individual codices of outstanding importance, and to
regions, periods, and scripts of especial interest to scholars. The series will be of interest not
only to scholars and students of medieval literature and history, but also to theologians,
art historians, and others working with manuscript sources.

ALREADY PUBLISHED

Bernhard Bischoff, translated by Michael Gorman *Manuscripts and Libraries
in the Age of Charlemagne*

Richard Gameson *The Early Medieval Bible: Its Production, Decoration and Use*

Nancy Netzer *Cultural Interplay in the Eighth Century: The Trier Gospels
and the Making of a Scriptorium at Echternach*

William Noel *The Harley Psalter*

Charles F. Briggs *Giles of Rome's* De regimine principum: *Reading and Writing
Politics at Court and University, c. 1275–c. 1525*

Leslie Brubaker *Vision and Meaning in Ninth-Century Byzantium: Image as Exegesis
in the Homilies of Gregory of Nazianzus*

Francis Newton *The Scriptorium and Library at Monte Cassino, 1058–1105*

Lisa Fagin Davis *The Gottschalk Antiphonary: Music and Liturgy
in Twelfth-Century Lambach*

Albert Derolez *The Palaeography of Gothic Manuscript Books: From the Twelfth
to the Early Sixteenth Century*

Alison I. Beach *Women as Scribes: Book Production and Monastic Reform in
Twelfth-Century Bavaria*

# THE BOBBIO MISSAL

*Liturgy and Religious Culture in Merovingian Gaul*

Edited by
YITZHAK HEN AND ROB MEENS

CAMBRIDGE
UNIVERSITY PRESS

CAMBRIDGE UNIVERSITY PRESS
Cambridge, New York, Melbourne, Madrid, Cape Town, Singapore,
São Paulo, Delhi, Dubai, Tokyo

Cambridge University Press
The Edinburgh Building, Cambridge CB2 8RU, UK

Published in the United States of America by Cambridge University Press, New York

www.cambridge.org
Information on this title: www.cambridge.org/9780521126915

First published 2004
This digitally printed version 2009

*A catalogue record for this publication is available from the British Library*

*Library of Congress Cataloguing in Publication data*
The Bobbio missal: liturgy and religious culture in Merovingian Gaul / edited by Yitzhak
Hen and Rob Meens.
p.    cm. – (Cambridge studies in palaeography and codicology; 11)
Includes bibliographical references and index.
ISBN 0 521 82393 5
1. Bobbio Missal – Congresses.   2. Missals – Gaul – Congresses.
3. Catholic Church – Liturgy – Texts – History and criticism – Congresses.   4. Bibliothèque nationale
de France. Département des manuscrits – Congresses.
I. Hen, Yitzhak.   II. Meens, Rob.   III. Series.
BX2037.A3G333   2003
264′.01403 – dc21   2003055170

ISBN 978-0-521-82393-7 Hardback
ISBN 978-0-521-12691-5 Paperback

# Contents

# Contents

# *Illustrations*

# Contributors

LOUISE P.M. BATSTONE  Magdalene College, Cambridge

DAVID GANZ  Department of Classics, King's College, University of London

MARY GARRISON  Department of History and Centre for Medieval Studies, University of York

YITZHAK HEN  Department of General History, Ben-Gurion University of the Negev

ROSAMOND McKITTERICK  Faculty of History, University of Cambridge, and Fellow of Newnham College, Cambridge

ROB MEENS  Department of History, University of Utrecht

MARCO MOSTERT  Department of History, University of Utrecht

ELS ROSE  Research Institute for History and Culture, University of Utrecht

IAN N. WOOD  Department of History, University of Leeds

CHARLES D. WRIGHT  Department of English, University of Illinois

ROGER WRIGHT  Department of Hispanic Studies, University of Liverpool

# *Acknowledgements*

The Bobbio Missal is one of the most intriguing liturgical manuscripts that were produced in Merovingian Francia. It is here argued that it was copied in south-eastern Gaul and it contains a unique combination of a lectionary and a sacramentary, to which a plethora of canonical and non-canonical material was added. Notwithstanding its richness and significance, no major study of the Bobbio Missal has been published since 1924, and scholars who used it throughout the twentieth century simply picked up from previous discussions whatever they deemed appropriate. On 28 April 2001 a group of scholars from various disciplines and universities gathered together in Utrecht for a one-day workshop on the Bobbio Missal. The present volume is essentially the revised and expanded version of the papers presented at the Utrecht gathering, to which three more papers have been added (by Ganz, Mostert and Wright and Wright), in order to cover issues which were raised (but not discussed) in the Utrecht workshop.

This volume could not have been published without the help and advice of many friends and colleagues. We would first like to extend our deep gratitude to the contributors for their cooperation and forbearance, and to those who participated in the discussions at the Utrecht gathering. Special thanks should go to Mayke de Jong, who took a special interest in the progress of this enterprise, and provided much encouragement and support. She also chaired the sessions held at Utrecht, and contributed immensely to the success of our workshop. We are equally indebted to the Research Institute for History and Culture of the University of Utrecht and the Netherlands Organisation for Scientific Research (NWO) for their generous financial support, and to Irene van Renswoude who masterfully helped us in organising things. Finally, we should like to thank Tessa Webber, William Davies, Caroline Bundy and the staff of the Cambridge University Press for their interest in this book and for seeing it through the press.

# Abbreviations

| | |
|---|---|
| AASS | Acta Sanctorum (Antwerp and Brussels, 1643–) |
| BAR | British Archaeological Reports |
| BAV | Biblioteca Apostolica Vaticana |
| BM | Bibliothèque Municipale |
| BNF | Bibliothèque Nationale de France |
| *Bobbio* | *The Bobbio Missal: A Gallican Mass-Book*, ed. E.A. Lowe, HBS 58 (London, 1920) |
| CCSL | Corpus Christianorum, Series Latina (Turnhout, 1952–) |
| *CLA* | *Codices Latini Antiquiores. A Palaeographical Guide to Latin Manuscripts Prior to the Ninth Century*, 11 vols. with a supplement (Oxford, 1935–71; 2nd edn of vol. II, 1972) |
| *CLLA* | *Codices Liturgici Latini Antiquiores*, ed. K. Gamber, 2 vols., Spicilegii Friburgensis Subsidia 1 (2nd edn, Freiburg, 1968); supplemented by B. Baroffio *et al.*, Spicilegii Friburgensis subsidia 1A (Freiburg, 1988) |
| Clm | Codices latini monacenses |
| *DACL* | *Dictionnaire d'archéologie chrétienne et de liturgie*, ed. F. Cabrol and H. Leclercq, 15 vols. in 30 (Paris, 1907–53) |
| HBS | Henry Bradshaw Society Publications |
| Lowe, 'Notes' | E.A. Lowe, 'Notes on the parallel forms in early texts', in *The Bobbio Missal: Notes and Studies*, ed. A. Wilmart, E.A. Lowe and H.A. Wilson, HBS 61 (London, 1924), pp. 107–47 |
| Lowe, 'Palaeography' | E.A. Lowe, 'The palaeography of the Bobbio Missal', in *The Bobbio Missal: Notes and Studies*, ed. A. Wilmart, E.A. Lowe and H.A. Wilson, HBS 61 (London, 1924), pp. 59–106 (repr. in E.A. Lowe, |

|  |  |
|---|---|
|  | *Palaeographical Papers*, ed. L. Bieler, 2 vols. (Oxford, 1972), I, pp. 142–81) |
| MGH | Monumenta Germaniae Historica |
| AA | Auctores Antiquissimi, 15 vols. (Berlin, 1877–1919) |
| SRG | Scriptores rerum Germanicarum in usum scholarum (Hannover, 1871–) |
| SRM | Scriptores rerum Merovingicarum, 7 vols. (Hannover, 1884–1951) |
| PL | Patrologiae cursus completus, series latina, ed. J.-P. Migne, 221 vols. (Paris, 1841–64) |
| PLS | Patrologiae latinae supplementum, ed. A. Hamman, 4 vols. (Paris, 1957–71) |
| Settimane | Settimane di studio del Centro italiano di studi sull'alto medioevo (Spoleto, 1954–) |
| Wilmart, 'Notice' | A. Wilmart, 'Notice du Missel de Bobbio', in *The Bobbio Missal: Notes and Studies*, ed. A. Wilmart, E.A. Lowe and H.A. Wilson, HBS 61 (London, 1924), pp. 1–58 |
| Wilmart, 'Palimpseste' | A. Wilmart, 'Le palimpseste du missel de Bobbio', *Revue Bénédictine* 33 (1921), pp. 1–18 |

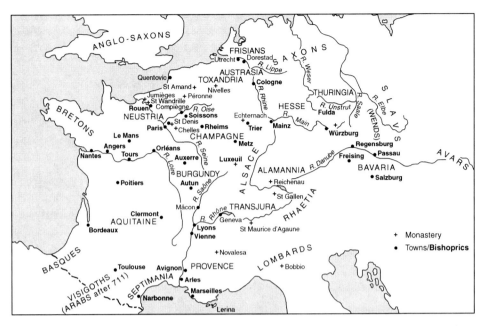

*Map 1*  Bobbio and other monasteries. After Paul Fouracre, *The Age of Charles Martel* (Harlow, 2000)

# I

## *Introduction: the Bobbio Missal – from Mabillon onwards*

In June 1686, on the way back from his manuscript-collecting campaign in Italy, the Benedictine monk Jean Mabillon visited the monastery of Bobbio.[1] This short visit (from 4 till 9 June 1686) was extremely fruitful. In the library of Bobbio, Mabillon found a unique treasure of old manuscripts, among them a small liturgical codex – commonly known nowadays as the Bobbio Missal. Mabillon immediately understood the importance of this codex, and he could hardly conceal his excitement in the initial report of his discovery.[2] A year later, an edition of the liturgical section of this manuscript was published by Mabillon under the title *Liber Sacramentorum Ecclesiae Gallicanae*.[3]

In his short introduction to the text,[4] Mabillon explained in eleven detailed points why he thought this liturgical codex was a *Sacramentarium Gallicanum* found in Bobbio, and not a sacramentary produced in Bobbio or used there. Mabillon constructed his argument with great care. First, he argued, the sacramentary found in this Bobbio manuscript represents the Gallican liturgy, known from other liturgical manuscripts of the early Middle Ages, such as the *Missale Gothicum*, the *Missale Gallicanum Vetus* and the Lectionary of Luxeuil.[5] He then proceeded

---

[1] On Mabillon's visit to Bobbio, see J. Mabillon, *Museum Italicum seu collectio veterum scriptorum ex bibliothecis Italicis* (Paris, 1687), I.1, pp. 218–19. See also, B. Barret-Kriegel, *Jean Mabillon, 1632–1707* (Paris, 1988), pp. 67–75.

[2] Mabillon, *Museum Italicum*, I.1, p. 219: 'Ex eadem bibliotheca mutuati sumus codicem Liturgiae Gallicanae optimae notae, literis maiusculis exaratum.'

[3] Ibid., I.2, pp. 278–397. This edition was reprinted in 1724. In 1748 L.A. Muratori published the same edition in his *Liturgia Romana Vetus*, II.3 (Venice, 1748), pp. 775–968, and in 1849 J.-P. Migne reprinted it in his PL 72, cols. 451–574. In 1858/67 G.H. Forbes reprinted a revised version of the Mabillon–Muratori edition in his *The Ancient Liturgies of the Gallican Church* (Bruntisland, 1855), pp. 205–368. However, neither Muratori nor Forbes had examined the manuscript itself. At the request of Mabillon, the codex was transferred from Bobbio to Saint-Germain-des-Prés, where it was given the shelf-mark 1488.

[4] Mabillon, *Museum Italicum*, I.2, pp. 273–7: 'Praefatio in sequens Sacramentarium Gallicanum'. Mabillon's introduction is reprinted in Appendix I, below, pp. 8–15.

[5] Ibid., I.2, pp. 273–4 and 277 (nos. I–III and XI respectively).

to eliminate other possibilities, arguing that this sacramentary is emphatically not Roman, Mozarabic, Ambrosian or African.[6] The diversity of liturgical practice in Merovingian Gaul, not only on the national, but also on the diocesan level, explains, according to Mabillon, the fact that his manuscript is not identical with the *Missale Gothicum* and the *Missale Gallicanum Vetus*.[7] Mabillon, then, reached the climax of his introduction, suggesting that this manuscript was produced in what he called *provincia Maxima Sequanorum*, that is, the diocese of Besançon, where the monastery of Luxeuil was located.[8] He even cautiously suggested that this codex might well have been brought to Bobbio by Columbanus and his disciples, but he also clearly pointed out that there is no indication of such a Columbanian connection in the manuscript itself.[9]

Mabillon's views were accepted by many of his immediate followers and later liturgists.[10] George Hay Forbes even named this sacramentary *Missale Vesontionense*, that is, 'The Missal of Besançon',[11] and Friedrich Wiegand called it *Burgundische Messbuch aus dem Kloster Bobbio*.[12] Yet, not all scholars agreed with Mabillon, and shortly after its first publication, the so-called Bobbio Missal was the subject of much heated debate.[13]

The *Nouveau traité de diplomatique*, published in 1757, although accepting Mabillon's argument, stressed the role of Columbanus in transferring the codex from Burgundy to Bobbio.[14] This was enough for Charles O'Conor to describe the script of the Bobbio Missal as Insular, and to argue that it represents the authentic rite of St Patrick and St Comgall of Bangor. He even called it *Missale Hibernicum Bobiense*,[15] and shortly afterwards John Lanigan referred to it as *Cursus Scotorum*.[16] The 'Irish' hypothesis fell on fertile ground and was adopted by scholars such as Ferdinand Probst,[17] Suitbert Bäumer[18] and Henry Marriot

---

[6] Ibid., I.2, pp. 274–5 (nos. IV–VI).     [7] Ibid., I.2, p. 275 (no. VII).

[8] Ibid., I.2, pp. 275–7 (nos. VIII–IX).     [9] Ibid., I.2, pp. 276–7 (no. IX).

[10] See, for example, A. Lesley, *Missale Mixtum* (London, 1755), pp. lxxvi–lxxxiv; P. Le Brun, *Explication de la messe*, III (Paris, 1777), p. 239; Wilmart, 'Notice', pp. 3–58 (a revised version of the entry published in *DACL* II.1 (Paris, 1907), cols. 939–62).

[11] See Forbes, *The Ancient Liturgies of the Gallican Church*, p. 205. This title was also accepted by F.E. Warren, *The Liturgy and Ritual of the Celtic Church* (Oxford, 1881), pp. 272–3 (reprinted with an introduction by J. Stevenson (Woodbridge, 1987)).

[12] F. Wiegand, *Die Stellung des apostolischen Symbols im kirchlichen Leben des Mittelalters*, I (Leipzig, 1899), pp. 147–8 n. 1 (from p. 145), § 5.

[13] For more details, see Wilmart, 'Notice', especially pp. 4–6, 35–58.

[14] *Nouveau traité de diplomatique*, III (Paris, 1757), pp. 210–11.

[15] C. O'Conor, *Rerum Hibernicarum scriptores veteres*, I (London, 1814), pp. cxxx–cxliii.

[16] J. Lanigan, *An Ecclesiastical History of Ireland from the First Introduction of Christianity to the Beginning of the Thirteenth Century*, 4 vols. (Dublin, 1829), IV, p. 371.

[17] F. Probst, *Die abendländische Messe von fünften bis zum achten Jahrhundert* (Münster, 1896), pp. 35–9 and 359–65.

[18] S. Bäumer, 'Das Stowe-Missale', *Zeitschrift für katholische Theologie* 16 (1892), pp. 446–90, at pp. 485–6.

Bannister,[19] all of whom attributed it to an Irish monk or an Irish missionary on the Continent. Even after it was clearly demonstrated by Ludwig Traube, Andrew Ewbank Burn and Frederick Edward Warren, the doyen of Irish liturgical studies, that Mabillon's *Sacramentarium Gallicanum* is independent of any Irish tradition,[20] the 'Irish' hypothesis did not die out. In 1918 the liturgist Edmund Bishop still argued that 'there can be no doubt that the missal is of Irish compilation, not improbably at Bobbio itself'.[21] In fact, it was Edmund Bishop who coined the name the Bobbio Missal, alluding to its supposedly Irish counterpart – the Stowe Missal – and thus canonising the Irish hypothesis.[22]

Other scholars, however, went astray in other directions. Based on the fact that Ambrose is mentioned in the *memento* of the *canon*, Louis Duchesne suggested, with some reservations, northern Italy as the place of production.[23] He noted that 'the Roman rite . . . is here combined with the Gallican in a peculiar fashion, quite different from that which obtains in the systems of combination which we find in the Frankish manuscripts of late Merovingian times. It is not exactly the Ambrosian liturgy, but it is somewhat analogous to it.'[24] Duchesne's suggestion was accepted by several scholars, among them Klaus Gamber,[25] but it was taken *ad absurdum* by the liturgist Paul Cagin. Cagin was in no doubt that the manuscript was produced in Bobbio itself. He dated its composition to 603–15, and he even argued that the compiler was Columbanus himself. Moreover, on account of the *Missa in honore sancti Michaeli* which mentions the dedication of a church to St Michael,[26] Cagin argued that this small codex was designed for use in a church dedicated to St Michael, which he identified with the small church of San Michelle della Spelunca del Curiasca in the vicinity of Bobbio.[27] Yet, Cagin, it seems, ignored the fact that this particular mass, part of which appears in the so-called *Sacramentarium Veronense*, was originally composed for the dedication of the church of St Michael

---

[19] H.M. Bannister, 'Some recently discovered fragments of Irish sacramentaries', *Journal of Theological Studies* 5 (1903/4), pp. 49–75, at pp. 53–4.

[20] See A.E. Burn and L. Traube, *Facsimiles of the Creeds from Early Manuscripts*, HBS 36 (London, 1909), pp. 44–7; Warren, *The Liturgy and Ritual of the Celtic Church*, pp. 272–3.

[21] E. Bishop, *Liturgica historica* (Oxford, 1918), p. 58 n. 3; see also pp. 90–2, 178–9.

[22] See E. Bishop, 'Liturgical note', in *The Prayer-Book of Aedeluald the Bishop, Commonly Called the Book of Cerne*, ed. A.B. Kuypers (Cambridge, 1902), pp. 234–83, at pp. 239–40, 244 and 247.

[23] L. Duchesne, *Origines du culte chrétien. Etude sur la liturgie avant Charlemagne* (5th edn, Paris, 1925), pp. 166–8.

[24] L. Duschesne, *Christian Worship: Its Origin and Evolution: A Study of the Latin Liturgy up to the Time of Charlemagne*, trans. from the 3rd French edn M.L. McClure (London, 1903), p. 159.

[25] See K. Gamber, *Sakramentartypen. Versuch einer Gruppierung der Handschriften und Fragmente bis zur Jahrtausendwende*, Texte und Arbeiten 49–50 (Beuron, 1958), pp. 39–40; CLLA 220, pp. 167–9.

[26] *Bobbio* 393–7, pp. 117–18.

[27] P. Cagin, *Avant-propos*, in *Paléographie musicale: les principaux manuscrits de chant grégorien, ambrosien, mozarabe, gallican*, V (Solesmes, 1896), pp. 96–184 and 195–8.

in the Via Salaria on the outskirts of Rome.[28] Cagin's argument was neatly refuted by Wilmart.[29]

In 1914 Germain Morin suggested the province of Septimania as the place of origin. Morin identified in the prayers of the Bobbio Missal several 'Spanish symptoms', which he could also trace in the Mozarabic liturgy. These 'symptoms', according to him, suggest that the compiler of the Bobbio Missal used Visigothic material, and thus Septimania was the most likely place for such an interaction.[30] Yet again, André Wilmart managed to demonstrate quite convincingly that Morin's argument was based on extremely shaky grounds, and, if accepted, both the *Missale Gothicum* and the masses of Mone should also be classified as Visigothic.[31]

Wilmart himself came up with a new suggestion – the province of Rhaetia. Given the fact that the Bobbio Missal is a complex codex, whose script cannot be located precisely, whose liturgy is Gallican, whose palimpsest leaves point to the region of Milan, and whose Irish connection is suggested by the fact that it was found in Bobbio in the seventeenth century, Wilmart looked for an intermediate location, and thus suggested Rhaetia.[32] Geographically, Rhaetia is situated in between Burgundy and northern Italy, and many Irish *peregrini* passed through it in the course of the seventh and the eighth centuries. But Wilmart was well aware of the fact that his suggestion was nothing but intellectual guesswork. It was, as he himself stated, an attempt to explain the unknown by the unknown. After all, 'nous ignorons tout de ce pays à l'aurore du moyen âge; nous ne savons même pas quand y débuta la civilisation chrétienne, ni sous quelle influence, cisalpine, franque ou alémanique'.[33]

The amount of interest in the Bobbio Missal shown by scholars in the past is not at all surprising.[34] After all, the Bobbio Missal is one of the most intriguing liturgical manuscripts from early medieval Francia. As it shall be argued in this present volume, Paris, BNF lat. 13246 was copied in south-eastern France (most conceivably in or around the city of Vienne), and it contains a unique combination of a lectionary and a sacramentary, to which some canonical material (such as a

---

[28] See *Sacramentarium Veronense*, c. 846, ed. L.C. Mohlberg, L. Eizenhöfer and P. Siffrin, Rerum Ecclesiasticarum Documenta, series maior 1 (Rome, 1956), p. 106.

[29] See Wilmart, 'Notice', pp. 37–8.

[30] G. Morin, 'D'où provient le missel de Bobbio?', *Revue Bénédictine* 31 (1914), pp. 326–32.

[31] Wilmart, 'Palimpseste', pp. 1–18; Wilmart, 'Notice', pp. 52–6.

[32] A. Wilmart, 'Une curieuse instruction liturgique du missel de Bobbio', *Revue Charlemagne* 2 (1912), pp. 1–16, at pp. 14–16; Wilmart, 'Palimpseste'; Wilmart, 'Notice', p. 52.

[33] Wilmart, 'Palimpseste', p. 16; Wilmart, 'Notice', p. 52.

[34] Although in the past mainly liturgists have dealt with the Bobbio Missal, it is worthwhile mentioning here the works of two scholars for their particular interest in the Bobbio Missal's penitential, namely, H. Wasserschleben, *Die Bußordnungen der abendländischen Kirche* (Halle, 1851), pp. 57 and 407–12; H.J. Schmitz, *Die Bußbücher und das kanonische Bußverfahren* (Düsseldorf, 1898; repr. Graz, 1958), pp. 322–6.

penitential) was added. At a later stage several other quires were also added to the original codex. These quires contain a plethora of miscellaneous material, such as a mass *pro principe*, an abridgement of Pseudo-Theophilus' commentary on selected passages from the four Gospels, a sermon entitled *De dies malus*, a copy of the so-called *Joca monachorum*, several incantation formulae, instructions on how to celebrate a mass, an Ordinal of Christ and some computistical material.[35] Thus the Bobbio Missal, which contains a unique combination of liturgical, canonical and pedagogical material, can teach us not only about the liturgical practices and traditions prevailing in late seventh- and early eighth-century Francia, but it can also shed some light on the status, education and duties of the Frankish priests, of whom we know next to nothing.[36] Moreover, the plethora of material appended to the Bobbio Missal can illuminate the cultural and ideological context within which this unique liturgical volume was produced.

The debate concerning the origins of the manuscript and its texts, as well as the preoccupation with the various aspects of 'Romanisation' which characterised the interest of eighteenth- and nineteenth-century scholars, and particularly liturgists, have, however, prevented the discussion from moving forward. Although providing crucial evidence on many cultural and religious matters, the Bobbio Missal has been largely ignored by scholars since the 1920s. In 1917 the Henry Bradshaw Society published a facsimile edition of the Bobbio Missal,[37] and three years later the first complete critical edition of Paris, BNF lat. 13246 was published.[38] Subsequently, in 1924, the last major study dedicated to the Bobbio Missal was published, again by the Henry Bradshaw Society, as a compendium to the facsimile and the critical edition.[39] Nevertheless, both E.A. Lowe and André Wilmart, who joined forces in this enterprise, admitted that the riddle concerning the origin of the Bobbio Missal was by no means solved. However, both seemed to accept the initial observations made by Mabillon. Wilmart stressed the fact that it is a Gallican sacramentary, produced, most probably, in Burgundy, in a centre influenced by Irish tradition, such as Luxeuil.[40] Similarly, E.A. Lowe concluded that 'a little over twelve hundred years ago, in an obscure village somewhere on this side of the Alps, in a district

---

[35] For a brief summary of the Bobbio Missal's contents, see Appendix II, below, pp. 16–18.

[36] See, for example, Y. Hen, 'Priests and books in Merovingian Gaul', in *Early Medieval Priests*, ed. Y. Hen and R. Meens (forthcoming). On Merovingian priests, see also R. Godding, *Prêtres en Gaule mérovingienne*, Subsidia hagiographica 82 (Brussels, 2001).

[37] *The Bobbio Missal: A Gallican Mass Book*, ed. J.W. Legg, HBS 53 (London, 1917).

[38] *The Bobbio Missal: A Gallican Mass Book*, ed. E.A. Lowe, HBS 58 (London, 1920).

[39] *The Bobbio Missal: Notes and Studies*, ed. A. Wilmart, E.A. Lowe and H.A. Wilson, HBS 61 (London, 1924).

[40] Wilmart, 'Notice', pp. 38–9. However, at the conclusion of his revised version, Wilmart argued that the codex was copied, most probably, in northern Italy, in the region of Bobbio, from an exemplar that came from Bobbio itself. See ibid., pp. 57–8.

where French was the spoken language, near a convent of nuns, an old cleric once copied a service-book'.[41]

Lowe and Wilmart's verdict on the Bobbio Missal, it appears, discouraged scholars from looking at the Bobbio Missal as an important piece of evidence for the history and culture of early medieval Gaul. No major study of the Bobbio Missal has been published since Lowe and Wilmart's *Notes and Studies*. Scholars who used the Bobbio Missal throughout the twentieth century simply picked up from previous discussions whatever suited their own argument. Thus, for example, J. Janini opted for Duchesne's Septimania hypothesis;[42] Geoffrey Willis classified the Bobbio Missal as an Hiberno-Gallican sacramentary;[43] northern Italy was chosen by Cyrille Vogel,[44] Frederick Paxton[45] and Rolf Busch;[46] whereas other scholars seem to prefer Mabillon's suggestion.[47] Moreover, although being an indispensable source for the study of many aspects of Merovingian culture, only a handful of scholars in recent years, such as Arnold Angenendt, had discussed the Bobbio Missal with a more general and cultural interest.[48]

Since our views on the early Middle Ages have changed dramatically in the last few decades, it seemed appropriate to re-examine the Bobbio Missal in light of modern research. Thus, on 28 April 2001 a group of scholars from various disciplines and universities gathered together in Utrecht (under the auspices of Utrecht University and the Netherlands Organisation for Scientific Research (NWO)) for a one-day workshop on the Bobbio Missal. The Bobbio Missal was then re-examined

[41] Lowe, 'Palaeography', p. 105. It should be added that subsequently, in *CLA* V.653, Lowe committed himself to 'probably south-eastern France'. However, one has to remember that the *CLA* entry was actually written by Bernhard Bischoff. For a fuller discussion of Lowe's impression, see the contribution by Rosamond McKitterick, below, pp. 19–52.

[42] See *Liber ordinum sacerdotal (Cod. Silos, Arch. monástico 3)*, ed. J. Janini, Studia Silensia 7 (Silos, 1981), pp. 31–2.

[43] G.G. Willis, *A History of Early Roman Liturgy to the Death of Pope Gregory the Great*, HBS subsidia 1 (London, 1994), pp. 1 and 19.

[44] C. Vogel, *Medieval Liturgy. An Introduction to the Sources*, trans. and rev. W.G. Storey and N.K. Rasmussen (Washington, DC, 1981), pp. 323–4.

[45] F. Paxton, *Christianizing Death. The Creation of a Ritual Process in Early Medieval Europe* (Ithaca and London, 1990), p. 31.

[46] R. Busch, 'Die vielen Messen für das Seelenheil. Beobachtungen zum frömmigkeitsgeschichtlichen Kontext der "Missa pro uiuis et defunctis" des Bobbio-Missale', *Regulae Benedicti studia* 19 (1997), pp. 141–73, at pp. 142 and 148.

[47] See, for example, R. McKitterick, 'The scriptoria of Merovingian Gaul: a survey of the evidence', in *Columbanus and Merovingian Monasticism*, ed. H.B. Clarke and M. Brennan, BAR International Series 113 (Oxford, 1981), pp. 173–207, at p. 177 (repr. in R. McKitterick, *Books, Scribes and Learning in the Frankish Kingdoms, 6th–9th Centuries* (Aldershot, 1994), ch. 1); Y. Hen, *Culture and Religion in Merovingian Gaul, A.D. 481–751* (Leiden, New York and Cologne, 1995), p. 47; Y. Hen, *The Royal Patronage of Liturgy in Frankish Gaul to the Death of Charles the Bald (877)*, HBS subsidia 3 (London, 2001), p. 29.

[48] See A. Angenendt, 'Missa specialis. Zugleich ein Beitrag zur Entstehung der Privatmessen', *Frühmittelalterliche Studien* 17 (1983), pp. 153–221. See also Paxton, *Christianizing Death*, pp. 31–2, 58–9, 63–4; Busch, 'Die vielen Messen für das Seelenheil'; Hen, *Culture and Religion*, pp. 180–9.

from various angles (palaeographical, linguistic, liturgical, theological, cultural and historical), and this re-examination offered a fresh look at this most remarkable manuscript and the context within which it was produced. For example, a careful re-examination of the palaeography and codicology of the Bobbio Missal (by Rosamond McKitterick, David Ganz and Marco Mostert) concludes that, contrary to Lowe's judgement, this manuscript was copied in an established *scriptorium*, by a competent scribe, who also had some access to patristic writings. The Latin of the manuscript as examined by Els Rose, Charles Wright and Roger Wright, reveals how creative the compiler of the Bobbio Missal was, and it further adds a new dimension to the ongoing debate concerning the passage from Latin to Romance. The compiler's creativity is also revealed when the liturgical content and theological themes hidden in the prayers of the Bobbio Missal are examined (by Yitzhak Hen and Louise Batstone respectively). Other papers connect the initial composition and the subsequent dissemination of various texts which the Bobbio Missal contains, with specific historical-cultural contexts. Hence the liturgical milieu of St Maurice of Agaune, the Merovingian reform movement initiated by Columbanus and his followers, as well as the rise of the Carolingians and their association with monasteries and church institutions in south-eastern Gaul are all evoked (by Ian Wood, Rob Meens and Mary Garrison, respectively) in order to provide a context for different parts of the Bobbio Missal. Although no attempt has been made by the editors to harmonise the various viewpoints these papers espouse, the end result is a remarkably harmonious and coherent picture which, in many respects, goes back to Mabillon and confirms many of his initial observations. This, of course, must not be taken to imply that the riddle of the Bobbio Missal is solved. However, we are closer now than ever to understanding some of its complexities and uniqueness.

APPENDIX I
# MABILLON ON THE BOBBIO MISSAL[49]

PRAEFATIO IN SEQUENS SACRAMENTARIUM GALLICANUM

I. Ordo Missae, quem mox subjiciemus, haud dubie pertinet ad Liturgiam Gallicanam. Primum hujus rei argumentum desumi potest ex collectionibus *post nomina*, *ad pacem*, et ex vocabulo *Contestationis*, quales notae in vera Liturgia Gallicana deprehenduntur, ut in opere de Liturgia Gallicana ostendimus.

II. Alterum argumentum petitur ex convenientia, quam habet hic Ordo cum Missali Gothico seu Gallicano, et cum Lectionario Luxoviensi a nobis editis, ut facta comparatione suis locis observabimus. Cur vero in omnibus non conveniat, inferius dicturi sumus.

III. Tertium argumentum suppeditant Sanctorum festa, quae paucissima in hoc ordine referuntur. Haec festa sunt sanctorum *Stephani protomartiris, Jacobi et Johannis apostolorum, Cathedrae sancti Petri, Depositionis seu Assumtionis sanctissimae Virginis, Inventionis sanctae Crucis, Nativitatis sancti Johannis Baptistae, ejusdemque passionis; apostolorum Petri et Pauli, Missa Sigismundi regis, festum sancti Martini episcopi Turonensis, et Michaëlis archangeli*, quibus adde *triduum Rogationum* ante Asscensionem. Ex his peculiaria Gallis erant Missa sancti Sigismundi Burgundiae regis; et festum sancti Martini, quod tamen extra Galliam antiquitus celebrari potuit. Ad haec Rogationes triduanae ante Asscensionem ritui Gallicano conveniunt, et Depositio seu Assumtio Deiparae in Ianuario, itidemque Cathedra sancti Petri in hoc ordine eodem mense, uti et in Gothico et Lectionario Luxoviensi assignantur. Praeterea in Canone fit commemoratio sancti Hilarii.

IV. Denique his Ordo non est Romanus ut primo intuitu evinci potest; neque ferme ullam habet, excepto Canone, cum Gelasiano aut Gregoriano Ordine convenientiam. In veteri nostro exemplari praemittitur quidem MISSA ROMENSIS COTTIDIANA, cum Canone item Romano. Verum in fine Missalis Gothici eadem Missa adscripta erat, sed mutila in codice Christinae reginae, quo usus est eruditus Thomasius in edendo primum illo Missali. An Canon etiam Romanus in eo codice relatus fuerit, affirmare non licet propter mutili codicis defectum. Attamen cum ad singulas Missas in illo Gothico habeantur singuli

---

[49] Mabillon, *Museum Italicum*, I.2, pp. 273–7. I have followed Mabillon's capitalisation, italics and emphases, but altered the punctuation in a few cases. The English translation was prepared by Rob Meens.

INTRODUCTION TO THE FOLLOWING GALLICAN SACRAMENTARY

I. The order of the Mass which we now publish, belongs without any doubt to the Gallican liturgy. The first argument for such a case is to be taken from the collections *post nomina*, *ad pacem* and from the formula of the *Contestatio*, the characteristics of which derive from the true Gallican Liturgy, as we showed in our book on the Gallican Liturgy.

II. The second argument derives from the correspondence between this ordo of the Mass and the *Missale Gothicum* or *Gallicanum* as well as the Lectionary of Luxeuil, which we edited and which we will indicate comparing them where they correspond. The reason why they do not conform in every way, we will discuss below.

III. The few feasts of the saints, appearing in the following order, supply the third argument. These are the feasts of the saints: Stephen the protomartyr, the apostles Jacob and John, the *Cathedra sancti Petri*, the Deposition and the Assumption of the holy Virgin, the invention of the holy Cross, the Birth of saint John the Baptist, his passion, the apostles Peter and Paul, the Mass of king Sigismund, the feast of saint Martin bishop of Tours and the archangel Michael, to which one should add a three-day Rogation before the Ascension. Of these the Mass for the Burgundian King Sigismund and the feast of St Martin are typically Gaulish, although the feast of St Martin from very early on was also celebrated outside Gaul. The three-day Rogations, moreover, before Ascension Day conform to the Gallican rite and the Deposition or Assumption of the Mother of God in January, and also the *Cathedra sancti Petri* in the same month in that order, as they are placed in both the *Missale Gothicum* and in the Lectionary of Luxeuil. Furthermore, in the Canon of the Mass St Hilary (of Poitiers) is commemorated.

IV. Therefore, this Order is not a Roman one as it may seem at first sight. It has almost no similarities with the Gelasian or Gregorian liturgy except for the Canon of the Mass. In the old manuscript which has been used here the first Mass is entitled *Missa Romensis Cottidiana*, containing a Roman Canon of the Mass. At the end of the *Missale Gothicum* the same Mass has been added, although it is damaged in the manuscript of queen Christina, which was used by the erudite Thomasius when he first edited this Missal. Whether this manuscript also contained the Roman Canon of the Mass cannot be ascertained because of the damage to the manuscript. But because in the *Gothicum* every Mass has its own Canon, different from the Liturgy which we publish here, it can be conjectured that the Roman Canon was not yet adopted in the *Gothicum*, which already appears in the Liturgy presented here, just like in the Frankish Missal of Thomasius. This thesis we reject. And to such

Canones, secus quam in Ordine quem hic vulgamus, conjici potest, in illo Gothico nondum fuisse receptum Canonem Romanum, qui in nostro Ordine jam admissus erat, uti etiam in Missalis Francorum Thomasiano, quod a nobis recusum est. Atque adeo, ut in libro primo de Liturgia Gallicana observatum, majores nostri prius Romanum Canonem, quam integrum Missae ritum Romanus susceperunt. Ex his manifestum est, hunc Ordinem nostrum non esse Romanum.

V. Sed neque Mozarabicus est, ut conferenti patet. Neque Ambrosianus, siquidem, praeter multas alias orationes, Rogationes in Ordine Ambrosiano celebrantur post Asscensionem; hic ante[50] illam ex ritu Gallicano. Praeter ea nullum est in nostro Ordine festum sanctorum Mediolanensium, ac demum non omnino eaedem sunt Missa partes in Ambrosiano, cui desunt Praefationes initio Missae, in hoc Ordine usitatissimae; item Collectiones *post nomina* et *ad pacem* aut Contestationem.

VI. At forte hic Ordo fuerit ecclesiae Africanae. Sed neque hoc dici potest. Quippe Liturgiae Africanae indicia duo ex Augustino discimus, quae huic, qua de agimus, nullo modo conveniunt. Primum indicium est, quod cum in ecclesia Gallicana tres lectiones ex libris sacris ad Missam cathecumenorum recitari mos esset; in Africanae duae tantum lectiones cum intermedio Psalmo recitabantur. Id patet ex sermonibus Augustini ad populum, editis in tomo quinto eius operum novae editionis, quae in posterum semper utemur. In sermo CXII: *Lectiones sanctae propositae sunt, et quas audiamus, et de quibus aliquid sermonis, adiuvante Domino, proferamus. In lectione apostolica gratiae aguntur Domino de fide gentium. In Psalmo diximus, DEUS VIRTUTUM CONVERTE NOS, etc. In Evangelio ad caenam vocati sumus.* Brevis in sermone CLXV: *Apostolum audivimus: Psalmum audivimus: Evangelium audivimus.* Idem colligitur ex sermonibus CLXX et CLXXVI, loquor de lectionibus sacris. Nam paullo [*sic!*] ante Missam in festis Martyrum acta eorum legebantur, ut patet ex sermonibus XXXVII et CCLXXVI: *Post sermonem sit Missa*, seu dimissio, *cathecumenis*, Augustini verba sunt in sermone XLIX num. 8: *manebunt Fideles; venietur ad locum Orationis*, scilicet Dominicae. Alterum indicium est, quod in Africana ecclesia, uti et in Romana et in Mediolanensi, *post sanctificationem sacrificii, et Orationem Dominicam, dicitur PAX VOBISCUM, et osculantur se Christiani in osculo sancto*, ex sermone CCXXVII. Contra in Gallicana et Mozarabica Liturgia Pax dabatur ante actionem, immo ante Praefationem sacrificii, quae Contestatio appellatur. Itaque sequens Ordo non est Africanus, ac proinde superest ut sit Gallicanus.

VII. Cur ergo, inquis, in omnibus non convenit cum Missali Gothico-Gallicano? Id ex eo factum esse existimamus, quod, etsi in ecclesia Gallicana primis saeculis,

---

[50] The first edition (1687) has *post*, which was corrected in the second edition (1724) as *ante*.

an extent that in the first book on the Gallican Liturgy it was observed that our forefathers adopted the Roman Canon earlier than the complete Roman liturgy of the Mass. From this the non-Roman character of this Liturgy is clear.

V. A comparison shows further that it is not Mozarabic, nor Ambrosian, since, apart from containing many different prayers, the Ambrosian Liturgy celebrates the Rogations after Ascension Day; here they are before it, as in the Gallican Liturgy. Apart from this there is no feast in our Liturgical book of the saints of Milan and in this Liturgy the regular parts of the Mass are not entirely the same as in the Ambrosian, where the Praefationes at the beginning of the Mass are lacking; the same is true for the *Collectiones post nomina* and *ad pacem*, and for the *Contestatio*.

VI. Possibly, however, this Liturgy is African, but this cannot be maintained either. Because we learned from Augustine two characteristics of the African Liturgy, which do not at all conform with the one we are dealing with. The first characteristic is that while in the Gallican church three lections from the sacred books are to be recited in the Mass for the catechumens, in the African church only two lections were recited with a Psalm in between. This is clear from the sermons of Augustine *ad populum*, edited in the fifth volume of the new edition of his works, which we from now on should be using. In sermon 112: 'the holy readings are introduced which we listen to and about which with the Lord's help we sermonise a little. In the apostolic reading we thank the Lord for the faith of the peoples. In the Psalm we say "God of virtues, convert us" etc. In the Gospel we are called to the table.' In sermon 165 [Augustine alludes] briefly to this: 'we hear the Apostle, a Psalm and the Gospel'. The same can be concluded from sermons 170 and 176. I speak about the sacred readings, because shortly before the Mass on the feast days of Martyrs their deeds are read, as is shown by sermons 37 and 276: After the sermon the Mass for the catechumens should be celebrated, or they should be sent out. Augustine's words in sermon 49, number 8 are: 'the Faithful will stay, they should come to the place of Prayer', that is the Lord's Prayer. Another indication is that in the African church, as in the churches of Rome and Milan, 'after the sanctification of the sacrifice and the Lord's Prayer they say "Pax vobiscum" and Christians kiss each other with the holy kiss': from sermon 227. In the Gallican and Mozarabic liturgy, however, the 'Pax' is given before the action, right before the *Praefatio* of the sacrifice, which is called the *Contestatio*. Therefore the Order of the Liturgy is not African, so it has to be Gallican.

VII. Why then, you might ask, does it not totally agree with the Gothic-Gallican Missal? We think this is so because, although in the Gallican church during the first centuries, that is before the kingdom of Charlemagne, the liturgy for celebrating Mass was uniform and consisted of the same parts, the place of

11

id est ante Caroli M. principatum, fuerit uniformis celebrandae Missae ritus, eaedemque partes, non tamen eaedem erant ubique Collectiones, Lectiones, et Contestationes, sed forsan in unaquaque metropoli diversae. Id colligere licet ex Concilio Venetico anni CCCCLXV, cujus haec verba sunt in canone XV: *Rectum quoque duximus, UT VEL INTRA PROVINCIAM NOSTRAM, sacrorum ordo et psallendi una sit consuetudo.* Quasi dicerent Patres, si non tota Gallia, saltem intra provinciam nostram, id est Turonensem, uniformis sit sacrorum ritus. Epaonense, anno DXVII celebratum, huic interpretationi suffragatur canone XXVII: *Ad celebranda divina officia Ordinem, quem metropolitani tenent, provinciales observare debebunt.* Hinc est quod ecclesia Lugdunensis peculiarem in sacris ritum semper retinuit. Non itaque mirum, si provincia Narbonensis, quae Gothorum imperio tunc parebat, non in omnibus consenserit cum aliis Gallicanis provinciis; immo non mirum, si singulae provinciae, quae rarissime in unum nationale Concilium convenire poterant, aliquid habuerint, diversi in Ordine rerum sacrarum, tametsi in plerisque atque in ipsa rei (ut ita dicam) substantia conveniebant.

VIII. Codicem antiquum, ex quo subsequentem Ordinem Gallicanum descripsimus, invenimus in bibliotheca percelebris et perantiqui monasterii Bobiensis. Scriptus est codex ante annos mille, et quidem litteris majusculis, ut ex apposito specimine periti intelligent . . .[51] BERTULFUS alicubi legitur in ora folii cujusdam, quem putamus esse ipsum Bertulfum loci abbatem medio saeculo septimo. In alio folio ELDERATUS; item in alio MUNUBERTUS. Illud in eo codice magni faciendum, quod sit integer, non mutilus, ut in illis vetustis libris evenire solet. Porro continet Collectiones, Lectiones Propheticas, Apostolicas, et Evangelicas, atque Contestationes ad Missam per totum annum. In fine etiam (quod rarissimum est, et paene singulare) habetur liber Paenitentialis, in quo multa scitu digna occurrunt ad veteris disciplinae ecclesiasticae cognitionem.

IX. Cujus porro provinciae fuerit hoc Missale, non obvium est definire. Forte ad usum erat provinciae Maximae Sequanorum, id est Vesontionensis, in qua situm est Luxoviense monasterium, unde Columbanus Bobium migravit. Favet huic conjecturae Missa de sancto Sigismundo rege Burgundionum. Certe hic codex non fuit ad usum monachorum Bobiensium. Nihil enim in eo de sanctis Bobiensibus, Columbano, ejusve discipulis. Nihil item de rebus monasticis, non benedictio Abbatis, aut monachorum; non benedictiones pro monasterii officinis, in ejusmodi libris monasticis usitatae. Fit quidem sancti Benedicti commemoratio in Canone Missae, sed haec itidem in plerisque aliis cathedralium ecclesiarum vetustissimis libris occurrit, ut in Canone ecclessiae Mediolanensis ante annos sexcentos scripto, immo in edito Missali

---

[51] Mabillon gives a facsimile of five lines from fol. 60v.

the *Collectiones*, *Lectiones* and *Contestationes* differed from one metropolitan see to another. This can be concluded from the Council of Vannes of the year 465, canon 15 of which reads: 'we also think it is right when the order of the office and of the psalms to be sung will be observed in a uniform way *in our province*'. As if the Fathers were saying that if not in all of Gaul, then at least 'in our province', that is the province of Tours, the office of the Mass should be uniform. The Council of Epaon, gathered in the year 517, confirms this interpretation in canon 27: 'the Order of the Holy Mass as maintained by the metropolitans, should be observed in their provinces'. This is the reason why the church of Lyons always maintained its distinctive liturgy. It comes as no surprise, therefore, when the province of Narbonne, which then was under Gothic rule, did not in everything conform to the other Gallican provinces. Therefore it is no wonder that, when singular provinces, which only very rarely were able to convene in a single national Council, show some differences in the Liturgy of the Mass, although they concord in most cases and in the essential ones (as I would say).

VIII. The old manuscript from which we have transcribed the following Gallican Liturgy, we found in the very famous and old monastery of Bobbio. The codex was written a thousand years ago in a majuscule script, as the experts will understand from the following specimen . . . At some place in the margin of a leaf 'Bertulfus' is to be read, whom we think to be the same Bertulf who was abbot of the monastery in the middle of the seventh century. On another leaf 'Elderatus' can be read and somewhere else 'Munubertus'. And it should be noted that this manuscript is complete, not mutilated, as is usual in such ancient books. It further contains Collectiones, Readings from the Prophets, the Apostles and the Gospels and Contestationes of the Mass for the whole year. At the end it also has – and this is extremely rare and almost unique – a Penitential, in which many noteworthy things are to be found for our knowledge of ancient ecclesiastical discipline.

IX. From which province this Missal comes, is not that easy to decide. Possibly it was in use in the province 'Maxima Sequanorum', i.e. Besançon, in which the monastery of Luxeuil is located, from which Columbanus moved to Bobbio. Such a hypothesis is supported by the Mass for St Sigismund, king of the Burgundians. Certainly this manuscript did not serve the monks of Bobbio, for it contains nothing about the Saints from Bobbio, Columbanus and his disciples. It contains nothing about monastic matters, nor the benediction of the abbot or the monks; nor benedictions for the monastic workshops, which we usually find in such monastic books. In the Canon of the Mass a certain St Benedict is commemorated, but this also occurs in various other ancient books from episcopal churches, as in the Canon of the Church of Milan written 600 years ago, or in the reformed Missal propagated by the holy

per sanctum Carolum reformato, quae tamen commemoratio in subsequentibus Ambrosianorum Missalium editionibus resecta est. Nihil ergo prohibet, quin hoc Missale fuerit ad usum ecclesiae et provinciae Vesontionensis, quod tamen aliis expendendum permittimus. Confer ea quae in Missa pro Principe dicuntur. In Canone post consecrationem commemoratur cum aliis sanctis *EUGENIA*, eademque laudatur in Contestatione Missae pro vigilia Natalis Domini. Haec est Eugenia virgo, quae Romae tempore Gallieni martyrium passa est. In ejus ecclesia extra portam Latinam sanctum virginis corpus requiescere dicitur in vita Leonis tertii, qui quaedam ornamenta eidem ecclesiae assignavit. Hadrianus ante Leonem ibidem monasterium puellarum construxerat. At quo apud Gallias in loco Eugenia cultum habuerit, nobis incompertum.

X. Superest ut sequenti Liturgiae Gallicanae titulum apponamus, quandoquidem nullus exstat in codice Bobiensi. Ne simplici vocabulo appellemus Liturgiam Gallicanam vetant aliae Liturgiae, quae hoc nomen occuparunt. Dici potest *LITURGIA BOBIENSIS*, at praeferendus videtur titulus *LIBER SACRAMENTORUM ECCLESIAE GALLICANAE*, propterea quod in fine codicis, ubi libri sacri recensentur, extremo loco ponitur *SACRAMENTORUM UNUS*, quo nomine librum de re sacra majores nostri solebant designare. Sic Liturgia Romana, qualis a Gregorio M. ordinata est, appellatur *LIBER SACRAMENTORUM DE CIRCULO ANNI*. At quemadmodum Gregorianus ille liber compendioso modo non tantum a recentioribus, sed etiam a Micrologo aliisque laudari solet sub titulo *Sacramentarii Gregoriani*; ita etiam noster hic liber dici poterit *SACRAMENTARIUM GALLICANUM*.

XI. Ceterum in Scripturae sacrae lectionibus, quae hoc in Ordine fiunt, adhibetur versio Vulgata, ut in Lectionario Luxoviensi, nisi quod lectiones nonnullae potius ad sensum, quam ad verbum referuntur, non consequenter, sed quasi centenos ex variis Scripturae locis. Haec in antecessum praemisisse sufficiat.

Charles; in subsequent Ambrosian Missals such a commemoration has been eliminated. So there is nothing to show that this Missal was not used in the province of Besançon, but we leave it to others to elaborate such a thesis.

Now let us turn to the things contained in the *Missa pro Principe*. In the Canon after the *Contestatio* Eugenia is commemorated among others and she is also commemorated in the *Contestatio* of the Mass for Christmas Eve. This is the virgin Eugenia who, in the time of Gallienus, suffered martyrdom in Rome. Her sacred body is said to rest in her church next to the Porta Latina according to the life of Leo III, who adorned her church with various ornaments. Before Leo, Hadrian had built a nunnery on the same spot. But where in Gaul there was a cult of Eugenia, we do not know.

X.  We now have to provide a name for the following Gallican Liturgy. We cannot simply name it 'Gallican Liturgy' because the use of this name by other Liturgical books forbids this. It could be called 'Liturgy from Bobbio', but the title 'Sacramentary of the Gallican Church' seems preferable, because at the end of the manuscript, where the holy books are tabulated, in last place we encounter a 'Sacramentary' (*Sacramentorum unus*), by which name our forefathers used to designate a book about the liturgy. So the Liturgy of Rome as it was devised by Gregory the Great, is called 'sacramentary for the whole year' (*Liber sacramentorum circuli anni*). And as that Gregorian book used to be praised briefly, not only in later times, but also by the Micrologus and others, under the title of *Sacramentarium Gregorianum*, so also our book may be called 'a Gallican Sacramentary'.

XI. Furthermore in the readings from Holy Scripture which are to be found in this Liturgy, the Vulgate version is used, as in the Lectionary of Luxeuil, although some readings refer to it rather according to the sense than according to the letter, not according to their original order but like a patchwork from various places of Scripture. This may suffice to serve as a foreword.

## APPENDIX II
# THE CONTENTS OF THE BOBBIO MISSAL

The following list is a brief summary of the contents of the Paris, BNF lat. 13246. The contents of the original codex are printed in normal script or italics, the additions are printed in bold, and the numbers in brackets denote the chapters in Lowe's edition.

**Excerpts from Pseudo-Theophilus' commentary on the Gospels**
**Pseudo-Augustine's sermon *De dies malus***
***Joca monachorum***
Daily readings (1–3)
*Canon missae* (4–33)
*Adventus* (34–63)
*Vigilia natalis Domini* (64–70)
*Natalis Domini* (71–9)
St Stephen (80–6)
The Holy Innocents (87–93)
St Jacob and St John (94–100)
*Circumcisio Domini* (101–7)
*Epiphania* (108–14)
*Cathedra sancti Petri* (115–21)
*In Sollemnitate sanctae Mariae* (122–8)
*In Assumptione sanctae Mariae* (129–33)
*Quadragessima* (134–73)
*Ad aurium apertionem* (174–82)
*Expositio Symboli* (183–8)
*Traditio Symboli* (189–93)
*Cena Domini* (194–201)
*Lectiones in Parasceue* (202–4)
*Sabbato Sancto* (205–13)
*Orationes in Vigilia Paschae* (214–26)
*Benedictio Caerei* (227)
*Ad Christianum faciendum* (228–33)
*Ordo Baptismi* (234–54)
*Vigilia Paschae* (255–61)
*Pascha* (262–87)
*Inventio sanctae Crucis* (288–92)

*Litaniae* (293–9)
*Ascensio Domini* (300–4)
*Quinquagesima* (305–11)
A daily reading (312)
St John the Baptist (313–21)
St John's Passion (322–6)
St Peter and St Paul (327–33)
St Sigismund (334–8)
Martyrs [unspecified] (339–44)
A Martyr [unspecified] (345–51)
A Confessor [unspecified] (352–9)
St Martin (360–7)
A Virgin [unspecified] (368–74)
Dedication of a Church (375–6 and 384–92)[52]
For the sick (377–83)
St Michael (393–7)
*Pro iter agentibus* (398–404)
For a priest [*sacerdos*] (405–11)
*Missa omnimoda* (412–18)
Votive masses (419–35)
For the living and the dead (436–40)
*In domo cuiuslibet* (441–4)
Sunday masses (445–82, 484–91 and 498)[53]
*Apologia* (483)
**Missa pro principe** (492–6)
**Devotiones sive imprecationes** (497)
*Missae cotidianae dominicales* [5 sets] (499–521)
*Depositio sacerdotis* (522–7)
For the dead (528–39)
*Exorcismi salis et aquae* (540–4)
*Oratio in domo* (545)
Various Benedictions (546–62)
*Orationes vespertina et matutina* (563–73)
*Exorcismum olei* (574–5)
**Benedictio olei** (576)

---

[52] The mass for the sick was copied in the middle of the mass for the dedication of a church (between the *collectiones* and the rest of the mass) probably because of a scribal confusion.

[53] The *Apologia* was copied between the fourth and the fifth sets of the Sunday masses. The small *libellus* which contains the *missa pro principe* and the *Devotiones sive imprecationes* was inserted between fols. 250 and 255, thus separating the last *contestatio* from the rest of the mass.

Penitential (577)
*Orationes super paenitentem* (578–9)
**Benedictio hominis cum domo sua** (580)
**De lege ad missam celebrandam** (581)
**De septem gradibus ecclesiae** (582)
**De peccatis ad infirmum ducentibus** (583)
**De tempore nativitatis Christi** (584)
**Orationes pro paenitentibus** (585–6)
**Benedictiones panis** (587–9)
**De omnibus cursibus** (590)
**Symbolum apostolorum** (591)
**De libris canonicis** (592)
**Orationes ad missam** (593–8)

# 2

## The scripts of the Bobbio Missal

ROSAMOND McKITTERICK

In 1924, E.A. Lowe concluded his contribution on 'The palaeography of the Bobbio Missal' for the Henry Bradshaw volume accompanying the facsimile and edition, as follows:

If palaeography were not, in the hands of certain experts, rapidly becoming an exact science, competent to fix within a decade the date of an undated manuscript, and to determine its home with enviable confidence, I should be tempted to sum up the impression made upon me by the Missal in some such unscientific language as this: A little over twelve hundred years ago, in an obscure village somewhere on this side of the Alps, in a district where French was the spoken language, near a convent of nuns, an old cleric once copied a service-book. His hand was not very steady, but he wrote with a will, and meant to do a good job. His parchment was not of the best, and his penmanship showed that he was no master of the craft. He had two kinds of ink: ordinary dark for the text, and red for the rubrics. He used the red as unskillfully as the black. He had little time, busy priest that he was, for over-care or refinements to bestow on titles and rubrics. But he could not deny himself the pleasure of some ornamentation, so when he could he copied a decorative initial, with results pathetic in their crudity. The old scribe was trying to follow his original page for page. When he came to passages he knew by heart, such as lessons from the gospels or prophets, he often cast a mere glance at his copy, and trusted his memory for the rest. He was a simple downright man – no purist in spelling or grammar. He wrote as he spoke, with ci for ti, soft g for j, and vice versa; and he had small regard for case or verb endings. Coming from a modest place, he could not afford many books, so he crowded into his missal much more than properly belonged there. And when his parchment went back on him, he borrowed fortuitous scraps . . . By some strange freak of fate, this homely copy by an obscure, unnamed cleric has survived to puzzle and edify us.[1]

Lowe's judgements were influenced by assumptions about the general historical context in which the book was written. These appear to have encouraged him to extrapolate from what he saw in a peculiar way. In the first place, his comments about the location of production being a place where 'French' was spoken were

[1] Lowe, 'Palaeography', pp. 105–6.

made at a time before the debate about Latin and Romance had clarified and extended the period of written and spoken Latin of different registers in Gaul well beyond the time of production of this book. Geographical differentiation remains possible and provides clues about the location of particular word forms. The oddities of the Latin, however, were associated in Lowe's mind with decline and decadence, for to him they were a departure from classical standards. Similarly, it seems to be an elaboration from Lowe's judgement, due to the shaky scripts of many of the pages, that the priest was an old man, though elsewhere in the chapter he had suggested 'illness or old age'. The unsteadiness of the hand in terms of the slightly wavering lines of the script is not in doubt, but it has to be said that it is not manifest on every page. One could offer the, no-doubt frivolous, suggestion that the scribe's inclusion of prayers concerning quartan fever (malaria) was because he himself was a sufferer and thus that the batches of shaky pages are written by someone in the first stages of recurrent fever.[2]

Even if the scribe were old, this does not entitle us to conclude that the quality of his work is an indication that he was also working in an 'obscure village' and was himself an 'obscure, unnamed cleric'. There is no justification for the assumption that if the text had been written by an old man he had to be some way removed from any 'centre' of book production. Even illustrious archbishops and master scribes get old. An old man in any case would have had major problems with the natural long-sightedness of old age, though the effect of this on reading ability would depend on whether he had been short- or long-sighted in his youth. The size of this script, neither excessively large nor excessively small, does not necessarily support any conclusion that the main scribe was someone much past the age of fifty or so. In this context it is germane to recall Boniface's letter, written when he was approximately seventy years old, concerning the size of the script for a book he had commissioned: 'I cannot procure in this country such a book of Prophets as I need, and with my fading sight I cannot read well writing which is small and filled with abbreviations. I am asking for this book because it is copied clearly, with all letters distinctly written out.'[3] In the light of these considerations I remain unconvinced that this scribe was necessarily an 'old man'.

The contents of the book are also used to condemn the scribe; an inappropriate model of what 'properly belongs' in a 'missal' is used to belittle the scribe's resources rather than considering the function of the compilation as a whole. How can a conclusion that he came from a 'modest place' with 'few books' be justified on the evidence of one liturgical book which includes a number of very interesting

---

[2] Below, pp. 211–12.

[3] Boniface of Mainz, *Ep.* 63 (742–6), ed. M. Tangl, *Die Briefe des heiligen Bonifatius und Lullus*, MGH Epistolae Selectae 1 (Berlin, 1916), p. 131; trans E. Emerton, *The Letters of Saint Boniface*, revised edn T.F.X. Noble (New York, 2000), no. LI, p. 94.

texts for use by a priest? The Bobbio Missal could equally be regarded as a useful handbook with all that was needed for particular purposes in one volume.[4]

Contents, mistakes in the Latin and script together, moreover, seem to have encouraged the implicit understanding of this book as a symptom of a decline in literary culture so marked that it could only be a book from some remote, unimportant and small place. With what, however, can the Bobbio Missal reasonably be compared? In relation to what is remoteness, size or importance to be determined? As we shall see, any 'centre' of book production is rather hard to define in Merovingian Gaul, especially during the seventh and early eighth centuries, which is the period with which we are largely concerned.[5] Certainly, there are places which we can identify as able to produce more than one book of greater elegance, with a greater range of script types and written on finer parchment than the Bobbio Missal. The centre producing Luxeuil minuscule or the Seine River basin's constellation of convents, for example, spring to mind.[6] Yet the precise function of the minuscule at Luxeuil, for example, should be stressed, for, as David Ganz has argued, it was elaborated as an appropriate script in which to copy homilies and patristic texts.[7] Such differentiation of status implies a very considerable scribal discipline, not necessarily achieved by many other writing centres.[8] This too needs to be borne in mind in any assessment of the scripts of the Bobbio Missal.

None of these factors, moreover, constitutes proof of the political or ecclesiastical, as distinct from intellectual or religious, importance of any book-producing centre. Until we have a clearer idea of the Bobbio Missal's date, the liturgical importance of its contents, and of its context, we cannot justifiably relate it to any other book or reach conclusions about the age of the scribe, his status and importance as a cleric, or the kind of place he served. Even then, it is essential to keep an open mind about the vigour of any ecclesiastical centre and not condemn it as of no significance as a result of subjective or aesthetic reactions to one of the books it produced. Certainly, there are lines of enquiry to be pursued. But it may be that

[4] See Yitzhak Hen, 'Priests and books in Merovingian Gaul', in *Early Medieval Priests*, ed. Y. Hen and R. Meens (forthcoming).

[5] I made some preliminary observations on this topic twenty years ago in R. McKitterick, 'The scriptoria of Merovingian Gaul: a survey of the evidence', in *Columbanus and Merovingian Monasticism*, ed. H.B. Clarke and M. Brennan, BAR International Series 113 (Oxford, 1981), pp. 173–207 (repr. in R. McKitterick, *Books, Scribes and Learning in the Frankish Kingdoms, 6th–9th Centuries* (Aldershot, 1994), ch. 1).

[6] On Luxeuil see David Ganz, 'Texts and scripts in surviving manuscripts in the script of Luxeuil', in *Ireland and Europe in the Early Middle Ages: Texts and Transmission*, ed. P. Ní Chatháin and M. Richter (Dublin, 2002), pp. 186–203 and his references. On the Seine basin convents see R. McKitterick, 'Nuns' scriptoria in England and Francia in the eighth century', *Francia* 19 (1992), pp. 1–35 (repr. in McKitterick, *Books, Scribes and Learning*, ch. 7).

[7] Ganz, 'Luxeuil', p. 189.

[8] See Armando Petrucci, 'Alfabetismo ed educazione grafica degli scribi altomedievali (secc. vii–x)', in *The Role of the Book in Medieval Culture*, ed. P. Ganz, 2 vols. (Turnhout, 1986), I, pp. 109–32.

Bobbio represents far more of a norm for its time and place than we realise, and that the Frankish sacramentaries of the late seventh and the eighth centuries, and the manuscripts of Luxeuil, which appear to provide appropriate comparanda, are exceptional.[9]

The Bobbio Missal, in short, is a crucial piece of evidence in its own right, and deserves to be judged on what it has to tell us on its own terms. Nevertheless, Lowe's verdict on the script, and his reluctance to identify a place of production, have strongly encouraged subsequent historians, palaeographers and liturgical scholars to regard the Bobbio Missal as a peripheral piece of evidence for the history and culture of early medieval Gaul. As I hope to demonstrate in this chapter, however, there is a case for regarding the Bobbio Missal as a vital piece of evidence for the history of south-east Gaul in the Merovingian period and one which raises many important questions about Merovingian culture as a whole.

In the forty pages preceding his concluding summary of 1924, Lowe provided an admirably clear, methodical and comprehensive description of the scripts of the Bobbio Missal, letter by letter. This description is summarised in the *CLA* entry,[10] though the necessary compression of the *CLA* summary has created some ambiguity that only the fuller description of 1924 clarifies.[11] Thus I refer to the latter in what follows.

The manuscript is small in format, 180 × 90 mm (130 × 70 mm) with an average of 22 long lines to the page. That is, it is slightly narrower and taller than a modern paperback book. It has the appearance of a chunky (at 300 folios/600 pages) and easily transportable working copy of the crucial mass texts it contains and is certainly different in this respect from the Frankish mass books of the eighth century. Thus the oldest portion of the *Missale gallicanum vetus* measures 245 × 175 mm (180 × 175 mm) and is written with 14–16 long lines to a page, though the number of pages of the original is not clear.[12] The *Missale Francorum* measures 233 × 145 mm (150 × 110 mm), has 150 folios and is written with 13 long lines to a page.[13] The *Gelasian Sacramentary* has a total of 261 folios, measures 260 × 172 mm (220 × 130 mm), is written with 23 long lines to a page and once

---

[9] For supporting remarks, see Y. Hen, 'A liturgical handbook for a rural priest', in *Organizing the Written Word*, ed. M. Mostert (Turnhout, forthcoming); and Y. Hen, 'The knowledge of canon law among rural priests', *Journal of Theological Studies* 50 (1999), pp. 117–34.

[10] *CLA* V.653.

[11] Incidentally, the *CLA* entry, presumably as a consequence of a conflation of notes made on the manuscript, says that the added mass *pro principe* mentions King Sigismund of the Burgundians but in fact it does not. No specific ruler is named. Sigismund, king and saint, on the other hand, as we shall see, has a separate mass to himself in the main text, starting on fol. 165r; on the latter, see Ian Wood's contribution to this volume.

[12] Vatican City, BAV, Pal. lat. 493 (France, north of the Loire, s. viii[1]); *CLA* I.92.

[13] Vatican City, BAV, Reg. lat. 257 (Seine basin, s. viii[1]); *CLA* I.103.

included a penitential in its last two quires (now Paris, BNF lat. 7193 (fols. 41–56)).[14] The *Missale Gothicum* is 255 × 170 mm (165–95 × 110–30 mm), contains 264 folios and pages are written with 12–20 long lines.[15]

Lowe commented that the gatherings of the Bobbio Missal were of an extraordinary variety (a judgement modifed in the *CLA* entry to 'gatherings [vary] greatly in size with eights predominating'). Lowe added that the variety was 'of a piece with other extraordinary features of the manuscript, which seem to point to some out-of-the-way village as its home'. I disagree profoundly with this judgement. Again it makes an illogical leap from extraordinariness to distant and out-of-the-way location. If standards are judged to have slipped, which is the burden of Lowe's characterisation of this manuscript, then logically they could do so as much in a central place as in an 'out-of-the-way' one. Alternatively, high standards could be maintained in a remote location far removed from any contaminating influences. As far as the Bobbio Missal is concerned, I shall propose instead that this manuscript's extraordinary features should not be exaggerated and that the book should be regarded as one produced in and for a thriving ecclesiastical centre. I shall return to the codicology of this book in a moment, but let us first look at the script.

### SCRIPT

Lowe distinguished four hands:

The Missal proper is written by one hand, designated as **M**, . . . the few pages in uncial – the Mass *pro principe*, written by another hand – are referred to as **M2**; . . . the pages containing added matter, in two different styles of crude writing, one showing distinct majuscule and the other as distinct minuscule traits, are referred to as **A** and **a**.[16]

If we set out these 'hands', without prejudging whether or not they are the work of different scribes, the manuscript can be apportioned as set out below (though it is important to compare this with the quiring discussed on pp. 46–50). I have also tabulated the letter forms of the different hands of sections of the manuscript for ease of comparison (see Fig. 1).

Fols. 1–8v additions by hand **A** in a script with some uncial elements though basically minuscule and letters are separated.

Fols. 9r–250v hand **M** 'Missal proper', that is the main hand, a 'mixed uncial' with some half-uncial and minuscule letter forms.

[14] Vatican City, BAV, Reg. lat. 316 (Chelles/Jouarre, s. viii^med); *CLA* I.105.

[15] Vatican City, BAV, Reg. lat. 317 (Burgundy, s. viii^in); *CLA* I.106.

[16] Lowe, 'Palaeography', p. 64.

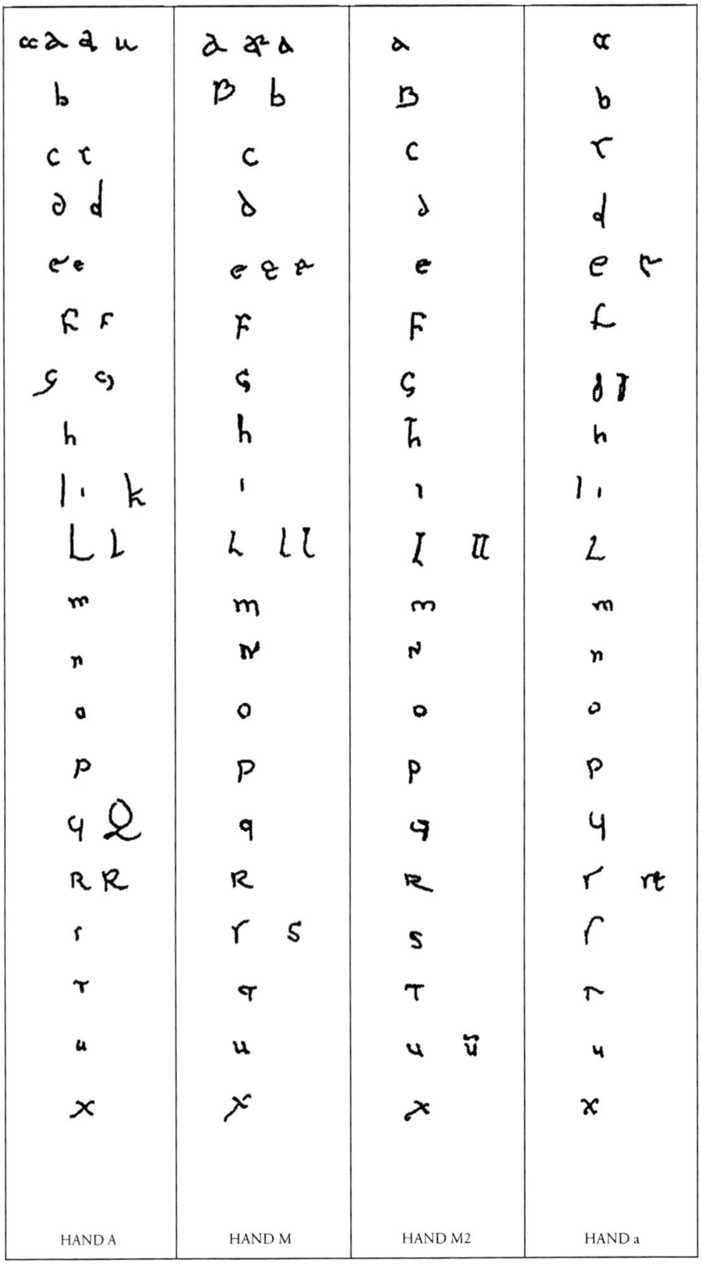

Figure 1   *The Bobbio Missal: letter forms*

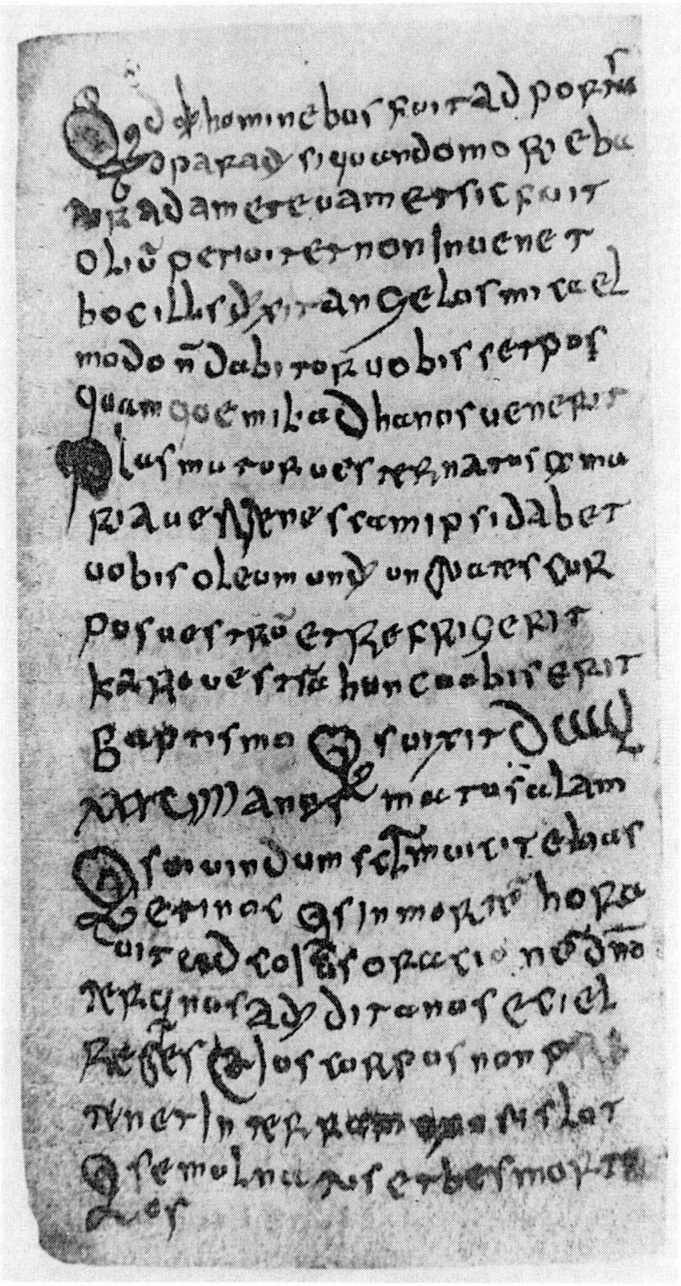

*Plate 1   Paris, BNF lat. 13246, fol. 7v: sample of a leaf from quire A*
*(Joca monachorum): scribe **A***

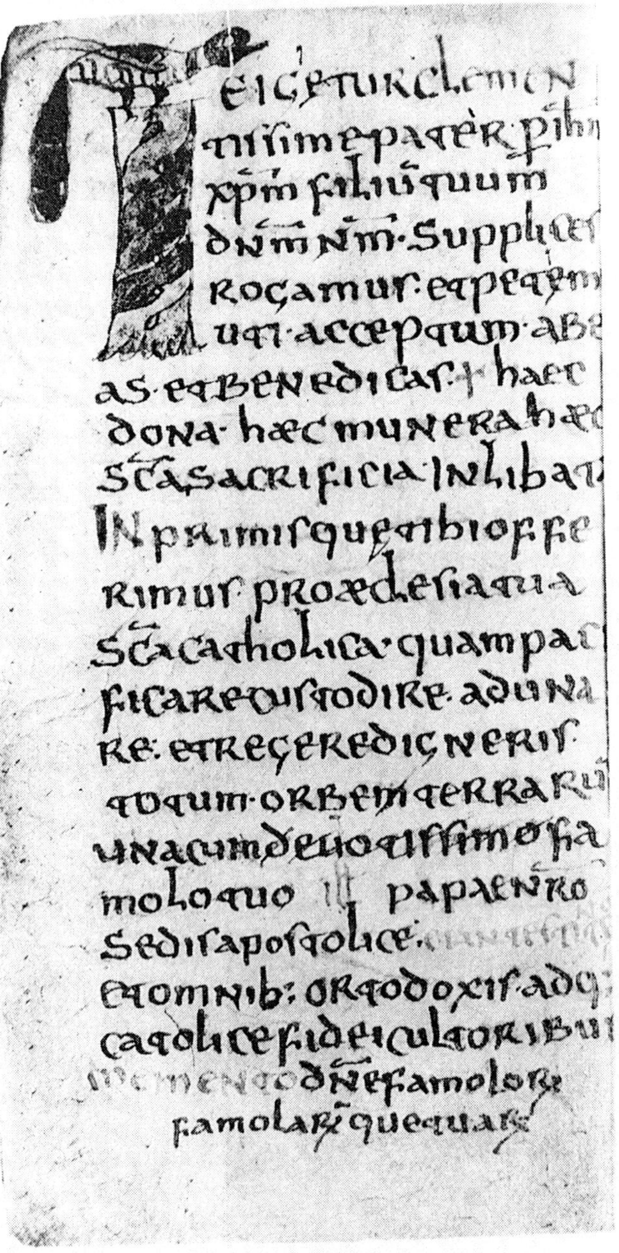

*Plate 2   Paris, BNF lat. 13246, fol. 11v: the beginning of the
canon missae (Te igitur): scribe **M***

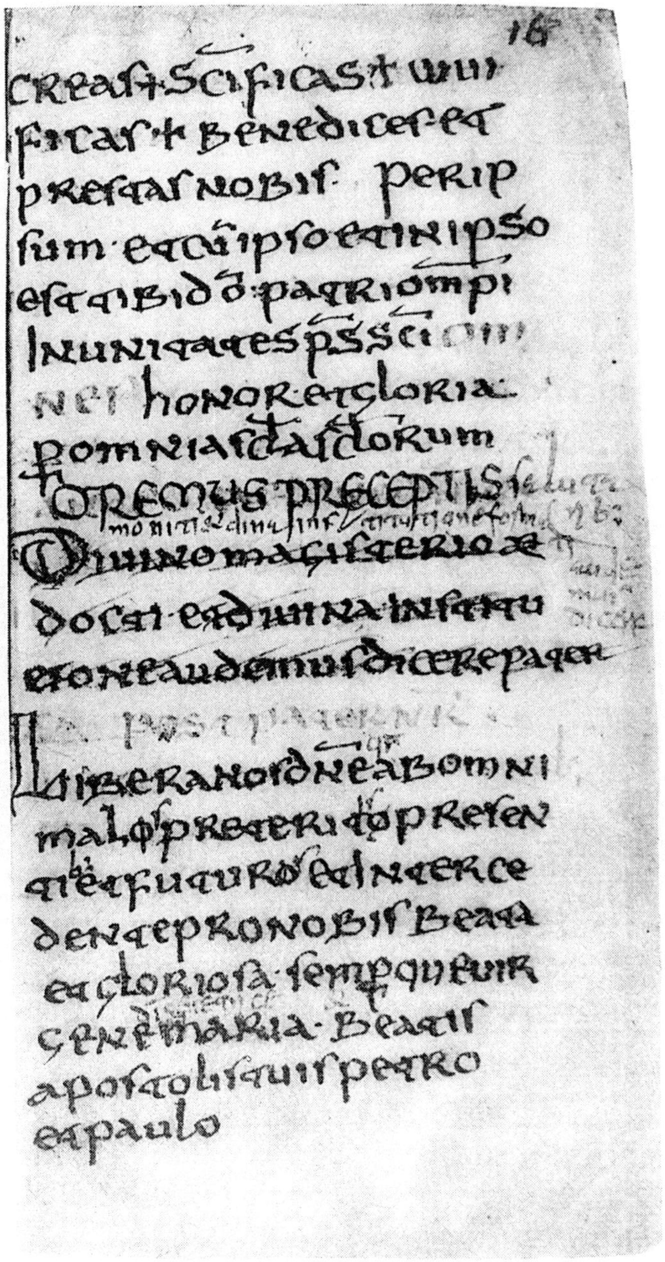

*Plate 3   Paris, BNF lat. 13246, fol. 16r: the* canon missae *with interlinear additions: scribe **M**, main hand*

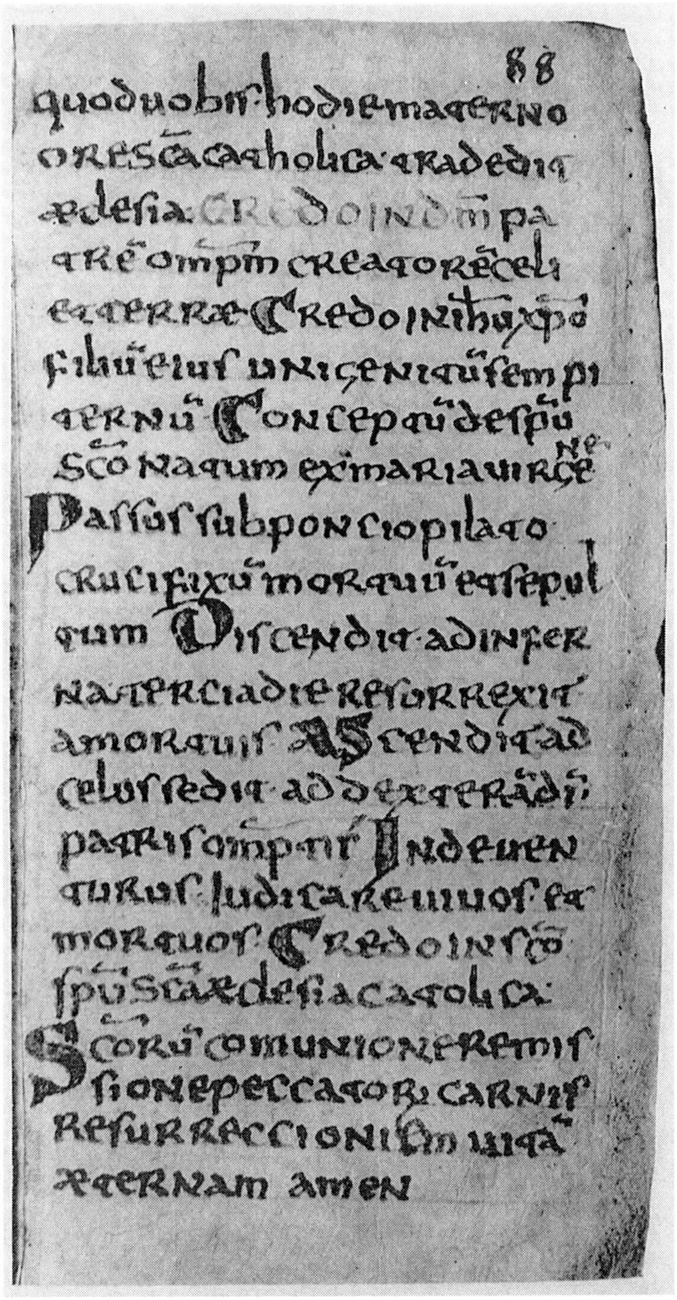

*Plate 4   Paris, BNF lat. 13246, fol. 88r: the Apostolic Creed: scribe* **M**

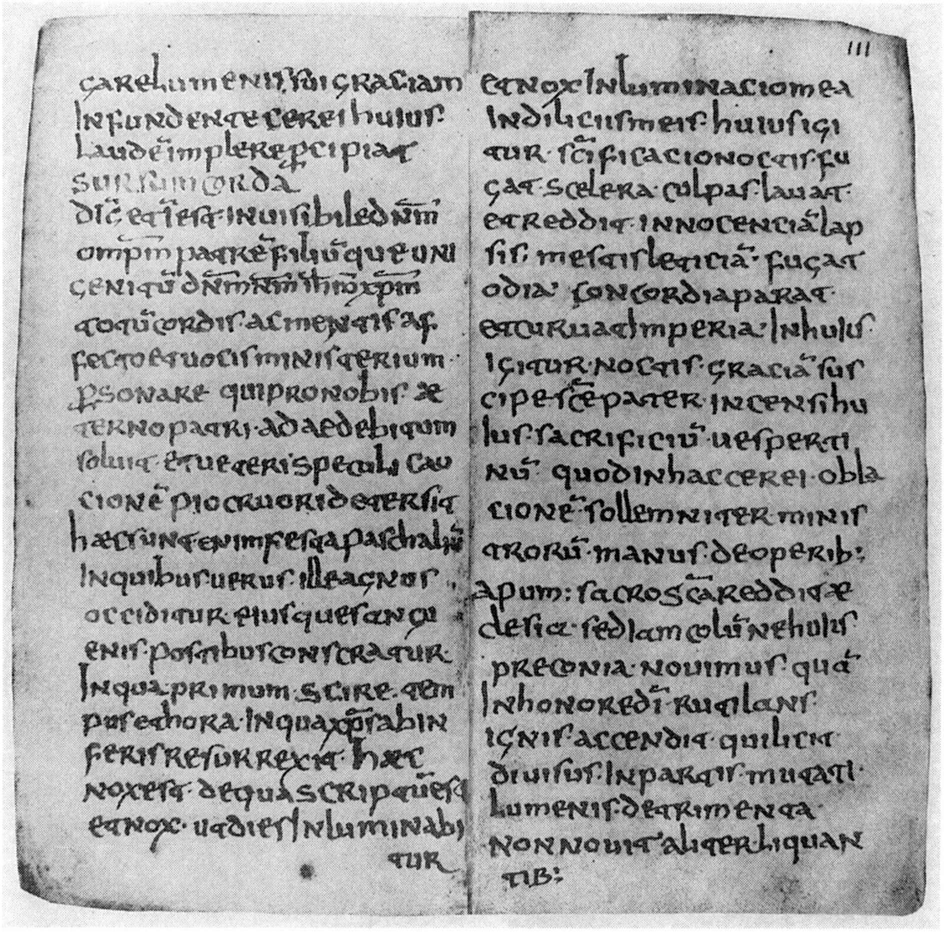

*Plate 5   Paris, BNF lat. 13246, fols. 110v–111r: sample of an opening (reduced): scribe* **M**

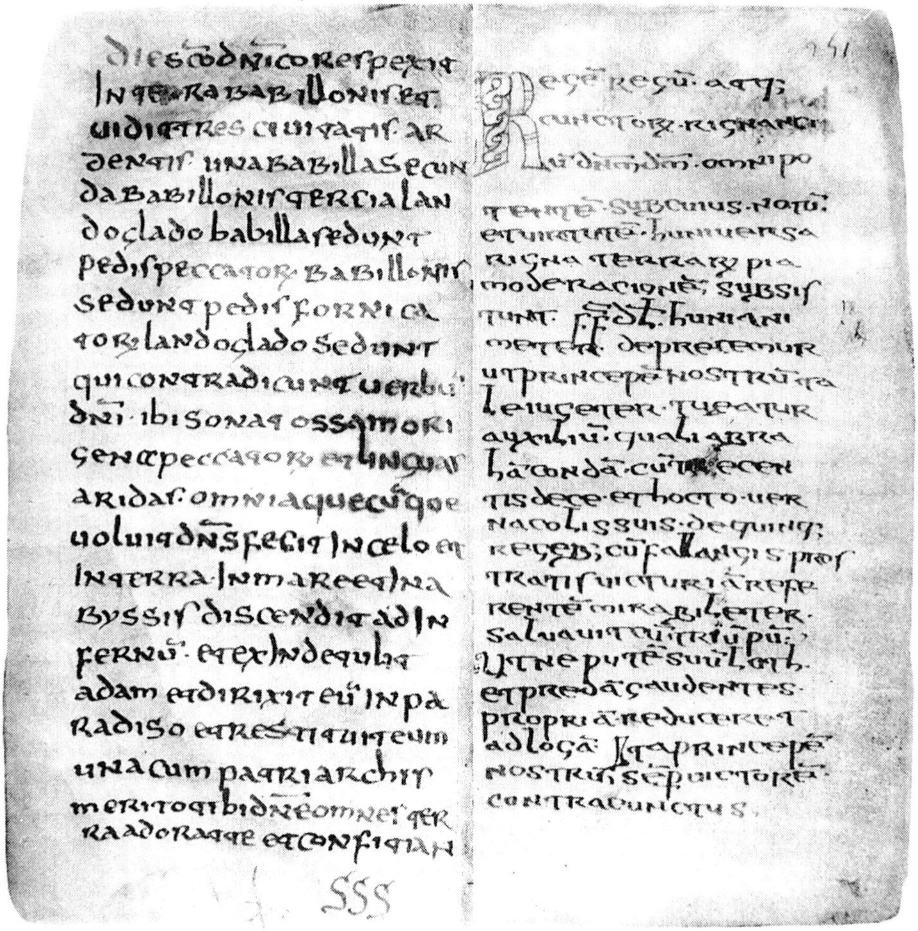

*Plate 6  Paris, BNF lat. 13246, fols. 250v–251r: the beginning of the* Missa pro principe *(reduced): scribe **M**, fol. 250v; scribe **M2**, fol. 251r*

*Plate 7   Paris, BNF lat. 13246, fols. 251v–252r: sample of an opening (reduced): scribe **M2***

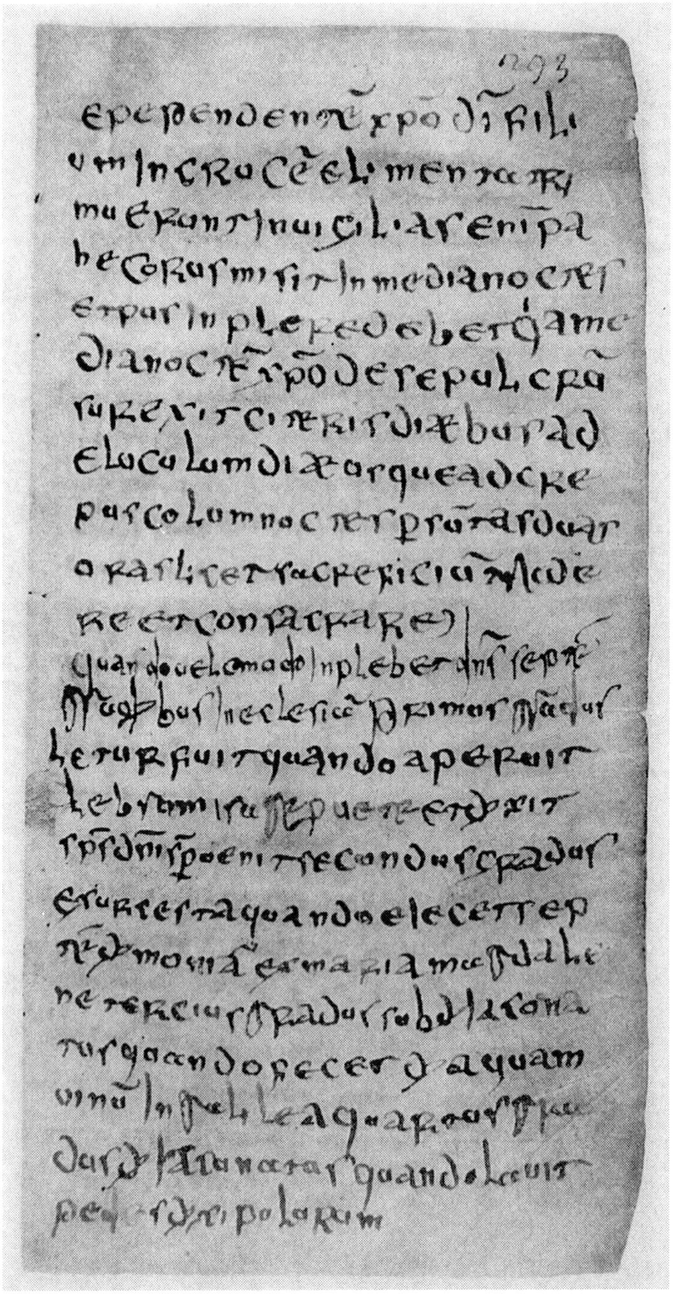

*Plate 8  Paris, BNF lat. 13246, fol. 293r: sample of a leaf with Merovingian cursive lines: scribe **A**, main hand*

Fols. 251r–253r **M2** the uncial script of the mass *pro principe*.

Fols. 253v–254r additions by hand **a** in a script with no uncial elements and with letter forms rather cursive in character even though the letters are usually separated.

Fol. 254v blank.

Fols. 255r–286r line 5 **M**, the main hand of the 'Missal proper' continues.

Fols. 286r lines 6–22 additions by hand **A**.

Fols. 286v–291r hand **M**.

Fols. 291v–292r additions by hand **a**.

Fols. 292v–295v additions by hand **A** (but note the Merovingian cursive lines 12–13 on fol. 293r).

Fols. 296r–299v hand **M** (?) (on palimpsest leaves).

Fols. 299v–300v hand **A** (?) (on palimpsest leaves).

On a number of folios are short Merovingian cursive and mixed minuscule script annotations or corrections, viz. fols. 14v, 15v, 16r, 56r, 208v, 209r, 241r, 278v, not all by the same hand.

Fols. 43v, 82v, fol. 113v line 16 last word, fol. 249v, 278v which might be **M**'s less formal hand and verges on Merovingian cursive, and fol. 17v line 8 which may be **A**. Note too the names in a larger crude script on fols. 197v (Bertulfus), 208v (Elderatus), 213v (Munubertus), 268v (Dacolena), 271v (Bonolo) and 284r (Aquilina) with possibly another on fol. 270r. Lowe thought these the work of a single hand, possibly **M**.[17]

I suggest that the sequence in which these hands were written is **M, A, M2, a**. The corrections and additions in the main text, added after it was completed, and in hands of the late seventh and early eighth century in appearance, point to dates no later than that for the main text.

In his 1924 characterisation of the script, Lowe retained his distinction of 'majuscule' and 'minuscule' traits with particular reference to hands **A** and **a**. None of the hands named **M, A** and **a** can be cleanly and without exception labelled as 'majuscule' or 'minuscule' (which Julian Brown with reference to Insular script at least found rather an insufficient distinction in any case). All three hands wrote mixed scripts and exhibit a wide spectrum from formality to rapid and informal script. **M** and **A** contain uncial letter forms to varying degrees.

It should be remembered that variations in letter forms could, in some palaeographers' opinion, be as much one scribe's lack of skill as evidence of several scribes at work. This would seem to me, however, to depend on the degree to which consistency of letter forms as a virtue was taught and how wide the range of options was when presented to the scribe. If we compare such manuscripts as Lucca, Biblioteca

---

[17] Ibid., p. 104 n. 2.

Capitolare Feliniana 490 or the Tours' Eugippius, for example, we find considerable variation in letter forms attributed to the scribes concerned.[18] The Bobbio Missal raises, indeed, many interesting questions about the formation of a scribe and what his work reflects of written culture in the context of Frankish Gaul. These need to be explored, together with the other evidence from the Merovingian period, along the lines of Petrucci's and Romeo's important work on early medieval Italy.[19]

In the *CLA* entry made by Bernhard Bischoff it is stated that what he calls the 'mixed uncial' of the main text uses uncial forms for **F**, **G**, **N** and **R** consistently, uncial, half-uncial or minuscule forms for **A**, **B**, **D**, **L** and **S** and minuscule forms consistently for **c**, **e**, **m** and **t**. It is also observed merely that the 'minuscule' sections, that is, those in the mixed script with predominantly minuscule traits, were in one 'rude untrained hand' which was *sui generis* and needed no description. In his long 1924 description of the script, however, Lowe had gone into more detail. The 'mixed uncial' of the main scribe was again stated by Lowe almost always to have **F**, **G**, **N** and **R** in the uncial form with the **A**, **B**, **D**, **L** and **S** in uncial, half-uncial or minuscule and **c**, **e**, **m**, **t** regularly in minuscule. **h**, **i**, **k**, **p**, **q**, **x** are 'minuscule of a neutral type', **u** sometimes has the **v** form, **y** dotted and undotted appears, **z** normally projects above the headline (see Fig. 1). Lowe further notes the distinctive form of **N** with the third stroke being formed something like a comma and often meeting the oblique second stroke well above the writing line (an observation repeated in the *CLA* entry).

Lowe offered the opinion (confirmed in the *CLA* entry) that the few names added, such as *bertulfus* on fol. 197v, were written in the same hand as the other additions. He also considered the possibility that the mixed script with predominantly minuscule traits of **a** and **A** was the work of the same scribe as the main text **M**. I doubt that this is the case. Not only are there some significant differences between the letter forms, suggesting a different ductus, but there is also no particular reason for changing the general type of script for these additions. Thus the different kinds of handwriting, that is, hands **M**, **A** and **a**, identified by Lowe seem to me to be the work of three different scribes rather than one, with an extra and different hand being responsible for the *Missa pro principe*. The occasional names added on fols. 197v, 208v, 213v, 268v, 271v and 284r as noted above are difficult to categorise but conceivably could have been made by either **A** or **a**. Essentially, therefore, the main text is by one scribe, with two more responsible for

---

[18] Lucca, Biblioteca Capitolare Feliniana 490 (Lucca, s.viii^ex); *CLA* III.303; L. Schiaparelli, *Il codice 490 della Biblioteca Capitolare de Lucca e la scuola scrittoria Lucchese (sec. VIII–IX ). Contributi allo studio della minuscola precarolina in Italia*, Studi e Testi 36 (Vatican, 1924); and Paris, BNF n.a. lat. 1575 (Tours, s. viii) *CLA* V.682; E.K. Rand, *The Earliest Books of Tours* (Cambridge, MA, 1934).

[19] A. Petrucci and C. Romeo, '*Scriptores in urbibus': Alfabetismo e cultura scritta nell'Italia altomedievale* (Bologna, 1992).

the additions on fols. 1–8, 292v–295 and the even more informal hand on fols. 253v–254 respectively. Still another scribe wrote the *Missa pro principe* on fols. 251–3. I am not certain whether fols. 299–300 represent yet another hand or whether they are the work of **A**.

A crucial element of Lowe's discussion was his argument in favour of the identity and thus date of the hands which wrote **A** and **a** and the main hand **M**. He stated that the first impression might indeed be that there were significant differences, but he pointed to the forms of **a**, **c** and **o**, the kicking **r** and **s** as supporting identity. Although he suggested that 'much can be said in favour of their identity', and produced a number of points in support of this, he added that the dissimilarity of the **t** forms presented 'an objection to the theory of identity which seems unanswerable'.[20] There he left the matter and it remained unresolved in the subsequent discussion. The similarities Lowe detected, whether or not he thought **M**, **A** and **a** to be the work of one, two or three scribes, led him to date all the hands to the same period, to underestimate the significance of the many differences in the abbreviations used by the various scribes, and to account for the many different spellings in the added sections as being a consequence of being 'more carelessly written' than **M** and therefore furnishing a 'richer quarry of corrupt forms'.[21]

Certainly there is a relation between all these scripts. Nevertheless, the differences make better sense if the additions are judged to have been made chronologically later than the original text than if they are attributed to carelessness and greater corruption. The contrasts between them cannot simply be attributed to the greater degree of informality and perhaps also rapidity with which they were written. An expansion of the chronological scope of the Bobbio Missal would render the book even more valuable as a witness to the written culture of its region over a longer period of time than used to be imagined. It also allows for the possibility that the production of the main text took place a little earlier than has been accepted hitherto if there is no longer a need to accommodate the manifestly later minuscule portions as the work of the same scribe. Of course the chronological span might not be very great (and this is addressed in greater detail below) but the codicology of the manuscript makes it clear that all these additions were made after the main text was complete.

Lowe himself stressed that the closest analogues in orthography to the Bobbio Missal's texts were manuscripts and charters from Merovingian Gaul in the seventh and eighth centuries. It is also important to note that the orthography so meticulously recorded by Lowe appears to have proceeded much further along lines already indicated in the famous papyrus manuscript of Bishop Avitus of Vienne's letters written in the early sixth century, most likely at Vienne itself.[22] This scribe

---

[20] Lowe, 'Palaeography', p. 72.    [21] Ibid., p. 86.
[22] Paris, BNF lat. 8913 (Burgundy/Vienne, s. vi); *CLA* V.573.

confuses **e** and **ae**, uses **e** more or less consistently for **i**, **h** at the beginnings of words is omitted where it should be and added where it should not, **u** is substituted for **o** and **c** sometimes for **t**.[23] While adding useful indications about the region in which this book was written, the orthography of the Bobbio Missal may suggest that the texts which may have acted as exemplars for the compiler of the Bobbio Missal already contained this characteristic spelling and choice of particular consonants. The full implications of this would merit further consideration on some future occasion but it points at the least to a Provençal origin of the Bobbio Missal's texts if not the Bobbio Missal itself.

Lowe's dating of the book overall, moreover, rested on the mixed character of the main script **M** and its similarity with dated examples such as the apparently Burgundian Gundohinus Gospels and the probably Frankish Bobbio Gregory, both of around 750.[24] Lowe rejected seventh-century manuscripts such as the Morgan Augustine as being too dissimilar.[25] Lowe also appears to have conflated the script types in the book as a whole by implying that the scripts of the additions were to be attributed to the same period as that of the main text, despite the contrary indications of the codicology and orthography. It should perhaps also be observed that Lowe's detailed understanding of the script recorded in 1924 was possibly formed without the benefit of the knowledge afforded by the comprehensive survey of many Frankish centres of book production recorded in volumes V and VI of the Paris and French collections in *CLA*. This survey was in any case largely carried out by Bernhard Bischoff when he was acting as Lowe's assistant.[26]

Further, the marked differences in particular between the main text and the various additions as far as the abbreviations are concerned, let alone the letter forms themselves, need to be given their due weight. The abbreviations of the *nomina sacra* and the regular (and ancient) suspensions of **-bus** and **-que** are very similar in the main text and the additions. In the 'literary abbreviations', on the other hand, there are significant differences between the main text and the additions and it is these differences which point most persuasively to different scribes.[27] The main

[23] See further the comments by Charles Wright and Roger Wright in this volume.

[24] Autun, BM 3 (?Burgundy [*Vosevi*]), s. VIII^med–754); *CLA* VI.716, and see L. Nees, *The Gundohinus Gospels* (Cambridge, MA, 1987); and Milan, Biblioteca Ambrosiana B 159 sup. (uncial Francia/Bobbio, s.viii^med); although written by the scribe Georgius for Abbot Anastasius and thus probably at Bobbio, this does not necessarily provide a location for the style of script which has a number of Frankish features, not least the heart-shaped bows on the **B**, the form of the **N** and the flesh side appearing on the outside of a quire; *CLA* III.309.

[25] New York, Pierpont Morgan Library M. 334 (Luxeuil, 669); *CLA* XI.1659. See E.A. Lowe 'The script of Luxeuil: a title vindicated', *Revue Bénédictine* 63 (1953), pp. 132–42 (repr. in Lowe, *Palaeographical Papers*, II, pp. 389–98).

[26] This is clear from the E.A. Lowe papers now in the Pierpont Morgan Library in New York, and was explained by Bernhard Bischoff in the address to the Bibliographical Society of Great Britain on the occasion of his receiving the Gold Medal of the society, 19 October 1982.

[27] These are meticulously recorded by Lowe in his 1924 discussion, pp. 76–85.

text's scribe was sparing in his use of liturgical abbreviations, but the scribes of the additions were more liberal. As a whole, the abbreviations are of a mixed character, with 'Merovingian' predominating and some Insular symptoms. In the past some of these abbreviations (such as n̄sīs, n̄sm̄ for *nostris* and *nostrum*) were labelled as 'Visigothic' but it is a little misleading to do so. Essentially they are so ubiquitous in Merovingian manuscripts as to deprive a differentiation of them from Frankish abbreviations of any value.[28] In any case, some of these abbreviations could have been taken over from the exemplar or exemplars.

It is not only the variety of abbreviations, however, which is of importance. The fact that all the scribes involved in this book were clearly accustomed to using a wide range of abbreviations as a matter of course adds up to an eloquent statement about the high level of competence of the scribes as scribes, without invoking aesthetic criteria.

The cursive insertions are important for any understanding of the use to which this manuscript was put.[29] On fols. 15v and 16r, for example, we can see what appear to be corrections and alterations to the text and the change of the order of certain saints in the list. Thus Felicity is inserted beside Perpetua, and Agatha is put before Agnes.

If one were to exercise aesthetic judgement one would also be bound to acknowledge again the confidence of the scribes in the consistency of their letter forms and ductus, their use of the writing space and the judgement of space required in the organisation of the text and its disposition within each gathering in the process of copying. This is, in short, despite its lack of elegance and its unpleasingness to the eye, not the work of scribes unaccustomed to the process of copying text. The question of exemplar or selection of exemplars providing a number of texts for compiling this book needs to be explored further, but cannot be done within the compass of this chapter.[30]

In many ways one might get no further than saying that these (with the exception for the moment of the Frankish hand of the *Missa pro principe*, possibly written somewhere else) are confident Frankish hands in a centre where writing at many levels was commonplace and where a range of texts was available. There are several other matters, however, which may indicate the origin of the main text of this codex.

In the first place, there are some differences between the mixed uncial in this book and the Frankish uncial, largely from the Seine River basin and the north of Francia

---

[28] See W.A. Lindsay, *Notae Latinae: An Account of Abbreviation in Latin MSS. of the Early Minuscule Period, c. 700–850* (Cambridge, 1915), and D. Bains, *A Supplement to Notae Latinae* (Cambridge, 1936), whose categorisation reflects early attempts at constructing a typology for abbreviations.

[29] See Rob Meens' contribution, below, pp. 154–67.

[30] Compare Lowe's hypothesis of page by page copying, 'Palaeography', pp. 96–8.

that I have discussed elsewhere.[31] In the latter, a distinctive character developed in the course of the seventh and eighth centuries. There is a square rather than round effect in the treatment of the letter forms, the bows of the uncial **B** form a curious heart shape, marked serifs on the **T**, a strong flourish to the **R** and exaggerated treatment of **L** and double **LL**. Some of this Frankish uncial was heavy and more monumental than other examples, but there remains sufficient similarity between the great variety of examples of uncial script written in Frankish Gaul north of the Loire and from the more northern part of Burgundy, such as Autun at least, to distinguish it from other uncial being produced in western Europe (especially Britain, Spain and Italy) at the time. Uncial linked with Flavigny, for example, has a marked double **LL** which resemble parallel columns and a thread-like descender on the uncial **G**. But the Bobbio Missal's uncial **B** also forms the distinctive Frankish heart-shaped bows and pronounced form of the double **LL** with the strong serifs on the top of the ascender as well as the slightly oblique bottom shaft. All Frankish manuscripts, including the Bobbio Missal, furthermore, show a preference for initials with birds and fish, zig-zag ornament and curled or leaf-shaped flourishes on the serifs, and hollow capitals with a simple infill of colour. All scripts show signs of contact with Merovingian cursive and a tendency to introduce minuscule letter forms. It is these last named aspects, the initials, particular letter forms, the influence of cursive scripts, the mixture of scripts within a book but a retention of a sense of display and command of abbreviations, which are also present in the Bobbio Missal. The script of the latter also certainly displays some superficial overall similarities with north Italian and Spanish uncials of the late seventh and eighth centuries, but the closest parallels are with codices apparently from the south and east of Merovingian Gaul.

As far as the main text is concerned, there are the similarities already signalled and noted in some cases also by Lowe, between the uncial letter forms in the Bobbio Missal and such books as the Luxeuil codex in the Pierpont Morgan Library (Morgan 334), not least the kicking **r**. But other comparanda may be observed.

Autun, BM 24 + Paris, BNF n.a. lat. 1629, fols. 17–20, dated to the late sixth century, for example, is an unevenly written half-uncial manuscript of Cassian's *Institutiones*, thought to be from the south of France.[32] It has a confusion of spelling between **d** and **t**, **b** and **p** and it is also rather 'blobby' in appearance. That is, the thickening at the ends of the shafts of both short and tall letters and of minims create a visual effect rather different from that of the scripts further north. Three seventh-century codices from the Lyons region, Lyons, BM 443 containing Origen, Lyons, BM 468 + Paris, BNF lat. 602 and Lyons, BM 604 + Paris, BNF lat. 1594, all

[31] R. McKitterick, 'Frankish uncial; a new context for the Echternach scriptorium', in *Willibrord zijn wereld en zijn werk*, ed. A. Weiler and P. Bange (Nijmegen, 1990) (repr. in McKitterick, *Books, Scribes and Learning*, ch. 5).
[32] *CLA* VI.724.

written in half-uncial, have more resemblance to the Bobbio Missal's mixed uncial of hand **M** than they do to the books produced further to the north and west.[33] The minuscule of the eighth-century manuscript remnants in Bern, Burgerbibliothek 611 fols. 42–93 + Paris, BNF lat. 10756, fols. 62–9, on the other hand, is ascribed to 'eastern France' by Lowe and Bischoff. It is reminiscent of the Bobbio Missal's hands **A** and **a** and does also have a round **d**.[34] Most of the other examples I have cited naturally persist in using the half-uncial straight **d**. In my view the mixed uncial of hand **M** of the Bobbio Missal has more in common with the original script of the seventh-century Ashburnham Pentateuch, though the origin of the latter is both unknown and hotly disputed and a north Italian origin rather than a Frankish one may need to be considered seriously.[35]

Such comparisons are inherently tentative. No exact parallels have been found and comparisons rest on what may be thought to be far too subjective visual impressions of letter forms. In this respect, more substantial corroboration of the suggestion that one may be dealing with regional practice is provided by the evidence of the preparation of the membrane and arrangement of leaves within the quire. In the manuscripts associated with the south-east of Merovingian Gaul mentioned above there is a certain persistence of the use of quires arranged with the flesh side outside and ruled on the flesh side, with flesh side occasionally facing hair side in the quire. The Bobbio Missal's membrane and arrangement of quires accord with this. These books also contain consistent peculiarities of orthography and a particular inclination in abbreviation practice. In the nature of things, if one is dealing with a possible solitary survivor from a particular place, then one is unlikely to come up with exact parallels as distinct from similar elements. It is also the case that some of the peculiarities of the Bobbio Missal's script might be attributable to a later stage of evolution of the characteristics of the few codices I have cited as possible comparanda.

So far, the evidence supports Lowe's original suggestion of France and the *CLA* attribution to south-east Gaul.[36] I take this to point to Provence. Let us look more closely at the evidence for book production, writing practice and book availability in Provence provided for the sixth and seventh centuries. This can be observed in such manuscripts as the famous papyrus codex of Avitus' letters mentioned earlier.[37] The cursive letter forms of this scribe could be seen in an evolutionary relationship with the cursive forms in the Bobbio Missal. Bede's *Historia abbatum*

---

[33] Ibid. VI.774a, 776, 783.    [34] Ibid. V.604d.

[35] Paris, BNF n.a. lat. 2334; *CLA* V.693. See Dorothy Verkerk's forthcoming monograph on the Ashburnham Pentateuch. It should be noted that the replacement leaves of the Ashburnham Pentateuch made in s. viii^med (fols. 3, 4, 8, 37–8, 60–4, 122, 129) are in Frankish uncial and possibly from eastern France.

[36] Lowe, 'Palaeography', p. 105.    [37] Above, p. 35.

testifies to the availability of books in south-east Gaul in the seventh century when he refers to Benedict Biscop's acquisition of various books which he then left with friends at Vienne while he went to Rome. He fetched them on his way back to Northumbria.[38] That writing continued in the Provençal region is clear from both the charter evidence and the abundant inscription evidence for the late sixth and seventh centuries. The cursive additions, moreover, for example on fols. 113v (last word, line 16), 249v, 278v, 293r lines 12–13 of the Bobbio Missal, indicate a scribe familiar with the conventional Merovingian documentary cursive script used in charters. The *Vita sancti Clari* recounts the career of the abbot of Saint-Marcel, a contemporary of Bishop Chaoldus (fl. 654, 664).[39] Although it was written possibly under episcopal auspices in the early Carolingian period, churches and monasteries in Vienne in the seventh and eighth centuries also imply the presence of written culture, documents and books.

Among the inscriptions assembled in the fine recent atlas of medieval inscriptions are examples from Ardèche, Vienne and Grenoble.[40] One inscription from Ardèche is dated 683 (the fourth year of the reign of King Theuderic) in memory of Bertigisilus. It is prefaced with a cross and is inscribed on a tall narrow stone with fairly even capitals in short lines. There is a capital **A** with a v-form for the cross bar often associated with Luxeuil.[41] The inscription on another stone from Ardèche in memory of the five-year-old boy Amatus is written in rather less stylish letters and the **A** has a straight cross bar.[42] The confusion of **i** and **e** (thus *menus* instead of *minus*) is similar to that noted above in the Bobbio Missal. From Vienne there is a rather more elaborate inscription in memory of the young man Maurolenus, dated 660 (that is, the third year of King Chlothar) and preserved in St Peter's church, Vienne.[43] It has some decorative leaf-work carved at the head of the inscription and there is a certain plastic and curved quality to the well-placed letter forms making them look more like rustic than square capitals. There is also the confusion of **e** and **i** in *menus* for *minus* and *rig(ni)* for *reg(ni)*. But another example from Vienne, in memory of Valiaricus and his wife Licinia and no more precisely dated than the seventh century, adopts a different method. The letter forms are more angular, including a diamond-shaped **O** and serifs on the finials, but the inscription is also set out as if between lines. Its spelling confuses **o** and **u**; **v** and **b**.[44] A Grenoble inscription of the late sixth or early seventh century, moreover, is even more ambitious. Underneath the inscription in memory of Populinia, written

[38] Bede, *Historia abbatum*, c.4., ed. C. Plummer, *Opera Omnia* (Oxford, 1896), pp. 377–9; also J.E. King, *Bede, Historical Works*, II (Cambridge, MA, and London, 1963), p. 400.
[39] AASS Ian.1, pp. 55–60.
[40] *Recueil des inscriptions chrétiennes de la Gaule antérieures à la renaissance carolingienne: XV Viennoise du Nord*, ed. F. Descombes (Paris, 1997).
[41] Ibid., no. XV.21.    [42] Ibid., no. XV.18.    [43] Ibid., no. XV.104.
[44] Ibid., no. XV.119.

in quite mannered and plastic capitals with an anvil-shaped top to the **A** and an elaborate **Q** with the tongue branching out of the middle of the letter, there is a decorated urn flanked by two doves.[45] These inscriptions, being in capitals, do not provide analogues for the uncial and minuscule forms in the Bobbio Missal, though the orthography and the decorative forms are undoubtedly similar. Nevertheless, a variety of styles and formulae is in evidence, in the letter forms, texts and the design of the inscriptions. They suggest different groups of skilled stone cutters who served communities throughout the seventh century still interested in erecting inscribed stones in memory of the departed. What they and the extremely meagre literary or documentary evidence from the region[46] do indicate, therefore, is a wide range of uses of literacy, skilled scribes and stone cutters, and letter forms available in the south-east region of Gaul throughout the early Middle Ages.

In terms of its history, moreover, the common understanding of Provence as removed from Frankish affairs cannot be sustained.[47] Quite apart from the extensive series of church councils convened at Orange, Vaison, Arles and Carpentras in the sixth century,[48] the recorded attendance, for example, of Landelenus bishop of Vienne at the council of Chalons (647–53) and the presidency of the council of Paris by Bishop Domnolus in 614, the career of Desiderius of Vienne is a further indication of how closely Vienne's bishop was involved in Merovingian politics as a whole.[49] That the decrees of these councils were also preserved within Gaul is a further indication of the persistence of literate modes of record keeping in the region.[50]

Bishop Desiderius himself, stoned to death in 607, was reputed to have been buried at St Peter's. The growth of his cult, the burials of successive bishops at

---

[45] Ibid., no. XV.237.

[46] According to the published volumes of the *Chartae Latinae Antiquiores*, none survives in the original from this region. For information about the documentary sources in the archdioceses of Vienne, Arles and Lyons, see *Topographie chrétienne des cités de la Gaule des origines au milieu du VIIIe siècle: III Provinces ecclésiastiques de Viennes et d'Arles*, ed. N. Gauthier and J.C. Picard (Paris, 1986), and *IV Province ecclésiastique de Lyon* (Paris, 1986); see also below on the will of Abbo, pp. 42–3.

[47] P.-A. Fevrier, *Provence depuis les origines à l'an mil: histoire et archéologie* (Rennes, 1989).

[48] C. de Clercq, *Concilia Galliae A. 511-A. 695*, CCSL 148A (Turnhout, 1963).

[49] For detail on Desiderius, see L. Duchesne, *Fastes épiscopaux de l'ancienne Gaule*, I (2nd edn, Paris 1907), pp. 207–8, and see also the comments in H. Leclercq's exhaustive entry on Vienne in *DACL* XV.2 (Paris, 1956), cols. 3038–94, which uses an early medieval episcopal list and Ado of Vienne's *Chronicle* (PL 123, cols. 75–138). But Françoise Descombes, 'Vienne', in *Topographie chrétienne*, ed. Gauthier and Picard, III, pp. 17–35, appears to accept him as Merovingian rather than place him in the second century as Duchesne had done, and dates his incumbency 594–610.

[50] See, for example, Vatican City, BAV, Pal. lat. 574 (origin uncertain but probably made for Autun, s. viii/ix); *CLA* I.96, which may represent a culmination of canon law transmission in Merovingian Burgundy and Provence. See also the material surveyed by H. Mordek, *Kirchenrecht und Reform im Frankenreich. Die Collectio Vetus Gallica, die älteste systematische Kanonessammlung des fränkischen Gallien. Studien und Edition*, Beiträge zur Geschichte und Quellenkunde des Mittelalters 1 (Berlin and New York, 1975).

Vienne, especially at the church of St Peter's and the associated monastery, and the importance of Vienne as a cult site should not be underestimated. The city possessed the relics of Gervasius and the relics of the martyr Ferreolus were translated to a new church within the city in the time of Bishop Willicarius. There may have been a cult of the Maccabees. The earliest reference to the relics of the martyr St Maurice in association with the cathedral of Vienne appears to be at the beginning of the early eighth century, though the structure to the west of the cathedral apparently built for St Maurice's relics dates from the late seventh century or early eighth century and may have been commissioned by Eoldus who was bishop at the time. More information survives from the reverence King Boso offered to the saint and embellishment of his shrine between 879 and 887.[51] The archaeological excavations of the nineteenth and twentieth centuries have not been able to indicate marked building activity in the seventh and eighth centuries, and there seems to be a resumption of activity only in the ninth. There is some hope that archaeological excavation may reveal more from the period from the seventh to ninth centuries, but as in many other instances, not least Rome itself, the early medieval history of church foundations and buildings has been left largely unexplored.[52]

In the early eighth century Charles Martel made a most determined effort to incorporate the region into his administrative and judicial arrangements for the Frankish realm. The Continuator to Fredegar's Chronicle describes Charles' conquest of Burgundy, which incorporated Roman *Provincia*, that is, Provence, between 736 and 738. It states that Charles subjected the chief men and officials of that province to his rule and placed his judges (*iudices*) over the whole region as far as Marseilles and Arles.[53] Probably a couple of years after this first episode and the siege of Avignon, Charles despatched an army under his brother Duke Childebrand and 'many dukes and counts' with orders to march on Provence. He was here dealing with the revolt of Duke Marontus. Once they had reached Avignon, Charles 'restored the whole country, down to the Mediterranean, to his rule'.[54] From 739 furthermore, we have the testament of Abbo, a major landowner and one of Charles Martel's staunch supporters and probably the last *patricius* of Provence. It was written by the 'venerable cleric' Hytbertus and witnesses to an

[51] See M. Jannet-Vallat, R. Lanxeroi and J.-F. Reynaud, *Vienne aux premiers temps chrétiens* (Lyons, 1986), and F. Descombes, 'Vienne', in *Topographie chrétienne*, ed. Gauthier and Picard, III, pp. 17–35.

[52] See R. Coates-Stevens' excellent corrective survey, 'Dark-age architecture in Rome', *Papers of the British School at Rome* 65 (1997), pp. 177– 232.

[53] Fredegar, *Chronicle*, cont. c. 18, ed. J.M. Wallace-Hadrill, *The Fourth Book of the Chronicle of Fredegar and its Continuations* (London, 1960), p. 93. See also the account of the capture of Avignon which linked Charles to Joshua capturing Jericho, and the laying waste of the cities of Agde, Nîmes and Béziers, ibid., c. 20, pp. 93–5.

[54] Ibid., c. 21, pp. 95–6.

extensive and accurate use of Roman legal forms and standard Merovingian testamentary formulae in the region, though the precise location of Hytbertus' training and of the redaction of the will itself are not known.[55] Fredegar's Continuator, on the other hand, clearly indicates that a subsequent count of Vienne, Theodoenus, was loyal to Pippin III, for it was he who had killed Pippin's troublesome brother Grifo, though Theodoenus was also killed in the fight.[56] Ewig speculated that this Theodoenus of Vienne was related by marriage to Charles Martel, and was possibly the brother of Charles' son-in-law Theudebert of Autun.[57] If correct, it is an indication of the importance of Vienne that it should be entrusted to a close associate of the Carolingian family.

Thereafter Provence retained its importance for the Carolingian royal house, for both strategic and logistic reasons, not least as their interests in Italy burgeoned. Vienne in particular was on the direct route from Lyons down the Rhône whether by river or Roman road towards Italy. At Vienne the road forked, with the southern route proceeding towards Valence, Avignon and Arles and the eastern route proceeding to Grenoble, Briançon and over the pass of Mt Geneviève into the Dora Riparia valley or via Saint-Jean de Maurienne and the Mont Cenis Pass to Susa. Certainly the Frankish host took that route to Italy in 754.[58] It was at Vienne itself that there was most probably a royal residence, or at least a residence sufficiently commodious for use by the members of the royal family and their entourage. It was there that Carloman, brother of Pippin, went with his sister-in-law Queen Bertrada in 755. He had come to Francia from Monte Cassino in 753, apparently to intervene in the Lombard–Frankish–papal discussions. It was in Vienne, moreover, that Carloman fell ill and died and from thence that his body was taken to Monte Cassino to be buried. In 767 Pippin III celebrated Easter there and it may well be that Pope Hadrian rested there as he travelled into Francia overland from Marseilles in 773.[59]

For episcopal and monastic activity, the sources yield even less. The attendance of archbishops of Vienne at Merovingian church councils has already been mentioned. The catalogue of bishops by Ado, archbishop of Vienne, and the Martyrology of Ado (usually dated 858–67) yield a list of twenty bishops of Vienne before the

[55] See P.J. Geary, *Aristocracy in Provence. The Rhône Basin at the Dawn of the Carolingian Age* (Stuttgart, 1985), pp. 27–35. See also U. Nonn, 'Merowingische Testamente. Studien zum Fortleben einer römischen Urkundenform im Frankenreich', *Archiv für Diplomatik* 18 (1972), pp. 1–129.

[56] Fredegar, *Chronicle*, cont. c. 35, ed. Wallace-Hadrill, p. 103.

[57] E. Ewig, 'L'Aquitaine et les pays Rhénans au haut moyen âge', *Cahiers de civilisation médiévale* 1 (1958), pp. 37–54, at p. 49.

[58] Fredegar, *Chronicle*, cont. c. 37, ed. Wallace-Hadrill, p. 105.

[59] *Annales regni Francorum*, s.a. 755, 767, 773, ed. F. Kurze, MGH SRG (Hannover, 1895), pp. 12, 24 and 34. The revised version of the annals records that Carloman's body was taken to Monte Cassino on the king's orders, ibid., p. 13.

seventh century and an apparently unbroken sequence of bishops throughout the seventh and eighth centuries, some of whom are mentioned in Merovingian royal diplomas.[60] Bishop Willicarius, given the *pallium* by Pope Gregory III,[61] is said to have gone into voluntary exile during the troubles in the late 730s.[62] Bishop Bertericus, according to Ado, was elevated to the see by Pippin III. Then in 794, there was the famous dispute brought to the synod of Frankfurt by Ursio, bishop of Vienne, concerning episcopal and metropolitan jurisdiction.[63] Difficult and late though the evidence of episcopal presence at Vienne in the seventh and eighth centuries may be, it is more abundant than for many other Frankish sees, not least Rheims, in this period. Ado, moreover, certainly succeeds in creating the impression of continuous religious activity at Vienne which also implies no break in written culture or liturgical observance. All this suggests that Vienne was not relegated to a backwater but retained throughout the seventh and eighth centuries a presence on the national stage as well as at a local level.

It is within the context of Vienne's importance to the emerging Carolingian house in the central decades of the eighth century, furthermore, that the incorporation of the *Missa pro principe* should be considered. The best place to do so is within the discussion that follows concerning the codicology of the Bobbio Missal, but it is appropriate here to offer a few comments on the script. Lowe in the remarks mentioned at the outset merely stated his opinion that the script of this mass was a 'pure uncial' of the eighth century and written in a different centre from the rest of the text. It is eighth century certainly, but not wholly pure: the scribe uses minuscule long **s** on occasion as well as an uncial **a** with such a truncated shaft as to make the letter look more like a minuscule **q** with a short shaft lying on its side. The **H** has an exaggerated horizontal bar on the top of the shaft, the **B** has the distinctive Frankish heart-shaped bows, The double **LL** and **L** are emphatic with a bar on the top of the shaft like that of the **H** and, when on its own, the **L** also has a strong comma shape on the end of its horizontal shaft. The fact that this portion of text was added later may account for the differences in type of script and in the forms of individual letters, and there may be no need to posit a different centre. On the other hand, given the fact that the leaves are inserted, it remains a possibility that these leaves did indeed come from somewhere else in the form of a liturgical *libellus* and were duly incorporated into the book. What light, therefore, can the palaeographical evidence throw on the question of the origin of these leaves? The uncial of these leaves has, in fact, far more in common with the characteristics of late seventh- and eighth-century uncial from north of the Loire that I described

[60] H. Leclercq, 'Vienne', in *DACL* XV.2 (Paris, 1956), cols. 3038–97, remains the classic account.
[61] *Liber pontificalis*, ed. L. Duchesne, 2 vols. (Paris, 1886–92) (repr. with vol. III by C. Vogel (Paris, 1955–7)), I, p. 421.
[62] Ado of Vienne, *Chronicon*, PL 123, cols. 75–138.
[63] *Concilium Frankofurtense*, c. 8, ed. A. Boretius, MGH Capitularia I (Hannover, 1883), p. 73.

earlier. Close analogues are manuscripts such as the Orosius fragments in Paris (especially the forms of **T**, **L**, **N** and **B**), the *Codex Salmasianus* and the earliest manuscript of Fredegar's Chronicle.[64] That there is uncertainty about the origin of all these books and fragments does not help us but the eighth-century dates do suggest that the *Missa pro principe* is also to be dated to the eighth century. I should be inclined to date it to the middle of the eighth century rather than much earlier, partly on the grounds of it being some way along a development into minuscule. As for origin there is a possibility that this could be simply a later manifestation of the uncial from the same centre that produced the main text, but the closest comparanda seem to me to be north Frankish. If *libelli* of certain mass texts were circulated, as seems likely from the extant palimpsest evidence in particular, studied by Yitzhak Hen,[65] and if the kings wished to promote liturgical acknowledgement of their rule as well as liturgical reform more generally, then the *Missa pro principe* in the Bobbio Missal could be the outcome of a deliberate attempt to promote the liturgical observance of the ruler's position as a consequence of the imposition of Carolingian rule in Provence.[66] A *libellus* might have been received and either inserted as it was into the Bobbio Missal or copied on to a fresh gathering for insertion. The Bobbio Missal may therefore come from a place where the king or members of his household might be, or where his loyal supporters were based. The appropriate place to start to disseminate such a new liturgical element would be the archbishopric. Further, in the light of the indications that Vienne was a royal residence in the middle of the eighth century, the insertion of the *Missa pro principe* leaves (probably written elsewhere and distributed to certain centres) may have been made at Vienne in the middle of the eighth century to mark the acknowledgement of Carolingian rule and the authority of Charles Martel and Pippin III in the region.

All these considerations taken together incline me to propose Provence and the archdiocese of Vienne, if not the city itself, as the origin of the Bobbio Missal.[67] Although nearby Lyons might seem to be a suitable candidate there seem to be sufficient differences between Lyons manuscripts and this one not to make this possible. There are in any case the well-known obstacles in the palaeographical evidence to determining any single centre of book production at Lyons and the difficulty of locating codices from the Lyons area to the later seventh and eighth

---

[64] Paris, BNF lat. 10399, fol. 3 + London, British Library Add. 24144 + Brussels, Bibliothèque Royale 19609 (1346) (uncertain origin, s. viii^in); *CLA* II.171; Paris, BNF lat. 10318 (uncial, ?N. Italy or S. France, s. viii^2); *CLA* V.593; Paris, BNF lat. 10910 (?Burgundy, s.viii^1); *CLA* V.608.

[65] Y. Hen, 'Liturgical palimpsests in the early Middle Ages', in *Early Medieval Palimpsests*, ed. G. Declercq (forthcoming).

[66] On the Carolingian rulers and the liturgy see Y. Hen, *The Royal Patronage of Liturgy in Frankish Gaul to the Death of Charles the Bald*, HBS subsidia 3 (London, 2001).

[67] This conclusion is supported by the findings of Charles Wright and Roger Wright concerning the additions made to the text; see below, pp. 79–139.

centuries.[68] It may also be the case that Vienne, prominent in Carolingian affairs around the middle of the eighth century, was actually eclipsed by Lyons towards the end of the eighth century with the installation of Leidrad there as archbishop.[69] Further, I should like to propose that the scripts of the book, seen in conjunction with the codicology of the manuscript, enable us to posit two stages in the compilation of this book, if not three, with these four different scribes involved. In what follows I shall offer suggestions of when these various stages should be dated, though I would wish to stress that these are tentative suggestions at present.

## CODICOLOGY

Closer examination of the codicology in particular makes the successive stages of the compilation of this manuscript very clear. The Collation reveals that the quiring is regular more often than not and that the arrangement of the gatherings has considerable significance for our understanding of the manuscript as a whole. Of the thirty-six quires, twelve only have an irregular number of leaves, greater or fewer than the standard eight. The non-standard quires, however, complete texts or sections of related texts; they therefore reflect methodical judgement about the length of texts. The run-on of text between quires is much more likely between successive regular quires of eight leaves. In the detailed summary of the gatherings below I indicate where the text has a natural break, whether minor in the sense of a break between lections or between prayers of a mass, or major in the sense of a new section or new group of related texts.

**A-8 fols. 1–8** There is a natural break to the text at the end of the *Interpretationes capitulorum* and *Joca monachorum.*

This quire contains explanations of holy writ and Christian morals and a dialogue on sacred history. It is written in the mixed script designated by Lowe as **A**.

**B-11 fols. 9–19** contains the *Lictio Libri Daniel prophetae in cottidiana legenda* and the *Missa Romensis Cotidiana.* These eleven leaves contain these texts which then allows the scribe to start a new quire for the lectiones.

**C-9 fols. 20–8** Incipiunt Liccionis.

**D-8 fols. 29–36.**

---

[68] On Lyons and the characteristics of manuscripts associated with the Lyons area, see E.A. Lowe, *Codices Lugdunenses antiquiores* (Lyons, 1924), and my comments in 'The scriptoria of Merovingian Gaul', pp. 177–84. Lenka Kolarova has in hand a major study of the scriptorium and library of Carolingian Lyons for her PhD in the University of Cambridge, which also makes important observations concerning the earlier book production to be associated with the city.

[69] B. Bischoff, 'Panorama der Handschriftenüberlieferung aus der Zeit Karls des Großen', in B. Bischoff, *Mittelalterliche Studien*, III (Stuttgart, 1981), pp. 5–38 at pp. 18–19 (English translation in B. Bischoff, 'Manuscripts in the age of Charlemagne', in B. Bischoff, *Manuscripts and Libraries in the Age of Charlemagne*, trans. M. Gorman (Cambridge, 1994), pp. 20–56 at pp. 33–5).

**E-8 fols. 37–45** (there is no fol. 38).
**F-8 fols. 46–53.**
**G-12 fols. 54–65.**
**H-11 fols. 66–76.**

Quires C–H are all lections and masses in continuous sequence with no obvious break between the quires and should be seen as a whole with the number of leaves having needed to be calculated carefully and distributed evenly.

But the next quire **I-8 fols. 77–84**, beginning on fol. 77, makes it clear that with *Item missa ieiunii* the scribe began a new mass text *in ieiunii* (the fifth of such masses) and deliberately spread out the text on the preceding page a little so that it would not be necessary to start this part of a text on the last page of a gathering. Again, this signals an orderly set of decisions about the grouping of the text in relation to the quires and copying sequence.

**K-8 fols. 85–92** also has a natural break after the preceding one and begins *In symbolum ad aures apercionis ad elictus*. This quire includes an exposition of the creed.[70]

**L-8 fols. 93–100** begins again after the natural break at the end of the preceding gathering with a *Missa symboli tradicti*. This runs on to the next quire.

**M-9 fols. 101–9** ends, with the help of one additional leaf with a natural break before the next quire.

**N-8 fols. 110–17** the *Benedictio Caerei sancti Agustini episcopi cum adhuc diaconus essit cecinit dicens ad Christianum faciendum*. This quire includes the *ordo baptismi* (fol. 114) and runs on to the next quire.

**O-8 fols. 118–25** includes the *Missa in vigiliis Pasche* and runs on to the next quire.

**P-8 fols. 126–33**, however, ends with a natural pause between lections for *Missa Paschalis* III.

**Q-8 fols. 134–41** includes the *Missa in inventione sancte +*, that is, the Holy Cross (fol. 138)[71] and ends with the *Lectio* from the prophet Joel and a pause before the next gathering.

**R-10 fols. 142–51** does have a break at the end on fol. 151, though not as obvious had another leaf been added, for the *Lictiones Cottidianas* section starts on fol. 151. Even the *Lectio* itself does begin a new gathering.

**S-6 fols. 152–7** has only six leaves and there is again a natural break at the end of the last page.

[70] For useful contemporary and near contemporary comparisons, see A.E. Burn and L. Traube, *Facsimiles of the Creeds from Early Manuscripts*, HBS 36 (London, 1909).

[71] On the knowledge of the legend of the Holy Cross in the west see J.W. Drijvers, *The Finding of the True Cross. The Judas Kyriakos Legend in Syriac* (Louvain, 1997); and S. Borghammer, *How the Holy Cross Was Found. From Event to Medieval Legend*, Bibliotheca theologiae practicae 47 (Stockholm, 1991). This is an early textual witness to the incorporation of the *inventio* prayers into the Frankish liturgy.

**T-8 fols. 158–65** includes the *Missa sancti Sigismundi regis*[72] and runs on to the next quire.

**V-8 fols. 166–73** runs on to the next quire.

**X-8 fols. 174–81** continues.

**Y-2 fols. 182–3** completes a section ending with a *Missa unius virgenis*, two Collectiones *post prophetia in dedicatione aecclesie*.

**Z-8 fols. 184–91** then starts a new group.

The editors added a heading *Lictiones in missa pro egroto* but the manuscript itself simply begins on fol. 184r with *Epistola iacobi apostoli* and then runs on to the next quire.

**AA-8 fols. 192–9** runs on to the next quire.

**BB-8 fols. 200–6bis** contains votive masses and runs on to the next quire.

**CC-14 fols. 207–20** with *Missa dominicalis* I, II, with two inserted leaves and running on to the next quire.

**DD-8 fols. 221–8** has *Missa Dominicalis* III and runs on to the next quire.

**EE-8 fols. 229–36** (with fols. 232, 233 as single inserted leaves), runs on to the next gathering.

**FF-8 fols. 237–44** runs on to the next quire.

**GG-12 fols. 245–56**. This quire includes the *Missa pro principe* on fols. 251–3. As already mentioned, this portion of the text is written in a different, and later, hand and intrudes itself into the main text between fols. 250 and 255, that is, leaves 6 and 7 of the original quire, interrupting the Fifth *Missa dominicalis* which then resumes on fol. 255. The diagram (Fig. 2) illustrates how this was done and what the recto opening of the mass *pro principe* looks like in conjunction with the preceding mass. Originally, therefore, this quire in the Bobbio Missal comprised eight leaves. The two inserted bifolia in their turn included three blank leaves (fols. 253v, 254r and 254v) subsequently used by scribe **a** to write in the texts entitled by the editors *Devotiones et imprecationes*. The last leaf of quire **GG** begins then with *legendas Cottidianis* and runs on to the next quire.

**HH-8 fols. 257–64** (includes *Missa Cottidiana*) runs on to the next gathering.

**II-8 fols. 265–72** includes *Lictiones in depositionis sacerdotis* and *Missa sacerdotis defuncti* and ends with a natural break before the next quire.

**KK-3 fols. 273–5** comprises a bifolium and singleton, containing prayers of exorcism, and ending half-way down fol. 275.

**LL-8 fols. 276–83** introduces a new section with the *Ordo ad consacrandas monachas* (the title *Benedictiones* provided by the editors is not in the manuscript) which runs on through *oracionis vespertinas* to the next quire.

[72] See Ian Wood's chapter in this volume and F. Paxton, 'Power and the power to heal: the cult of St Sigismund of Burgundy', *Early Medieval Europe* 2 (1993), pp. 95–110.

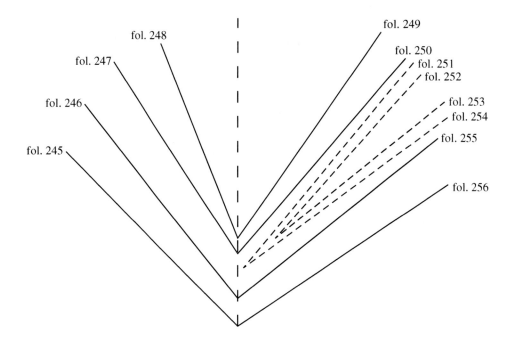

*Figure 2   The Bobbio Missal: quire GG, showing insertion of leaves with the* Missa pro principe

**MM-12 fols. 284–95** completes the *oracionis vespertinas* four lines short of the bottom of the page on fol. 284r and begins the *oraciones de matutinis* on fol. 284v. Fol. 286 had originally been left blank but hand **A** inserts a prayer (*benedictio olei*) with no heading. The original text and main hand then continues on fol. 286v with

*In d(e)i nomen incipit iudicius penetencialis*
*1 Si quis clericos humicidium fecerrit et proximum suum occideret X annos exsol peneteat*
*in patriam cui conmisit satisfaciat parentibus eius quem occidit . . . etc.*
The *oratio super penitentem* ends on fol. 291r.
On fols. 291v–292r the very informal hand (probably **a**, the hand of fols. 253v–254v) has copied another *Benedictio*.
On fol. 292v *Incipit inquisitio de lege ad mesam celebrare*, that is, instruction about the hours at which mass should be celebrated, is added by the same hand who wrote quire **A**, probably continuing the process of filling up a gathering whose end leaves had been left blank. On fol. 293, moreover, the scribe of the informal minuscule hand, that is, probably **a**, who wrote fols. 291v–292r inserted a title, viz. *quando vel comodo inplebet dominus septem gradibus eclesiam*. In other words this later informal minuscule-writing scribe inserted a title into the text he found and also wrote the first two words *primus gradus* (wrongly stated by the editors to

be part of the original text).[73] This establishes that fol. 292v, including the texts beginning *incepet di tempore nativitatis christi* on fols. 294r–295v (that is, the dates of the life of Christ), was written before the minuscule of **a**. The writing on fol. 295v is now so worn as to be virtually illegible but it appears to break off one line short of completing the *Benedictiones panis at que acepeset abiant ha . . .* This last line (*. . . biant corpores sanetatem*) is then put as the last line (line 21) on the first page of the following quire.

**NN-5 fols. 296–300** (fol. 296 is a single leaf bound in). This last quire comprises palimpsested leaves. The lower sixth-century half-uncial text is the commentary by Ambrose on Luke,[74] but the upper text, apart from the intruded line 21, is the beginning of a new set of texts on the hours of the day, on the division of the phrases of the apostles' creed among the twelve apostles and a list of the canonical books of the Old and New Testaments in an unconventional order. These texts are written in a hand closely resembling, if not identical with, the main mixed uncial hand of the manuscript. From fol. 299v various prayers are also added in a ragged mixed uncial hand.

The codicology, therefore, clearly establishes a sequence of additions made to the Bobbio Missal. They have a crucial bearing on the dating of the manuscript overall. This is not a manuscript produced on one single occasion but a book compiled over a period of as much as fifty years between the main text's compilation and the latest additions. Study of the codicology also enables us to challenge one of the bases on which Lowe reiterated his view that the book was produced in an 'obscure village', namely, that the quire arrangements were allegedly 'extraordinarily haphazard'.

The effect of this judgement, coupled with Lowe's own meticulous observations on the abbreviations and orthography, was to date the manuscript to the eighth century. I propose rather that the main text was written at the very end of the seventh century or early eighth century and that the additions of **A** and **a**, culminating in the insertion of the *Missa pro principe*, were made in the course of the first half of the eighth century.

In conclusion, I should like first to make a personal observation. I have in my possession the Bible given to my father, in his thirtieth year, and on his ordination to the priesthood on the 16th Sunday after Trinity (2 October 1949), by the bishop of Derby. When considering gospel books and mass books from the early Middle Ages, it seems to me that we should not forget the possibility of a particular gift marking particular occasions in the relevant career or history of the person or

[73] For the text on the circumstances in which Christ entered the seven grades or orders of the church see R. Reynolds, *The Ordinals of Christ from their Origins to the Twelfth Century*, Beiträge zur Geschichte und Quellenkunde des Mittelalters 7 (Berlin and New York, 1978).

[74] *CLA* V.654 (?N. Italy [half-uncial], s. v) and see David Ganz, below, pp. 53–9.

community owning or using the book. The book itself, therefore, may be witness to a complex web of social and pastoral association, and possibly to the relationship between a bishop and his clergy. Such a gift would, as my father's Bible was, most likely have been a working copy, designed for constant reference and use. The most likely occasion for the acquisition of a sacramentary like the Bobbio Missal, therefore, might have been the first owner's ordination as priest when a youngish man, though whether he received it as a gift, had it written for him or wrote it himself is not known. He or the community to which he belonged may then have used it thereafter and at some stage, still in relation to the work required of the book's owners, other additions, notably those by **A**, who may have been one of the owners of the book during its early history, were made. To envisage the first owner and writer of the book as an old man cobbling together something in a remote village is not only to understate severely the importance of the book's contents, but also marks a failure of the practical imagination.

In the light of the suggestions I have offered in this chapter, therefore, let me now return to Lowe's summing up of almost a century ago and modify it. A little over thirteen hundred years ago, that is, in the later seventh or early eighth century, in a diocese in the south-east Provençal region of the Frankish kingdoms, conceivably Vienne itself, in a region where written traditions in book production, use of documents for legal records and inscriptions remained strong, a book was written for a priest's use, possibly to mark and equip his entry into the priesthood. The book was not primarily intended for a monastic community, though service to nuns and monks may have been part of this priest's role. Further, the priest could have belonged to a group of clerics in a community who together shared pastoral responsibilities in a city or region. It is conceivable that the person first compiling the book was also its first owner. Subsequently, in the first half of the eighth century, another user or other users of the book inserted leaves containing the mass *pro principe* and extra texts concerning penance, the biblical canon and various *benedictiones*. These later additions indicate that certain scribal habits remained current in the region, though the move towards a more informal script and towards minuscule as a book script was well underway, as was the development of the local Latin towards Romance. The script of the *Missa pro principe* is fully in line with Frankish uncial elsewhere in the first half of the eighth century which serves to indicate that this place was not so out of the way that it was not in touch, directly or indirectly, with the royal court or with other churches offering liturgical prayers for the king and was thus in a position to receive this text. The scribe who added the leaves at the beginning on penance could conceivably have been the same person as the main scribe at a much more advanced age. Alternatively, the similarities to be observed between uncial and minuscule elements may point more to the maintenance of certain letter forms within the region, not least the kicking **r**. One of those involved in a second stage of compilation also made use of the palimpsested leaves originally containing Ambrose on Luke, added texts concerning the creed and the canon of the Old and New Testaments. If these texts were also the work of the first scribe, however, they seem to have been added after the calculation of leaves for the main text had been done, making the resort to second-hand parchment necessary, presumably because it was to hand.[75] It is also a possibility that the texts on the palimpsested leaves represent part of the original campaign; but second-hand parchment was all that by then was available to the scribe. Hand **A** also made additions to this section. All this also argues for a stability of location of ownership within a particular church. The owner of the book may also have served a convent of nuns nearby. The occasional shakiness of the main hand **M** which Lowe attributed to age or illness could, with only some facetiousness, be linked with the inclusion in the book of the prayers for those suffering from quartan fever, that is, malaria, for such a common affliction in this region might have struck this scribe at regular intervals.[76]

The scribe of the main text certainly 'wrote with a will'. He made a good job of organising his text and the complicated gatherings of leaves necessary to form coherent sections within the manuscript. He was well versed in scribal conventions, not least the technical abbreviations used in liturgical texts as well as those more widespread among scribes. He wrote with great energy and consistency. His penmanship in red ink for headings and black ink for the main text shows that he was a competent scribe even if one cannot describe his script as either elegant or beautiful. By great good fortune, this extraordinarily interesting compilation by an unnamed cleric has survived to raise important questions that the rest of this volume will address.

---

[75] Compare the various observations on the recycling of parchment and circumstances in which palimpsests may have been appropriate, *Early Medieval Palimpsests*, ed. Declercq.
[76] See Wood below, pp. 211–12.

# 3

# The palimpsest leaves in the Bobbio Missal

DAVID GANZ

Leopold Delisle seems to have been the first to notice that the last quire of the Bobbio Missal, fols. 296–300, is a palimpsest, and among the plates which he provided for *Le Cabinet des manuscrits de la Bibliothèque nationale* he included a line of the primary script on fol. 297v.[1] In 1921 Dom André Wilmart deciphered the primary script of the ten palimpsest pages, identified their text and discussed their palaeography, their probable date and the bearing of these leaves on the question of where the Missal might have been copied.[2] In the *Notes and Studies* which accompanied the Henry Bradshaw Society's edition of the Missal E.A. Lowe included a note on the primary script of the palimpsest leaves,[3] and he returned to them in the entry for the Paris volume of *Codices Latini Antiquiores* (V.654). Most recently Caroline Hammond Bammel has discussed this fragment in a survey of early half-uncial and informal half-uncial Latin manuscripts.[4]

This final quire comprises five leaves, for the last leaf is missing. They were added to the Missal in order to complete a blessing entered on to the verso of fol. 295, the last leaf of the previous quire, and to supply additional texts on the canonical hours and the apostles' creed. They do not appear to have been treated in order to efface the primary script, which remains fairly legible.

The original manuscript from which the leaves were taken contained Ambrose's Commentary on Luke copied in two columns of 30–2 lines. While the outer margin and some lines of text at the top and bottom of each column have been lost, the inner margin of *c.* 8 mm makes it possible to estimate the original page layout, which must have had a squarish format; Lowe suggested this would have

---

[1] L. Delisle, *Le Cabinet des manuscrits de la Bibliothèque nationale*, III (Paris, 1881), pp. 225, 228, and pl. XVII.6; E. Châtelain, 'Les palimpsestes latins', *Annuaire de l'Ecole des Hautes-Etudes* (Paris, 1903), no.103, p. 36, reprints Delisle's account.

[2] Wilmart, 'Palimpseste', pp. 1–18.

[3] Lowe, 'Palaeography', pp. 73–6. He also discusses the palimpsest leaves on pp. 102–3.

[4] C. Hammond Bammel, 'Products of fifth-century scriptoria preserving conventions used by Rufinus of Aquileia: script', *Journal of Theological Studies* 35 (1984), pp. 347–93.

measured 225 × 185 mm. There is no visible evidence of ruling. The Bobbio Missal was copied in a tall narrow single column format, and, before the leaves of the Ambrose manuscript were palimpsested, each was folded down the centre between the two columns, so that each column of the Ambrose became one page of the Missal. During this process, the order of the text was disturbed: the first leaf was folded to form fols. 298 and 299 (in the order 298v, 299r, 299v, 298r). The outer columns of the original second leaf were lost; the inner columns are now fol. 296 (in the order 296r, 296v). The third leaf was folded to become fols. 297 and 300 (in the order 300v, 297r, 297v, 300r). Between the original first two leaves a leaf is missing; between the second and third leaves two leaves are probably missing.

The text can be identified with passages from Book VII of Ambrose on Luke in M. Adriaen's *Corpus Christianorum* edition:[5]

| Original order | Folio | Begins | Ends |
| --- | --- | --- | --- |
| 5 | 296r | c. 94 p. 245 line 962 | c. 95 p. 246 line 980 |
| 6 | 296v | c. 95 p. 246 line 984 | c. 96 p. 247 line 1000 |
| 8 | 297r | c. 117 p. 253 line 1200 | c. 119 p. 253 line 1214 |
| 9 | 297v | c. 119 p. 253 line 1218 | c. 120 p. 254 line 1233 |
| 4 | 298r | c. 84 p. 242 line 842 | c. 86 p. 242 line 858 |
| 1 | 298v | c. 78 p. 240 line 783 | c. 81 p. 240 line 796 |
| 2 | 299r | c. 82 p. 240 line 800 | c. 82 p. 240 line 808 |
| 3 | 299v | c. 83 p. 242 line 825 | c. 85 p. 242 line 840 |
| 7 | 300v | c. 116 p. 241 line 1183 | c. 117 p. 253 line 1196 |
| 10 | 300r | c. 119 p. 254 line 1237 | c. 122 p. 254 line 1250 |

The other surviving early copies of this text are two palimpsested uncial leaves in Zurich, Zentralbibliothek C. 79, fols. 17–18 (*CLA* VII.1018) and the sixth-century half-uncial volume Milan, Biblioteca Ambrosiana H 78 sup. + Turin, Biblioteca Nazionale G.V.15 (*CLA* III.347) which came from Bobbio. The Milan–Turin volume is the best witness for the text, and the palimpsest leaves of the Missal seem very close to it, though they are not its source. Wilmart reported most variants and Adriaen gives a full list in the apparatus of his edition. Since Petrus Chrysologus, Eusebius Gallicanus and Fulgentius quoted Ambrose's Commentary, the early reception cannot be used to localise the Bobbio leaves.

The text of Ambrose's Commentary was copied in a neat, elegant and fluent cursive script, with several letters consistently in ligature with the following letter. Features of the script include open and closed **a**, open bows of **b**, **d** and **p**, high

[5] Ambrosius, *Expositio in Lucam*, ed. M. Adriaen and P.A. Ballerini, CCSL 14 (Turnhout, 1957).

c and flat-topped **g** with no bow, **m** with the second bow higher than the first, uncial **N** and half-uncial **n** and **q** with an oval bow. The most prominent ligatures are **fi** (on fol. 299v the top of **f** curves down, but elsewhere the cross stroke joins the top of **i**), **ti** as a curving monogram, and **ra** and **re** with the curve of **r** going down to the base of the following letter. Ligatures are standard practice after **e**, **g** and **t**. Citations are indented. There is no punctuation beyond a blank space for major pauses, followed by a somewhat larger letter.

The choice of script to copy such a substantial text deserves a commentary. Wilmart described this script as a 'semionciale fort menue' and affirmed that 'cette fine écriture a tous les traits de l'ancienne et pure semionciale, rapprochée de la cursive jusqu'à l'extrême limite',[6] and Lowe agreed 'this type of half-uncial has all the marks of great antiquity'. In *CLA* Lowe compared the script of the palimpsest leaves to that found in half-uncial fragments of Augustine *De civitate Dei* which have survived as patches on the flyleaves of two manuscripts in Milan, Biblioteca Ambrosiana C 238 inf. + E 26 inf. (*CLA* III.325), and to the elegant half-uncial Fleury fragments of Augustine *Contra duas epistulas Pelagianorum* in Paris, BNF lat. 13368. Neither is copied in a script as cursive as the Ambrose: all the letters in the Milan manuscript are clearly separated.

The cursive half-uncial of this primary script (which Traube once called quarter-uncial)[7] has only survived in a very few examples, most of which are palimpsested or are fragments. Cursive half-uncial is a rapid and cursive form of half-uncial, found in papyrus fragments of classical, legal and patristic texts, and in parchment codices of grammatical and patristic writings. It is also found in the marginalia of classical and patristic texts, which sometimes supply omissions and sometimes provide scholia. For Wilmart it was at the origin of half-uncial, the 'écriture littéraire' derived from Roman cursive. Bischoff saw cursive half-uncial as preceding half-uncial, whose earliest specimen (St Gall, Stiftsbibliothek 1395) dates to the late fourth century. No specimen of cursive half-uncial can be securely dated. I list the surviving examples below.

PAPYRI

A rapid cursive, rich in ligatures, is used in a very few papyrus copies of patristic texts: the fifth-century Pommersfelden papyri lat. pap. 7–13 with fragments of Evagrius carelessly written (*CLA* IX.1359) and lat. pap. 14, which Nicetas copied in

---

[6] Wilmart, 'Palimpseste', p. 4.
[7] L. Traube, *Vorlesungen und Abhandlungen*, II (Munich, 1910), p. 27. The term was used by Lowe in the preface to *CLA* IV (Oxford, 1949), p. xvi, but was rejected by J. Mallon, *Paléographie romaine* (Madrid, 1952), p. 100, and by Bischoff.

a rapid expert cursive (*CLA* IX.1349).[8] A later development is the Milan, Biblioteca Ambrosiana C 1, a papyrus codex of Josephus *De antiquitatibus Iudaicis* generally dated to the sixth century (*CLA* III.304). All these papyri have many more ligatures than the Bobbio palimpsest leaves. No surviving parchment codex of the fifth or sixth century containing patristic texts is copied in this script, but a ligature-rich informal cursive was used in the seventh and eighth centuries at Bobbio, Vercelli and Verona and in northern Francia.

### PARCHMENT CODICES

There are three grammatical texts, all copied without ruled lines, in a rapid small cursive half-uncial:

> Naples, Biblioteca Nazionale 2: Probus and Charisius (*CLA* III.397a), s. v., grammatical treatises and excerpts.
> Naples, Biblioteca Nazionale 2: Claudius Sacerdos (*CLA* III.398), s. v., in which the text has been adapted for school use.
> Turin, Biblioteca Nazionale G.V.4: Probus (*CLA* IV.462), s. v.

The script is also used in three legal manuscripts, all dated to the fifth century and rich in legal abbreviations:

> Autun, BM 24: Gaius commentary (*CLA* VI.726), s. v.; with uncial **N**, fewer **r** ligatures, a distinctive **eg** ligature and *Notae Iuris*.
> Geneva, Bibliothèque Publique et Universitaire Pap. lat. VI: Legal fragment (*CLA* VII.886), s. v.
> St Gall, Stiftsbibliothek 908, pp. 277–92: Legal fragment (*CLA* VII.964) s. v.

The following manuscripts copied in an early and rapid half-uncial contain biblical and patristic texts. All are copied in a more formal script, which has fewer ligatures than the Ambrose leaves.

> St Gall, Stiftsbibliothek 1395: Gospels (*CLA* VII.984), early fifth century, copied in two columns of 24 lines.
> Orléans, BM 192, fols. 32–3 + Paris, BNF lat. 13368, fol. 256: fragments of Augustine *Contra duas epistulas Pelagianorum* (*CLA* VI.815), s. v., 23 long lines.
> St Gall, Stiftsbibliothek 193 and 564: *Prophetae* (*CLA* VII.916) s. v., copied in 21 long lines.

---

[8] Both the Pommersfelden papyri are illustrated and transcribed in R. Seider, *Palaeographie der lateinischen Papyri*, II.2 (Stuttgart, 1981).

Vatican City, BAV, Pal. lat. 24, fols. 47–52: oratorical fragment (*CLA* I.73), copied in 28 long lines.

Milan, Biblioteca Ambrosiana C 238 inf. and E 26 inf.: fragments of Augustine *De civitate Dei* (*CLA* III.325), perhaps 28 long lines.

St Gall, Stiftsbibliothek 722: Hilary on Psalms (*CLA* VII.947), 27 long lines.

## MARGINALIA

In addition the script is found in marginalia which comprise several important Arian texts copied into the margins of a manuscript of works of Hilary of Poitiers and Ambrose: Paris, BNF lat. 8907, fols. 298–311v and fols. 336–49 (*CLA* V.572), comprising Arian materials attacking the council of Aquileia copied around the middle of the fifth century. These have been the subject of a full facsimile with elaborate palaeographical analysis.[9]

Additional manuscripts with extensive marginalia in cursive half-uncial include:

Milan, Biblioteca Ambrosiana R 57: scholia in a manuscript of Cicero's speeches, now a palimpsest (*CLA* III.363).

Vatican City, BAV, Vat. lat. 3226: Codex Bembinus of Terence (*CLA* I.12), the scholia by two hands dated by Mountford to the sixth century.[10]

Verona, Biblioteca Capitolare XIII: Hilary on Psalms (*CLA* IV.484), according to *CLA* quarter-uncial marginalia supply insertions.

The most substantial cursive half-uncial marginalia are found in the Weingarten Prophets (*CLA* IX.1174), fifth-century marginalia in a neat, regular and careful tiny script of which there is a near complete facsimile edited by Paul Lehmann.[11] The marginalia and Latin translations of Greek passages in the fifth-century copy of Lactantius, now Bologna, Biblioteca Universitaria 709 (*CLA* III.280) are also written in this script.

Of these manuscripts, the script of the Naples Sacerdos and Probus is characterised by frequent ligatures, uncial **N**, curved **d**, often high **e** in ligature with **r**, **m** or **n** and a long **s** with a high head. There is little contrast between thick and thin pen strokes, which may indicate that they were written with a reed pen. The contrast between thick and thin penstrokes is present in the half-uncial manuscripts, all of which have fewer ligatures than the Bobbio Missal Ambrose. The Fleury and Milan Augustine fragments, which Lowe considered to be the closest parallels, both have

[9] R. Gryson and L. Gilissen, *Les Scolies Ariennes du Parisinus Latinus 8907*, Armarium Codicum Insignium 1 (Turnhout, 1980).

[10] J. Mountford, *The Scholia Bembina* (Liverpool, 1934), pp. 4–6.

[11] P. Lehmann, *Die Konstanz-Weingartener Propheten-Fragmente in phototypischer Reproduction; Einleitung von Paul Lehmann* (Leiden, 1912).

fewer ligatures than the Ambrose. The Milan Augustine is copied in a larger script with no ligatures; **b** is always open; both uncial **N** and **n** occur; and **r** does not join following letters. The St Gall Hilary has open **a**, tall **c** turned to the right, a larger bow of flat topped **g**, and always uses the uncial **N**. All of these volumes are copied in an informal but elegant bookscript, which may have derived from a script more commonly used for annotations. The Arian cursive half-uncial marginalia in the Paris manuscript of Hilary copy a substantial text, unlike the other marginalia listed here which represent glosses or corrections. In addition these latter are written in very small scripts, some of which make extensive use of ligatures but others have the letters much more separated. Dr Hammond Bammel characterised the Fleury leaves as follows:

the scribes of the Augustine fragments are themselves accustomed to using the script they employ in a more rapid and cursive form for less formal purposes. Their work represents not the laborious efforts of second-rate imitators of an already long established style, but rather the products of highly skilled experts, who are disciplining a swift and fluent script in order to produce a pleasing calligraphic effect.[12]

The two-column format of these palimpsest leaves is almost unique for a manuscript in cursive half-uncial; the only other examples are a fragment of Arator preserved as an offset in a manuscript now in Oxford (*CLA* Sup. 1140), which Lowe dated to the sixth century, and the fragments of a perhaps fifth-century codex with a Manichean text, of which only the inner column is preserved, Paris, BNF n.a. lat. 1114 (*CLA* V.680) in two columns of perhaps 30 lines.

Half-uncial is generally considered to derive from the letter forms of New Roman cursive. In the case of the palimpsest leaves the script retains many cursive features, but lacks some of the elaborate looping ligatures found in the Pommersfelden and Milan patristic papyri. Because cursive half-uncial script is smaller, more rapid and more informal than that of half-uncial patristic manuscripts, it has been suggested that it was used for private copies, rather than for library books.[13] Both the grammatical manuscripts in Naples and Turin, where texts have apparently been adapted, and the two-column Manichean codex in a crude half-uncial seem to have been written in informal and individual scripts. But a complete copy of Ambrose on Luke would have been a much larger volume than those books, and perhaps required the work of several scribes. The text, even in the two-column format of this palimpsest, would have required over 270 folia. The St Gall Hilary and the Milan *De civitate Dei* were also substantial volumes; 14 of some 250 leaves of the Hilary are now wholly or partially legible. These three fragments reveal that cursive half-uncial was used to copy major texts. Hammond Bammel implies that they might be the work of scholars copying texts for personal use, rather than the work

---

[12] Hammond Bammel, 'Products of fifth-century scriptoria', p. 350.    [13] Ibid., p. 388.

of professional scribes. The three grammatical manuscripts contain texts which may have been adapted for teaching purposes, as she suggests, and so support her suggestion of privately made books. But whether this suggestion can serve to characterise all instances of copying in an informal script is less certain.

It seems safer to underline how very little we know about these early instances of book production. In the entries for *CLA* Lowe assumed that they were all Italian, probably from the north, but Traube had considered the possibility that the Fleury fragments of Augustine *Contra duas epistulas Pelagianorum* might have been copied in Gaul, and in 1924 Lowe had cautiously said of the Bobbio leaves that 'The probability is that they are Italian; but the possibility of French origin is not to be excluded.'[14] Julian Brown explicitly cited this fragment, together with the Naples grammatical manuscripts, in his discussions of the origins of Insular letter forms. He assumed that specimens of cursive half-uncial are representative of a widely used script: two later but relevant items are Rome, Biblioteca Vittorio Emmanuele Sess. 55, Augustine *Confessiones* (*CLA* IV.420) in 43 to 47 long lines, and the offsets of Arator in Oxford, Bodleian Library e Museo 66, in a very small two-column format.

The decision to add palimpsested leaves to the Missal must indicate that this discarded fragment was regarded as a more convenient writing surface than fresh parchment. This surely implies that, whatever the cultural context where the Missal was copied, the additions were not made in a place where fresh parchment was available, such as a major writing centre. That might confirm the view that the script is not that of a library book. But it seems safer to suggest that we are in the presence of one of the more substantial texts copied in an elegant and accomplished script generally used for annotations. The script is the earliest true 'minuscule', a script which allowed scribes to save space without sacrificing legibility. Only the investigation of scribal errors in later copies of patristic texts will offer clues as to whether such cursive half-uncial manuscripts were important in the transmission of such texts. In that case, the tendency towards minuscule scripts would be a major palaeographical feature throughout the history of the Latin book.

[14] Lowe, 'Palaeography', p. 75.

# 4

## Reading and writing the Bobbio Missal: punctuation, word separation and animated initials

MARCO MOSTERT

Written texts, whatever else they may have been used for, were first of all meant to be read. Skill in reading a written text depends, among other things, on the reader's knowledge of the language in which the text is written. A literate native speaker will encounter fewer problems in rendering the visual symbols of his own written language audible, than when he is asked to do the same with texts written in other languages. An early medieval native speaker of Latin, for example, will therefore have needed fewer extra-alphabetical signs to help him understand written Latin than someone who had had to learn Latin as a second language. Similarly, when late Latin developed into early Romance, a literate native speaker of late Latin, because of linguistic changes which had taken place meanwhile, would probably have welcomed the aid of extra-alphabetical signs in Latin texts copied several centuries before. These linguistic differences and developments have caused manuscripts of the same Latin texts to vary enormously in the way they look and, more importantly, the ease with which they can be read. Changes in the forms of the Latin alphabet's letters are now thought by some to have been less important for medieval manuscripts' 'grammars of legibility'[1] than have been changes in layout, punctuation and word spacing.[2] The choice of one script rather than another, or the inclusion of animated letters,[3] may have suggested the esteem in which a written text was held or the way in which it was meant to be interpreted, but the ability to give voice to written words was determined by other signs on the page. Recent work on punctuation and, more recently, space between words, has provided a first outline of the grammar of legibility's history. Manuscripts of the early Middle Ages can be shown in all probability to obey other visual conventions than those of the later Middle Ages, and manuscripts written by early medieval Latin speakers may obey other conventions than those written by Insular scribes. Much remains as yet

[1] M.B. Parkes, *Pause and Effect. Punctuation in the West* (Aldershot, 1992), pp. 20–9.
[2] P. Saenger, *Space between Words. The Origins of Silent Reading* (Stanford, CA, 1997).
[3] L. Kendrick, *Animating the Letter. The Figurative Embodiment of Writing from Late Antiquity to the Renaissance* (Columbus, OH, 1999).

hypothetical. However, it seems possible to use the results of the pioneers' research in this field to formulate cautious hypotheses as to the origin and Latinity of the scribes of individual early medieval manuscripts.

In the Bobbio Missal, at least four hands, belonging to at least two and quite possibly four – or even more – scribes, can be identified.[4] Most quires have been written by hand **M**, while the first quire, **A$^8$**, was written by one or two hands, together called **A** by Lowe. This 'hand' also made additions to **MM$^{12}$** (on fols. 292v–295v and fol. 286r) and the final quire **NN$^{12}$** (on fols. 299v–300v). Hand **A** used empty pages to add miscellaneous materials. Before hand **A** made its additions to the main body of the book, another hand, **a**, seems to have already made additions to a gathering (fols. 251–254), inserted in what is now called quire **GG$^{12}$** (the additions occur on fols. 253v–254r),[5] and to quire **MM$^{12}$** (additions on fols. 291v–292r).[6] Before **a** made its additions, however, fols. 251–254, in which hand **M$^2$** wrote the *Missa pro principe* (fols. 251r–253r), seem already to have become part of the MS, although it is impossible to say whether they were already inserted in the present quire **GG$^{12}$** (fol. 254v remained blank after **a** made his additions to **M$^2$**). The most likely sequence of the four hands, then, is **M** (datable to the very end of the seventh century on the basis of letter forms, ligatures and abbreviations), **M$^2$**, **a**, **A** (all three datable to the first half of the eighth century).[7]

In considering the grammar of legibility of the Bobbio Missal, we have to distinguish between these four 'hands'. The possibility cannot be excluded that the scribes producing some or all of the additional hands came from another linguistic background than the scribe of hand **M**. It may seem probable on palaeographical

---

[4] Because there is a possibility that several hands were produced by the same scribe, it is necessary, contrary to current terminology, to distinguish hands from scribes. Unfortunately, this occasionally leads to cumbersome phrasing.

[5] **GG$^{12}$** is not a single quire, as Lowe the palaeographer erroneously states in his 'Palaeography', p. 6. Rather, as he himself explains as the editor, fols. 251–4 form a separate gathering (*Bobbio*, p. 151 n. 2), which must have been inserted in an original **GG$^8$**. Corroboration for Lowe the editor's observation is provided by the ruling (see Lowe, 'Palaeography', p. 65): contrary to the rest of the manuscript, fols. 251–4 are ruled for 28 rather than for 21 or 22 lines to a page. Fol. 255 therefore originally followed fol. 250, so that c. 498 followed c. 491 (curiously, Lowe the editor (*Bobbio*, p. 153 n. 3) seems to think that c. 498 follows c. 496, suggesting that fols. 251–4 were situated in their present place from the moment they were written; however, there is no reason why c. 498 should be a part of the *Missa pro principe*). This does away with the otherwise incomprehensible skipping of fols. 251–4 by **M**. Unfortunately, therefore, Lowe the palaeographer is curiously at odds with Lowe the editor. I have not been able to ascertain whether as an editor Lowe made, after all, a mistake, as the manuscript is too tightly bound to make sure.

[6] The relative chronology is suggested by the fact that in **MM$^{12}$** hand **A** starts its additions on the pages which had been left blank by **M** after the additions in hand **a**, suggesting **a** preceded **A**.

[7] See the contribution of Rosamond McKitterick, above, pp. 19–52. The sequence is, however, hypothetical at best: if 'hand' **A** is assumed in fact to consist of more hands, then only the additions by '**A**' to fol. 292v have been made later than those by **a**, and the other additions by '**A**' may well have been made either before or after those by **a**.

grounds that all of the Bobbio Missal was produced in one and the same area (Provence, and perhaps the archdiocese of Vienne),[8] but the hands each represent a different type of script or kind of handwriting. It remains possible, even if improbable, however, that scribes were trained in these scripts after arriving in this area. Differences between the origins of scribes and scripts may be detectable through differences in the grammar of legibility. Hence we will look at the conventions for punctuation and word separation apparently followed by all four hands individually. In addition, we will also consider those initials that may give us clues to the ways in which the scribes intended the texts they copied to be read.

According to Lowe, who was baffled by the script of the additions and merely considered hand **M**, no strict system of punctuation was used.[9] The punctuation seems consistent, however, with that of texts meant for public worship and aural responses to the written word as studied by Parkes.[10] The use of 'points placed medially or high' (Lowe), *positurae*, here suggests the indication of 'pauses dictated by sense and rhythm',[11] with the 'points placed . . . high' possibly corresponding to the *punctus elevatus*, the 'points placed medially' to the *punctus versus* as employed, for example in the ninth-century *Sacramentarium Gelasianum mixtum* now Oxford, Keble College, Millard 41 (binding fragment).[12] The sign 'shaped like an arabic figure nine with the loop very open at the top' (Lowe) seems another form of the *punctus versus*. Although Lowe was right to observe that '[t]hese points . . . do not always correspond to what would seem to us suitable division', they do nevertheless make reading the text aloud easier. Consultation of the manuscript shows that the colour of the ink of the punctuation is identical to that of the letters, suggesting, even if not proving, that the punctuation was supplied (or copied from his exemplar) by hand **M** rather than added afterwards.

The edition of the Bobbio Missal has carefully reproduced the punctuation of the manuscript, inasmuch as typography has the means to distinguish between signs that in their handwritten form may closely resemble one another, yet are perceived to be different. In the edition words, however, are separated according to modern conventions, in which '[a]n unambiguous distinction between interword and interletter space is fundamental to the modern reading of separated writing and to the economy of mental effort that today's reading habits represent'.[13] The edition uses what Saenger calls 'canonical separation', a term which

describes the configuration of space that has since the twelfth century become characteristic of almost all written or printed Latin texts. In canonically separated manuscripts, all words, including conjunctions (except, as in modern printed Latin, the postpositional *-cum*, the

---

[8] McKitterick, above, pp. 39–46.    [9] Lowe, 'Palaeography', p. 96.
[10] Parkes, *Pause and Effect*, pp. 76–80 and Plates 16–19.    [11] Ibid., p. 77.
[12] Ibid., Plate 16.    [13] Saenger, *Space between Words*, p. 29.

enclitics -que and -ve), monosyllables, and particles (except the interrogative -ne and the inseparable in- and ve-), were separated solely by space with interword space equivalent to an average minimum of twice the unity of space.[14]

The 'unity of space' is defined as the distance between the minim strokes of the 'lower case' letters **u**, **m**, or **n**.[15] The manuscript, however, looks quite different. Hand **M** seems to have followed the conventions of late antique manuscripts that were either unseparated or separated only by interpuncts accompanied by minimal space. These conventions may have been suggested by his exemplars rather than by his own predilection, because quite often he inserts space, even if at first sight it seems to be done capriciously. Saenger calls this type of insertion of intratextual space 'aeration', the script 'aerated script'. The purpose of aeration is ease of reading: 'The insertion of intratextual space at irregular intervals implied the possibility of fixations and fewer regressions [of the eye], with greater quantities of text decoded at each fixation, potentially measurable by an enhanced eye–voice span.'[16] While on the Continent aeration was sufficient for native speakers of Latin at least until the end of the tenth century, Insular scribes writing in Latin developed word separation early on, the practice becoming prevalent in the eighth century.[17] The more characteristics of canonical separation one may observe in an early medieval manuscript, the greater the probability that it has been written by an Insular scribe, or at least a non-native speaker of Latin. The absence of anything resembling canonical separation in the work of hand **M** corroborates the arguments against assuming **M** to have been an Insular or Irish scribe.[18] The evidence of the absence of word separation suggests the scribe of hand **M** to have been a native speaker of Latin who tried to follow the conventions of late antique (liturgical) manuscripts to the best of his ability.

It is uncertain whether hand **M** is responsible for the gold added to the initial **D** on fol. 219r. Lowe suggested that the initial itself might have been a later addition.[19] However, there is no difference with the large initials on fols. 10r and 11v, and there are no reasons to suggest that all three may not have been made by hand **M**. Of the three, the **T** on fol. 11v (the initial letter of the *Te igitur*) is most eloquent: it consists of a peacock sitting on a pillar; the pillar is partially obscured by a plant resembling ivy, but more probably representing vines. A peacock could signify the senses of Scripture other than its literal sense, because of its tail's many colours. Cassiodorus had compared the meanings in the Book of Psalms to the peacock's tail, and two centuries later John Scotus was to apply the metaphor to Scripture

---

[14] Ibid., p. 44.    [15] Ibid., p. 27.    [16] Ibid., p. 33.    [17] Ibid., p. 41.

[18] The argument concerns merely the manuscript of the text, of course, and not the text: Insular influence on the contents of what **M** copied cannot be excluded.

[19] Lowe, 'Palaeography', p. 96.

in general.[20] Possibly, our scribe was conversant with this interpretation, extending it to the meanings of liturgical texts – unless he merely copied the initial from his exemplar. He may also have understood animated letters to be appropriate for Christian books, or he may have thought of the peacock as a symbol for eternal life. Vines suggested Christ, 'the true vine' (John 15.1), and were particularly apt for animating the **T** of the *Te igitur*, opening the canon of the mass, the words by which bread and wine were thought to be transformed into the real presence of Christ.[21] The initial **D** (the first letter of 'Deus') on fol. 10r may with some imagination also be seen as sprouting vines; the sign abbreviating the word *Missa*, in 'Missa Romensis cotidiana', one line above the initial **D**, certainly sprouts leaves. If our interpretation of the **D** on fol. 10r is correct, then the rather similar gilded **D** on fol. 219r (the first letter of 'Domine') is sprouting vines, too.

The scribe of hand **M** has thus taken care to present his texts according to the conventions of late antique books, using punctuation to help reading aloud the liturgical texts he collected. He used animated letters to give his readers to understand that they embarked on reading Christian texts filled with the mysteries of the faith. He may not have been capable of writing a very beautiful hand, but the product of his labours was adequate for the liturgical use intended. The absence of attempts at systematic word separation suggests that he was a native speaker of Latin.

The scribe of hand **M²**, too, meant to write a liturgical text to be read aloud. He follows the same conventions as hand **M**, and his initials are also meant to be perceived as 'animated', even if his vines are sketchy. It is not even clear whether his capitals **D** and **M** show twigs, blossoms or merely ornaments to complement the vines. Most probably, the additions of **M²** were meant as a supplement to **M**.

Had fols. 251–4, whose unusually narrow dimensions may have been meant to match that of **M**'s work, been ruled for **M**'s usual 21 or 22 lines rather than for 28 lines, fols. 253v and 254r would have been filled by **M²**; as it was, the scribe of hand **a** found these pages blank and added his *Deuotiones seu Imprecationes* (as they are known to scholarship). Hand **a** has dispensed (as he did in the *Benedictio* on fols. 291v–292r) with punctuation and word separation altogether. This suggests that the texts this time were not meant for reading aloud. The absence of word separation does not, of course, of necessity preclude oral delivery. Contemporaries were most probably more accustomed to reading cursive minuscule hands, and did not need as many visual clues for legibility as later readers of the same hands would. However, word separation arguably would have enhanced legibility also for

[20] Kendrick, *Animating the Letter*, pp. 74–5 and p. 249 (quoting Cassiodorus, *De institutione divinarum litterarum* 4 (PL 70, col. 1115), and John Scotus, *De divisione naturae* 4.5 (PL 122, col. 749 C)).

[21] Ibid., pp. 82–4, discussing the vine-wrapped initial of the **T** of the *Te igitur* page in the Drogo Sacramentary (Paris, BNF lat. 9428, fol. 15v).

expert readers of cursive minuscule. Possibly, then, these texts were to be recited (if they were meant to be voiced at all by anyone other than the scribe of hand **a** himself) after a performer had prepared himself through something resembling *praelectio*: an initial reading in which the words were voiced 'aloud or in a muffled voice, because overt physical pronunciation aided the reader to retain phonemes of ambiguous meaning'.[22] For the *reader*, ambiguity might arise through the use of many word forms which are not found in classical Latin – even if for a *listener* from the area where the copy of the texts was made the texts would have contained little he did not understand.[23]

If the additions in hand **a** must have been readily understandable to their scribe (who may have also been their author or compiler), the additions in hand **A** try to follow the conventions of hands **M** and **M²**. Quire **A⁸** was certainly intended as a supplement to the original manuscript, as is suggested by its format, ruling and the animation of the initial **R** of *De dies malus* (fol. 6r) as indeed that of the title of that text itself. Although there are marked differences between the letter forms of the different texts copied in this quire (most probably caused on fol. 8v by the scribe's realisation that he was running out of parchment), all texts show the same absence of punctuation as the additions made in hand **a**. The legibility of the texts is helped by the use of capitals, some of which are coloured, and there is some aeration (especially on fols. 1r–6r and 7r–8r), but otherwise the reader is not assisted in his task. Most probably the scribe never intended these texts to be read aloud.

The additions in hand **A** to quire **MM¹²** (on fols. 292v–295v, after hand **a** had already filled fols. 291v–292r) also try to follow the conventions of **M** and **M²**, with the letters of *Incepit inquisitio de lege* animated, but without any punctuation and only little aeration. These texts, too (with the exception of the benedictions of fol. 295v), were most probably not meant to be read aloud. The grammar of legibility of the various additions made by **A** to fols. 299v–300v resembles that of the additions made on fols. 292v–295v.

To sum up. In considering the scribes of the four 'hands' and the uses they seem to have envisaged for the texts they copied into the Bobbio Missal, we have tried to look at letter forms, abbreviations and ligatures only to distinguish the different hands working on the manuscript. We have tried to establish the genesis of the book from its original composition up to the copying of its last additions. Our aim has not been to date the various hands, but merely to establish their relative chronology, because the grammar of legibility of the additions may have been influenced both by the exemplars of the texts copied and by the conventions of those parts of the book

---

[22] Saenger, *Space between Words*, p. 8 and n. 36, referring to I. Taylor and M. Taylor, *The Psychology of Reading* (New York, 1983), pp. 35–6.

[23] Assuming, that is, that the allusions in the texts were as understandable to the audience as was their language.

already extant at the time of copying. Having considered the punctuation and word spacing of the oldest quires, we have found the conventions of **M** to be consistent with those of late antique (liturgical) books meant for reading aloud by a native speaker of Latin – even if the consistency of the punctuation may leave something to be desired. The use of animated initials, despite their lack of artistic merit, clearly suggested something about the nature of the texts and their possible meanings. $\mathbf{M^2}$ followed **M**'s conventions, as did **A**. The scribe of **a**, however, does not seem to have meant his texts to be read, read aloud (or performed) by anyone but himself. The absence of any punctuation and the lack of aeration in the additions made by **a** and **A** would in any case have made their reading very difficult indeed for any non-native speaker of Latin. The suggestion is that the book was intended for use by native Latin speakers whose literate skills enabled them to understand the visual conventions of the book well enough to know what they were meant to do with the different texts included in it.

These findings seem on the whole to corroborate the results of the study of the texts, their language and their script presented elsewhere in this volume. The interest of these notes lies not so much in their results as in their use of arguments of a nature different from those used elsewhere in this volume. Apart from adding something to our knowledge of the Bobbio Missal, it is hoped that they also show something of the potential of continued study of the grammar of legibility.

5

# Liturgical Latin in the Bobbio Missal*

ELS ROSE

## THE STUDY OF LITURGICAL LATIN

The Swedish expert in the field of late and vulgar Latin, Bengt Löfstedt, must have been in a proud and optimistic mood when he stated in an article on the *status quaestionis* of the study of vulgar Latin: 'We can even maintain that there are only a few late Latin texts to which no Swedish dissertation has been dedicated so far.'[1] He adds that these days – he was writing in the early 1980s – it is hardly worth the effort to write a commentary on a vulgar Latin text of the kind produced by Einar Löfstedt for Egeria's travel journal at the beginning of the past century, as: 'Most of the well-edited vulgar Latin texts of some importance as far as content is concerned, and well edited, have already been given an exhaustive treatment as regards their linguistic features.'[2] If one combines this assertion with the fact that no thorough linguistic study has been dedicated to the liturgical language of the Bobbio Missal, only two conclusions seem possible: either the Bobbio Missal is 'of no importance as far as content is concerned', or there is no adequate edition of the manuscript at our disposal. As the latter argument cannot be upheld in view of the excellent accessibility of the manuscript in the tripartite edition produced by the Henry Bradshaw Society, we are left with the sad conclusion that the Bobbio Missal is of no importance if measured by its content. Still, there is a third possible conclusion, which I would prefer to the other two: that the corpus of liturgical Latin texts from the early medieval period has been strangely ignored by those who, during the last fifty years, have made an

---

* I would like to thank Roger Wright, who carefully read and commented on a first draft of this article.

[1] B. Löfstedt, 'Die vulgärlateinische Sprachforschung in diesem Jahrhundert. Rückschau und Ausblick', *Aevum* 56 (1982), pp. 200–4, at p. 200: 'Es lässt sich sogar behaupten, dass es recht wenige spätlateinische Texte gibt, denen bisher keine schwedische Dissertation gewidmet worden ist.'

[2] Ibid., p. 202: 'Die meisten inhaltlich einigermassen wichtigen und gut edierten vulgärlateinischen Texte sind bereits in sprachlicher Hinsicht so ziemlich erschöpft.'

effort to give the study of late and vulgar Latin its own place in the field of Latin philology.

Bengt Löfstedt is not the only specialist in the field of late and vulgar Latin whose work gives rise to this observation. Joseph Herman, another expert who is hard to ignore, produced a description of the Merovingian Latin corpus in which legal, historiographical and hagiographical texts are enumerated, as well as charters and diplomatic documents – but no mention is made of liturgical texts.[3] In the early fifties, the lack of thorough studies of liturgical Latin texts had already been noticed by the liturgist W. Dürig, in a *status quaestionis* published in the first issue of the German *Liturgisches Jahrbuch*. In this article Dürig surveyed the publications in the field of liturgical Latin, referring mostly to lexicological studies. Dürig concluded this overview with the same complaint that Bernard Botte had uttered several years before: 'On the whole, we know very little about liturgical language. We are still dealing with preliminary matters.'[4] Dürig's *status quaestionis* is now exactly fifty years old and, fortunately, things have changed since then. The study of liturgical Latin texts of the early period has been facilitated considerably by the publication of studies like Ellebracht's *Remarks on the Vocabulary of the Ancient Orations in the Missale Romanum*[5] and Blaise's liturgical dictionary.[6] Still, these are only lexicological studies. Systematic studies of the language of the early medieval liturgical documents, especially those not originating from Rome, are still lacking.[7]

It is astonishing that none of the specialists in Latin philology during the past century chose such a remarkable book as the Bobbio Missal or any of its contemporaries as an object of study. Various phenomena may have contributed to this lack of interest in the linguistic study of early medieval non-Roman liturgical writings.

[3] J. Herman, 'Sur quelques aspects du latin mérovingien: langue écrite et langue parlée', in *Latin vulgaire – latin tardif III. Actes du IIIème Colloque international sur le latin vulgaire et tardif*, ed. M. Iliescu and W. Marxgut (Tübingen, 1992), pp. 173–86, at p. 175.

[4] W. Dürig, 'Die Erforschung der lateinisch-christlichen Sakralsprache', *Liturgisches Jahrbuch* 1 (1951), pp. 32–47, at p. 47: 'La langue liturgique nous est, en somme, mal connue. Nous en sommes encore aux besognes préliminaires.' Dürig here refers to B. Botte, 'Paschalibus initiata mysteriis', *Ephemerides liturgicae* 61 (1947), p. 77–87, at p. 87.

[5] M. Ellebracht, *Remarks on the Vocabulary of the Ancient Orations in the Missale Romanum* (Nijmegen, 1963).

[6] A. Blaise, *Le vocabulaire latin des principaux thèmes liturgiques* (Turnhout, 1966).

[7] Wright paid some attention to the language of contemporary Spanish (Visigothic) liturgical documents: R. Wright, *Late Latin and Early Romance in Spain and Carolingian France* (Liverpool, 1982), pp. 73–8. See also M.C. Díaz y Díaz, 'El latín de la liturgia hispánica', in *Estudios sobre la liturgia mozárabe*, ed. J. Rivera Recio (Toledo, 1965) pp. 55–87 (Roger Wright kindly drew my attention to this study). I myself made an attempt to fill at least some of this gap in my dissertation on the Gothic Missal: E. Rose, 'Communitas in commemoratione. Liturgisch Latijn en liturgische gedachtenis in het Missale Gothicum (Vat. reg. lat. 317)' (PhD thesis, Utrecht, 2001). I dedicated one part of this study to the analysis of the language of this Gallican sacramentary, examining its orthography, morphology, syntax, lexicology and semantics (an English translation of this dissertation, which includes a revised edition of the Gothic Missal, is in preparation for CCSL).

Liturgical texts in general were for a long time perhaps seen as too sacred to be submitted to the clinical and detached approach of methodical scholarly research. We must not forget that for centuries liturgical studies had been conducted largely by monks and other people who considered their material primarily as their historical, cultural and religious heritage. This hypothesis, however, is difficult to prove. Moreover, a possible cause of the neglect of non-Roman liturgical texts dating from the pre-Carolingian period is to be found in the early Middle Ages themselves, and, more precisely, in the attitude of the Carolingians towards the liturgy of their day. The second half of the eighth and the early ninth centuries bore witness to important reform activities in the field of both liturgy and language.[8] This reformation not only left the Bobbio Missal and similar liturgical texts in the shadows, but also, because of the Carolingian propaganda-like promotion of the reformed liturgy, had a negative effect on the image of the liturgical activities of the preceding period.[9]

There is, I believe, a third possible reason for the lack of attention paid to the linguistic features of the Bobbio Missal and contemporary liturgical texts: attitudes such as those found in the work of two modern scholars in the field of liturgical Latin. The first is found in the work of the Dutch Latinist Christine Mohrmann who paid considerable attention to the Latin of the liturgy. Her most important ideas on this subject can be found in a collection of lectures given at the Catholic University of America in May 1957.[10] The picture of liturgical Latin drawn here is that of a highly stylised, hieratic language. Liturgical language, in Mohrmann's view, is a 'Kunstsprache', an artificial language with its own vocabulary and fixed expressions, comparable, for example, to the language of Homer's epic: 'The earliest liturgical Latin is a strongly stylized, more or less artificial language ... This language was far removed from that of everyday life, a fact which was certainly appreciated, since, at the time, people still retained the *sens du sacré*.'[11] In liturgical texts there is, according to Mohrmann, no room for elements inspired by external traditions,

---

[8] On the liturgical reform in the Carolingian period see Y. Hen, *The Royal Patronage of Liturgy in Frankish Gaul to the Death of Charles the Bald (877)*, HBS subsidia 3 (London, 2001), pp. 65–95; R. McKitterick, *The Frankish Church and the Carolingian Reforms, 789–895* (London, 1977), pp. 123–38; M. Metzger, *Histoire de la liturgie. Les grandes étapes* (Paris, 1994), pp. 174–85; E. Palazzo, *Histoire des livres liturgiques: le Moyen Age. Des origines au XIIIᵉ siècle* (Paris, 1993), pp. 69–79. On the reform of the Latin language see for example G. Calboli, 'Aspects du latin mérovingien', in *Latin vulgaire – latin tardif I. Actes du Iᵉʳ Colloque international sur le latin vulgaire et tardif*, ed. J. Herman (Tübingen, 1987), pp. 19–35, especially p. 32; K. Heene, 'Merovingian and Carolingian hagiography. Continuity or change in public and aims?', *Analecta Bollandiana* 107 (1989), pp. 415–28, especially pp. 419–20; M. Richter, 'Die Sprachenpolitik Karls des Großen', *Sprachwissenschaft* 7 (1982), pp. 412–37, especially pp. 422–4. On both see Wright, *Late Latin and Early Romance*, especially pp. 104–44.

[9] On anti-Merovingian propaganda by the Carolingians in general, see Y. Hen, *Culture and Religion in Merovingian Gaul, A.D. 481–751* (Leiden, New York and Cologne, 1995), pp. 197–205 and *passim*.

[10] C. Mohrmann, *Liturgical Latin: its origins and character* (Washington, 1957).

[11] Ibid., p. 54.

---

such as secular poetry, or non-Christian religious traditions.[12] The occurrence of vulgar elements in liturgical texts is all the more inconceivable: 'All the more, the presence of a vulgarism . . . is contrary to the general character of language and style of liturgical Latin: a hieratic language, highly stylised with hardly any popular features.'[13] This rather one-sided view of liturgical Latin is due to the narrow interpretation Mohrmann gives to the concept of liturgical Latin which she invariably confines to the liturgical texts of the *Patres* and the liturgy of the church of Rome, choosing her examples from these undoubtedly rich but restricted treasuries. Moreover, she states that the regions outside Rome followed, broadly speaking, the use of Christian language of which Rome set the norm.[14] In her consideration of liturgical language, however, Mohrmann passes over the Latin liturgical traditions which do not belong to the Roman church, such as the Gallican rite, represented, for example, by the Bobbio Missal. Unfortunately, she does not always make her choice of liturgical texts explicit. Therefore the reader of Morhmann's studies is confronted with an opinion on liturgical Latin based on a select corpus of sources but presented as a general view on the subject.[15]

Another scholar whose work has, more recently, contributed to the neglect of non-Roman liturgical texts from a linguistic point of view is Robert Coleman.[16] He does not entirely ignore the sources of the non-Roman liturgy, but he does not give them a serious place in the discussion of liturgical language either. Coleman compares the vulgar character of the Latin of the Vulgate to the elevated style of the language of liturgical (prayer) texts. His choice of liturgical texts is, again, remarkably limited, as he confines himself to highlights such as the *Gloria*, the *Te Deum* and the Roman canon. The liturgical sources of the seventh and eighth centuries are disposed of in one paragraph as examples from a period in which 'the devotional literature suffered extensive vulgarization'.[17] As an example Coleman refers to the way the Roman canon is handed down in the Bobbio Missal, whose 'garbled forms' gave rise to 'doubts about the validity of the rites enacted by them'

---

[12] C. Mohrmann, 'Notes sur le latin liturgique', in C. Mohrmann, *Etudes sur le latin des chrétiens*, II (Rome, 1961), pp. 93–108, at pp. 102–3.

[13] C. Mohrmann, 'Missa', in C. Mohrmann, *Etudes sur le latin des chrétiens*, III (Rome, 1965), pp. 351–76, at pp. 357–8: 'De plus, la présence d'un vulgarisme . . . est très peu compatible avec le caractère général de la langue et du style de la liturgie latine: langue hiératique rigoureusement stylisée et très peu populaire.'

[14] C. Mohrmann, 'Les origines de la latinité chrétienne à Rome', in Mohrmann, *Etudes*, III, pp. 67–126, at pp. 125–6: 'Sauf des divergences très légères, la terminologie chrétienne de Rome et celle de Carthage sont identiques', and 'quand . . . la Gaule et l'Espagne nous fournissent des textes chrétiens ceux-ci s'ajusteront dans le même cadre général'.

[15] See also E. Rose, 'Liturgical Latin in the *Missale Gothicum* (Vat. reg. lat. 317). A reconsideration of Christine Mohrmann's approach', *Sacris Erudiri* 42 (2003) [in press].

[16] R. Coleman, 'Vulgar Latin and the diversity of Christian Latin', in *Latin vulgaire – latin tardif*, ed. Iliescu and Marxgut, pp. 37–52.

[17] Ibid., p. 47.

so that 'the motivation to restore was strong'.[18] This view of the Bobbio Missal as nothing more than a motivation for the Carolingians to restore the liturgy and its language not only ignores the individuality and the irrefutable value of this unique source, but also fails to live up to the expectations aroused by the title Coleman chose for his article: 'Vulgar Latin and the *diversity* of Christian Latin' (my emphasis).

Thus the neglect of the language of the early medieval non-Roman liturgical sources of the Latin church is, partly, due to a more or less general preference for the liturgical texts elaborated during the golden age of western liturgy, and in particular for those of the Roman rite. This is regrettable, as the Bobbio Missal and similar liturgical books provide a most interesting source for the process of continuity and change in which the Latin language was involved during the early medieval period.

## LITURGICAL LATIN IN THE BOBBIO MISSAL

Since it is impossible to discuss the Latin of the entire Bobbio Missal in this short contribution, I have chosen to focus upon the prayer texts alone. The Latin of the biblical lections is a matter for separate discussion. The same goes for the text of the penitential, and the other additions to the sacramentary, such as the sermon *De dies malus* and a collection of riddles, the so-called *Joca monachorum*.[19]

Lowe, in his introduction to the palaeography of the Bobbio Missal, paid some attention to the linguistic peculiarities of the book, dedicating two chapters to orthography and grammar.[20] In these sections, Lowe mentioned those features of the manuscript which are most striking to the reader. The orthography is marked by the frequent occurrence of incorrect vowels and consonants. These orthographic peculiarities give the text a rather unusual appearance, but after some practice the reader becomes accustomed to them, so that the orthography is not the greatest problem in the intelligibility of the text. A second chapter is dedicated to the grammatical problems raised by the Missal's texts. In this chapter, Lowe enumerated some morphological and syntactical peculiarities common to the Latin of the

---

[18] Ibid., p. 47: 'Like all forms of written Latin this devotional literature suffered extensive vulgarization in the 7C and 8C. This can be seen even in a brief extract from the 8C Bobbio Missal, where towards the end of the *canon* the words *intra quorum nos consortium non aestimator meriti sed ueniae, quaesumus, largitor admitte* appear in the garbled form *intra quorum nos consorcio non stimator meritis sed ueniam quesomus largitur admitte.* But in a religion where departures from the prescribed form of words could raise doubts about the validity of the rites enacted by them, the motivation to restore was strong.'

[19] On the sermon *De dies malus* and the *Joca monachorum* see the contribution by Charles Wright and Roger Wright below, pp. 79–139.

[20] Lowe, 'Palaeography', pp. 85–95, 95–6.

period, such as the use of anomalous cases after prepositions or verbs, and the use of the accusative absolute instead of the ablative absolute, a well-known feature of the Latin of the early medieval period.[21] He did not, however, attempt a systematic analysis of the enigmatic language of this manuscript.

One of the ways to discover and to evaluate the eccentricity of the Latin of the Bobbio Missal is to compare its prayer texts with contemporary sources containing the same prayers. In this chapter I want to set the Bobbio Missal beside the *Missale Gothicum*, a Gallican sacramentary, probably written in the region of Burgundy around 700.[22] This sacramentary has many prayers in common with the Bobbio Missal and it is interesting to see how these books treat the prayer texts in different ways. At the same time, while drawing this comparison, some of the orthographic and syntactic peculiarities of the Bobbio Missal will come to the fore. Compared with their equivalents in the *Missale Gothicum*, the prayers of the Bobbio Missal are drastically shortened. In some cases the result is still a correct prayer text, as regards both syntax and content. But in others, the scissor and paste work of the compiler of the Bobbio Missal has led to grammatically incorrect and incomprehensible texts. The examples that follow are not intended to suggest that the compiler of the Bobbio Missal had the *Missale Gothicum* itself as his or her exemplar. Rather, it is highly probable that both sacramentaries shared a common ancestor for part of the prayers.

First I will consider the mass for Our Lord's Circumcision, celebrated on the eighth day after Christmas, i.e. New Year's Day, 1 January. The only prayer that the Bobbio Missal and the *Missale Gothicum* have in common for this mass is the *contestatio*. The *contestatio* (or *immolatio*) forms the heart of the Gallican mass-forms. We are dealing here with the first part of the Eucharistic prayer preceding the *Sanctus*. The *Missale Gothicum* and the Bobbio Missal are similar as far as the broad outlines of this text are concerned, but the extent to which the latter shortens the text as found in the *Missale Gothicum* is striking. It is as if the Bobbio compiler wanted to reproduce only the main thoughts of the prayer. Given below is the entire text as found in the *Missale Gothicum*, with those passages found in the Bobbio

---

[21] Compare, for example, the use of the ablative absolute, accusative absolute and nominative absolute in the writings of Gregory of Tours: M. Bonnet, *Le Latin de Grégoire de Tours* (Paris, 1890; repr. Hildesheim, 1968), pp. 558–68; in the travel journal of Egeria, E. Löfstedt, *Philologischer Kommentar zur Peregrinatio Aetheriae. Untersuchungen zur Geschichte der lateinischen Sprache* (Uppsala, 1911), pp. 158–9; in the *Missale Gothicum*: Rose, 'Communitas in commemoratione', pp. 247–50. For general literature on these syntactic phenomena, see J.B. Hofmann and A. Szantyr, *Lateinische Syntax und Stilistik* (= Lehmann, Hofmann, Szantyr, *Lateinische Grammatik. Handbuch der Altertumswissenschaft* II.2.2) (2nd edn, Munich, 1972), pp. 137–44; V. Väänänen, *Introduction au latin vulgaire* (3rd edn, Paris, 1981), pp. 166–9.

[22] Vatican City, BAV, Reg. lat. 317 (Burgundy, s.viii^in); *CLA* I.106; *Missale Gothicum*, ed. L.C. Mohlberg, Rerum Ecclesiasticarum Documenta, series maior 5 (Rome, 1961); revised edition in Rose, 'Communitas in commemoratione', pp. 7–177.

Missal reproduced in italics, and with additional passages or words suggested by the Bobbio Missal placed within square brackets.

[Uere] *dignum et iustum est*, uere aequum et iustum est nos tibi gratias agere, teque benedicere in omni tempore, *omnipotens* aeterne *deus*, quia in te uiuimus, mouemur et sumus, et nullum tempus nullumque momentum est, quo a beneficiis pietatis tuae uacuum transagamus. His autem diebus, quos uariis sollemnitatum causis salutarium nobis operum tuorum et munerum memoria signauit uel innouante laetitia praeteriti gaudii uel permanentis boni tempus agnoscimus et *propterea exultamus uberius quia sicut*[a] in recens gaudium de uenerabilis gratiae recordatione reuiuiscimus. Unde [in] *hodiernum diem* a die *salutiferi*[b] *natalis octauum, legitima domini secundum carnem geniti circumcisione signatum,* ordinata commemoratione recolentes sacrificium pacis in uotis sollemnibus honoramus, et tantae dignationis opus in domini altissimi pia humilitate ueneramur. *Qui*[c] *sicut mortalitatem nostram adsumpsit, ut mortem consumeret, ita et iugum legis in sua carne suscepit, ut* iugum diabuli a *nostra ceruice discuteret.* Circumcisus est in carne corporis nostri, ut nos per uerbum spiritus sui in corde purgati sine carnis uulnere circumcideremur in spiritu, ut utrique sexui proficeret circumcisio spiritalis, *quia pro uniuersitate generis humani saluator aduenerat.* Unde utrumque sexum sacramentum incarnationis amplexus est, suscipiens uirum natus ex faemina. Quam ob rem, domine, sacrificium circumcisionis sollemnitate uotiua pro nostrae aeternitatis gaudio suppliciter offerentes, placido dignare conspectu respicere, et offerentium praeces placatus exaudi, per Christum dominum nostrum. Per quem maiestatem tuam [quem] *laudant* angeli.[23]

   [a] *Bobbiense* scimus    [b] *Bobbiense* salutaris fieri    [c] *Bobbiense* quia

The result in the Bobbio Missal is a prayer in which the main lines of thought from the original text are rearranged into a new, more or less coherent text:

Uere dignum et iustum est omnipotens deus, propteria exultemus uberius quia scimus in hodiernum diem salutaris fieri natalis octauum legitimam domini secundum carnem geniti circumcisionis signatum. Quia sicut mortalitatem nostram adsumsit ut mortem consumarit, ita et iugum legis in sua carne suscepit ut nostra ceruice discuterit, quia pro uniuersitate humani generis saluatur aduenerat, quem laudant.[24]

There are, however, still some problems hidden in this text. To begin with the minor problems: the orthography of *propteria* for *propterea* is not unusual, the interchange of *i* and *e* being frequent in Latin texts of the period. The sentence from *quia* onwards constitutes a more serious problem. *Scimus* should be followed by an accusative + infinitive construction. This construction could be formed by *hodiernum diem . . . signatum*, given that the preposition *in* after *scimus* is superfluous. The infinitive *fieri* is, implausible as it may seem, not impossible in this construction. This leaves us with two words which make no sense in this text of the prayer, namely *legitimam* and *circumcisionis*. Together they should have formed

[23] *Missale Gothicum* 55, ed. Mohlberg, pp. 17–18; ed. Rose, in 'Communitas in commemoratione' pp. 27–8.
[24] *Bobbio* 107, p. 33.

the ablative which gives the whole sentence its original meaning: 'It is just and fair <that we praise thee>, omnipotent God, <and that> we rejoice all the more abundantly as we know this day – the eighth after the birth of the Saviour – to be marked with the legitimate circumcision of our Lord, born in the flesh.' In the second sentence it is only the word *ceruice* that causes a problem, or, rather, two problems. The first is that it should be an accusative, instead of the ablative, as is written down here. This may have resulted from the fact that the final *m* of *ceruice* and *nostra* has been dropped, a common feature in Latin texts of the period, due to phonetic causes.[25] But the sentence also falls short with respect to the content, for it is not 'our neck' (*ceruice*) which Christ shattered through his Incarnation, but 'the devil's yoke' (*iugum diabuli*) weighing upon it. This yoke is lost in the rendition of the Bobbio compiler.

A similar case is found in the mass for the Holy Innocents, celebrated on 28 December, a few days after Christmas. Again, the example is taken from the *contestatio*. It displays the same pattern as the *contestatio* of the Circumcision-mass. It seems as if the Bobbio compiler chose haphazardly some sentences from his exemplar, and rearranged them into a new, more or less intelligible whole.

[Uere] *dignum et iustum est*, uere dignum et iustum est, nos tibi semper et ubique gratias agere, domine, sancte pater, *omnipotens* aeterne *deus* [per christum dominum nostrum]. Pro his praecipue, quorum hodierno die annua festiuitate recolentes memoriam passionis celebramus, quos Herodianus satelles lactantum matrum uberibus abstraxi*t*. *Qui* iure dicuntur martyrum flores, qui in medio frigore infedilitatis exorti uelut primas erumpentes eclesiae gemmas quaedam persecutionis pruina pruina discussit, *rutilante fonte in Bethleem ciuitatem. Infantes* enim *qui aetate loqui non poterant, laudem domini cum gaudio resonabant. Occisi praedicant, quod uiui non poterant. Loquuntur* sanguine, quod lingua nequiuerunt. Contulit his martyrium laudem, quibus abnegauerat lingua sermonem. Praemittit infantes *infans Christus* [transmittit] *ad caelos*; transmittit *noua exenia patri; primicias exhibet genetori* paruulorum prima martyria Herodis scelere perpetrata; praestat hostis corpori, dum nocet; benificium tribuit, dum occidit: moriendo uiuitur, cadendo resurgitur, uicturia per interitum conprobatur. Pro his ergo beneficiis et pro praesenti sollemnitate inmensas pietati tuae gratias referentes potius quam rependentes, cum sanctis angelis et archangelis, qui unum te deum dominantem, distinctum nec diuisum, trinum nec triplicem, solum nec solitarium, consona laudamus uoce, dicentes: Sanctus, sanctus, sanctus.

[per christum dominum nostrum cuy merito][26]

Again, the result of this compilation is a more or less comprehensible prayer as far as content is concerned, with, however, some grammatical problems.

---

[25] In the process during which the pronunciation became more and more visible in the orthography of the Latin of the post-classical and early medieval period, no longer perceptible phonemes such as the final *m* of nouns in the accusative were often dropped in writing.

[26] *Missale Gothicum* 49, ed. Mohlberg, pp. 15–16; ed. Rose, p. 25.

Uere dignum et iustum est; omnipotens deus per christum dominum nostrum *qui* rutilante fonte in betthelem ciuitate infantes; qui aetate loqui non poterant laudem domini cum gaudio resonabant. Occisi predicabant quod uiui nequiuerant; *loquentur* infans christus transmittit ad celus noua exsenia patri primicias exhibit geneturi per christum dominum nostrum cuy merito[27]

It is just and fair <that we praise thee>, omnipotent God, through Christ our Lord. While the spring in the city of Bethlehem coloured blood red, the children, who because of their age could not speak yet, made resound the praise of the Lord with joy. Slain, they proclaimed what they could not when they were still alive. The infant Christ sends new presents to heaven; he presents the first fruits to the father, the creator.

This translation leaves two words in the Latin text unaccounted for: the first *qui* before *rutilante*, which has no following clause, and the verb *loquentur*, which has no subject. These two words make no sense in this shortened version of the prayer.

The mass for the Assumption of Our Lady, a feast which the Gallican liturgy used to celebrate in the middle of the month of January, provides us with the third and final example of the way the Bobbio compiler treated his texts. Several prayers from this mass have been chosen to serve as examples. All have been shortened by the Bobbio compiler in such a way that the grammatical constructions of the sentences are disturbed. In some cases, the meaning of the prayer has undergone a drastic change.

The first example comes from the *praefatio*. In the Gallican mass this prayer served as an introduction to the Eucharistic part of the mass. The *praefatio* here is a kind of transition from the first part of the mass of which the readings from Scripture form the core to the actual celebration of the Eucharist. There is an interesting passage in the *praefatio* for the feast of *Assumptio Mariae* in the *Missale Gothicum* in which Mary is called admirable, 'not only because of the pledge she conceived, but also because of the praiseworthy ascent by which she departed from this life'. The latter part is omitted in Bobbio:

Non solum mirabilis pignore quod fide concepit, sed translatione praedicabilis qua migrauit. Speciali trepudio, affectu multimodo, fideli uoto, fratres dilectissimi, corde depraecemur attento, ut eius adiuti muniamur suffragio.[28]

Non solum mirabiles pignore quod fidem concepit, fratres karissimi deprecimur ut eius adiuti moniamur suffragium.[29]

The construction of the original sentence is disturbed in the Bobbio Missal: after the introduction *non solum* the anticipated counterpart *sed (etiam)* does not follow.

---

[27] *Bobbio* 93, p. 30.
[28] *Missale Gothicum* 94, ed. Mohlberg, p. 28; ed. Rose, pp. 41–2.      [29] *Bobbio* 131, p. 40.

The second example is chosen from the *collectio ad pacem*, a prayer which accompanies the kiss of peace which is exchanged in the Gallican liturgy between the celebrant and the faithful, before the Eucharistic prayer is started. In this prayer, constructions also suffer from the way the Bobbio compiler shortened the original text.

*Deus uniuersalis* machinae propagator, *qui in sanctis spiritaliter, in matre uero uirgine etiam corporaliter habitasti,* quae ditata tuae plenitudinis ubertate, mansuetudine florens, *caritate uegens, pace gaudens, pietate praecellens, ab angelo gratia plena, ab Elisabeth benedicta, a gentibus* merito *praedicatur beata, cuius nobis fides mysterium, partus gaudium,* uita prouectum, discessus attulit hoc festiuum, praecamur supplices, ut *pacem, quae in adsumptione matris tunc praebuisti discipulis* sollemni nuper largiaris in cunctis, saluator mundi, qui cum patre et spiritu sancto uiuis.[30]

Deus uniuersalis qui in sanctis spiritaliter in matre uero uirgene etiam corporaliter habitasti caretate degens pace gaudens pietate precellens ab angelo gracia plena ab helisabet benedicta ab gentibus predicatur beata cuius nobis fides mistirium partus gaudium pacem quam in adsumcione matris tunc prebuisti discipolis nobis miserire supplicibus.[31]

The grammatical construction is disturbed since after *habitasti* a relative pronoun is lacking, and there is no verb governing the direct object *pacem*.

In the last example, the *contestatio* of the mass of Mary's Assumption, the Bobbio compiler again pruned in such a manner that a rather remarkable error creeps in. Instead of the sentence *nesciens damna de coitu*, with which Mary's virginal quality is indicated in the Gothic Missal ('she was not acquainted with the damage caused by sleeping with a man'), the Bobbio compiler writes *damna de coetu*. The most important word of this sentence, *nesciens*, is dropped. This yields a strange sentence with, if it makes any sense at all, a very peculiar meaning.

## CONCLUSION

The relationship between the Bobbio Missal and the *Missale Gothicum* has been discussed by several scholars.[32] Some of them still defend the proposition that the texts in the Bobbio Missal represent the older layer.[33] According to them, where the Bobbio Missal deviates from the *Missale Gothicum*, it is the *Missale Gothicum* that has lengthened the text, rather than the opposite. I regard this opinion as untenable

[30] *Missale Gothicum* 97, ed. Mohlberg, p. 29; ed. Rose, p. 43.   [31] *Bobbio* 132, pp. 40–1.
[32] *Missale Gothicum. A Gallican Sacramentary*, ed. H.M. Bannister, HBS 52 and 54 (London 1917 and 1919), II: *Notes and Indices*, p. 12; B. Capelle, 'La messe gallicane de l'Assomption: son rayonnement, ses sources', in *Miscellanea liturgica in honorem L. Cuniberti Mohlberg*, 2 vols. (Rome, 1949), II, pp. 33–59, here p. 34; A.H.M. Scheer, *De aankondiging van de Heer. Een genetische studie naar de oorsprong van de liturgische viering van 25 maart* (Baarn, 1991), pp. 104–7.
[33] Scheer, *De aankondiging van de Heer*, pp. 104–7.

after studying the results of the efforts of the Bobbio compiler. It is unthinkable that the original prayers could have been the Bobbio texts, whose sense and grammar are both confused. It is obviously more likely that the Bobbio compiler shortened the prayers as witnessed by the *Missale Gothicum* than the reverse.[34]

Apart from the relationship between the two liturgical books as such, the study of these sources draws a sharper outline of their position in the history of liturgical Latin in general. Christine Mohrmann, picturing her image of liturgical Latin as a language in an ivory tower, suggests that the process of development during which the Latin language changed gradually from vulgar Latin into the Romance languages did not touch the language of the liturgy. Instead, liturgical Latin survived the developments within the colloquial language.[35] In Mohrmann's view, the Latin of the liturgy was an impregnable entity. The Latin of the liturgical sources transmitted in the early medieval, especially the Merovingian, period is depicted by her as a mangling of the original texts, which had obviously become incomprehensible to the celebrating priest.[36] As an example she quotes the famous orthography of the baptismal formula *Baptizo te in nomine patri et filiae*. But I do not think that there was any bishop in early medieval Gaul who thought he was baptising the candidates in the name of the Father and the Daughter, although the orthography in his *Rituale* would suggest this heresy. Rather, this example is one of many instances where the influence of spoken language on the written account of liturgical texts becomes visible. Both the Bobbio Missal and the *Missale Gothicum* contain innumerable appearances of such orthographic peculiarities, which can be explained by the developments of the Latin language in the period to which these sacramentaries belong. These liturgical texts are, however, not merely confused and mangled representations of originally 'correct' Latin texts. Rather, they are highly important documents at the transitional period for the Latin language, including the language of the liturgy, *before* reaching the stage in which the liturgical language was released from the developing vernaculars. That the orthography in the liturgical manuscripts did not follow the classical rules any longer does not necessarily imply that the makers and users of these manuscripts did not understand what they were writing or reading any more.

Still, some gradation must be indicated. For it cannot be denied that, where the *Missale Gothicum* provides us with comprenhensible prayer texts, as regards both grammar and content, the Bobbio Missal raises some problems. The examples discussed above give a good impression of the way the modern reader has to struggle in order to reconstruct the original meaning of the prayers in the Bobbio Missal. A good example of confusion is the fragment of the *contestatio* of the feast

[34] Here I agree with Bannister; see *Missale Gothicum*, ed. Bannister, II, p. 12.

[35] C. Mohrmann, 'Sakralsprache und Umgangssprache', in C. Mohrmann, *Etudes*, IV (Rome, 1977), pp. 161–74, here p. 170.

[36] Mohrmann, 'Sakralsprache und Umgangssprache', p. 167.

of *Assumptio Mariae*, in which Mary seems to have lost her maidenhood. Was this confusion observed by the officiating celebrant, or by those who attended mass? This is a difficult question. The *Missale Gothicum* and the Bobbio Missal seem to represent different stages in the period in which the liturgical language 'survived colloquial language'. This process was completed in the Carolingian period, in which liturgical language was subject to the reform activities in the field of language. This is precisely the period in which the intelligibility of liturgical texts became a real problem, especially for the laity in the church, as was pointed out by Donald Bullough:

One of the paradoxes of 'Carolingian reform' is that the more successful it was in training the clergy in 'good Latin', with a traditional syntax and carefully articulated in ways that served clearly to distinguish it from the 'Romance' vernaculars in a direct line of descent from earlier spoken Latin . . . the less accessible the liturgy of mass and office became to the ordinary faithful in both Romance and Germanic regions.[37]

To what extent the Latin prayers as discussed above were understood in the pre- ceding period remains a matter that is open to discussion. Whereas the question of intelligibility has been addressed with respect to hagiographical texts of the early medieval period,[38] in the case of liturgy it has hitherto remained a largely unex- plored field. Before this question can have a chance of receiving an answer, the sources which raise them should be taken out of the shadowy corners to which they have been dismissed by previous generations of scholars. In this contribution I can do no more than lift a corner of the veil. Further research may shed more light on the questions raised, which concern essential aspects of early medieval life and thought.

[37] D. Bullough, 'The Carolingian liturgical experience', in *Continuity and Change in Christian Worship*, ed. R.N. Swanson, Studies in Church History 35 (Woodbridge 1999), pp. 29–64, at p. 52.
[38] For instance Heene, 'Merovingian and Carolingian hagiography'; M. Van Uytfanghe, 'Le latin des hagiographes mérovingiens et la protohistoire du français. Etat de la question', *Romanica Gandensia* 16 (1976), pp. 5–89; M. Van Uytfanghe, 'L'hagiographie et son public à l'époque mérovingienne', *Studia patristica* 16 (1985), pp. 54–62.

# 6

## *Additions to the Bobbio Missal:* De dies malus *and* Joca monachorum *(fols. 6r–8v)*[*]

CHARLES D. WRIGHT AND ROGER WRIGHT

## I  TEXTS AND TRANSMISSION

The additions to the Bobbio Missal in the first quire include a sermon headed DE
DIES MALVS (*DDM*) and an untitled question-and-answer dialogue mainly on
biblical and ecclesiastical history (for the extracts from the Gospel commentary
of Pseudo-Theophilus on fols. 1–6r, see below, p. 153). The sermon[1] has never
been studied in detail. Wilmart noted two other copies in Zurich, Zentralbibliothek, Rheinau 140, and Sélestat, Bibliothèque Humaniste 2 (1073).[2] Machielsen's
*Clavis Patristica Pseudepigraphorum Medii Aevi* lists a copy in Munich, Bayerische
Staatsbibliothek, Clm 28135,[3] although Machielsen was unaware that this sermon
occurs in the Bobbio Missal and elsewhere. Two further copies were noted (again
without reference to the other manuscripts) by Manfred Oberleitner in Cesena,
Biblioteca Malatestiana S.XXI.5, and Venice, Biblioteca Marciana II.46 (2400).[4] It
has not previously been noted that an extended quotation from the sermon occurs
within an addition to Isidore's *De natura rerum* in certain manuscripts.

---

[*] Part I is by Charles D. Wright, with the assistance of Roger Wright in the establishment of the
texts and translations; Part II is by Roger Wright.

[1] We refer to this text as a 'sermon' because of its general hortatory content, its address to an audience
of 'fratres' and its concluding doxology. Its brevity suggests that it might be an outline or notes for a
sermon to be elaborated upon extemporaneously by the preacher; but it is hardly possible to specify
the acceptable length of a 'sermon' in the early Middle Ages, and in any case none of the surviving
manuscript copies contains any significant expansions, so it may have been deemed complete as written.
Its context in **B** suggests that it may have functioned as a catechetical instruction (see below, p. 123).

[2] Wilmart, 'Notice', p. 42. For details on these manuscripts see below, pp. 82–4.

[3] J. Machielsen, *Clavis Patristica Pseudepigraphorum Medii Aevi*, IA–B: *Opera Homiletica*, Corpus
Christianorum (Turnhout, 1990), no. 3314. Hereafter cited as *CPPM* I, by entry number.

[4] M. Oberleitner, *Die handschriftliche Überlieferung der Werke des heiligen Augustinus* 1/2, Sitzungsberichte der Österreichischen Akademie der Wissenschaften, phil.-hist. Klasse 267 (Vienna, 1970),
pp. 59 and 368. The *In Principio* database (version 7) registers the copies in Zurich, Munich, Cesena
and Verona, but not Sélestat, Bibliothèque Humaniste 2 (1073) or the Bobbio Missal. For details on
these manuscripts see below.

The dialogue is one of the earliest surviving copies of a genre known as *Joca monachorum* (*JM*), a title found in four early manuscripts and one fifteenth-century copy, though not in the Bobbio Missal itself. For purposes of comparative analysis, however, it is convenient to adopt this title (and the standard edition's spelling with *J*) here. The Latin *JM* dialogues and their relationships have been analysed by Walther Suchier, who also edited many previously unpublished versions.[5] Since Suchier's study a few additional *JM* and similar dialogues have come to light.[6]

We provide herein a new edition of these two texts as found in the Bobbio Missal (**B**), together with an analysis of their sources, discussion of the relationship of **B**'s texts to other surviving versions (Part I), and a detailed linguistic commentary (Part II). Suggestions as to the possible functions of these texts are given at the end of each Part; while our conclusions are complementary, they are derived from essentially independent considerations of the texts' sources and manuscript trans-mission on the one hand (Part I) and their Latinity on the other (Part II), so we have thought it appropriate to frame them separately within each context.

To facilitate reference in the linguistic commentary, we have divided the texts into short numbered sections. For the *JM* dialogue these sections correspond to individual questions and their answers (and to Suchier's numbering), but for the sermon they are simply convenient divisions into one or more clauses or sentences. For each numbered section we print the Latin text in two forms, followed by a literal English translation. We first provide a semi-diplomatic transcript of the texts, without supplying punctuation or expanding abbreviations. (We do not attempt an exact reproduction of the form of the scribe's abbreviations, but have contented ourselves with approximate representations; the original forms can be seen in the facsimile.) The rationale for this step, despite the ready availability of the facsimile edition, is to avoid prejudging how the scribe would have spelled abbreviated words had he written them out in full, since his orthography is irregular and inconsistent. Moreover, the scribe's abbreviations, especially for the forms of the relative and interrogative pronouns, are themselves inconsistent and idiosyncratic, and it is not always certain what form was intended. For example, the scribe uses three different forms of abbreviation where the word *quia* is presumably intended: qa, ꝗa, and q̄a. Lowe ('Palaeography', p. 79 n. 4) suggests that the last abbreviation 'may be due to phonetic confusion: quaea = quia', and expands it as 'qu*ae*a' (with italics indicating the uncertainty in this case, whereas he resolves other abbreviations silently). An editor must decide in favour of one of these possibilities even if he cannot rule out the other, but such decisions should not affect the initial data upon which a

---

[5] W. Suchier, *Das mittellateinische Gespräch Adrian und Epictitus nebst verwandten Texten (Joca Mona-chorum)* (Tübingen, 1955). Suchier did not print the Bobbio Missal text, though he did include it in his comparative table of *JM* questions (pp. 94–5).

[6] For these see below, pp. 107–9.

linguistic analysis is to be based. Again, a frequent scribal combination (represented here as 'd/') takes the form of d followed by an oblique stroke that often curves back at the top and touches the shaft of the letter. Despite the fact that (as Lowe notes, 'Palaeography', p. 73 n. 2) certain other seventh- and eighth-century manuscripts use a final d with intersecting stroke to represent -de, -di, or -dum, Lowe asserts that for the Bobbio Missal additions 'an analysis of the usage goes to show that the stroke is a form of the letter *i* and not a mere abbreviation stroke' (*Bobbio*, p. 1 n. 3). Unfortunately Lowe does not 'show his work', and it is not clear to us that the symbol cannot equally represent -de, as W.M. Lindsay assumed.[7] The scribe also uses this oblique stroke in writing 'secund/' (fol. 6v/23, and again at fol. 6v/26 without the additional mark indicating a nasal consonant), which Lowe refrains from expanding as 'secundim'. The scribe's unabbreviated spellings afford many examples of hesitancy between *e* and *i*, and if this grapheme is taken to stand for -du in 'secundum', it is hard to see why it must be regarded as a form of *i* everywhere else. It is better simply to concede that the original vowels [e] and (short) [i] were often pronounced identically (see Part II, sect. 1), and that 'd/' may have been a convenient 'fuzzy' notation for a vowel the scribe was not really sure how to spell (or was willing to spell more than one way). Finally, while the abbreviation of uncial R with a stroke through the tail at the end of a word surely represents the ending conventionally spelled –rum, the scribe sometimes spells out this ending as –rom.

Even some individual letter forms are problematic to transcribe. Lowe noted (*Bobbio*, p. 1 n. 2) that 'the scribe formed the letters *o* and *u* so much alike that it is often impossible to say with certainty which he really meant', but in editing the text he is forced to choose one or the other. In cases where we cannot distinguish clearly between *u* and *o*, we have generally followed Lowe's judgement, but the fact that this is sometimes mere guesswork should be borne in mind.[8]

The purpose of the transcript, therefore, is to provide a preliminary text that does not resolve potentially ambiguous abbreviations. Letters that are only partially legible due to the condition of the manuscript (as represented by the facsimile) are enclosed in parentheses. A vertical bar indicates the end of a manuscript line. The transcript is 'semi-diplomatic' in that we have supplied word division, because a printed transcription in *scriptura continua* would be a typographical monstrosity, and because defining morphemic boundaries does not materially affect the issues that are significant for determining the scribe's own linguistic habits. In only one

---

[7] W.A. Lindsay, *Notae Latinae: An Account of Abbreviation in Latin MSS. of the Early Minuscule Period, c. 700–850* (Cambridge, 1915), p. 328.

[8] Unambiguous examples of a particular spelling with *u* or *o* do not serve to clarify the scribe's intention in other occurrences of the same word, for he can write 'duriciam' (5v/16) and 'doriciam' (5v/19) in close proximity.

case (*De dies malus*, sect. 20) does editorial word separation involve a substantive choice between alternative readings.

In order to produce a translatable text, we have also supplied a minimally edited version with expanded abbreviations and punctuation. Since the texts as they survive in **B** are the targets of our investigation, we do not normalise the scribe's spelling or grammar, but because we must resolve scribal 'd/' one way or the other, by default we expand it according to the conventional orthography of the word in question. (In the linguistic commentary such cases are not counted in statistics regarding the relative correctness of the scribe's orthography.) Special attention is drawn in the commentary on individual sections to certain abbreviations that appear to be ambiguous. We do not emend the text except where assuming a scribal blunder is necessary to make any sense of a passage.

Because the other versions of the sermon are all unpublished, and because the idiosyncrasies of **B** render its text unsuitable as a basis for literary and source analysis, we have also provided a critical edition based on the other manuscripts, all of which employ more conventional grammar and orthography than does **B**. We draw attention to substantive divergences from **B** in our commentary on the latter.

## DE DIES MALUS

In addition to **B**, the complete sermon occurs separately in five manuscripts:

**C** Cesena, Biblioteca Malatestiana S.XXI.5 (north-east Italy, s. ix$^{1/3}$), fols. 274v–275r. See J.M. Mucciolus, *Catalogus codicum manuscriptorum Malatestianae Caesenatis Bibliothecae*, 2 vols. (Cesena, 1780–84), II, pp. 249–51; B. Bischoff, 'Panorama der Handschriftenüberlieferung aus der Zeit Karls des Großen', in B. Bischoff, *Mittelalterliche Studien: Ausgewählte Aufsätze zur Schriftkunde und Literaturgeschichte*, 3 vols. (Stuttgart, 1966–81), III, pp. 5–38, at p. 31; B. Bischoff, *Katalog der festländischen Handschriften des neunten Jahrhunderts I: Aachen–Lambach* (Wiesbaden, 1998), no. 855; C.D. Wright, *The Irish Tradition in Old English Literature*, Cambridge Studies in Anglo-Saxon England 6 (Cambridge, 1993), p. 72; M. Gorman, 'The Carolingian miscellany of exegetical texts in Albi 39 and Paris lat. 2175', *Scriptorium* 51 (1997), pp. 336–54, at p. 351, with further references. According to Bischoff, **V** is a copy of **C**, but see p. 84 below for difficulties with this assumption.

**E** Sélestat, Bibliothèque Humaniste 2 (1073) (Lake Constance region, s. ix$^{2/4}$), fols. 1r–2r. See G. Morin, 'Textes inédits relatifs au symbole et à la vie chrétienne', *Revue Bénédictine* 22 (1905), pp. 505–24, at pp. 510–11; P. Adam, *L'Humanisme à Sélestat: l'école, les humanistes, la bibliothèque* (Sélestat, 1962), pp. 98–9; R. Haggenmüller, 'Das Paenitentiale Sletstatense – ein weiteres anonymes fränkisches Bußbuch. Anmerkungen zum Schlettstädter Codex 2', *Deutsches Archiv* 48 (1992), pp. 615–19 (see p. 617 for the manuscript's date and origin); *Paenitentialia minora Franciae et Italiae saeculi VIII–IX*, ed. R. Kottje, L. Körntgen and U. Spengler-Reffgen, CCSL 156 (Turnhout, 1994), p. xxxvii. For evidence of losses and misplacement of the final two quires, see below, n. 16.

**M** Munich, Bayerische Staatsbibliothek, Clm 28135 (Freising, s. ix in.), fols. 89v– 90v. See A. Werminghoff, 'Zu den bayrischen Synoden am Ausgang des achten Jahrhunderts', in *Festschrift Heinrich Brunner* (Weimar, 1910), pp. 39–55; G. Morin, 'Un nouveau feuillet de l'*Itala* de Freising', *Revue Bénédictine* 28 (1911), pp. 221–7; B. Bischoff, *Die südostdeutschen Schreibschulen und Bibliotheken in der Karolingerzeit*, I: *Die bayrischen Diözesen* (2nd edn, Wiesbaden, 1960), pp. 61 and 93; R. Etaix, 'Un manuel de pastorale de l'époque carolingienne (*Clm 27152*)', *Revue Bénédictine* 91 (1981), pp. 105–30, at pp. 112–13, 115; H. Hauke, *Katalog der lateinischen Handschriften der Bayerischen Staatsbibliothek München: Clm 28111–28254* (Wiesbaden, 1986), pp. 31–7; M.F. Wack and C.D. Wright, 'A new Latin source for the Old English "Three Utterances" exemplum', *Anglo-Saxon England* 20 (1990), pp. 187–202; Wright, *The Irish Tradition*, pp. 217–18, 264; H. Mordek, *Bibliotheca capitularium regum Francorum manuscripta*, MGH, Hilfsmittel 15 (Munich, 1995), pp. 364–7, with further references.

**V** Venice, Biblioteca Marciana II.46 (2400) (north Italy, s. xi, according to M. Ferrari; north Italy or southern Germany, s. x in., according to R.E. McNally), fol. 131r. See J. Valentinelli, *Bibliotheca manuscripta ad S. Marci Venetiarum*, 6 vols. in 2 (Venice, 1868–73), II, pp. 46–9; R.E. McNally, 'Isidorian pseud-epigrapha in the early Middle Ages', in *Isidoriana: Estudios sobre San Isidoro de Sevilla en el XIV centenario de su nacimiento*, ed. M.C. Díaz y Díaz (León, 1961), pp. 305–16, at p. 308; Wright, *The Irish Tradition*, p. 72; Gorman, 'The Carolingian miscellany', p. 351. A copy of **C**, according to Bischoff. However, in addition to evidence (cited below, p. 84) that **V** may be an independent copy of **C**'s exemplar, **V** has many corrections that seem to be based on collation with another manuscript. Valentinelli (mis)prints a reference in one text (fol. 136r) to Charles Martel's campaign against Chilperic II and Raginfrid (Ragamfred, Neustrian mayor of the palace) with the dating clause, 'Modo restant anni de sexto [sexio *ms.*] miliario L.XXX. [LXX, Val.] post isto anno quando carulus pugnauit in [n]eustria contra regem et rangifrido [*sic*; Elrangifrido, Val.]' (i.e., AD 719).[9]

---

[9] For the campaigns against Raginfrid, see *The New Cambridge Medieval History*, II: *c. 700–c. 900*, ed. Rosamond McKitterick (Cambridge, 1995), pp. 87–8.

**Z** Zurich, Zentralbibliothek, Rheinau 140 (probably Switzerland, s. viii[2]; *CLA* VII.1021), fols. 109r–110v. K. Halm, *Verzeichnis der älteren Handschriften lateinischer Kirchenväter in den Bibliotheken der Schweiz* (Vienna, 1865), p. 14; L.C. Mohlberg, *Katalog der Handschriften der Zentralbibliothek Zürich*, I: *Mittelalterliche Handschriften*, fasc. 3 (Zurich, 1936), pp. 228–30; A. Bruckner, *Scriptoria Medii Aevi Helvetica*, 8 vols. (Geneva, 1935–55), IV, p. 38; Wright, *The Irish Tradition*, pp. 57, 67–8, 74–7, 105.

The contents of **C** and **V** are virtually identical until **C** ends, and Bischoff has stated that **V** is a copy of **C**. If so, it would be difficult to explain why the scribe of **V**, whose script is not Insular, would have introduced so many Insular and specifically Irish abbreviations (such as those for *hoc*, *est*, *quia*, *tibi*, *quomodo*, *homines*) that are not present in **C**. **V** may thus rather be a copy of **C**'s exemplar or a congener that contained the material corresponding to **V** fols. 133v–140v now missing from **C**.

An analysis of a partially overlapping exegetical collection has been made by Michael Gorman,[10] but the contents of **CV** require further study. The context of the sermon *De dies malos* in **CV** may be laid out as follows:

1. Isidore of Seville, *Etymologiae* (**C**, fols. 1–273v; **V**, fols. 3–130v).
2. 'Epistula sancti Augustini episcopi. Primum quidem decet nos audire iusticia[m]' (**C**, fols. 274rv; **V**, fols. 130v–131r). The so-called 'Three Utterances' sermon (*CPPM* I.1930). See R. Willard, *Two Apocrypha in Old English Homilies*, Beiträge zur englischen Philologie 30 (Leipzig, 1935), pp. 1–35; R. Willard, 'The Latin texts of *The Three Utterances of the Soul*', *Speculum* 12 (1937), pp. 147–66; R.E. McNally, ' "In nomine Dei summi": seven Hiberno-Latin sermons', *Traditio* 35 (1979), pp. 121–43, at pp. 133–6; Wack and Wright, 'A new Latin source'.
3. 'Sermo sancti Augustini de dies malos' (**C**, fols. 274v–275r; **V**, fol. 131r).
4. 'Incipit nomina prophetarum. Esaias, Hieremias' (**C**, fol. 275r; **V**, fol. 131r). Unidentified; states that the prophets will intercede at the day of Judgement on behalf of anyone who recalls their names.
5. 'De uia iustorum et uia peccatorum. Via sanctorum fides catholica' (**C**, fol. 275rv; **V**, fol. 131r). *Liber de numeris* II.18, PL 83, cols. 1297D–1298B. Cf. R.E. McNally, 'Der irische Liber de numeris: Eine Quellenanalyse des pseudo-isidorischen Liber de numeris' (diss. Munich, 1957), pp. 41–2. This extract has been edited from **MVZ** by R. Etaix, 'La collection de sermons du codex 152

---

[10] **C** and **V** are mentioned briefly by Gorman, 'The Carolingian miscellany', p. 351. A fuller list of their contents, but without identification of many of the anonymous items, was formerly available at Gorman's web-site <http://ccat.sas.upenn.edu/jod/genesis>. The description of **C** by Jose Carlos Martin, *Isidori Hispalensis Chronica*, CCSL 112 (Turnhout, 2003), pp. *61–*64, appeared after the present chapter was completed.

de la Faculté de médecine de Montpellier', *Revue Bénédictine* 106 (1996), pp. 134–50, at pp. 147–48.

6. 'De anima et eius uirtutibus. Per auditum credit' (**C**, fol. 275v; **V**, fol. 131rv). *Liber de numeris* II.14, PL 83, col. 1296C; cf. McNally, 'Der irische Liber de numeris', pp. 37–8. This extract is also in **Z**.

7. 'Credo in Deum patrem omnipotentem' (**C**, fol. 275v; **V**, fol. 131v). The Niceno-Constantinopolitan creed.

8. 'Crux Deum mecum [Domini mei **V**]' (**C**, fol. 275v; **V**, fol. 131v). A variant form of Calbulus Grammaticus, *Versus sanctae crucis*, ll. 5–6 (*Anthologia Latina* 379): D. Schaller and E. Könsgen, *Initia Carminum Latinorum Saeculo Undecimo Antiquiorum* (*ICL*) (Göttingen, 1977), no. 2902. Cf. B. Bischoff, 'Ursprung und Geschichte eines Kreuzsegens', in Bischoff, *Mittelalterliche Studien*, II, pp. 275–84; here combined with *ICL* no. 2903, as in the Manual of Dhuoda, for which see Bischoff, 'Ursprung und Geschichte eines Kreuzsegens', p. 280. See also A. Wilmart, 'Prières médiévales pour l'adoration de la Croix', *Ephemerides Liturgicae* 46 (1932), pp. 22–65, at p. 38 n. 7; Maddalena Spallone, 'Ricerche sulla tradizione manoscritta dell' "Anthologia Latina" (AL 181, 186–188, 379 Riese): itinerari testuali nell'età carolingia', *Studi medievali* 3rd ser. 29 (1988), pp. 607–24, at pp. 618–21; Joachim M. Plotzek, 'Zur Geschichte der Kölner Dombibliothek', in *Glaube und Wissen im Mittelalter. Katalogbuch zur Ausstellung* (Munich, 1998), pp. 15–64, at pp. 62–3.

9. 'Incipit homelia sancti Augustini de die iuditii [iudicii **V**]. O fratres karissimi, quam timendus est' (**C**, fols. 275–276r; **V**, fol. 131v). A Pseudo-Augustinian Doomsday sermon (App. 251; *CPPM* I.1036), which often circulated with the Three Utterances.[11]

10. 'Incipit interrogationes. Quia uideo te de scripturis contendere uelle' (**C**, fols. 276r–277v [defective]; **V**, fols. 131v–135v). Partial ed. from **V** by Mucciolus, *Catalogus*, II, pp. 249–51. Includes (in **V**) separately rubricated questions on Genesis and Exodus, among which occurs the reference to Charles Martel's campaign against Raginfrid. See F. Stegmüller, *Repertorium Biblicum Medii Aevi*, 11 vols. (*RBMA*) (Madrid, 1950–80), nos. 5263–4; cf. 9545–6 (=Leiden, Bibliotheek der Universiteit, Voss. lat. Q.122, part II); 10321–2 (=Paris, BNF lat. 614A).

11. 'Incipit cronica sancti Eusebii presbyteri de principio celi, creatione terrę, et omnem firmatione mundi. Mundus de tribus uisibilibus' (**V**, fol. 135v). Ed.

---

[11] For some examples, see C.D. Wright, 'Apocryphal lore and Insular tradition in St. Gall, Stiftsbibliothek MS 908', in *Irland und die Christenheit: Bibelstudien und Mission*, ed. P. Ní Chatháin and M. Richter (Stuttgart, 1987), p. 136. Material from the two sermons is also conflated in a sermon found (uniquely?) in Prague, Knihovna Metropolitní Kapitoly (*olim* Universitní Knihovna) III.F.6 (509) (provenance Opatowitz, s. xii), ed. F. Hecht, *Das Homiliar des Bischofs von Prag. S. XII.*, Beiträge zur Geschichte Böhmens I/1 (Prague, 1863), pp. 66–7.

from Munich, Clm 22053 (Augsburg diocese, ca. 814; Bischoff, *Schreibschulen*, pp. 18–21) by U. Schwab, *Die Sternrune im Wessobrunner Gebet*, Amsterdamer Publikationen zur Sprache und Literatur 1 (Amsterdam, 1973), pp. 85–90, and from Sélestat, Bibliothèque Humaniste 1 (1093) (probably Italy, s. viii; *CLA* VI.829), fols. 67r–71r, by C. Munier, 'La chronique pseudo-hiéronymienne de Sélestat: un schéma de catéchèse baptismale?', *Revue Bénédictine* 104 (1994), pp. 106–22, at pp. 108–9. Apparently a distinct work from item 10, but often appended to it along with item 12. For additional manuscripts of items 10–12, see Wright, *The Irish Tradition*, pp. 70–2; Gorman, 'The Carolingian miscellany', p. 351.

12. 'De octo pondera unde factus est homo. In primis pondus humi' (**V**, fols. 135v–136v). This tract appears elsewhere headed *De plasmatione(m) Adam* and appended to the *Cronica* (ascribed to Jerome) in Sélestat, Bibliothèque Humaniste 1, fols. 71r–78r; Karlsruhe, Badische Landesbibliothek, Aug. 229 (near Chieti in the Abruzzi, ?821; Bischoff, *Katalog*, no. 1719), fol. 69rv; Cologne, Dombibliothek 15 (perhaps western Germany, s. ix$^{3/4}$ or $^{4/4}$; Bischoff, *Katalog*, no. 1872), fol. 95rv; and Vatican City, BAV, Reg. lat. 846 (France; ?provenance Saint-Sulpice, Paris; s. ix$^{1/4}$), fols. 106v–107r. Ed. from Sélestat, Bibliothèque Humaniste 1, by M. Förster, 'Das älteste mittellateinische Gesprächbüchlein', *Romanische Forschungen* 27 (1910), pp. 342–8 (repr. PLS 4, 938–41), and by Munier, 'La chronique pseudo-hiéronymienne', pp. 110–12; ed. from Vatican City, BAV, Reg. lat. 846, by W. Schmitz, *Miscellanea Tironiana aus dem Codex Vaticanus Latinus Reginae Christinae 846* (Leipzig, 1896), pp. 35–8. On the Vatican manuscript see also Mordek, *Bibliotheca capitularium*, pp. 830–3; M. Hellmann, *Tironische Noten in der Karolingerzeit am Beispiel eines Persius-Kommentars aus der Schule von Tours*, MGH, Studien und Texte 27 (Hannover, 2000), pp. 255–6. On the Cologne manuscript, see also Wright, *The Irish Tradition*, pp. 62ff; *Handschriftencensus Rheinland: Erfassung mittelalterlicher Handschriften im rheinischen Landesteil von Nordrhein-Westfalen*, ed. Günter Gattermann *et al.*, I (Wiesbaden, 1993), pp. 583–4; and for a complete digital facsimile, see *Codices Electronici Ecclesiae Coloniensis*, <http://www.ceec.uni-koeln.de/>. On an additional passage 'Dicamus de arcu' in some manuscripts see below, p. 94 and n. 57.

13. 'Incipit glosas euangeliorum. Fyson insufflatio' (**V**, fols. 136v–137r). *RBMA* no. 5268 (the only copy listed).

14. 'Interrogatio. Dic mihi sol ubi ambulat per xii. horas diei?' (**V**, fol. 137r). A brief dialogue, not graphically distinguished from the preceding item.

15. 'De figuris. .iiii. libris moysi .iiii.`or´euangelistas significant' (**V**, fol. 137rv). Miscellaneous biblical motifs, mainly enumerative; perhaps a continuation of items 13–14.

16. 'Incipit epistula Iohannis . . . tria sunt qui testimonium perhibent' (**V**, fols. 137v–138r). Brief tract on the *comma Iohannem* (1 Io. 5.7).

17. 'Incipit commemoratorium in apocalypsim sancti Iohannis. Iohannes gratia Dei interpretatur' (**V**, fols. 138r–140v). *RBMA* no. 5271 (cf. 8933); B. Bischoff, 'Wendepunkte in der Geschichte der lateinischen Exegese im Frühmittelalter', in Bischoff, *Mittelalterliche Studien*, I, pp. 205–73, no. 37.

R.E. McNally, who was not aware of **C**, characterised the contents of **V** as 'an Irish *collectaneum*'.[12] Items 2, 5–6 and 17 had previously been identified as Hiberno-Latin. Charles D. Wright drew attention to further manuscripts with parallels for some of this material.[13] The origins of the other anonymous pieces have not been determined, but items 13 and 15 have contacts with Hiberno-Latin exegesis on the Gospels, and item 14 (which may be part of a single text comprising items 13–15) includes two lists of the names of the seven heavens that agree in part with those found in the apocryphon of the Seven Heavens and its vernacular Irish and Anglo-Saxon avatars.[14] Extracts from items 10–12 (possibly constituent parts of a single work) also occur in a group of manuscripts recently discussed by Michael Gorman.[15]

**E** has lost several quires and has at least one and possibly two others out of position.[16] The manuscript in its current order begins defectively with the

---

[12] McNally, 'Isidorian pseudepigrapha', p. 308.

[13] Wright, *The Irish Tradition*, pp. 70–2, with further references.

[14] **V**, fol. 137r: 'Dic mihi nomen vii. cęlorum. Dico tibi, ager, arpharius, galfahel, galphuher, thot-thiam, iaciam, seluc, seruch ubi Dominus omnipotens habitat. Interrogatio. Alia nomina vii. celorum. Eleothim, eleothin, edat, edam, eleothi, iuhim, firmamentum id est [Insular symbol] ecclesia in quorum [*sic*] lumina'. Compare the names of the heavens (or of their doors) in the texts cited by Willard, *Two Apocrypha*, p. 7. On the Seven Heavens apocryphon see also Wright, *The Irish Tradition*, pp. 217–18.

[15] See Gorman, 'A Carolingian miscellany', pp. 351–2. Some of these manuscripts also transmit material with Irish associations, including a recension of *Das Bibelwerk* (Bischoff, 'Wendepunkte', no. 1B), Recension II of Pseudo-Jerome, *Expositio in IV Euangeliorum* ('Wendepunkte', no. 11B) and the 'Ordinals of Christ' in the Hibernian Chronological version (see R. Reynolds, *The Ordinals of Christ from their Origins to the Twelfth Century*, Beiträge zur Geschichte und Quellenkunde des Mittelalters 7 (Berlin and New York, 1978), pp. 70–1, n. 9). On the relationship of items 10–12 see further below, p. 94, n. 57.

[16] According to Adam, *L'Humanisme*, p. 99, and *Paenitentialia minora*, ed. Kottje *et al.* p. xxxvii, the manuscript consists of ten quaternios and two ternios, and Adam states that the ternios (fols. 81–6 and 87–92) are from another manuscript. The script is the same as the main hand of the rest of the manuscript, however, and it seems rather that the two ternios are remnants of quaternios belonging to the original manuscript. To judge from the quire signatures visible in the printouts, four quires (presumably quaternios) are missing from the beginning of the manuscript, two quires are missing after fol. 32, two more after fol. 48, and one after fol. 56. No quire signatures are visible at the end of either ternio, probably due to loss of their last two (or first and last) leaves. The second ternio contains the first part of Isidore's *Synonyma*, the second part of which occurs on fols. 49r–56v (quire 'xv'). The second ternio, therefore (and possibly also the first), should be placed between fol. 48, the end of quire 'xii', and fol. 49, the beginning of quire 'xv'. The last quire would then either be the ternio fols. 81–6 (without signature) or fols. 73–80 ('xviii'), but since the texts on both fols. 80v and 86v end abruptly, one must assume that one or more leaves or quires have also been lost at the end.

conclusion of an unidentified and mostly illegible sermon (fol. 1r), followed by *De diebus malis* (fols. 1r–2r) and the Pseudo-Augustinian Doomsday sermon (fols. 2r–3r, with 'metuendus' for 'timendus' in the incipit); a hagiographical dossier on St Martin of Tours (fols. 3r–22v);[17] three sermons *De natali S. Mariae* (fols. 22v–32v);[18] Pseudo-Basil, *Admonitio ad filium spiritualem* (fols. 33r–48v), with losses at the beginning and end;[19] Isidore's *Synonyma*, book II, also defective (fols. 49r–56v);[20] the Athanasian and Niceno-Constantinopolitan creeds, the latter both in a bilingual Greek–Latin text and Latin only (fols. 57r–59v);[21] a version of the *Joca monachorum* (fols. 59v–64v; see below, p. 105); riddles[22] and *sententiae* on faith and charity drawn from Isidore and Caesarius (fol. 65rv);[23] an 'ordo angelorum' (fols. 65v–66r);[24] an 'orologius' (fol. 66rv);[25] a penitential (fols. 66v–69r);[26] extracts from the *Rule* of Benedict (cc. 5–7, fols. 69v–72v; ends defectively); a sermon (with some verbal parallels with *De dies malus*) 'Timor Domini expellit peccatum' in a form closely similar to **M**, fols. 69r–74r/2, but here with a different

---

[17] *Bibliotheca Hagiographica Latina* (*BHL*), 2 vols., Subsidia hagiographica 6 (Brussels, 1898–1901), with supplements in 1911 (Subsidia hagiographica 12) and 1986 (Subsidia hagiographica 70), nos. 5619, 5631, 5622, 5623, 5624c, 1451 (*Vita S. Briccii*), 5610, 5613.

[18] *CPPM* I.979, 156 and 1830; the last sermon ends defectively.

[19] Corresponding to the edition by P. Lehmann, *Erforschung des Mittelalters*, V (Stuttgart, 1962), pp. 221.40/1–242.516.

[20] II.28/9–62/3 = PL 83, cols. 851D/852A–859D/860A (due to damage in the first and last folios of the quire, it is not possible to determine from the printouts precisely where the text begins and ends). This copy is not registered in M.C. Díaz y Díaz, *Index Scriptorum Latinorum Medii Aevi Hispanorum* (Madrid, 1959), no. 31.

[21] See Morin, 'Textes inédits relatifs au symbole', pp. 510–11. Morin notes that the Niceno-Constantinopolitan creed here lacks the *filioque*.

[22] The riddles include a version of *Anthologia Latina* no. 281, ed. F. Büchler and A. Riese (Leipzig, 1894) I/1: 'Vidi hominem simul cum uia pendentem . . . cui latior?', followed by a sentence from Caesarius, *Sermo* 119.2, l. 16 (CCSL 103, 498).

[23] 'Non posse ad ueram beatitudinem . . . errore pietate' (Isidore, *Sententiae* II.2.1, 3, 6; CCSL 111, 94–5); 'De caritate nulum praemium pensatur. Karitas enim uirtutum omnium . . . ab amicus [*sic*; apostolo *Isid.*] dicit' (*Sententiae* II.3, 3; CCSL 111, 97); 'Nemo [te] potest mortem tua . . . suscipere non permittit' (Caesarius, *Sermo* 33.3, ll. 9–11; CCSL 103, 145).

[24] This unusual text states what responsibilities are given to particular archangels, including non-canonical ones (Geruhel, Tubihel).

[25] Other copies are printed by A. Staerk, *Les Manuscrits latins du Ve au XIIIe siècle conservés à la Bibliothèque impériale de Saint-Pétersbourg*, 2 vols. (St Petersburg, 1910), I, p. 201, from St Petersburg, Saltykov-Shchedrin State Public Library Q.V.II. no. 5, fol. 53r; *Liber sacramentorum Gellonensis*, addita s. ix, CCSL 159, 523 (no. 3070); *Ælfwine's Prayerbook*, ed. B. Günzel, Henry Bradshaw Society 108 (London, 1993), pp. 107–8 (cf. p. 199 for parallels in other Anglo-Saxon manuscripts); PL 78, col. 477; cf. also A. Cordoliani, 'Les MSS de comput de l'abbaye du Mont-Saint-Michel', *Sacris Erudiri* 17 (1966), p. 59 (Avranches, BM 236 [s. xi], fol. 97). Another copy is in Cologne, Dombibliothek 15, fol. 99v (on this manuscript see above, p. 86). The *In Principio* database lists several other manuscripts, but not Sélestat, Bibliothèque Humaniste 2.

[26] *Paenitentialia minora*, ed. Kottje *et al.*, pp. 81–5.

conclusion and ascribed to Isidore (fols. 73r–77r);[27] extracts from the *Vitaspatrum* (fols. 77r–80v);[28] extracts from Gregory's *Dialogues*, book II (fols. 81r–86v, perhaps to be placed after fol. 48); and Isidore, *Synonyma*, end of book I and part of book II (fols. 87r–92v, which should be placed before fol. 49).[29]

**M** is a collection of conciliar statutes, pastoral materials and sermons.[30] Four quires (fols. 51–80) of approximately the same date are additions to the original compilation. The conciliar and pastoral texts include *capitula de examinandis ecclesiasticis*; the statutes of the Councils of Reisbach, Freising and Salzburg (*c.* 800/3); Charlemagne's (Alcuin's) *Epistola ad Elipandum*; the Nicene creed and canons (drawn from the *Collectio Dionysio-Hadriana*);[31] an extract from Gregory's *Cura pastoralis* (I.11); and Arno of Salzburg's *Instructio pastoralis*.[32] The sermons include four by Caesarius of Arles,[33] one attributed to Sedatus,[34] several falsely attributed to Augustine[35] and a number of rare anonymous sermons.[36] Scattered

[27] *CPPM* I.5318; the first half corresponds to Pseudo-Augustine *Sermo 62 ad fratres in eremo* (PL 40, cols. 1345–7). The sermon occurs with ascription to Isidore also in St Gall, Stiftsbibliothek 194 (?Switzerland, St Gall, s. viii med.; *CLA* VII.917), pp. 225–31.

[28] *Vitaspatrum* (*Verba seniorum*) VII.1.1, PL 73, col. 1025A; V.5.36–38, PL 73, cols. 883C–885C; V.10.76, PL 73, cols. 925B–C (defective); cf. *BHL* 6530v; J.G. Freire, *A versão latina por Pascásio de Dume dos Apophthegmata Patrum* (Coimbra, 1971).

[29] I.71–II.23, PL 83, cols. 843C–850C.

[30] For incipits and bibliographical details on texts not discussed below, see Hauke, *Katalog der lateinischen Handschriften*, and Mordek, *Bibliotheca capitularium*.

[31] For this identification see Etaix, 'Un manuel de pastorale', p. 106.

[32] Ed. Etaix, 'La collection de sermons du codex 152', pp. 116–23.

[33] Sermo 16 [*CPPM* I.1051] (fols. 47v–50v); Sermo 13 [*CPPM* I.1050] (fols. 60v–63v); Sermo 158A, rec. B [*CPPM* I.4387] (fols. 65r–69r); Sermo 10 [*CPPM* I.1029] (fols. 94v–97v).

[34] *CPPM* I.6425 (fols. 39r–44r).

[35] *CPPM* I.2290 (fols. 33v–39r); *CPPM* I.1930 (the Three Utterances sermon, fols. 44r–47v); *CPPM* I.1036 (the Doomsday sermon, fols. 63v–65r; without ascription in the manuscript); *CPPM* I.1172 (fols. 81r–83v; without ascription); *CPPM* I.3328 (fols. 88r–89v); *CPPM* I.1187 (fols. 90v–94v, with considerable variation). Two of the four sermons of Caesarius are also attributed to Augustine in the manuscript.

[36] The sermon on fols. 13v–15r ('Audite uerbum Domini et intellegite et custodite et facite omnia mandata Domini et iudicia eius') seems to occur only here. The sermon on fols. 15v–18r ('Predicatio cottidiana. O fratres karissimi recordemur dignitatis regni celestis'; not in *CPPM*?) occurs in Munich, Bayerische Staatsbibliothek, Clm 6293 (Freising, s. ix; Bischoff, *Schreibschulen*, pp. 88–9), fols. 148v–150r, as noted by Hauke, *Katalog der lateinischen Handschriften*, and also in St Gall, Stiftsbibliothek 682 (?St Gall, s. ix[1]; Bruckner, *Scriptoria*, III, p. 116), pp. 311–23, and as part of a collection found in three manuscripts: Vatican City, BAV, Pal. lat. 212 (Germany, s. viii ex.; *CLA* I.85; Upper Rhine region or Lake Constance, s. ix in.: Bischoff, *Mittelalterliche Studien*, I, p. 155; III, p. 21 n. 73), Pal. lat. 220 (Middle or Upper Rhine region, provenance Lorsch, s. ix in.; Bischoff, *Mittelalterliche Studien*, III, p. 88), and Berlin, Staatsbibliothek, Phillipps 1716 (?Holland, s. ix[1/4]; Bischoff, *Katalog*, no. 415). On this collection, see McNally, '"In nomine Dei summi"'; Wack and Wright, 'A new Latin source', p. 188. The sermon on fols. 57r–60v ('Incipit omelia Romensis de die iudicii. Audiamus fratres karissimi de die iudicii magnam resurrectionem') is possibly identical to *CPPM* I.3315, from Munich, Bayerische Staatsbibliothek, Clm 6329 (north Italy, Burgundy or Switzerland, provenance Freising, s. viii ex.; *CLA* IX.1276). That on fols. 75r–79v ('Dixit Ihesus discipulis suis, Petite et dabitur

among the sermons are extracts from Defensor's *Liber scintillarum* (cc. 1–4), Benedict's *Rule* (c. 4) and the *Liber de numeris* II.18, *De uia iustorum et uia peccatorum* (fols. 11v–13r, the first of the two extracts found in **V** and **Z**), as well as miscellaneous enumerative and etymological motifs.[37] Material probably of Irish origin, in addition to the extract from the *Liber de numeris*, includes a list of the twelve abuses of the world (fol. 15r), here attributed to Gregory as in several other early manuscripts,[38] and the Three Utterances sermon, which occurs twice, in a

uobis . . . Dominus creator et redemptor noster ad gaudia celestis beatidudinis') occurs in Munich, Bayerische Staatsbibliothek, Clm 14380 (prob. Bavaria, s. ix[1/3]; Bischoff, *Schreibschulen*, p. 240), and in abbreviated form in Prague, Knihovna Metropolitni Kapitoly III.F.6, ed. Hecht, *Das Homiliar*, p. 43, and in Munich, Bayerische Staatsbibliothek, Clm 27152 (Bavaria, s. ix in.; Bischoff, *Schreibschulen*, p. 165), where it occurs along with several items also found in Munich, Bayerische Staatsbibliothek, Clm 28135 (for these see Etaix, 'Un manuel de pastorale', p. 108, no. 30). For the sermon on fols. 69r–75r ('Predicatio de timore Domini ad diuitis. Timor Domini expellit peccatum'), see above, n. 27. That on fols. 79v–80v ('Incipit de hoc quod dicit apostolus, Nemini quicquam debitis . . . Quantum cupio sancitatis uestre debitum reddere') also occurs in Munich, Bayerische Staatsbibliothek, Clm 14380, fols. 86v–88r (as noted by Hauke, *Katalog der lateinischen Handschriften*, who states that it is not identical to *CPL* no. 832). Finally, the sermon on fols. 83v–87v ('Beatus Hieronymus presbyter sic predicauit dicens: non quaeris gloriam et non delebis cum gloriosus fuerit') is also in Munich, Bayerische Staatsbibliothek, Clm 14364 (south Germany, s. ix[1]; Bischoff, *Schreibschulen*, pp. 239–40), fols. 38v–40r, and corresponds in part to a sermon in Prague, Knihovna Metropolitni Kapitoly III.F.6, ed. Hecht, *Das Homiliar*, pp. 76–77, and in part to Pseudo-Augustine, *Sermo 67 ad fratres in eremo* (PL 40, col. 353).

[37] E.g., fanciful 'Hebrew' etymologies of the words *gloria* and *alleluia* (fol. 15r), ed. from Munich, Bayerische Staatsbibliothek, Clm 6364 (s. x), fol. 1, by M. Thiel, 'Grundlagen und Gestalt der Hebräischkenntnisse des frühen Mittelalters', *Studi medievali* 3rd ser. 10/3 (1970), p. 233, with reference to **M**. In addition to the parallel cited by Thiel from London, BL Cotton Vespasian A.i (the Vespasian Psalter: Canterbury, St Augustine's, s. viii[1]; *CLA* II.193), fol. 6rv, see B. Löfstedt, 'Miscellanea grammatica (Zur grammatischen Schwindelliteratur)', *Rivista di cultura classica e medioevale* 23 (1982), pp. 159–64 ('Chaldean' etymology of *gloria*), and Manchester, John Rylands Library, 116 (the Psalter of St Maximin: provenance Trier, St Maximin, s. ix/x), printed by M.R. James, *A Descriptive Catalogue of the Latin Manuscripts in the John Rylands Library at Manchester*, 3 vols. (Manchester, 1899), I, p. 213 ('Chaldean' and 'Hebrew' etymologies of *alleluia* and *gloria*), both cited by D. Ó Cróinín, *Early Medieval Ireland 400–1200* (London, 1995), p. 213. In these sources the etymologies are of progressively smaller constituent parts of the words (*gloria, glori, glor, glo, gl, g*), a nicety lost on the compiler of Munich, Bayerische Staatsbibliothek, Clm 28135. For similar etymologies of 'alleluia', cf. *Collectanea Pseudo-Bedae*, ed. Bayless and Lapidge, pp. 251–4.

[38] Derived from the Hiberno-Latin treatise *De duodecim abusiuis saeculi*, ed. S. Hellmann, Texte und Untersuchungen zur Geschichte der altchristlichen Literatur 24/1 (Leipzig, 1909). See Wright, *The Irish Tradition*, pp. 64ff. In two of these manuscripts (Munich, Bayerische Staatsbibliothek, Clm 22053 and Cologne, Dombibliothek 15), the list of twelve abuses (with attribution to Gregory) occurs near an enumeration of six damnations of the soul and seven rewards of the just, which partly overlaps the lists in Munich, Bayerische Staatsbibliothek, Clm 28135 *De sex cogitationibus sanctorum et de septem damnationibus anime* (fols. 14v–15r). Cf. Wright, *The Irish Tradition*, pp. 69–70. The *sex cogitationes sanctorum* theme also occurs in Stuttgart, Württembergische Landesbibliothek, HB VII.5, fol. 24r, as noted by Hauke, *Katalog der lateinischen Handschriften*, as well as St Gall, Stiftsbibliothek 230 (St Gall, s. viii[2]; *CLA* VII.993), p. 538; Milan, Biblioteca Ambrosiana, M 79 sup. (Piacenza, between 1078 and 1095), fol. 46va, for which see B. Bischoff and M. Lapidge, *Biblical Commentaries from the Canterbury*

standard form (inc. 'Primum quidem decet nos audire iusticiam', fols. 44r–47v) and also in an apparently unique abbreviated redaction (inc. 'Anima homnis peccatoris cum exigerit de corpore', fol. 13rv) which must have circulated in Anglo-Saxon England, where it was translated into Old English.[39] A sermon contained in one of the interpolated quires on fols. 51v–54v (inc. 'Querite ergo primum regnum Dei . . . Primo oportet nos querere regnum per bona opera') is an expanded version of another of the Hiberno-Latin sermons 'In nomine Dei summi' edited by R.E. McNally.[40] The Pseudo-Hieronymian sermon on fols. 83v–87v is perhaps also Hiberno-Latin. It incorporates a series of characteristically Irish enumerative motifs, most of which are found in the *Liber de numeris*:[41] a list of the qualities of heaven in the form 'x sine y' (cf. VII.18),[42] the three unhappy ones in the law (III.19), a 'thought, word, deed' triad (cf. III.40), the three kinds of fear (III.47) and the three kinds of vocation (III.46). The sermon also quotes the opening lines of the Three Utterances sermon. The rather peculiar expressions *plebs peccatorum* and *plebs iustorum* may reflect vernacular Irish idiom.[43] There is other evidence for the circulation of Hiberno-Latin (or Insular) texts at Freising, as witnessed by the florilegium copied by the Anglo-Saxon scribe Peregrinus, Munich, Clm 6433 (s. viii ex.; *CLA* IX.1283),[44] as well as by the collection of (probable) Hiberno-Latin texts in Munich, Clm 6302 (s. viii$^{4/4}$; *CLA* IX.1267).[45]

---

*School of Theodore and Hadrian*, Cambridge Studies in Anglo-Saxon England 10 (Cambridge, 1994), p. 281; and Brussels, Bibliothèque Royale 1373 (s. xii), fol. 77r.

[39] See Wack and Wright, 'A new Latin source', with the Latin text at pp. 189–90.

[40] '"In nomine Dei summi"', p. 140. Another version of this text is found in St Gall, Stiftsbibliothek 682, pp. 396–7.

[41] These are noted by McNally ('Der irische Liber de numeris', p. 206); references are to his numbering of items.

[42] 'uita sine morte iuuentus sine senectute lux sine tenebras gaudium sine tristitia satietas sine uastidium claritas sine nube' (fols. 83v–84r). Briefer variations are found in other sermons: 'lucem habitat sine tenebras, habet regnum sine commutatione et uitam sine fine' (fol. 14rv), 'gaudium sine fine serenitas sine nube, gaudium sine commutatione' (fol. 52v) and 'regnum sine commutatione et uitam sine fine' (fol. 54r). For further examples, cf. Wright, *The Irish Tradition*, pp. 102–5. The motif was modelled on phrases in the 'x sine y' pattern from Augustine (e.g., *In Iohannis euangelium tractatus*, CCSL 36, 281), but often extended into lists of seven or more items, including some recurrent distinctive (non-Augustinian) phrases such as 'regnum sine commutatione'.

[43] Compare Irish expressions with *áes* ('people, folk') such as *ais fírian* 'folk of justice, the righteous'; *ais amprom*, 'folk of the wicked ones' [gl. *improborum*], cited in the *Dictionary of the Irish Language*, Compact Edition, gen. ed. E.G. Quin (Dublin, 1983), s.v. 2 *áes*.

[44] See A. Lehner, *Florilegia: Florilegium Frisingense (Clm 6433); Testimonia Diuinae Scripturae*, CCSL 108D (Turnhout, 1987). On the Irish background of some of this material, which includes extracts from the *Prouerbia Grecorum* and a copy of the Three Utterances sermon (the latter not edited by Lehner), see also Wright, *The Irish Tradition*, pp. 56–61, 104, 217, 247.

[45] See Bischoff, *Schreibschulen*, pp. 81–2; C.D. Wright, 'Bischoff's theory of Irish exegesis and the Genesis commentary in Munich Clm 6302: a critique of a critique', *Journal of Medieval Latin* 10 (2000), pp. 115–75.

**Z** contains primarily homilies, including one by Augustine,[46] two by Gregory,[47] two by Caesarius,[48] one attributed to 'Flaustus',[49] and a variety of Pseudo-Augustinian and other pseudonymous or anonymous sermons,[50] accompanied by extracts from Gregory's *Moralia in Iob*, three letters by Jerome, the *Fides Isatis*[51] and miscellaneous extracts and commonplaces.[52] Here again we find the extract *De uia sanctorum et uia peccatorum* from the *Liber de numeris* II.18 (fols. 38v–40r), coupled with the extract II.14 *De sancta anima et eius uirtutibus* (fols. 40r–41r) as in **V**. A section headed 'Testimonium Sancti Hyeronimi' (fols. 33r–36v) is a sequence of enumerations with extensive parallels in Hiberno-Latin compilations, and there is a subsequent group of triads from Irish tradition (fol. 123r), closely paralleled in the Bobbio Missal (*Bobbio* 582, pp. 178–9).[53] The Three Utterances sermon occurs on fols. 8v–11v, and the pseudo-Augustinian Doomsday sermon on fols. 93r–94v.

In addition to these manuscripts, a substantial extract from the sermon survives in the form of an addition to Isidore's *De natura rerum* in some late manuscripts [**Is**]. This was printed by Arévalo in a note (reprinted in PL 83, cols. 1003–5),

---

[46] Sermo 279, PL 38, cols. 1275–80 (fols. 76r–87r).

[47] *Hom. in Hiezechielem* II.viii.8–10, CCSL 142, 342–4 (fols. 1r–8v), which corresponds to *CPPM* I.2002, cf. M. Ferrari, 'Die älteste kommentierte Bibelhandschrift und ihr Kontext. Das irische Ezechiel-Fragment Zürich, Staatsarchiv W3.19.XII', in *Mittelalterliche Volkssprachige Glossen*, ed. Rolf Bergmann *et al.* (Heidelberg, 2001), pp. 47–76 at p. 57 n. 35; and an extract from *Hom. in Hiezech.* II.3.10, CCSL 142, 243 (fols. 112r–113r, part of a quire that belongs at the beginning of the manuscript) that also appears in the *Collectanea Pseudo-Bedae*, ed. Bayless and Lapidge, p. 160.

[48] *CPPM* I.4400 = 889 (Sermo 179, fols. 95r–106v); *CPPM* I.4400 = 862 (Sermo 157, fols. 124r–125v, incomplete).

[49] *CPPM* I.4720 (fols. 11v–15v).

[50] *CPPM* I.2302 (fols. 87v–92v); I.1036 (the Doomsday sermon, fols. 93r–94v); *CPPM* I.1721 (fols. 106v–109r); *De dies malos* (fols. 109r–110v); 'Iterum sancti Augustini. Quicumque enim cum peccato uiuit, mortuus est Deo' (fols. 110v–112r; not in *CPPM*, see below, p. 93); 'De apostulo. Orate, inquid, sine intermissione, et Deus pacis erit uobiscum. Audite fratres karissimi presens lectio recitata quid loquimur' (fols. 113r–124r).

[51] CCSL 9, 335–43.

[52] These include three extracts not identified by Mohlberg, *Katalog der Handschriften der Zentralbibliothek Zürich* and one that remains unidentified: 'De predestinacione sancti Esido: Gemena est predistinatio' (fols. 73v–74r) and 'De peccati recordacione. Bonum est homeni semper ante oculos propria adibere dilecta' (fols. 74v–75r) are from Isidore's *Sententiae* II.6 and 24 (CCSL 111, 103 and 141); 'Excarpsus sancti Hieronimi de euangelio. Regina austri surgit in iudicio cum generatio ista, ceterum. Interpretatio. Quod simpliciter futurum ad confessionem populi illius' (fols. 43r–45r) corresponds to an extract attached to the *Expositiunculae* of Arnobius the Younger in Munich, Bayerische Staatsbibliothek, Clm 6434 (Freising, s. viii/ix; *CLA* IX.1284; Bischoff, *Mittelalterliche Studien*, I, p. 221), see CCSL 25A, 260, and below, p. 96; 'In ueteris testamenti. Ignis semper in altare ardebat' (fols. 32r–33r, unidentified).

[53] See P. Sims-Williams, 'Thought, word and deed: an Irish triad', *Ériu* 29 (1978), pp. 78–111, repr. with original pagination and addenda in his *Britain and Early Christian Europe: Studies in Early Medieval History and Culture* (Aldershot, 1995), no. XIII, pp. 86–7; Wright, *The Irish Tradition*, pp. 64–73. To the examples cited there, add Milan, Biblioteca Ambrosiana, M 79 sup., fol. 46rb (see above, n. 38) and Paris, BNF 5596, fol. 136v.

but unfortunately he did not specify which manuscripts the addition occurs in, and Jacques Fontaine's critical edition does not address this particular addition.[54] It begins with an allegorical exposition of the colours of the rainbow, and abruptly shifts to a general discourse on sin and death:

Quicunque enim cum peccato vivit, mortuus est Deo, vivit diabolo. Si autem audieret Evangelium Christi, et conversus fuerit ad Deum, resurgit et vivit cum Christo. Qui vero cum peccato suo moriuntur, vadunt in poenam, resurgunt ad mortem. Multi vero hic pereunt putantes se diu vivere, ideo non corriguntur. Fallit illos spes sua, non vivit homo quantum putat, non quantum sperat. Audite, ubi dicitur: *Non tardes converti ad Deum* [Sir. 5.8].

Thus far the discourse agrees closely with the opening of an anonymous sermon that immediately follows *De dies malos* in **Z** (fols. 110v–112r).[55] Then comes the quotation from *De dies malos*:

Dies malos habemus, quandiu inter homines malos vivimus, testante Apostolo: *Videte quomodo caute ambuletis, non ut inspientes, sed ut sapientes, redimentes tempus, quoniam dies mali sunt.* Tolle homines malos, et non erunt dies mali. Appetentes res alienas, adulteri, periuri, calumniatores, oppressores. Per homines malos sunt dies mali. Dies ergo malos habemus, quandiu inter homines malos vivimus.

The citation agrees with **BCVEZ** against **M** in repeating the sentence 'Dies (ergo) malos habemus, quandiu inter homines malos vivimus' (corresponding to **B**.21 and 24), but whereas in **Is** the first occurrence immediately precedes the quotation of Eph. 5.15–16, in **BCVEZ** it follows these biblical verses. There is, however, a striking connection specifically between **Is** and **B**. The passage quoted above from Arévalo is followed quite abruptly by the sentence, 'Qui vivendo saeculum vicerunt, Elias et Enoch.' This has a loose connection to what preceded and what follows (a discussion of the six ages of the world): the discussion of the colours of the rainbow ends with an allusion to the Last Judgement, which is to be heralded by the return of Enoch and Elijah during the reign of Antichrist; and the allusion to these two Old Testament figures who are to return alive in the last days is followed by a list of the ages of the world. But the source of this sentence can be identified: it has been detached from a *JM* dialogue. Moreover, it is a very rare *JM* item, found elsewhere only in **B** and one other Latin version [**G**] in Munich, Bayerische

---

[54] *Isidore de Séville. Traité de la nature*, ed. J. Fontaine (Bordeaux, 1960).

[55] Halm, *Verzeichnis*, p. 14, notes another copy of this sermon in St Gall, Stiftsbibliothek 907 (St Gall, s. viii[2]; *CLA* VII.952), pp. 297–8, which I have not seen. **Z** has the following variants from Migne: quicunque] quicumque || diabolo] diabulo || ad Deum . . . Christo] ad Christum resurget uiuit in Christo. Audi apostolum dicentem, Surge qui dormis exsurge a mortuis et inluminabit tibi Christus, qui autem in fide uiuunt securi hic moriuntur || vadunt in poenam] uiuent in poena || resurgunt] resurgent || corriguntur] conuertuntur || fallit illos spes sua] fallet sua spes || non quantum] nec quantum || audite] audi || tardes] tardis || Deum] dominum.

Staatsbibliothek, Clm 19417 (southern Germany or Switzerland, s. ix$^{1/3}$; Bischoff, *Schreibschulen*, p. 164), and in an Old Icelandic translation:[56]

**B**.10: 'Quis uiuindum seculum uicit? Elias et Inoc'.
**G**.4: 'Quis vivit dum seculum vicit? Helias et Enoc et Johannes'.
*VLM*.32: 'Hverir ero, er enn lifa ok hafa sigrad heimen?' 'Enoch ok Helias ok Iohannes gudspialla madr'.

('Who are they who still live and have overcome the world?' 'Enoch and Elijah and
John the Evangelist')

It appears, then, that whoever cobbled together this particular addition to Isidore's chapter XXXI *De arcu* had access to a manuscript that combined the sermon *De dies malos* with a version of a *JM* dialogue that shared this rare question with **B** and **G**, but that shared its answer (omitting John) with **B** alone. It must also have contained a copy of the sermon 'Quicumque enim cum peccato uiuit' that survives in **Z**, though in a form textually at some remove from **Z**. The manuscript used by the compiler of **Is** was probably related to the lost exemplar from which the scribe of **B** copied both the sermon and the *JM* dialogue, and **Is** thus affords evidence that the sermon and dialogue circulated together apart from **B**. **Is** contains additional matter not paralleled in **B**, but its discussion of the colours of the rainbow is also found as part of the larger compilation headed *Cronica Sancti Eusebii presbyteri de principio celi* in **V**, fol. 136rv, and in some other manuscripts of the *Cronica*, including Karlsruhe, Badische Landesbibliothek, Aug. 229, fol. 69rv, and Cologne, Dombibliothek 15, fol. 100rv (though here the passage on the rainbow occurs separately from the *Cronica*, which is at fols. 94r–95v). It is not entirely clear whether the passage on the rainbow was originally part of the *Cronica*,[57] and resolution of its textual status must await the critical edition in preparation by Michael Gorman. Part of it also occurs separately in the *Liber de numeris*.[58]

---

[56] For bibliographical details on these texts see pp. 106 and 110 below.

[57] The text in **V** and Cologne, Dombibliothek 15 corresponds essentially verbatim to **Is** from 'Arcus autem qui in nubibus' (PL 83, col. 1003C) to 'ante diem judicii visus non erit' (PL 83, col. 1004B), with some additional matter towards the end that has been omitted by **Is**. Part of the passage from Karlsruhe, Badische Landesbibliothek, Aug. 229 was printed by McNally, 'Der irische Liber de numeris', p. 88. The other manuscripts of the *Cronica* (see above, p. 86) do not include the passage on the rainbow (though the Sélestat manuscript is defective). Judging from Gorman's table of correspondences ('The Carolingian miscellany', p. 353), the passage does not occur in the group of manuscripts containing extracts from the *Cronica*, but I have been able to consult only Paris, BNF 614A and Cologne, Dombibliothek 85. The tract *De arcu* may thus have been a separate item that became attached to *De plasmatione Adam*, which in turn became attached to the *Cronica*. That some of this material circulated independently is shown by **Is** and the *Liber de numeris* (see following note).

[58] *Liber de numeris* IV.39, corresponding to two brief passages, 'Arcus autem quatuor colores . . . nigrum de terra' (PL 83, col. 1003CD) and 'per igneum colorem Spiritum sanctum . . . significat persecutionem carnis' (cols. 1003D–1004B), but with an additional sentence also found in **V**, Karlsruhe, Badische Landesbibliothek, Aug. 229, and Cologne, Dombibliothek 15. I have consulted the text in Munich, Bayerische Staatsbibliothek, Clm 14392 (prob. Freising, s. ix$^{1/4}$; Bischoff, *Schreibschulen*,

*De dies malus* is based on two passages from the Pauline Epistles. The theme of 'evil days' derives from Eph. 5.15–16 (quoted in section 20), which the preacher develops in connection with Rom. 2.1, 4–6 (sections 12, 17–18). The quotations are Vetus Latina of a mixed type that cannot be precisely localised. There are, however, some recurring (though not exclusive) agreements with two **I**-type manuscripts whose text is north Italian:[59] 61 (= Vulgate [V] siglum D) = the Book of Armagh, Dublin, Trinity College 52 (Armagh, 807/8; *CLA* II.270) and 86 = Monza, Biblioteca Capitolare I-2/9 (Monza–Milan region, s. ix[2]).[60] Particularly striking are parallels for Rom. 2.5 in Augustine that seem not to be attested in any Vetus Latina or Vulgate biblical manuscripts,[61] but these are probably due to familiarity with Augustine rather than independent use of an otherwise unattested text-type.

The biblical quotations would be consistent with an origin for the sermon in north Italy, where manuscripts **C**, presumably **V** and possibly **B** (according to Wilmart, Bischoff and Gamber, though Lowe prefers Luxeuil) were written; but one cannot exclude an origin within the range of the other surviving manuscripts, that is, Alemannia–Rhaetia (**E**, **Z**) and Bavaria (**M**). The quotation in **Is** is conflated with an extract from another sermon ('Quicunque enim cum peccato vivit') that survives (to my knowledge) in only two manuscripts, both from Switzerland, together with a rare *JM* item found only in **B** and another *JM* manuscript (**G**) that may also be from Switzerland – though the material on the rainbow had a wider range, from the Abruzzi to western Germany. Given the circulation of *De dies*

pp. 98–9), fol. 87rv. See McNally, 'Der irische Liber de numeris', pp. 87–8, who notes the parallels in **Is** and Karlsruhe, Badische Landesbibliothek, Aug. 229. It is difficult to say whether the text found in **Is** and some manuscripts of the *Cronica* has conflated the passage on the *four* colours of the rainbow from the *Liber de numeris* with material on the *three* colours from another source, or whether instead the *Liber de numeris* has eliminated the contradiction by abbreviating the longer text.

[59] Sigla and variants for Ephesians are based on *Epistula ad Ephesios*, ed. H.J. Frede, Vetus Latina. Die Reste der altlateinischen Bible 24/4 (Freiburg, 1964), supplemented by Frede, *Ein neuer Paulustext und Kommentar*, 2 vols., Vetus Latina. Aus der Geschichte der lateinischen Bibel 7–8 (Freiburg, 1973–4), I, p. 46. For Romans I have been able to consult complete collations generously provided to me by P. Hugo S. Eymann, the editor of the forthcoming Beuron edition. Because the quotations are so heterogeneous, it does not seem worthwhile to document the variants fully here. I wish to thank Dr Eymann for his advice on the textual affiliations of these quotations, but I am solely responsible for the conclusions I have drawn. For descriptions of the biblical manuscripts, see Roger Gryson, *Altlateinische Handschriften. Manuscrits vieux latins. Répertoire descriptif, Première partie: MSS 1–275*, Vetus Latina. Aus der Geschichte der lateinischen Bibel 1/2 A (Freiburg, 1999). Citations from the Vulgate cited for purposes of comparison in the commentary on **B** are from Bonifatius Fischer *et al.*, *Biblia Sacra iuxta Vulgatam versionem*, ed. R. Weber, 2 vols. (3rd edn, Stuttgart, 1983).

[60] Rom. 2.4 ignoras; Rom. 2.5 sua [suam **B**]; Eph. 5.15 non ut [*om.* ut **EM**, *with* quasi *added above the line in* **E**] (*non ut* occurs only as a correction in 86). Readings paralleled in 61 but not in 86 are Rom. 2.5 tu autem secundum duriciam (-tiam 61); Eph. 5.16 *om.* ut[2] [**B** only].

[61] Rom. 2.5 + cordis tui (tuae **B**); *om.* et inpaenitens cor (c. inp., c. sine paenitentiam). The entire sequence *tu autem secundum duritiam cordis tui* [*-ciam c. tuae* **B**] *thesaurizasti* [*temsauricas* **B**, *thesaurizas* **E**] is paralleled outside of (or independently of) Augustine's writings only in Gregory of Elvira (Granada) and the Pseudo-Bede commentary on the Pentateuch (PL 91, col. 301B).

*malus* with texts that have been identified as Irish or Irish-influenced – notably the Three Utterances sermon and extracts from the *Liber de numeris* – it may have been compiled in a north Italian or Rhaetian centre frequented by Irish *peregrini*.[62] The biblical readings shared with the Book of Armagh, an Irish witness to a north Italian text type, point in the same direction. The use of Arnobius the Younger[63] in the commentary on the four Gospels wrongly attributed to Theophilus of Antiochon (fols. 1–6r) may afford further circumstantial confirmation, since the very limited transmission of Arnobius is concentrated in south Germany and north Italy, and the three earliest of four primary manuscripts (apart from **B**) all have Irish connections: one is a fragment in Irish script, another was copied from an Irish exemplar and the third contains the Hiberno-Latin *Catechesis Cracoviensis*.[64] Such a hypothesis would be consistent with the character of the Bobbio Missal as a whole: a Gallican sacramentary with Irish elements both in the liturgical core and among the additions,[65] including the 'Ordinals of Christ' in a variant of the Hibernian-Chronological version (fol. 293rv; *Bobbio* 582, p. 178),[66] and the immediately following sequence of enumerations.[67]

The sermon *De dies malus* is certainly pre-Carolingian, since the two earliest manuscripts, **B** and **Z**, dating from the eighth century, are textually already at some remove from one another. There are no quotations from ecclesiastical writers (save for a possible echo of Augustine in **B**.14) that would fix a *terminus post quem*.[68] In Wilmart's opinion ('Notice', p. 54), **B** originated 'dans son ensemble, c'est à dire avec tout son cortège d'additions', in the seventh century rather than the eighth; given the character of the sermon's Latinity (even as represented in the other manuscripts), a seventh-century date for this text seems most likely.

[62] The question of the sermon's place of origin is, of course, not the same as the question of the home of the scribe of **B**; for a suggestion that the scribe was from southern France (Burgundy), see Part II, sect. 17.

[63] The extracts in **B** are edited in CCSL 25A, 262–6. Cf. also n. 52, above. On this commentary see Yitzhak Hen, 'A Merovingian commentary on the Four Gospels (CPL 1001)', *Revue des Etudes Augustiniennes* 49 (2003), pp. 167–87.

[64] For these manuscripts see Bischoff, *Mittelalterliche Studien*, I, pp. 221, 257, 229 and 256; CCSL 25A, 254–6. The first two manuscripts are Bavarian, the third north Italian (the fourth is twelfth century).

[65] For arguable Irish elements cf. Wilmart, 'Notice', *passim*; G. Morin, 'D'où provient le missel de Bobbio?', *Revue Bénédictine* 31 (1914–19), pp. 326–32; P. Salmon, 'Le texte biblique des lectionnaires mérovingiens', in *La Bibbia nell'alto medioevo*, Settimane 10 (Spoleto, 1963), pp. 491–517, at p. 499; and the references cited by Sims-Williams, 'Thought, word and deed', p. 87 n. 52. Close parallels with the text of the Stowe Missal are often dismissed because it is also Gallican, but the liturgical classification does not eliminate their potential significance as evidence for contacts between Ireland and north Italy.

[66] See Reynolds, *The Ordinals of Christ*, pp. 58 and 72–3.  [67] See above, p. 92.

[68] There are some verbal parallels in a sermon ('Timor Domini expellit peccatum') found in **EM** and the corresponding part of Pseudo-Augustine, *Sermo 62 ad fratres in eremo* (see below, sections 4, 7 and 23). This sermon must be later than Isidore, who is quoted, but it is not clear if it draws on a form of *De dies malus*, or vice versa, or if they share an unidentified common source.

## *Edition and translation of* De dies malis

1. [f. 6r/24] DE DIES | MALVS.

    De dies malus.

    About evil days.

**B** lacks the attribution to Augustine found in the other manuscripts. **EM** have the grammatically regular title *De diebus malis*, as does **V** by correction.

2. Rapes ali|enā gaudens male | operares [f. 6v] et letares

    Rapes alienam, gaudens male operares et letares.

    You seize another's property, rejoicing you behave evilly and are happy.

The other manuscripts agree in adding *Audi* [+ *O* **EZ**] *homo* at the beginning, and in reading *aliena et gaudis* [corr. to *gaudes* **EV**].

3. an potas Proximom | tuum male facere et tibi bene

    An potas proximom tuum male facere et tibi bene?

    Do you think to treat your neighbour badly and yourself well?

**V** has a form of the question mark after *bene*; **E** places it at the end of sentence no. 4.

4. qa | elu spolias et te uestes

    Quia elu spolias et te uestes.

    For you despoil him and clothe yourself.

On forms such as *elu* and *ele* for *illum*, *ille* see Part II, sect. 7. Cf. the sermon 'Timor Domini expellit peccatum' in **EM**, *unum expoliat et* [om. *et* **M**] *alium se sperat uestire* [*unum exspoliant, alterum vestiunt*, Migne].

5. cum male fe|ceres carnē alterios te ipsum ⏤pdes |

    Cum male feceres carnem alterios, te ipsum perdes;

    Whenever you harm another's body, you will ruin yourself;

As Lowe notes (*Bobbio*, p. 4 n. 20), the scribe's abbreviation of *per* here and in *perdit* (*DDM* 6) is the one standard in Spain, which stands for *pro* elsewhere.

6. cum elom espo(li)as ele ⏤pdit tunica et | tu anima et iu(sti)ciā ante dm̄

    cum elom espolias, ele perdit tunica, et tu anima et iusticiam ante Deum.

    when you despoil him, he loses his tunic and you lose your soul and justice
      before God.

In *iusticiam* the *c* seems to be written over a *t*. The other manuscripts all omit *et . . . anima et* and *ante Deum*, reading *ille perdit tunicam* [*tonicam* **Z**, *tunica* **C**], *tu iustitiam* [*iusticiam* **CV**].

7. adten|dis Q d/ripias et non atendis qd p |das

    Adtendis quod diripias, et non atendis quod perdas.

    You give heed to whatever you are taking away, but not whatever you are losing.

The scribe normally abbreviates *quod* with a following *d*, while *q* alone with a stroke through the descender normally represents *que*. Here the unusually elaborate form of the capital Q and its tail-stroke seems to stand for *quod*, but perhaps the following *d-* in *diripias* is a phonetic Janus. Cf. the sermon 'Timor Domini expellit peccatum' in **EM**, *adtendunt quod adquirunt* [*quid adquerunt* **M**] *et non adtendunt quid perdunt* [*attendunt quid acquirunt, et non perpendunt quid amittunt*, Migne].

8. nõ uis ut neq; tiui mintiatur et | ipse fidem ñ seruas

   Non uis ut neque tiui mintiatur, et ipse fidem non seruas;

   You do not wish that one should lie to you, yet you yourself do not keep faith;

Lowe expands neq; to *neque*, but the scribe's abbreviation of *que* is not usually followed by the semi-colon, and it might have been intended to represent *nequis*, the reading of **CVZ** [ . . . *quis* **E**, *uel quis* **M**]. On the other hand, elsewhere the scribe abbreviates *quis* as qs, so with some reluctance we have allowed the less satisfactory *neque* to stand. The first *t* in *mintiatur* seems almost a hybrid of *t* and *c*.

9. uis ut hab elum ti|bi fedes seruetur

   uis ut hab elum tibi fedes seruetur.

   you want faith to be kept by him towards you.

The other manuscripts read *fidem seruari*.

10. ama in te ipso qood | spectis in altero

   Ama in te ipso qood spectis in altero.

   You love in yourself what you despise in another.

The first *o* in *qood* may be a smudged *u*. For *Ama*, seemingly an indicative form here, see Part II, sect. 5. The other manuscripts read *expetis* (**CVE**) or *expedis* (**MZ**), and *Ama* is imperative: 'Love in yourself what you require of another.'

11. ledere ñ uis et alte|rum led/re uis

   Ledere non uis et alterum ledere uis.

   You do not want to be hurt, yet you want to hurt another.

For *alterum ledere* **M** reads *laetare alterum*, presumably a variant spelling of *laedere*. On the form *ledere* (for standard *laedi*), see Part II, sect. 13.

12. alter/ iud/cas et ab alte|r/ iud/care non uis

   Alterum iudicas et ab alterum iudicare non uis.

   You judge another yet you do not want to be judged by another.

Cf. Rom. 2.1, which in the Vulgate reads 'o homo omnis qui iudicas in quo enim iudicas alterum [~alterum iudicas 89 75] te ipsum condemnas'. On the Vetus Latina variants in the sermon's Pauline quotations see p. 95 above. The other manuscripts of the sermon omit *Alterum iudicas et ab alterum* (recte *altero*), presumably due to haplography in a common archetype, but **E** has *et alterum iudicas* added in the margin. In **EV** *iudicare* has been corrected to *iudicari*.

13. alter/ damnas | et ab alter/ dānare ñ uis

   Alterum damnas et ab alterum damnare non uis.

   You harm another yet you do not wish to be harmed by another.

**E** reads *damnari* (*dampnari* corr. from *dampnare* **V**).

14. quod ergo | ibas et p̱ibas capit te paradysus dī | redi ad dōm

   Quod ergo ibas et peribas, capit te paradysus Dei: Redi ad Dominum.

   Thus because you have lived and gone to ruin, there is room for you in the
   paradise of God: return to the Lord!

In the other manuscripts the first clause takes the form of an independent question
(we have adopted the readings of **E**): *Cur* [*Cum* **M**] *ergo sic ibas* [*sitiebas* **CZ**, *siciebas*
**V**, *scibas* **M**] *et peribas* [*periebas* **CV**]: 'Why then were you living thus and perishing?'
(**E** punctuates with a form of the question mark). With **B**'s *ibas et peribas . . . Redi ad
Dominum* cf. Augustine, *Sermo xiii de Vetere Testamento*, CCSL 41, 178–9: 'Quid
est quod superbus ibas et peribas? Redi ad cor tuum'. **B**'s *Quod* is thus perhaps
an error for *Quid*. For the sense we assign to *capere*, see Part II, sect. 15. The
abbreviation of *Dominum* is what Lindsay would call a 'freak' (cf. *Notae Latinae*,
p. 403); the other manuscripts read *Deum* (abbreviated *dm̃*).

15. Quando exelera faci|ebas nonq̄ estatē ad sopliciom ra|piebat

   Quando exelera faciebas, nonquam estatem ad sopliciom rapiebat.

   When you were committing crimes, he never immediately took you away
   to punishment.

Lowe expands 'nonq̄' to *non quae*, but Lindsay (*Notae Latinae*, p. 218) has examples of 'numq̄' for *numquam*, and the spelling *nonquam* would easily fall within
our scribe's repertoire. The other manuscripts have at this point a question with
*numquid*, with the passive *rapiebaris* instead of *rapiebat*: 'When you were committing crimes, were you immediately taken away to punishment?' (**EV** punctuate
with question marks). This may establish an antecedent probability in favour
of resolving **B**'s abbreviation as *nonquid*, but *nonquam* makes sense and does
not require assuming a capricious suspension. On *exelera* and *estatē* see Part II,
sect. 7.

   With sections 15–18 compare a Pseudo-Augustinian sermon (inc.: 'Fratres karissimi istas res terrenas non habent homines sine labore'; not in *CPPM*), ed. M. de la
Bigne, *Maxima Bibliotheca veterum patrum*, XXVII (London, 1677), pp. 346–7,
which introduces the same quotation from Romans with statements similar to sections 15–16: 'tu quando malum facis, & Deus non vindicat, sua patientia emen-
dationem expectat. Quare thesaurisas in terra & non in Coelo? Thesaurizate in
coelo ait Dominus, quia nec fur nec latro, nec vicinus malus potest tollere. Ignoras miser quia Poenitentia ad Paradisum te adducit?' On this sermon see Wright,
'Apocryphal lore', p. 128 n. 24. To the manuscripts cited by Morin, CCSL 104,
996, add Orléans, BM 116 (94), fols. 31r–33v, and two manuscripts cited in the
*In Principio* database: Troyes, BM 239, fol. 50v, and BM 710. A partially overlapping sermon (inc.: 'Dilectissimi fratres oportet nos humilitatem habere'; not
identical to *CPPM* I.1194) in Vatican, BAV, Pal. lat. 216, fol. 109v, and Paris,
BNF lat. 5596, fol. 114, has essentially the same sequence (citation from Paris,
BNF lat. 5596): 'Homo quando male facit et Deus non uindicat sua pacientia tua

emendacione expectat. Sed quantum plus expectat ut conuertas tantum grauius damnat si non emendas. Apostolos ait, "An ignoras quia benignitas Dei ad penitentiam te adducit? Tu autem secundum duriciam tuam et cor inpenitens thensaurizas tibi iram in die irae et reuelacionis iusti iudicii Dei.'"

16. quare tibi pacipatur q̄a te | ad penetenciam espectabatur

    Quare tibi pa[r]cipatur? Quia te ad penetenciam espectabatur.

    Why was it spared you? Because it was hoped you (would come) to repentance.

Our emendation of **B**'s *pacipatur* is based on *parcebatur* of the other manuscripts. Instead of *te ad penitenciam*, the other manuscripts read *tua p(a)enitentia*: 'Because your repentance was hoped for.'

17. er|go benenote dī cūtemnis ignoras q̄a | benenetas dī ad penetenciam te adu|cit

    Ergo 'benenote Dei cuntemnis, ignoras quia benenetas Dei ad penetenciam te
        aducit'.

    Thus 'you despise the benevolence of God, you do not realise that the
        benevolence of God leads you to repentance'.

The quotation is from Rom. 2.4–5, which is continued in the following passage. In the Vulgate this passage reads, 'an divitias bonitatis eius et patientiae et longanimitatis contemnis / ignorans quoniam benignitas Dei ad paenitentiam te adducit'. **EV** punctuate *ignoras . . . adducit* as a question.

  On the form *benenote*, see Part II, sect. 1.

18. noli facere quod seq̄tur tu autem | secund̄/ duriciam cordis tuae temsauri|cas
        tibi ira in diae ire et reuelacionis | iusti iudicium dī q̄ retet oniquoiq̄ se|cun
        d̄/ hopera suā

    Noli facere quod sequitur: 'tu autem secundum duriciam cordis tuae temsauri-
        cas tibi ira in diae ire et reuelacionis: iusti iudicium Dei, qui retet oniquoique
        secundum hopera suam'.

    Do not do what follows: 'But you according to the hardness of your heart
        are storing up wrath for yourself on the Day of Wrath and of revelation:
        the judgement of the just God who will reward each according to his works.'

For the scribe's use of the 'd/' symbol for -dum cf. Lindsay, *Notae Latinae*, p. 363. The quotation is from Rom. 2.6; the Vulgate reading is 'secundum duritiam autem tuam et inpaenitens cor / thesaurizas tibi iram in die irae et revelationis iusti iudicii Dei / qui reddet unicuique secundum opera eius'. The other manuscripts have the standard reading *iusti iudicii* [**EMZ**; *iuditii* **CV**] *Dei*. **B**'s *iudicium* is probably a scribal error, but might have been construed as translated above. On the form *retet* (for *reddet*) see Part II, sect. 6.

19. hec ered/tatē cori|gete uos dum uiuites q̄a mortui n̄ re|dibetes

    Hec ereditatem corigete uos dum uiuites, quia mortui non redibetes.

    Rectify this inheritance (?) while you live, for when you are dead you will not be
        coming back.

Lowe prints *eriditatem corigite*. **B**'s reading here is probably a mere corruption of the reading found in the other manuscripts: *H(a)ec credite et timete*, 'Believe and fear this.' **EM**'s *uiuetis* (corr. from *uiuites* **E**) supports **B**'s *uiuites*, which has been corrupted in the other manuscripts to *uicis* (**CV**) and *uiciis* (**Z**). The variant readings for **B**'s *redibites* suggest some confusion between *redeo* and *rideo*, perhaps under the influence of Luke 6.25.

20. ait apustulus ued/te quo|modo cauti amboletes ñ ut insipi|ente set sapientes
    [f. 7r] redementes tẽpus quod d/es mali | sunt

Ait apustulus: 'Vedite quomodo cauti amboletes, non ut insipiente[s] set sapientes redementes tempus quod dies mali sunt.'

The apostle says: 'See that you tread carefully, not as the foolish do, but as wise men redeeming the time, for the days are evil.'

Eph. 5.15–16, which provides the author with his central theme concerning 'evil days'. The Vulgate reading is 'videte itaque fratres quomodo caute ambuletis / non quasi insipientes sed ut sapientes / redimentes tempus quoniam dies mali sunt'. As Lowe noted, the stroke through the descender of q in *quomodo* is otiose. **B**'s *cauti* probably represents the biblical adverb *caute*, but it could also be construed as a plural adjective (a common use of adjectives in Romance if they refer to the verbal subject). For *amboletes*, see Part II, sect. 16. In our transcript we follow Lowe in resolving MS *insipienteset* as *insipiente set*; *insipientes et* is also possible but is not elsewhere attested as a biblical variant. The other manuscripts of the sermon read *insipientes* [corr. from *insipientis* **V**] *sed* [*set* **CV**] *ut sapientes*. For *redimentes tempus*, **Z** reads *redemites uos*, **C** *redimentes uos*, and **V** *redimentes* with *tenpus* added in the margin by another hand.

21. dies malus habemus quamdios | inter hominis malus uiuim/ |

Dies malus habemus quamdios inter hominis malus uiuimus.

We have evil days for as long as we live among evil men.

In **Is** this sentence occurs just before the citation of Eph. 5.15–16 above. The form *quamdios* may be significant in narrowing down the scribe's origins; see Part II, sect. 5.

22. tole ho|menes malus et ñ ﬆ d/es mali ad pe|netentes

Tole homenes malus et non sunt dies mali ad penetentes.

Take away the evil men, and the days are not evil for those who repent.

For *Tole* [*tolle* **EVZ**, **Is**], **M** has the plural *tollite*; **C** has *tolles*. For **B**'s *ad penetentes*, **EMZ** have *appetentes*, **CV** *appendentes*, which must be taken with the following sentence as part of the list of types of evil men, with *res alienas* as object (there is nothing in the other manuscripts corresponding to **B**'s *cuncopitores*): 'those desiring (*appetentes*) / weighing out (? *appendentes*) other people's possessions'. The phrase *appetentes res alienas* occurs in Augustine, *Enarrationes in Psalmos* XCIX.12 (CCSL 39, 1401).

23. cunco(pi)tores res alie|nas adolteriõ p(iu)riaes calumnia|tures opresores p̱ os
    hominis p̱ dies | mali

    Cuncopitores res alienas, adolteriom, periuriaes; calumniatures, opresores: per
    os hominis [sunt] dies mali.

    Those who covet other people's possessions, adultery, perjuries; those who
    spread lies and oppress others: on account of these men the days are evil.

For **B**'s *adulteriom, periuriaes*, parallel with *res alienas*, the other manuscripts have
*adulteri*, and **MV**, **Is** also have *periuri* [*periures* **CZ**], parallel with *calum(p)niatores,
oppressores*. On the grammar of *cuncopitores res alienas*, see Part II, sect. 10. For **B**'s
*per os hominis per*, **CV**, **Is** read *Per homines malos sunt*, **EMZ** *Per homines sunt*. Cf.
the sermon 'Timor Domini expellit peccatum' in **EM**, *res alienas concupiscitis et
thaesauros caelestis neglegitis* [not in Migne's text].

24. dies ergo malus abemus Quam|d/us inter hominis malus uiuimus

    Dies ergo malus abemus quamdius inter hominis malus uiuimus.

    So we have evil days as long as we live among evil men.

This sentence, which repeats no. 21 save for the addition of *ergo*, is omitted by
**M**.

25. ita | uiuamus ff̃ ne nusmed ipsus in diae ela | malis adamus quod dies mali s̄ p̱
    ho|menes malus d/ cos nos d̄s pios libera|re dinetur IN

    Ita uiuamus, fratres, ne nusmed ipsus in diae ela malis adamus, quod dies mali
    sunt per homenes malus, de cos nos Deus pios liberare dinetur.

    Let us live, brothers, in such a way that we do not add ourselves to the (number
    of the) evil men on that day, because the days are evil on account of evil
    men, from whom may holy God deign to deliver us.

For **B**'s *in diae ela malis adamus*, the other manuscripts read *in diebus malis addamus*.
**B**'s *d/ cos*, which Lowe transcribed as *dicos* and attached to the preceding word
*malus*, instead almost certainly represents *de quos* (see Part II, sect. 10). The other
manuscripts do not help here; **CVZ** conclude with the doxology *Qui uiuis et regnas*
[**Z**; + *in sęcula sęculorum amen* **CV**], and **M** has *Adiuuet nos Dominus qui uiuit
et regnat in s. s. a.* The 'IN' at the end of the sermon in **B** might conceivably
be a vestige of a rubric INCIPIT for the following text, or even of a closing IN
SAECULA SAECULORUM, but makes no sense as it stands.

The following critical edition of the sermon takes **M** as its base, with corrections
from **CVEZ**. **M** stands somewhat apart in its omission of the sentence corresponding to **B**.24, but it offers some superior readings, has the best orthography and is
clearly legible. **CV** are closely related, either as exemplar and copy or as copies of a
common exemplar; **E** and/or **Z** often agree with **CV** against **M**, though there are
a few cases in which **EMZ** agree against **CV**. **B** represents a distinct line of transmission. Because a complete transcript of **B** has already been given, its readings are
not recorded in the variants.

The manuscripts were consulted in microfilms and/or printouts; in the case of **E** the printouts were darkened due to apparent water-damage to the opening folios, and some words or parts of words could not be recovered. In the apparatus periods indicate approximately how many letters are obscured; letters or words added above the line are marked thus: ʿquasiʾ. Abbreviations have been expanded silently.

INCIPIT SERMO SANCTI AUGUSTINI DE DIEBUS MALIS. Audi homo, rapis aliena et gaudis, male operaris et laetaris. An putas proximo tuo male facere et tibi bene? Quia illum spolias et te uestis. Cum male feceris carni alterius, te ipsum perdis; cum illum spolias, ille perdit tunicam, tu iustitiam. Adtendis quid rapias,
5 non adtendis quod perdas. Non uis ut nequis tibi mentiatur, et ipse fidem non seruas; uis ab alio tibi fidem seruari. Ama in teipso quod expetis in altero. Ledi non uis et laedere uis alterum. Iudicas et ab altero iudicari non uis, alterum damnas et ab altero damnari non uis. Cur ergo sic ibas [fol. 90r] et peribas? Capit te paradysus Dei. Redi ad Deum! Quando scelera faciebas, numquid statim ad supplicium rapiebaris?
10 Quare tibi parcebatur? Quia tua paenitentia expectabatur. Ergo ʿbenignitatem Dei contemnis, ignoras quia benignitas Dei ad paenitentiam te adducitʾ. Noli facere quod sequitur: ʿTu autem secundum duritiam cordis tui thesaurizasti tibi iram in die ire et reuelationis iusti iudicii Dei, qui reddit unicuique secundum opera suaʾ. Haec credite et timete, corrigite uos cum uiuetis, quia mortui non redebitis. Ait
15 apostolus, ʿVidete quomodo caute ambuletis, non ut insipientes sed ut sapientes: redimentes tempus, quoniam dies mali suntʾ. Dies malos habemus quamdiu inter homines malos uiuimus. Tolle homines malos et non sunt dies mali: appetentes res alienas, adulteri, periuri, calomniatores, oppressores. Per homines malos sunt dies mali; dies ergo malos habemus quamdiu inter homines malos uiuimus. Ita
20 uiuamus, fratres, ne nosmet ipsos in diebus malis [fol. 90v] addamus, quoniam dies mali sunt per homines malos. Adiuuet nos Dominus qui uiuit et regnat in secula seculorum amen.

*1* INCIPIT] *om.* **CV** AUGUSTINI] Agustini **EZ** + episcopi **Z** diebus] dies **CZ**, diebus *corr. from* dies **V** malis] malos **CZ**, malis *corr. from* malos **V** homo] O homo **EZ** *2* gaudis] gaudes *corr. from* gaudis **EV** male] mala **M** laetaris] lętaris **Z**, letaris **CV** proximo] proxiʿmoʾ**V**, pro(. . .)m(.) **E** tuo] *om.* **CVZ** male facere] mala facereʿsʾ**V** tibi] t(.)bi **Z** *3* illum] illu(m?) **C** spolias] expolias **CVZ**, (. . . . .)as **E** uestis] uestes **M**, *with* i *added above line* cum male . . . perdis] *om.* **E** carni] carnali **M** *4* illum] illu **C** spolias] expolias **Z** tunicam] tonicam **Z**, tunica **C** iustitiam] iusticiam **CV** adtendis] adtendes **M** quid] que **CV** rapias] rapis **V** *5* quod perdas] quid perdis **CV**, quid perdas **E**, quiʿdʾperdas **Z** Non] ut non **Z** nequis] uel quis **M**, (. .)quis **E** fidem] fide **C** *5–6* non seruas] non (. . .)uas **E** *6* alio] illo **CVZ** fidem] *added above line* **E** in] *om.* **M** expetis] expetis **CVE**] expedis **MZ** Ledi] laedi **E**, ledere **Z** *7* ledere] laetare **M**, laedere **E** uis²] *om.* **M** alterum] altero **C** Iudicas et ab altero] *om.* **MCVZ**, et alterum iudicas *added in margin* **E**; *cf.* iudicas et ab alterum **B** iudicari] iudicare **MC**, iudicari *corr. from* iudicare **E**(?)**V**, indicare **Z** alterum] et alterum **M** damnas] dampnas **VZ** *8* altero] alterum **Z** damnari **E**] *om.* **M**, damnare **C**, dampnari *corr. from* dampnare **V**, dampnare **Z** Cur] cum **M** sic ibas **E**] scibas **M**, siciebas **V**, sitiebas **CZ** peribas] periebas **CV** capit te] capit `te´ **M** paradysus] paradysum **V** *9* Quando] quan`do´ **E** supplicium] *corr. from* suppliciunt **V** *10* tua] tu`a´ **Z** paenitentia] penitentia **CVZ** expectabatur] (. . . .)ctabatur **E** benignitatem] benignitate **E** *11* contemnis] contempnis **VZ** paenitentiam] penitentiam **CVZ** adducit] adducet **Z** *12* duritiam] duriciam **VZ** thesaurizasti] thesaurizas **E**, thessaurizasti **Z** *13* die ire] die irae **E**, diẹ irẹ **CV**, die irẹ **Z** iudicii] iuditii **CV** reddit] r(.)ddet **E** *14* Haec] h- **M**, hẹc **CVZ** corrigite] corregite **CEZ** uiuetis] uicis **CV**, uiuitis *corr. from* uiuetis **E**, uiciis **Z** quia] qui **E** mortui] morti **M** redebitis] ridebitis **CM**, ridebitis *with* ri *over correction* **E**, ridebitis *corr. from* redebitis **V**, ridebites **Z** *14–15* Ait apostolus] Dies malos habemus quandiu inter homines malos vivimus, testante Apostolo **Is**, *cf. ll. 16–17* *15* caute] cautẹ **Z** ut[1]] *om.* **M**, `quasi´ **E** insipientes] *corr. from* insipientis **V** sed] set **CV** *16* redimentes tempus] redimentes uos **C**, redimentes *with* tenpus *added in margin by another hand* **V**, redimentis uo(. . . . .) **E**, redemites uos **Z** quoniam] (. . . .) **E** *16–17* Dies malos . . . uiuimus] *in* **Is** *the corresponding sentence occurs just before the citation of Eph. 5.15* *16* habemus] habimus **Z** quamdiu] quamdio **C**, quamdio *with* i *expunctuated?* **V** *17* uiuimus] uiu(. . . .) **E** Tolle] tollite **M**, tolles **C** et] *om.* **CVZ** sunt] erunt **Is** mali] (. .)l(.) **E** appetentes] (.)pp(. .)entes **E**, appendentes **CV** *18* alienas] alie(. .)s **E** periuri] periures **CZ**, periur(.) **E** calomniatores] calu(. . . .)tores **E**, calumniatores **C**, **Is**, calumpniatores **V** oppressores] opp(.)essores **E** malos] *om.* **EMZ** *19* dies ergo . . . uiuimus] *om.* **M** quamdiu] quamdio **CV**, quandiu **E**, **Is** *20* malis] malos **Z** *21* Adiuuet nos Dominus] *om.* **CVZ** *21–22* qui uiuit . . . amen] qui uiuit . . . saecula saeculorum amen **E**, qui uiuis et regnas in sẹcula sẹculorum amen **CV**, qui uiuis et regnas **Z**

*JOCA MONACHORUM*

Most surviving *JM* dialogues have been edited elsewhere, so I note here only those variants that materially affect the establishment or understanding of **B**'s text, or that involve a significant difference in the formulation of a question or the substance of its answer. I list all known parallels in other *JM* dialogues, the related *Adrianus et Epictitus* (*AE*) dialogues and similar Latin catechetical dialogues, as well as medieval vernacular dialogues (but not the vernacular translations of *AE*, the late French dialogue designated Text **S** by Suchier, or the late medieval vernacular dialogues edited by Suchier under the title *L'Enfant sage*).[69] Parallels that correspond closely in the formulation of both question and answer are cited first; 'cf.' indicates that any parallels cited thereafter differ in some substantive way. I also note briefly the ultimate source (usually biblical) of each item; but because Suchier's study of the

[69] W. Suchier, *L'Enfant sage. Das Gespräch des Kaisers Hadrian mit dem klugen Kinde Epitus* (Dresden, 1910); for Welsh, German and Provençal translations of *AE*, see Suchier, *Das mittellateinische Gespräch*, pp. 53–76.

Latin *JM* dialogues has been further supplemented by extensive source analysis of parallel material in recent editions of the *Collectanea Pseudo-Bedae* and the Old English *Prose Solomon and Saturn* and *Adrian and Ritheus* dialogues, to avoid duplication I provide only minimal commentary here.

Though no other surviving *JM* dialogue corresponds exactly to that in **B**, some overlap substantially in content, sequence and wording. The manuscript sigla in the list below are those assigned by Suchier, *Das mittellateinische Gespräch*. Only those with parallels for **B** are included. Additional Latin and vernacular dialogues with parallels for **B** (some unknown to Suchier) are listed subsequently.[70]

*JM* manuscripts

  **A** St Gall, Stiftsbibliothek 913 (Germany, s. viii[2]; *CLA* VII.976), pp. 149–61. Ed. G. Baesecke, *Der Vocabularius Sancti Galli in der angelsächsischen Mission* (Halle, 1933), pp. 7–8.

  **B** Bobbio Missal. Ed. Lowe, *Bobbio*, pp. 5–7, rpr. in PLS IV, 926–7; previous ed. P. Meyer, 'Joca Monachorum', *Romania* 1 (1872), pp. 485–8; corrections by A. Boucherie, *Revue des langues romanes* 5 (1874), pp. 491–2; H. Leclercq, 'Joca monachorum', in *Dictionnaire d'archéologie chrétienne et de liturgie*, 15 vols., ed. F. Cabrol (Paris, 1907–53), VII/2, pp. 2569–72.

  **C** St Gall, Stiftsbibliothek 908 (north Italy or Switzerland, s. viii–ix; *CLA* VII.953), pp. 68–72. Ed. Suchier, pp. 108–11. Cf. Wright, 'Apocryphal lore'.

  **D** Einsiedeln, Stiftsbibliothek 281, pp. 1–178 + 199, pp. 431–526 (Rhaetia, s. viii–ix; *CLA* VII.875; Bischoff, *Katalog*, no. 1118), pp. 50–3. Ed. Suchier, pp. 114–17.

  **E** Sélestat, Bibliothèque Humaniste 2 (1073) (Lake Constance region, s. ix[2/4]), fols. 59v–65v. Ed. E. Wölfflin-Troll, 'Joca monachorum, ein Beitrag zur mittelalterlichen Räthsellitteratur', in *Monatsberichte der Preußischen Akademie der Wissenschaften aus dem Jahre 1872* (Berlin, 1873), pp. 109–14; Leclercq, 'Joca monachorum' (giving the shelfmark incorrectly as '1173'); Suchier, pp. 114–18 (nos. 1–38 as variants of **D**, nos. 39, 41–7, 62–4, 72–4, 80,

---

[70] For further bibliography and information on the contents of these manuscripts see C.D. Wright, 'From monks' jokes to sages' wisdom: the *Joca monachorum* tradition and the Irish *Immacallam in dá Thúarad*', forthcoming in *Spoken and Written Language: Relations between Latin and the Vernaculars*, ed. M. Mostert and M. Garrison. I have not been able to consult the late unpublished dialogues cited by M. Bayless in *Collectanea Pseudo-Bedae*, ed. Bayless and Lapidge, p. 14 n. 3. Two manuscripts, Paris, BNF lat. 7558 (s. ix[1], France; provenance St Julien, Tours), fol. 2r, and Munich, Bayerische Staatsbibliothek, Clm 642 (s. xi), fol. 45, contain a biblical riddle from the *JM* tradition, 'Dic mihi quis dedit quod non accepit? HOA ΛΑΧΘΗΜ (eua lactem).' See Bischoff, 'Das griechische Element in der abendländischen Bildung des Mittelalters', in Bischoff, *Mittelalterliche Studien*, II, p. 255 n. 46, and *Handschriftenarchiv Bernhard Bischoff*, ed. Arno Mentzel-Reuters, MGH, Hilfsmittel 16 (Munich, 1997), fiche 36, 1.53. The database *In Principio: Incipitaire des textes latins*, Release 7 (Turnhout, 1999), lists a work 'Joca monachorum' in Angers, BM 1582 (37) (s. xv), fol. 22rv (inc.: 'Unus est Christus qui regnet et qui sunt duo / due sunt tabulae Moysi').

82, 85 as variants of **F**; parallels cited below are numbered according to **E**'s sequence). On this manuscript, which also includes the sermon *De diebus malis*, see above, pp. 82–3 and 87–9.

**F** Munich, Bayerische Staatsbibliothek, Clm 19410 (Passau, s. ix med.), pp. 13–16. Ed. Suchier, pp. 114–19 (nos. 1–27 as variants of **D**; parallels cited below are numbered according to **F**'s sequence). The *Joca*-sequence here comprises the second part of a composite set of *Interrogationes* that have recently been edited in their entirety by Franz Brunhölzl, *Studien zum geistigen Leben in Passau im achten und neunten Jahrhundert*, Abhandlungen der Marburger Gelehrten Gesellschaft 26 (Munich, 2000), pp. 51–2; his question nos. 71–135 correspond to Suchier's $JM_1$ from **DEF**, but **F** continues with an additional 34 questions omitted by Suchier. Cf. also Wright, *The Irish Tradition*, pp. 63ff.[71]

**G** Munich, Bayerische Staatsbibliothek, Clm 19417 (southern Germany or Switzerland, s. ix$^{1/3}$; Bischoff, *Schreibschulen*, p. 164), fols. 71r–74r. Ed. W. Wilmanns, 'Ein Fragebüchlein aus dem neunten Jahrhundert', *Zeitschrift für deutsches Altertum* 15 (1872), pp. 167–9.

**H** Autun, BM S184 (*olim* G.III) (Tours region, s. ix$^{3/4}$; Bischoff, *Katalog*, no. 170), fols. 113v–114v. Ed. H. Omont, 'Interrogationes de fide catholica (*Joca monachorum.*)', *Bibliothèque de l'Ecole des chartes* 34 (1873), pp. 60–2.

**I** Florence, Biblioteca Medicea Laurenziana, S. Croce Plut. XVIII dextr. 10 (s. x), fols. 160r–161r. Ed. Suchier, pp. 119–21.

**K₁** Paris, BNF n.a. lat. 2171, pp. 1–34 (Silos, between 1067 and 1073), pp. 12–16. Ed. Omont, 'Interrogationes', pp. 62–70.

---

[71] Brunhölzl (p. 34, n. 94) criticises me (with reference to an essay reprinted as ch. 2 of *The Irish Tradition*) for associating these 'Interrogationes' with the 'Irish enumerative style', because, he states, the passages I cite 'gehören eindeutig in den Kreis der vorausgehenden Interrogationes, d. h. in deren zweiten Teil, die sogenannten Joca monachorum'. In fact I distinguished clearly between the various parts of these composite *Interrogationes*, and related to Irish tradition only those questions following the *JM* dialogue on pp. 13–23 (as well as a brief sequence on pp. 32–3); moreover, it is clear that these questions are a later supplement to the original *JM* dialogue, even if the conflation had already occurred in the exemplar from which the scribe of Munich, Bayerische Staatsbibliothek, Clm 19410 copied the *Interrogationes*. That conflation may, indeed, have taken place in an Irish-influenced milieu, since (as I pointed out in *The Irish Tradition*, p. 64 n. 80) the *JM* dialogue in Munich, Bayerische Staatsbibliothek, Clm 19410 incorporates a list of the 'Ordinals of Christ' in a form related to the 'Hibernian Chronological' version. In any case, I have nowhere suggested that the *JM* dialogues themselves (or the questions preceding the *JM* dialogue in Munich, Bayerische Staatsbibliothek, Clm 19410) are Irish, only that the Irish were active in disseminating *JM* and similar dialogues; and I cautioned that 'Despite the extensive agreement between these dialogues [i.e. the supplementary questions in Munich, Bayerische Staatsbibliothek, Clm 19410, pp. 13–23 and 32–3 and several dialogues in other early manuscripts] and the Irish florilegia and dialogues which I have surveyed, it would be rash to label them "Hiberno-Latin"' (*The Irish Tradition*, p. 64, repeated from the earlier article cited by Brunhölzl). My suggestion that the supplementary questions in Munich, Bayerische Staatsbibliothek, Clm 19410 reflect Irish tradition would, however, be consonant with Brunhölzl's arguments on other grounds for strong Irish influence in Passau at this period.

**K₂** Paris, BNF n.a. lat. 2171, p. 18a. Ed. Omont, 'Interrogationes', pp. 70–1.

**L** Munich, Bayerische Staatsbibliothek, Clm 21576 (s. xiii), fols. 127r–128v. Ed. Suchier, pp. 123–7.

**M** Munich, Bayerische Staatsbibliothek, Clm 8885 (s. xiv ex.), fol. 278va. Ed. Suchier, pp. 123–7 (as variants of **L**; parallels cited below are numbered according to **M**'s sequence).

**N** Wolfenbüttel, Herzog-August-Bibliothek, Helmst. 433 (between 1415 and 1429), fol. 173v. Ed. Suchier, pp. 123–7 (as variants of **L**; parallels cited below are numbered according to **N**'s sequence).

**P** Salzburg, Stiftsbibliothek St Peter, NA.III 13 (s. xv), fols. 13v–15r. Ed. Suchier, pp. 130–3.

**Qa** Troyes, BM 1916 (s. xii/xiii), fol. 144ra–144va. Ed. Suchier, pp. 134–6.

**Qb** Munich, Bayerische Staatsbibliothek, Cgm 444 (a. 1422), fols. 11r–12r. Ed. M. Förster, 'Two notes on Old English dialogue literature', in *An English Miscellany: Presented to Dr. Furnivall in Honour of his Seventy-fifth Birthday* (Oxford, 1901), pp. 86–106, at p. 105.

**Qe** Tübingen, Universitätsbibliothek, MC 114 (s. xv in.), fol. 1r. Ed. Förster, 'Two notes', pp. 105–6.

**Qg** Munich, Bayerische Staatsbibliothek, Clm 14574 (s. xv), fol. 184v. Ed. Suchier, pp. 134–6 (as variants of **Qa**).

**Qh** Vienna, Schottenstift 280 (s. xv), fol. 87vb. Ed. Suchier, pp. 134–6 (as variants of **Qa**).

**R** *Collectanea Pseudo-Bedae*, ed. M. Bayless and M. Lapidge, Scriptores Latini Hiberniae 14 (Dublin, 1998).

Not included in Suchier's list:

**Qj** Vatican City, BAV, Ottobon. lat. 1212 (s. xiv in.; among additions to originally blank leaves). Ed. E. Langlois, *Notices des manuscrits français et provençaux de Rome antérieures au XVIe siècle* (Paris, 1889), p. 285. Corresponds to Suchier's **Q**, items 2, 8, 3, 7, 10, 12; 'Quis vivit non natus et non maritur? Raphael'; 5; 'Quis occidit quartam partem mondi? Cayn'; 16. The answers for Suchier's questions 10, 12, 5 are displaced and that for 16 is missing.

**Qk** Frankfurt am Main, Stadt- und Universitätsbibliothek, Praed. 105 (Valle Eni, a. 1429), fol. 1v. Unpublished. Contents analysed by Gerhardt Powitz, *Kataloge der Stadt- und Universitätsbibliothek Frankfurt am Main*, II/1: *Die Handschriften des Dominikanerklosters und des Leonhardstifts in Frankfurt am Main* (Frankfurt am Main, 1968), p. 241. Powitz states that this version is closely related to **Qe** and **Qh**; he lists the parallels and prints the items not found in other versions of **Q**.

**Ql** Munich, Bayerische Staatsbibliothek, Cgm 632 (Bavaria, 1459), fol. 2r. Unpublished. Similar to **Qb**, according to Karin Schneider, *Die deutschen*

*Handschriften der Bayerischen Staatsbibliothek München Cgm 501–690* (Wiesbaden, 1978), p. 280.

**Qm** Munich, Bayerische Staatsbibliothek, Cgm 660, pt I (Bavaria, 1459–75), fol. 222vb. Unpublished. Similar to **Qb**, according to Schneider, *Die deutschen Handschriften*, p. 352.

**T** Dublin, Trinity College 341, Part E (C.4.32) (England, s. xiii²), fol. 175v. Ed. M.L. Colker, 'Anecdota Dublinensia II. A series of riddles and answers', *Mediaevalia et Humanistica* 16 (1964), pp. 41–3. On the manuscript see M.L. Colker, *Trinity College Library Dublin: Descriptive Catalogue of the Mediaeval and Renaissance Latin Manuscripts*, 2 vols. (Dublin, 1991), II, pp. 686–707.

**U** Basel, Universitätsbibliothek B V 24 (France, s. xiv in.). Unpublished. Contents analysed by G. Meyer and M. Burckhardt, *Die mittelalterliche Handschriften der Universitätsbibliothek Basel, Abteilung B: Theologische Pergamenthandschriften*, 2 vols. (Basel, 1960), I, p. 512. Cf. E. Dekkers and A. Gaar, *Clavis Patrum Latinorum (CPL)* (3rd edn, Turnhout, 1995), no. 1155*f* (i).

**V** Paris, BNF lat. 2796 (France, c. 813–15?), fol. 56r. Unpublished; I have transcribed the text from the manuscript. See P. Lauer, *Bibliothèque nationale. Catalogue général des manuscrits latins*, 7 vols. (Paris, 1939–52), III, p. 95; L. Deslisle, *Le Cabinet des manuscrits de la Bibliothèque (imperiale) nationale*, 4 vols. (Paris, 1868–81), III, p. 244; *Catalogue des manuscrits en écriture latine portant des indications de date, de lieu, ou de copiste*, ed. C. Samaran and R. Marichal (Paris, 1959–), II, p. 129, and pl. 1; Bischoff, 'Die Bibliothek im Dienste der Schule', in Bischoff, *Mittelalterliche Studien*, III, p. 228 n. 75; D. Bullough, *Carolingian Renewal: Sources and Heritage* (Manchester, 1991), p. 228 n. 107; H. Mordek, *Kirchenrecht und Reform im Frankenreich. Die Collectio Vetus Gallica, die älteste systematische Kanonessammlung des fränkischen Gallien, Studien und Edition*, Beiträge zur Geschichte und Quellenkunde des Mittelalters 1 (Berlin and New York, 1975), p. 148 n. 242. Closely related to **R**, with parallels for **R**.194, 18, 196, 199, 195, 3, 128, 10, 9, 14, 15, 110, 137, 138, 132. My numbering follows the manuscript order, including an initial sequence of 'Vidi' riddles.

**Y** Paris, BNF lat. 5596 (probably Rheims, s. ix in.), fols. 155r–156v. Unpublished. 31 questions, headed INCIPIUNT INTERROGACIONIS MONACHORUM. See Bischoff, *Handschriftenarchiv*, fiche 35, 4.17–16 (the correct order of the pages dealing with this manuscript should be 4.22, 20, 15, 13, 18, 17, 16, 21). Identified as 'Ioca monachorum' in the *In Principio* database. I have transcribed the dialogue from the manuscript, and have also consulted a transcript by Elisabeth Pellegrin in the files of the Institut de recherche et d'histoire des textes (IRHT), part of a very extensive description of the entire manuscript. The dialogue occurs within a context of numerical, apocryphal and erotematic material characteristic of Insular learning, including several enumerations discussed in Wright, *The Irish Tradition*, pp. 65ff. The manuscript contains on fols. 156v–162v another dialogue consisting of 60 questions, headed INCIPIUNT INTERROG<A>C<IONES> and provided with an unusual introduction: 'Conuencio duorum summorum scolasticorum quorum pericia [-a < o] deuulgata est in omnibus locis. Et interrogauit alter alterum, Perhibe mihi frater quid te procedit in domo tua idannela mea. Dic mihi: Quid nigridior coruo? Animae peccatorum in info[>e?]rno . . .'. One item from this dialogue was printed by Bischoff in 'The study of foreign languages in the Middle Ages', in Bischoff, *Mittelalterliche Studien*, II, p. 234 n. 33. There is also an *AE* dialogue (overlooked by Suchier), from which Bischoff published 'Die älteste lateinische Fassung des Flachrätsels (frühes neuntes Jahrhundert)', in Bischoff, *Anecdota Novissima: Texte des vierten bis sechzehnten Jahrhunderts* (Stuttgart, 1984), pp. 101–2.

**Z** Zurich, Zentralbibliothek C. 65 (?St. Gall, s. viii/ix; *CLA* VII.1017), fols. 89r–90v. Ed. Jean-Pierre Bodmer, 'Ioca Monachorum um 800. Scherze der Mönche', in *Zentralbibliothek Zürich. Alte und neue Schätze*, ed. Alfred Cattani *et al.* (Zurich, 1993), pp. 11–13, 140–3. Transmits only nine items, headed INCIPIUNT IOCAM MONACHORUM. On the manuscript see also Mohlberg, *Katalog der Handschriften der Zentralbibliothek Zürich*, I, p. 38.

## Related Latin dialogues

*AE:* *Adrianus et Epictitus*. Ed. Suchier, *Das mittellateinische Gespräch*, pp. 10–41. Surviving in two redactions, $AE_1$ab and $AE_2$. Vernacular versions (Old French, Old Provençal, Welsh and Middle High German) are ed. Suchier, pp. 53–76.

*PA:* *De plasmatione Adam*. For manuscripts and editions, see p. 86 above.

*PME:* *Prebiarium de multorium exemplaribus*, ed. R.E. McNally, CCSL 108B, 161–71. A catechetical–exegetical dialogue, regarded by McNally as Hiberno-Latin or Irish-influenced, found in Munich, Bayerische Staatsbibliothek, Clm 6302, fols. 64r–69v (Freising, s. viii[2]; *CLA* IX.1267).

**Co** Cologne, Dombibliothek 15 (perhaps western Germany, s. ix[3/4 or 4/4]; Bischoff, *Katalog*, no. 1872), fols. 88v–91v. Unpublished. On this manuscript, see above, pp. 86 and 94.

**Ox** Oxford, Bodleian Library, Bodley 839 (SC 2572) (France, s. xi/xii), fols. 30r–31v. Unpublished. On the manuscript see F. Madan *et al.*, *A Summary Catalogue of Western Manuscripts in the Bodleian Library at Oxford*, 7 vols. (Oxford, 1895–1953), II/1, pp. 432–3; H. Schenkl, 'Bibliotheca patrum latinorum Britannica, pt. III', *Sitzungsberichte der kaiserlichen Akademie der Wissenschaften in Wien*, Philosophisch-historische Klasse 124 (1891), pp. 10–11.

Vernacular dialogues

   **O** Vienna, Österreichische Nationalbibliothek 3085 (a. 1475). Ed. Suchier, pp. 128–9. German version closely related to the Latin *JM* texts **LMN**.

   *CG: Cesta Grega* ('Greek questions'). Ed. and trans. W. Stokes, *Celtic Review* 1 (1904), pp. 132–5. A brief Irish dialogue.

*SS, AR: The Prose Solomon and Saturn and Adrian and Ritheus*. Ed. and trans. J.E. Cross and T.D. Hill (Toronto, 1981). Closely related Old English dialogues.

   *VLM: Vipræða Lærisveins ok Meistara* ('Dialogue of a student and a teacher'). Ed. J.W. Marchand, 'The Old Icelandic *Joca monachorum*', *Medieval Scandinavia* 9 (1976), pp. 99–126.

   *YG: Y Gorcheston* ('The questions'). Ed. and trans. C. Byfield and M. Bayless, 'Y Gorcheston: the Welsh *Ioca monachorum*. Texts, translations and commentary', *Studia Celtica* 30 (1996), pp. 197–222. Surviving in three main recensions (*YG$_{1-3}$*) and four anomalous versions (*YG* hmno).

Suchier's conclusions regarding the interrelationships of the *JM* manuscripts (insofar as they involve **B**) can be summarised briefly. He distinguishes two main groups: I (**AK$_2$**) and II (**BCDEFHLMNO**). Within Group II (which he would derive from a common archetype, itself ultimately based on a Greek original) are further distinguished *JM$_1$* (**DEF**) and *JM$_2$* (**LMNO**). **B** shows significant points of contact with *JM$_2$*, especially with **L**, and to a lesser extent with **G** and **C**. But there are other correspondences that cut across these subgroupings, and Suchier does not believe that the evidence permits more definitive conclusions.

Suchier believed that the *JM* archetype originated in southern Gaul in the sixth century, a time and place in which the requisite knowledge of Greek still obtained. That there was a significant Insular role in the early medieval transmission of these dialogues has been demonstrated by Charles D. Wright and Martha Bayless,[72] though Marcel Dando's claim that they are Irish in origin goes further than the evidence allows.[73] It appears, however, that certain 'rare' questions or batches of questions circulated predominantly in Insular contexts. The content of the *JM* dialogue in **B** is more or less standard, but as Lowe pointed out ('Palaeography', p. 79 and n. 1), it uses an Insular abbreviation of *per-* taken over from the exemplar.

---

[72] Wright, 'Apocryphal lore'; Wright, 'From monks' jokes to sages' wisdom'; Bayless, 'The *Collectanea* and medieval dialogues and riddles', in *Collectanea Pseudo-Bedae*, ed. Bayless and Lapidge, pp. 13–24.

[73] Marcel Dando, 'Les chaînes médiévales de Questions et de Réponses: des "Joca monachorum" irlandais au "Razoumik" vieux-slave', *Cahiers d'études cathares* 90 (1981), pp. 30–42; 91 (1981), pp. 23–38; 92 (1981), pp. 3–30.

*Edition and translation of the* Joca monachorum

1. Quit primus ex dō p̄ceset uerbū |
   Quit primus ex Deo proceset? Verbum.
   What first proceeded from God? The Word.

**N.**1; cf. **A.**46, **C.**1, **DEF.**1, **H.**1, **L.**1, **P.**1, **R.**4, **Y.**1, **Z.**1; *AE*$_2$.9–10; *AR.*31, *SS.*2, *VLM.*9; cf. also **I.**2, **K$_1$.**2–3.

**LN** *AE*$_2$ read *ex ore Deo* (*Domini* **L**), and *SS* has the vernacular equivalent. **B** and **N** are the only versions in which the answer is *Verbum* alone; **CDEFLPYZ** have instead *Fiat lux*, and *SS* / *AR* and *VLM* the vernacular equivalents; **AHIR** combine both answers, while *AE*$_2$ distinguishes *Verbum de principio* and *Fiat lux* as the first and second things spoken by God. **K$_1$.**2 has *Cogitatum*. In **I** and **K$_1$** the questions are differently formulated. For a parallel in a (?Hiberno-Latin) Genesis commentary, see the commentary on **R.**4 in *Collectanea Pseudo-Bedae*, ed. Bayless and Lapidge, p. 202.
Gen. 1.1 and John 1.1.
On the form *quit primus* see Part II, sect. 11. The analogues read *quid primum* or *quid primo*.

2. q̄ regeneratū filiū procria|uit terrā adam
   Qui regeneratum filium procriauit? Terram, Adam.
   Who gave birth to a reborn son? The earth, Adam.

Unique to **B**. Apparently based on Gen. 3.19, Adam being a 'son' of the earth (as the earth is Abel's 'grandmother' in no. 6 below).

3. Q̲ dimmortoos | et non es natus adā
   Qui dimmortoos et non es natus? Adam.
   Who died and was not born? Adam.

In *dimmortoos* it is not certain whether we have the *to* ligature as in *obtolet* (fol. 7r/23) or the *tu* ligature as in *moriebatur* (fol. 7v/3). The Latin analogues all read *mortuus* (*mortuos* **C**).

**C.**2, **DEF.**2, **G.**20, **H.**3, **I.**18, **LMN.**3, **P.**2, **Qagh.**2, **Qb.**2, **Qc.**2, **Qe.**2, **Qjk.**1, **U.**1, **Y.**2, **Z.**2; *AE$_1$*a.50, *AE$_1$*b.39, *AE$_2$*.11; *VLM.*43, *YG$_1$*.7, *YG$_2$*.1, *YG$_3$*.1, YGm.2, YGn.1, *YG*o.b1, e2; cf. **R.**123; **Ox**, fol. 30v; *AR.*28, *SS.*15.

**R** adds to the question *atque in utero matris suae post mortem baptizatus*; **Ox**, *SS* and *AR* ask 'who was *buried* in his mother's womb', but *AR* lacks the reference to the post-mortem baptism. Some of the *YG* dialogues add one or both of these allusions (burial and baptism) as distinct questions. For a parallel in the Irish *Immacallam in dá Thúarad* see the commentary on **R.**123 in *Collectanea Pseudo-Bedae*, ed. Bayless and Lapidge, p. 228, and Wright, 'From monks' jokes to sages' wisdom'.

4. quantus | anus uixit adam ᴅᴄᴄᴄᴄxxx
   Quantus anus uixit Adam? ᴅᴄᴄᴄᴄxxx.
   How many years did Adam live? 930.

**C.**5, **DEF.**4, **H.**7, **I.**7, **LMN.**6, **P.**38, **R.**27, **Y.**3, **Z.**5; *AE*$_2$.12; *PA.*11; **Co**, fol. 95v; *SS*.12, *YG*n.2; cf. *YG*$_1$.1; *YG*m.5 (which gives the incorrect answer 932), *YG*h.14 (970 years). See also Munich, Bayerische Staatsbibliothek, Clm 22053, fol. 57r, ed. Schwab, *Die Sternrune*, p. 107.

Gen. 5.5.

5. quan|tus filius habuit exseptis kain | et habel et sunt xxx filius et xxxx fili|as
   Quantus filius habuit exseptis Kain et Habel? Et sunt xxx filius et xxxx filias.
   How many children did he have apart from Cain and Abel? Both thirty sons and forty daughters.

**C.**6, **DE.**5, **G.**21, **K**$_1$.78, **LMN.**7, **P.**48, **R.**127, **Y.**3, **Z.**6 (thirty sons and thirty daughters, with sixty-two and fifty-three as an alternative); *AE*$_2$.14; *PA.*10; **Co**, fol. 95v; *SS*.24, *VLM*.44, *YG*$_1$.14, *YG*h.10 (thirty-two sons and thirty daughters), *YG*m.7, *YG*n.4 (thirty-two sons and thirty-two daughters). See also Munich, Bayerische Staatsbibliothek, Clm 22053, fol. 57r (ed. Schwab, *Die Sternrune*, p. 107). Probably based on the apocryphal *Vita Adae et Evae* 24, ed. W. Meyer, Abhandlungen der königlich-bayerischen Akademie der Wissenschaften, Philosoph.-philolog. Kl. 14/3 (Munich, 1878), p. 229; trans. J.H. Charlesworth, *The Old Testament Pseudepigrapha*, II (New York, 1985), p. 266. Apart from **B** and the variant counts specified above, the standard answer is thirty sons and thirty daughters, but three versions (**K**$_1$, **R**, *SS*) with this answer do not explicitly exclude Cain and Abel (or Seth) from the count of sons. The *Vita Adae* specifies that Adam had thirty sons and thirty daughters *after* the birth of Seth, for a total of sixty-three. **CDPYZ** and *VLM* explicitly exclude Cain, Abel and Seth, while **B**'s exclusion of just Cain and Abel is paralleled in **EGLMN**, *AE*$_2$, *PA*, **Co**, *YG*$_1$ and *YG*mn (*YG*h, whose count of thirty-two sons implicitly *includes* Cain and Abel, works out the same as **B**). It seems likely, however, that **B**'s *et sunt* is an error for *et seth*. For examples outside the dialogue tradition see the commentary on **R.**127 in *Collectanea Pseudo-Bedae*, ed. Bayless and Lapidge, p. 229. **B**'s count of forty daughters is unparalleled and likely a mere slip, although the Old English poem *Christ and Satan*, l. 473, states that Adam and Eve had forty *sons*: *Christ and Satan: A Critical Edition*, ed. R.E. Finnegan (Waterloo, Ontario, 1977).

6. Q d/ sorore sua natus est et ha|uiam suam uirgenē d/uiholauet | abel terram
   Qui de sorore sua natus est et hauiam suam uirgenem deuiholauet? Abel terram.
   Who was born from his sister and raped his virgin grandmother? Abel; the earth.

Cf. **C.**4, **DE.**3, **G.**42, **I.**16, **Z.**4; *YG*$_2$.12, *YG*$_3$.7, *YG*n.11, *YG*o.g3; **H.**4, **K**$_1$.43, **LN.**10, **P.**4; *AE*$_1$a.51; *YG*$_1$.12.

For Icelandic examples of this riddle outside the dialogue tradition, see Marchand, 'The Old Icelandic *Joca monachorum*', p. 105, who also refers to an example in Wolfram von Eschenbach's *Parzifal*. Like Wolfram, the versions listed after 'cf.' identify Cain rather than Abel as the one who 'violated' the earth. **H**, **K**$_1$ and **P**, together with *YG* (except *YG*n) specify that the violation of the earth consisted in the concealment of Abel's body in it. **B** is unique in saying that Abel was 'born from his sister'. Since Eve was created from Adam, he could be regarded (in the logic of riddling) as Eve's 'father', making her Abel's sister as well as his mother. Based on Gen. 4.11.

7. Q primus obto|let olocaustū abel agnum [f. 7v]

Qui primus obtolet olocaustum? Abel agnum.

Who first offered a sacrifice? Abel; a lamb.

**H.**6, **M.**12, **R.**6; $AE_1$a.52, $AE_1$b.70, $AE_2$.15; $YG_1$.11; cf. **A.**10, **C.**7, **DE.**6, **G.**22, **LN.**12, **Z.**7.

Some versions add *Deo* or *Domino* after *holocaustum*; those listed after 'cf.' add to the answer a clause stating that Abel's offering led to his murder by Cain. Gen. 4.4.

8. Qd d/ hominebus fuit ad porta`s´| parad/si quando morieba|tur adam et euam
et sic fuit | oliū petiuit et non inuenet | hoc illis d/xit angelus micael | modo
ñ dabitor uobis set pos | quamque milia D hanus uenerit | Plasmatur uester
natus ex ma|ria uergene scam ipsi dabet | uobis oleum und/ unguates
cur|pus uestrū et refrigerit | karo uestra hunc uobis erit | Baptismo

Quid de hominebus fuit ad portas paradisi quando moriebatur Adam? Et Euam
et sic fuit: olium petiuit et non inuenet. Hoc illis dixit angelus Micael: Modo
non dabitor uobis, set pos quamque milia D hanus uenerit plasmatur uester
natus ex Maria uergene s[an]c[t]am, ipsi dabet uobis oleum unde unguates
curpus uestrum et refrigerit karo uestra. Hunc uobis erit baptismo.

Who first among mankind was at the gates of paradise when Adam was dying?
Both Eve [and Seth?] and it was thus: [Seth?] sought for the oil [of life] and did
not find it. The angel Michael said this to them [Eve and Seth?]: 'It will not be
given to you now, but after five thousand five hundred years your creator
will come, born from the holy virgin Mary, and He will give you oil with which
you may anoint your body and your flesh will be cooled. Hence (*hunc* = *hinc*?)
will be your baptism.'

**C.**23, **DE.**15, **L.**28, **Y.**10 (fol. 155rv, transcribed by Bischoff, *Handschriftenarchiv* fiche 35, 4.17).

Based either on the *Vita Adae et Evae* 42, ed. Meyer, pp. 235–6, or on its source, the *Euangelium Nicodemi* 19, ed. C. Tischendorf, *Evangelia Apocrypha* (2nd edn, Leipzig, 1876), pp. 372–3 (Redaction A; cf. B, pp. 403–4). The wording, however, while similar, is not identical to either text. In these apocrypha Seth seeks the oil of life and receives essentially the same answer from Michael. Seth is included in the answer in **DELY** (Seh **E**; Seht **L**, Se`th´**Y**). **C** reads *Quando moriebatur Adam et Eva ipi fuerunt,* and Suchier assumes that Seth's name has accidentally been omitted. Although **B**'s *et sic fuit* can be translated as above, it is probably a corruption. There is a light stroke after the *f* in *fuit*, and the reading is conceivably *sicf iuit* with *sicf* a corruption of Seth's name. Even so, the abrupt switch from the singular verbs *petiuit, inuenet* to the plural pronouns (*illis, uobis*) suggests that in **B** Michael is speaking to both Seth and Eve. The parallels in **CDELY** do not suggest a simple emendation of **B**'s reading. In **Y** Eve and Seth together seek the oil and are refused (*quesierunt sed non acceperunt*). In **CDEY** the question begins with a clause specifying that this took place after the expulsion of Adam from Paradise. The *JM* analogues do not name Michael, and only **C** specifies that the reply came from an 'angel'. We assume that **B**'s *quamque* is a corruption of *quinque* (**C** reads . v., **DEY** *quinque milia quingentus* (*-is* **Y**; but **E** omits *quinque*), **L** *quinque milia.cc.xxviiii*). The *Vita Adae* gives the number as 5,500 in agreement with **DY**, but among the variants occurs **L**'s 5,228. **L** has nothing corresponding to the final sentence.

9. Qs uixit DCCCCL | XXXVIIII anus matusalam |
   Quis uixit DCCCCLXXXVIIII anus? Matusalam.
   Who lived 989 years? Methuselah.
Cf. **H**.13; *SS*.13.
Gen. 5.27, which gives 969 years. **H**.13 states that Methuselah lived 968 years. Errors in Roman numerals are common, but one might have expected more care in this case, since the biblical life-span of Methuselah, which is the same in the Hebrew, Septuagint, Vetus Latina and Vulgate, and which appeared to make Methuselah survive the Flood by fourteen years, was the crux of what Jerome termed a *famosa quaestio*. See Thomas O'Loughlin, 'The controversy over Methuselah's death: proto-chronology and the origins of the western concept of inerrancy', *Recherches de théologie ancienne et médiévale* 62 (1995), pp. 182–225.

10. Qs uiuindum scłm uicit elias | et inoc
    Quis uiuindum seculum uicit? Elias et Inoc.
    Who by living overcame time? Elias and Enoch.
**G**.4; *VLM*.32.
Based on Gen. 5.24, Ecclus. 44.16, and 4 Reg. 2.11.
The allusion is to the biblical assertions that Elias and Enoch were taken up alive by God, and their identification in standard Christian exegesis with the two witnesses (*testes*) of Apoc. 11.3–7 who will be slain by the Antichrist at the end of the world (cf. Mal. 4.5). Unlike **B** and **Is**, **G** and *VLM* include John in the answer (see p. 94, above). In other *JM* versions questions regarding Elias and Enoch are differently formulated (usually *Quis est natus et non mortuus?*; **L** reads *Qui non gustaverunt mortem?*); for these see the commentary on **R**.5 and 82 in *Collectanea Pseudo-Bedae*, ed. Bayless and Lapidge, pp. 202 and 220.

11. Qs in mortē hora|uit ad coius oraciōe dnō | ter qnus ad/dit anus eciel | reges
    Quis in mortem horauit ad coius oracionem Domino ter quinus adidit anus?
       Eciel reges.
    Who prayed at the moment of death, at whose prayer God added fifteen years?
       King Ezechiel (?).
Unique to **B**. As Lowe noted, the answer should be 'Ezechias'.

IV Kgs. 20; Isa. 38.

On nominative singular forms such as *reges* and *precepes* (no. 20) see Part II, sect. 12.

12. Cuius corpus non pre|tinet in terram oxoris lot

    Cuius corpus non pretinet in terram? Oxoris Lot.

    Whose body does not go into the earth? Lot's wife's.

Lowe reads *curpus*.

Cf. **P**.20, **R**.126; *AE*₁b.42; *YG*o.g4.

**B**'s formulation of the question is not precisely paralleled; **PR** and *AE*₁ ask whose body did not decay, but **R** (which lacks the answer) and *YG* also ask whose body was not buried. For additional parallels in a Byzantine collection of riddles and in the Latin *Vita S. Pachomii*, see the commentary to **R**.125–6 in *Collectanea Pseudo-Bedae*, ed. Bayless and Lapidge, pp. 228–9.

Based on Gen. 19.26.

13. Q semul natus et bes mortu|os [f. 8r] Lacarus

    Qui semul natus et bes mortuos? Lacarus.

    Who was born once and died twice? Lazarus.

**G**.38, **LMN**.19, **Qgh**.2a, **Qb**.11, **Qk**.4, **R**.124, **U**.4; *AE*₂.40; *CG*.11, *VLM*.50, *YG*n.9, *YG*o.e6, f2; cf. *YG*₃.4 ('Jonah and Lazarus').

John 11.43–4.

On *semul* (here and in no. 14) see Part II, sect. 16.

14. qd bis natus et se|mul mortuos noae

    Quid bis natus et semul mortuos? Noae.

    Who was born twice and died once? Noah.

Unique to **B** with this answer, but the question is paralleled (with Jonah rather than Noah as the answer) in **C**.9, **H**.44, **I**.19, **K**₁.68, **M**.19a, **P**.7; *AE*₁a.62, *AE*₁b.43; *YG*n.8; cf. *YG*₂.3. **B** may simply be wrong (the next two items are Jonah-riddles), though it is just possible that Noah could be regarded as having been 'born' twice by surviving the Flood and re-emerging from the ark (Gen. 7–8).

15. qs tribus | d/ebus et tribus noctebus | orauit ne ce(l)um uidit nec | terram tetegit iunas in uentre | citi

    Quis tribus diebus et tribus noctebus orauit ne celum uidit nec terram tetegit? Iunas in uentre citi.

    Who prayed for three days and three nights and neither saw the sky nor touched the earth? Jonah in the belly of the whale.

There is a stroke after the *u* in *noctebus* that Lowe regards as a false start of the final *s*.

**G**.23, **MN**.19b, **Y**.21; *AE*₂.65 (with *ieunavit* for *orauit*); *VLM*.45; cf. **C**.9, **H**.44, **Z**.8; **P**.8, **T**.2.

**P** conflates the question with one concerning Habacuc (no. 27, below); in **CHZ** the question corresponding to **B**.14 is answered not with 'Noe' but with a declarative form of the question in **B**.15 (*Ionam propheta(m), qui . . . tetigit*).

This and the following item are based on Ionas 2.

16. Qs est uiuus sepultus uiuit | et sep·lcrū eius iunas in uen|tri citi

    Quis est uiuus sepultus uiuit et sepolcrum eius? Iunas in uentri citi.

    Who was buried alive and his grave is also alive? Jonah in the belly of the whale.

The dot after the *p* in *sep·lcrū* might be a weakly executed example of a scribal form that Lowe notes on fol. 300r, where *o* is 'reduced to a mere thick dot' ('Palaeography', p. 182 n. 6).

**G**.10, **ML**.20, **P**.9, **Y**.22; **O**.8; **Ox**, fol. 30r; cf. **T**.2; *AE*₁b.44.

**T** conflates the question with a clause ('nec in celo nec in terra erat') based on the type of question found in **B**.15.

17. Qs prius monastirio fe|cit elias et eliseus Iam pos eliā | paulus erimita et antonios | habas

    Quis prius monastirio fecit? Elias et Eliseus. Iam pos Eliam Paulus erimita et Antonios habas.

    Who first founded a monastery? Elias and Eliseus. And after Elias, Paul the hermit and abbot Anthony.

**C**.14, **G**.27, **H**.62; *SS*.53, *VLM*.48 (omits Paul); cf. **I**.14, **N**.22a, **Qb**.15; *AE*₂.25; *YG*₁.22, *YG*m.11, *YG*n.15.

In the question, instead of **BHN**'s *fecit* or **C**'s *constituit*, some of the analogues have a verb (*construxit AE*, *hecdificavit* **I**) suggesting actual construction of a building. See the commentary on *SS*.53 in Cross and Hill, p. 118, who refer to Jerome's *Epist. 58 ad Paulinum* (PL 22, col. 583) and *Vita S. Pauli* 7–13 (PL 3, cols. 22–7) and Isidore, *De ecclesiasticis officiis* II.xvi.1 (CCSL 113, 74) as sources for these three figures as prototypes or founders of the monastic life. Instead of *pos(t) Eliam*, **CH** (in the answer) read *post baptismum* (**G**: *Ante adventum Elias et Eliseos et post adventum Paulus heremita et Antonius abba*). In the answer, **N** mentions only Elias and Eliseus, **Qb** only Eliseus; the remainder listed after 'cf.' mention Anthony and Paul, or only one of these, but not Elias and Eliseus.

18. q sene glad/o et fustē dra|conē ociset daniel profeta

    Qui sene gladio et fustem draconem ociset? Daniel profeta.

    Who killed a dragon without a sword and club? The prophet Daniel.

**G**.24, **LN**.23, **Y**.27; *VLM*.46; cf. **C**.15, **E**.85, **F**.43.

**C** reads *leonem* instead of *draconem*, perhaps by conflation with a closely similar *JM* question (**I**.33, **N**.22b, **Y**.26; **O**.12) referring to Samson (Jud. 14.6) rather than Daniel. In **EF** the question is differently formulated.

Dan. 14.25–7. The Vulgate reading is *absque gladio* (cf. Part II, sect. 16).

19. Qs asinam p̄siquendum renum | inuenet saul rex

    Quis asinam persiquendum renum inuenet? Saul rex.

    Who found a kingdom when following an ass? King Saul.

**C**.17, **DE**.8, **F**.6, **G**.26, **H**.46, **K₁**.22, **L**.24a, **Y**.6; *AE₁*a.63, *AE₁*b.47; *VLM*.47.

1 Sam. 9.3, 10.14. Most of the analogues read *qu(a)erendo* (*-dum* **CEG**, *querit* **F**, *querens AE₁*b) in agreement with biblical *quaere(re)*.

20. q prius fac|tus est precepes ninius
    Qui prius factus est precepes? Ninius.
    Who was first made a ruler? Ninius.

**C**.20, **D**.11, **E**.12, **F**.9, **L**.26, **R**.13.3.

The first ruler's name is properly Ninus (see discussion on the following item), but the spelling varies widely in the *JM* analogues. Only **R** specifies that he was the son of Bel. **F** adds *Apud romanos uero iulius caesar*.

21. Q | ciuitas priu facta est | niniuin
    Qui ciuitas priu facta est? Niniuin.
    What city was built first? Nineve.

**C**.19, **DE**.10, **F**.8, **G**.12, **H**.47, **LN**.25, **R**.134; *AE₂*.24; cf. **E**.50, **P**.62; *SS*.25, *VLM*.36.

The city of Nineve was built by Assur according to Gen. 10.11 (the form of the name *Niniuin* with final *-n* appears to reflect the accusative form *Nineuen*; among the analogues, only MS D of *AE₂* also has the form with final -n), but by Ninus son of Bel according to Augustine, *De ciuitate Dei* 16.3 (CCSL 48, 502). His status as first 'ruler' has apparently influenced the designation of Nineve as the first city, though according to Gen. 4.17 the first city was Henoch, built by Cain. See the commentary on *SS*.25 in Cross and Hill, pp. 89–91, who posit **B**.20–1 as an intermediate stage in the conflation of questions regarding the city built by Ninus and the biblical first city Henoch. See also the commentary on **R**.134 in *Collectanea Pseudo-Bedae*, ed. Bayless and Lapidge, pp. 134–5.

22. quod miliarios habet | ut eā tutam circis xxi
    Quod miliarios habet ut eam tutam circis? xxi.
    How many milestones has it got, as you go around it all? Twenty-one.

Cf. **C**.19, **D**.12, **E**.11, **G**.14; *SS*.25.

According to Ionas 3.3, *Nineve erat ciuitas magna itinere trium dierum*, and in the other *JM* versions the dimensions are given as *mansiones* (i.e. stations or day's journeys), but with different numbers (fifteen in **CDE**, twelve in **G**). In **C**, the dimensions are given as an addendum in the answer to the question 'Who built the first city?' (see preceding item). As Cross and Hill note in their commentary on *SS*.25 (p. 92), the physical size is also noted in Diodorus Siculus, *Library of History* 2.3–4.

For the sense of *ut* here, see Part II, sect. 15.

23. qsi | Prius inperatur fuit | iulius cesares [f. 8v]
    Quis prius inperatur fuit? Iulius cesares.
    Who was the first emperor? Julius Caesar.

The *i* following the abbreviation of *quis* seems to be an error; or was it the first stroke of a lower-case *p* that the scribe abandoned before he wrote the ornamented capital *P* on the following line?

**A**.40, **C**.21, **DE**.13, **LMN**.27, **P**.49; cf. **F**.9, **H**.64, **R**.136, **Y**.8; *PA*.36. Only **BY** and the addendum to **F**.9 (see commentary to no. 20, above) add the title 'Caesar' to the name. **Y** adds 'Antea consules fuerunt qui regebant rei publica'. **H** identifies the first emperor as Gaius, *PA* 'Iulianus et Octabianus' and **R** (by conflation with a question parallel to the next item) Saul.

24. Q̄s prius rex factus est in isrł saul |

> Quis prius rex factus est in israhel? Saul.

> Who was first to become king in Israel? Saul.

Lowe reads *factos*.

**A**.41, **C**.22, **DE**.14, **F**.10, **N**.27a, **P**.50, **Qb**.19, **Y**.9; *PA*.31; cf. **R**.136 (*imperator* for *rex . . . in israhel*, by conflation with no. 23).

1 Sam. 10.

25. quod anus renauit xlvi.

> Quod anus renauit? xlvi.

> How many years did he reign? Forty-six.

Unique to **B**.

26. q̄s | cū asinam locutos ē balā prou`e´ |ta

> Quis cum asinam locutos est? Balam proueta.

> Who spoke with an ass? Balaam the prophet.

**C**.28, **DE**.20, **F**.13, **G**.31, **H**.48, **Y**.14; *AE*₂.35. Only **BCG** identify Balaam as a 'prophet' (*propheta gentiles* **G**).

Num. 22.28–30.

27. Q̄s nec celū uidit nec terrā | tangit et in alia prouincia ceeci|dit abaco proueta

> Quis nec celum uidit nec terram tangit et in alia prouincia ceecidit? Abaco
> proueta.

> Who neither saw the sky nor touched the earth yet came down in another
> province? Habacuc the prophet.

**C**.29, **D**.21, **E**.22, **F**.15, **H**.49, **L**.30, **P**.52, **Qb**.23, **Y**.15; *AE*₂.32; cf. **K**₁.84, **P**.8. The usual phrasing of the question (with *tetigit* instead of *tangit*) seems to have been influenced by the phrasing of question no. 15 above regarding Jonah. Two *JM* versions show conflation of these two items: **K**₁.84 conflates the first part of the Jonah question with the second part of the Habacuc question (with Habacuc as the answer), and **P**.8 answers the question proper to Habacuc with *De ventre ceti*.

Dan. 14.35.

28. Q̄d p̄uincias sū | cxxxviii

> Quod prouincias sun? cxxxviii.

> How many provinces are there? 138.

After writing *su* and running out of space, the scribe may have used the abbreviation stroke to avoid writing *nt* on the next line, in which case *sū* would not represent 'sun' with phonological loss of [t].

Cf. **A**.45, **C**.30, **D**.22, **E**.23, **F**.16, **H**.56, **G**.32, **I**.13, **R**.137; *AE₂*.36; **V**.16; *PME*.36. Answers vary widely, but 138 is unique to **B**. Arno Borst, *Der Turmbau von Babel: Geschichte der Meinungen über Ursprung und Vielfalt der Sprachen und Völker*, 4 vols. (Stuttgart, 1958–63), II/1, p. 508 (cf. II/1, pp. 462, 470, 507), notes the parallel in **V** and suggests that the source is either Esther 8.9, which puts the number of provinces at 127 (though these are for the territory from India to Ethiopia) or Pseudo-Aristeas. According to Suchier (p. 122) those which give the answer as twelve (**AGI**) refer to the Roman dioceses established by Diocletian (**I** specifies how they came to be distributed among the Saracens, the Byzantine empire and Gaul).

29. Q̂d linguas sunt LXXII |

    Quod linguas sunt? LXXII.

    How many languages are there? Seventy-two.

On the syntax of *Quod linguas*, see Part II, sect. 10.

**C**.24, **DE**.16, **F**.11, **P**.32, **H**.50, **K1**.82, **R**.138, **V**.17, **Y**.11; cf. *SS*.79.

In **EF** the answer is twenty-two.

Based on Gen. 10. See Borst, *Der Turmbau*, IV, p. 1970 n. 272, and Hans Sauer, 'Die 72 Völker und Sprachen der Welt: ein mittelalterlicher Topos in der englischen Literatur', *Anglia* 101 (1982), pp. 29–48.

30. Q̂d uolocrū genere sunt XX

    Quod uolocrum genere sunt? XX.

    How many kinds of birds are there? Twenty.

**C**.50, **D**.24, **E**.25, **F**.18, **H**.53, **G**.15, **R**.131; *AE₂*.45; *SS*.51, *AR*.33, *VLM*.37.

The standard answer is fifty-four; twenty is unique to **B**. In their commentary on *AR*.33–6, Cross and Hill, p. 152, give a chart showing the various numbers of birds, serpents, fish and quadrupeds according to *JM* and related dialogues.

On the plural form *genere*, see Part II, sect. 11.

31. Qoʻdʻ| genera serpentina sunt XXIIII |

    Qod genera serpentina sunt? XXIIII.

    How many kinds of snakes are there? Twenty-four.

**C**.32, **H**.55, **G**.33, **I**.25, **R**.132, **V**.18; *AE₂*.37; *AR*.34, *VLM*.38.

The standard answer is thirty-three or thirty-four, but twenty-four is paralleled in *AE*.

32. Qs illi inposuit nomen adā

    Quis illi inposuit nomen? Adam.

    Who first gave it a name? Adam.

**C**.51, **G**.36; *AE₂*.38; cf. **L**.32; *AR*.36.

In **CG** *AE* Adam is credited with naming all the creatures whose species have been enumerated, not just the snake; **L** (which lacks these enumerations) says simply that he named 'things'; *AR* specifies that he named the species of fish.

Based on Gen. 2.20.

33. Q pri|us conouet filium quam maria | x̄p̄m

    Qui prius conouet filium quam [maritum]? Maria Christum.

    Who first knew her son before her husband? Mary; Christ.

**D**.32, **E**.33, **I**.26, **K**$_1$.35, **Y**.19; cf. **F**.23; **P**.6.

The analogues all have *maritum*. **F** formulates the question differently (*Quae femina concepit filium sine marito?*); **P** answers '.ccxii.'

34. qs de noae risit filius eius

    Quis de Noae risit? Filius eius.

    Who laughed at Noah? His son.

**C**.34; cf. **D**.26, **G**.37, **L**.33.

In **DGL** the question involves the origins of slaves, said to descend from Cham, who laughed at his father.

Gen. 9.22–5.

35. qs | prius sacerdus fuit sēp̄ ipsē mel|cesedic

    Quis prius sacerdus fuit semper? Ipsem Melcesedic.

    Who was the first priest forever? Melchesidech himself.

**I**.15, **R**.11; *YG*$_1$.13, *YG*m.13, *YG*n.18; cf. *AE*$_2$.19 (*presbiter*), *AE*$_1$a.54 (*episcopus*; M. and Aaron), *AE*$_1$b.74 (*sacerdos*; M. and A.); *AR*.13 ('bishop'; M. and A.); cf. also **L**.36 and **A**.12, **K**$_2$.12.

Instead of **B**'s awkward *semper ipsem*, **RL** read *in uetere testamento* and identify either Melchesidech (**R**) or Abiuth (**L**, cf. *AE*$_2$.72; Exod. 28.1, Lev. 10.2) as the first 'priest' of the Old Law, Peter being the first priest of the New (cf. no. 40 below, which in other versions is usually paired with this question). On the varying terms for Melchesidech's priestly office, and Aaron's role as the first 'bishop', see the commentary on *AR*.13 in Cross and Hill, pp. 139–40.

Gen. 14.18; cf. Ps. 110.4.

36. Qs uidit dm̄ abrā ad elecē | ambrē

    Quis uidit Deum? Abram ad elecem [M]ambrem.

    Who saw God? Abraham at oak of Mambre.

**C**.10, **H**.36, **N**.20a; *AE*$_1$a.61, *AE*$_1$b.80.

Gen. 18.1, but *elecem* (=*ilicem*) reflects the Vetus Latina (type **L**) reading (Vulgate *in convalle*). **C** reads *hilicet*, **H** *AE* read *radicem*; **N** does not specify the location. **CN** add that Abraham was the first priest in circumcision.

37. Cuius sepolcrō n̄ inuentum | in terra mose

    Cuius sepolcrom non inuentum in terra? Mose.

    Whose grave is not found in the earth? [That of] Moses.

**C.**16, **E.**81, **H.**43, **G.**25, **L.**24, **N.**17, **P.**72; *AE*$_2$.44; cf. *SS.*44, *VLM.*18.

Only **BG** have *in terra*.

Based on Deut. 34.6. *SS* and *VLM* the burial place as *F(i)egor*, reflecting the Vetus Latina reading *Phegor* (see Cross and Hill, p. 111).

38. Q(s) dm̄ negauit | Petrus
    Quis Deum negauit? Petrus.
    Who denied God? Peter.

**F.**27; cf. **D.**36, **E.**37, **P.**17; *AE*$_2$.28.

Matt. 26.69–75; Mark. 14.66–72; Luke. 22.55–62; John. 18.16–18, 25–7.

39. qs in altom axsend/rit | a sidira simon macus
    Quis in altom axsenderit a sidira? Simon Macus.
    Who would have ascended on high to the stars? Simon Magus.

Unique to **B**, although **L.**18 and **N.**12 have a different question regarding Simon Magus (*Quis voluit expugnare paradysum?*).

Based on the Acts of Peter 31–2, in W. Schneemelcher and E. Hennecke, *New Testament Apocrypha*, 2 vols., trans. R. McL. Wilson (Philadelphia, 1965), II, pp. 314–16. Simon employs magic to fly, but is brought down to earth and to his death by the prayers of Peter.

On the form *axsend/rit*, see Part II, sect. 8; for *macus*, see sect. 6.

40. Qs p̄ clere|cos factus ē petros
    Quis primus clerecos factus est? Petros.
    Who was the first cleric? Peter.

**A.**8, **R.**12; cf.**L.**37; *AE*$_1$b.73; *AR.*14.

The analogues listed after 'cf.' identify Peter and James as the first 'bishops' of the New Law.

Based on Matt. 16.18–19.

41. Q uiui sepol|ti sunt datan et abiron
    Q[ui] uiui sepolti sunt? Datan et Abiron.
    Who were buried alive? Dathan and Abiron.

Unique to **B**.

Num. 16.31–4.

42. Qs uid/ isca|lam suspiontā ad celū iacob
    Quis uidi iscalam suspiontam ad celum? Iacob.
    Who saw a ladder suspended towards heaven? Jacob.

**C.**61, **G.**50; *AE*$_1$a.64, *AE*$_1$b.48.

Gen. 28.12. The form *suspiontam* is not readily explicable, but seems to represent *suspensam*. **C** reads *subiuncta*, **G** *posita*, *AE*$_1$ab *erectam*. The Vulgate reading is *stantem*; the many Vulgate and Vetus Latina variants do not afford a parallel for *suspensam*.

43. Quan|ti milites d/uiserunt uistimenta x͞pi | ɪɪɪɪ

   Quanti milites diuiserunt uistimenta Christi? ɪɪɪɪ.

   How many soldiers divided Christ's garments? Four.

**A**.6, **C**.54, **K1**.87, **K2**.6; *AE*2.42; *AR*.37, *VLM*.52; cf. **G**.45 (*Quantas sortes fecerunt milites . . .?*).

John 19.23.

44. in c(o) mont͞e nonquam plouet us͞q in | eternum in gelbue ubi saul ucisus e͞

   In co montem nonquam plouet usqui in eternum? In Gelbue ubi Saul ucisus est.

   On what mountain will it never rain unto eternity? In Gelboe where Saul was slain.

**C**.18, **DE**.9, **F**.7, **H**.45, **G**.28, **I**.21, **N**.24b, **Y**.7; *AE*₁b.45; *AE*₂.26; *VLM*.49; cf. **K₁**.81 (*In Sinaa*).

There are many minor verbal variants among the analogues; those closest to **B**'s formulation are **EGN** *numquam*; **E** *ubi Saul occisus est*; **CFH** *AE*₁b *in (a)eternum*.

1 Sam. 31.4 and 2 Sam. 1.21.

45. Qs d/ cel͞o pluit extra aquam mana | et coturnix

   Quis de celom pluit extra aquam? Mana et coturnix.

   What rains from heaven besides water? Manna and quail.

Paralleled only in **Y**.31, which reads 'Quae pluit de celo extra aqua? R. Coturnix in castris quando pauit dominus filios israhel de manna quadraginta annis.'

Exod. 16.

46. qs posed/ parad/|su abraam

   Quis posede paradisu? Abraam.

   Who possesses paradise? Abraham.

**C**.46, which adds *qui filium immolavit Christum*.

Apparently based on Luke 16.22 (the 'bosom of Abraham').

47. q erat mortuos et mor|tuos et mortous sussetauit iliseus

   Qui erat mortuos et mortuos et mortous sussetauit? Iliseus.

   Who had died and even when dead brought the dead back to life? Eliseus.

**C**.13, **G**.46; cf. **H**.61, **K₁**.80, **L**.22, **N**.15, **Y**.25.

In the answer **CGHLN** add *in Galgalis* [+ *in suo sepulcrho* **G**], **K₁** *in monasterio*. Those listed after 'cf.' formulate the question differently ('Who first raised the dead?'). See also the Hiberno-Latin (?) prayer *Oratio S. Gregorii*, 'Oret pro me sanctus Heliseus, qui suscitauit mortuum post mortem': *Collectanea Pseudo-Bedae*, ed. Bayless and Lapidge, p. 194; cf. Lapidge, 'A new Hiberno-Latin hymn on St Martin', *Celtica* 21 (1990), 240–51, at pp. 241–2.

4 Reg. 13.21.

On the form *erat mortuos*, see Part II, sect. 13.

## THE CONTEXT AND FUNCTION OF *DE DIES MALUS*
### AND *JOCA MONACHORUM*

The variety of materials included among the additions to **B** makes generalisation hazardous, but the liturgical context of the sermon and dialogue raises the possibility that both were intended for use in catechetical instruction. It seems unlikely that the *JM* dialogues were originally intended for instruction of catechumens, since the questions focus on biblical esoterica (as opposed to the essential narrative summaries of the catechetical *narratio*), and generally lack questions relating to creed or dogma. Probably their intended function was to instruct oblates and students in a monastic setting, as the title in four of the earliest manuscripts (but not **B**) implies (*Joca monachorum* might be translated as 'Bible quiz for monks'). However, as I have shown elsewhere, *JM* and related dialogues often circulated with creeds and other catechetical material, and *JM* questions came to be conflated with questions from catechetical dialogues.[74] The well-established early title *Joca monachorum* subsequently disappears, surfacing again only in one fifteenth-century copy. In a recent study Charles Munier has suggested that the closely similar dialogue *De plasmatione Adam* (see above, p. 86) in Sélestat, Bibliothèque Humaniste 1 (1093) (whose main content is a lectionary) was used in pre-baptismal catechesis.[75] According to Germain Morin, there are close connections between the Bobbio Missal and the sermons of Caesarius of Arles, especially 'ses catéchèses bibliques préparatoires au baptême de Pâques'.[76] Without prejudice to the question of the origins of **B** (Morin on this basis urged south-east France), I would suggest that the materials in the first quire – which consist of interpretations of the Gospels, *De dies malus* and the dialogue – were intended for use in Lenten catechetical instruction. As such they are para-liturgical materials, written in a lower grade of script than the sacramentary proper. As Roger Wright suggests (Part II, sect. 18), they were meant to be read aloud, but only by the scribe himself, who, according to my hypothesis, would have been a priest serving a community in which there were still a significant number of adult converts.

[74] Wright, 'From monks' jokes to sages' wisdom'.
[75] Munier, 'La chronique pseudo-hiéronymienne'.
[76] Germain Morin, 'Le Symbole de S. Césaire d'Arles', *Revue Bénédictine* 46 (1934), pp. 180–9, at pp. 187–8.

## II THE LANGUAGE OF *DE DIES MALUS* AND THE *JOCA MONACHORUM* IN THE BOBBIO MISSAL

Many of the linguistic features in these two texts that would seem strange to a literate member of the Roman Empire, or to a nineteenth-century schoolmaster, are explicable in terms of the nature of early Romance speech. It is notoriously difficult to locate texts such as this geographically on the basis of their language, but it is worth stating here at the outset that such evidence as there is is consistent with the placing and dating to the Rhône valley around 700 as is suggested by other contributors to this volume. That does not mean it would necessarily be inconsistent with other times or places.

The scribe must have been taught to write, since writing is not a skill that comes naturally in the way that speech does, and presumably he will have been taught the tricks of the trade that were in general use to make texts look acceptable (perhaps partly via one of the treatises *De Orthographia*, or perhaps not); and even in texts not designed for posterity, as these are not, his training will inevitably prevent him from coming up with an accurate transcription of his speech habits. But on the whole there is nothing particularly surprising about those details which, perhaps unbeknownst to the scribe, attest non-classical linguistic features.

The majority of the linguistic developments mentioned below are explained further by Herman, who includes a large bibliography;[1] there is a huge specialist literature which will not normally be referred to here.

### SPELLING

Not all mis-spellings are linguistically significant, but the majority are, since they may well be attributable, often directly, to features of early Romance speech. The scribe was not, of course, deliberately trying to write in a phonetic script; the Latin orthography is far too accurate for that.

It is essential for these analytical purposes not to resolve the manuscript abbreviations. Whichever way they are resolved, they can distort the analysis. Charles Wright follows Lowe, for example, in resolving *isrl* in the edition as *israhel* (*JM* 24); and indeed it is possible that the scribe would have spelt this word that way if it had not been abbreviated; but it would be quite misleading for me to use this as any kind of data in the linguistic discussion of the use of the letter *h*, which this scribe often omits. Similarly, in this analysis I have left unresolved the *d* with the long tail, presenting it as *dl*, since any guess whether that would otherwise have been *de* or *di* seems pointless.

---

[1] J. Herman, *Vulgar Latin*, trans. R. Wright (Philadelphia, 2000).

In the ensuing analyses, symbols in square brackets indicate sounds, and those in italics indicate letters; thus, for example, the letters *qu* usually represent the sound [kw]. And since it is not clear if the scribe was following a standard procedure for Semitic names, these are omitted from the statistics, although comparisons with forms used in the Vulgate can at times be instructive.

1. *Vowels.* The main developments in the vowel system of early Romance were consequences of the breakdown in phonemic length during the Imperial period; that is, of the fact that the old length distinction, between the long and short versions of each of the five vowels, was no longer usable to distinguish between words. Since it was in any event the case that the originally longer vowels were pronounced more closed than the corresponding short vowel, a further consequence, in most of the western Romance area, was that, among the front vowels, originally long [e:] and originally short [i] came to be pronounced identically, along with originally short [e] in unstressed syllables; and in the same way, among the back vowels, originally long [o:] and originally short [u] came to be pronounced identically, along with originally short [o] in unstressed syllables. This means that for each of these two sounds, it was not immediately clear to a scribe whether or not the standard spelling was with *i* or *e*, *u* or *o* respectively. Thus the 'mistake', if there is one, could be either way round, and an ostensibly correct choice could often merely be the result of similar guesswork which happened this time to be correct. More often than not the scribe gets these written forms right, of course, but there are four cases of *i* for standard *e*, and twenty-five of *e* for standard *i*, in the *De dies malus*; sixteen cases of *i* for *e*, and twenty-one of *e* for *i*, in the *Joca monachorum*; there are approximately thirteen cases of *u* for standard *o*, and approximately fifteen of *o* for standard *u*, in the *De dies malus*; and fourteen cases of *u* for standard *o*, and eighteen cases of *o* for standard *u*, in the *Joca monachorum*. There is no great significance in these statistics, which in the case of the back vowels are anyway necessarily approximate because (as Charles Wright points out) it is often difficult to determine whether a particular letter in the text is actually *u* or *o*.

As for the spellings *benenetas* and *benenote* (*DDM* 17), the first is understandable as an attempt at writing *benignitas*, but the *o* in the other is not explicable in phonetic terms; [i] > [o] is effectively an impossible change, so the influence of the biblical form *bonitatis* (which occurs in the passage from Rom. 2.4. being quoted) is all that can be suggested as a reason.

2. *Diphthongs.* The diphthong [aj] had long since levelled to [e], which is why it had become so common to spell *ae* for standard *e* and *e* for standard *ae*; in these two texts together there are three cases of *ae* for *e* and fourteen of *e* for *ae*, including on all occasions the forms of *celum* and *penite-*. Whether this helps explain the aberration of spelling in *ceecidit* is unclear (*JM* 27), but there seems to be no better explanation available. Noah is *Noe* in the Vulgate, but he is not included in the present conjectures.

Not only [kwi] (nine times in *JM*) but also [kwo] is often represented by an abbreviation, as in $\widetilde{Qd}$ or $Q\bar{d}$ for *quot* (*JM* 28, 29, 30); but on three occasions we can see the *u* being omitted from this sequence: *cos* for *quos* (*DDM* 25), *qo^d* for *quod* (*JM* 31) and *co* for *quod* (*JM* 44). If these forms without *u* have a phonetic inspiration, that could be a reason for our not locating the texts in Italy or Spain, where [wo] usually survived intact.

3. *Aspiration.* The [h] had long since fallen from speech, and *aspiratio* was merely seen as a spelling peculiarity at this time, with a name modelled originally on the Greek 'breathing'. The contemporary grammarians were unsure what to say about it. Even Alcuin, in his *De Orthographia* of a century later, was uncharacteristically unhelpful on the topic: 'Asspiratio ante uocales omnes poni potest, post consonantes autem quattuor tantummodo ponitur c t p r, ut habeo heres hiems homo humus Chremes Thraso Philippus Rhodus. H ideo uocalibus extrinsecus ascribitur, ut minus sonet, consonantibus autem intrinsecus, ut plurimum sonet' (section 180 in the edition by Sandra Bruni).[2] Meanwhile, scribes either knew where to put the letter in or did not. Initial *h* was added on seven occasions in these two texts to words that the standard spelling did not give one (e.g. *hopera*, *DDM* 18) and omitted four times when the standard would have had one (e.g. *abemus*, *DDM* 24). An *h* was also inserted inside *diuiolauit*, giving *d/uiholauet* in *JM* 6, which is more interesting; this spelling seems designed to represent two vowels in hiatus, rather than a diphthong (that is, [io] rather than [jo]). This train of thought seems to have stemmed from the word *mihi*, often reinforced in writing to *michi*. As Alcuin says, the *h* was also available as the second part of a digraph to represent Greek sounds; but here it is omitted even so from *temsauricas* (*DDM* 18, rather than *the-*) and *sep.lcru* and *sepolcrō* (*JM* 16 and 37, rather than *-chrum*). It is also noticeable that the *h* is, probably deliberately, never here inserted into Semitic names that might seem to need them, such as those otherwise elsewhere spelt *Michael* (or often *Michahel*), *Abraham*, *Habakkuk*, *Methuselah*, *Enoch*, *Ezechiel*, *Dathan*, *Melchizedech*, as well as *Nineveh*.

4. *Consonants in general.* Several changes in the consonants of speech were underway at this time, and the scribe is much better at resisting mis-spelling consonants for phonetic reasons than he is with vowels. If we can conclude anything from this, it is that phonemic merger was not, or not yet, the normal resolution of consonantal developments, and that as a result even an evolved pronunciation could often be unambiguously allotted the standard spelling without the phonetic ambiguity characteristic of the vocalic symbols.

5. *Final consonants.* Word-final consonants tended to be lost from speech unless they were alveolar (and even those were on their way out in Italy). The main perceived problem for scribes in this respect seems to have been the spelling of

---

[2] Alcuin, *De Orthographia*, ed. S. Bruni (Florence, 1997).

a word-final dental consonant, with confusions of final -*d* and -*t* being explicitly mentioned, e.g. by Isidore of Seville (*Etymologiae* I.27.1–3), in pairs of words identically pronounced such as *at* and *ad*, *aut* and *haud*; and in practice there were also cases of total loss of both -*d* and -*t*. We find here *quit* for standard *quid* and *set* for standard *sed* (*JM* 1, 8), but also inversely six cases of *quod* for standard *quot*, in which the word must have meant 'how many?' in view of the answers given (*JM* 22, 25, 28–31). The letter *d* in *nusmedipsus* (*DDM* 25) probably comes under this heading also, for the original word division was *nosmet ipsos*; but in speech the word division came to be perceived as *nos metipsos*, since *metipse* is what gives rise eventually to Catalan *mateix* (with a surprisingly unvoiced [t]) and the reinforced form *metipsimum* is what led to French *même*, Spanish *mismo*, Italian *medesimo*, etc. That both sounds were at risk of disappearing in word-final position can be seen here in one use of *a* for standard *ad* (that is, meaning 'to' rather than 'from', as *a* had originally meant), *posed*/ for *possidet* and, if it is the correct reading, *uid*/ for *uidit* (*JM* 39, 46 and 42); and *es* for standard *est* (that is, third person singular rather than second). The inverse case, with the written *quid* apparently twice used for standard *qui* (that is, meaning 'who' rather than 'what': *JM* 8 (at the start), 14), is similarly explicable if the final letter *d* regularly corresponded to no sound at all (i.e. was 'silent'). Final *c* also disappears from *nec* (*JM* 15); this is before an initial *c*- in the following word, so haplography helped here, but this [k] was indeed being lost (eventual Romance *ni* or *nè*).

Final -*s* is lost in *priu* for *prius* (*JM* 21, although not elsewhere), and again in *ama* for *amas* (*DDM* 10), if we are right in interpreting *ama* here as indicative rather than imperative. Final written -*s* is lost sporadically in texts all over the Empire at an earlier date, but at this time the loss may just conceivably be geographically significant, for only in Italy is the corresponding sound-change regularly found in Romance.[3] The form *quamdius* (or *quamdios*) for normal *quamdiu* has twice acquired a final letter *s* (*DDM* 24, 21); this could correspond to an [s] sound rather than being silent, perhaps acquired by analogy with the formally and semantically similar *prius*; for temporal terms tended to acquire such a final, etymologically inexplicable, [-s] (e.g. Spanish *antes*, from *ante*). In the event, the form survived in Romance in Provence, and, it seems, only in Provence (according to Meyer-Lübke).[4] It appears in two early Romance texts from the area; on three occasions in the *Vie de Saint Léger* (*c.* AD 1000): 'Quandius visquet ciel reis Lothiers' (49), 'Quandius al suo consiel edrat' (69) and 'Quandius in ciel monstier instud' (111), being described by the editor as a *provençalisme* meaning 'for as long as'; and in the first line of the *Boecis* (*c.* AD 1115), which begins 'Nos ioue omne, quandius que

[3] A. Varvaro, 'Latin and Romance: fragmentation or restructuring?', in *Latin and the Romance Languages in the Early Middle Ages*, ed. R. Wright (London, 1991; repr. Philadelphia,1996), pp. 44–51.
[4] W. Meyer-Lübke, *Romanisches Etymologisches Wörterbuch* (2nd edn, Heidelberg, 1924).

nos estam,/ de gran follia per folledat parllam'.[5] The use of this word in the *De dies malus* could thus be regarded as slight evidence in favour of a textual origin in southern France.

Why the form *niniuin* (*JM* 21) acquired its final *n* is probably explicable, if at all, within morphology, and morphology also complicates our analysis of the loss of an expected letter *m* or tilde. Sometimes there is no such factor: the tilde is absent, for example, from *precepes* (for standard *princeps*, *JM* 20), which is probably just an error of omission with no phonetic significance, since Romance derivatives of this word all contain a nasal. The other cases are all at the end of a word where the developed morphology and phonetics combine in creating potential for confusions; these will be considered in the morphological section below. Why the nominative form *ipsē* has a tilde is not directly explicable (*JM* 35), for a written form *ipsem* was never recommended and a spoken [ipsem] never existed; there seem to be one or two other rogue unattached tildes in the text as well.

6. *Voicing*. The lack of spelling phenomena in these texts due to voicing is remarkable. The voicing between vowels of [t], [p], [k] and [f] (to [d], [b], [g] and [v] respectively) often gives rise in texts of this time, even in manuscripts of the hyper-correct Visigoths, to spellings between vowels of *d* for standard *t*, *b* for *p*, *g* for *c* and *v* for *f* or *ph*. This indeed happens occasionally in this manuscript: the first folio offers all of *luporum*, *lopos* and *lubis* for 'wolves', a variation which is not only a delight in itself but also an instructive indication to us not to see spellings as phonetic transcriptions, because the actual pronunciation probably corresponded unvaryingly to the one combination of stressed vowel and intervocalic consonant that is not directly attested on that folio, [lob-] (that is, there is here no case of written *lob-*). All that the scribe of our two texts offers in this category are two cases (*JM* 26, 27) of *proueta* for *propheta*; the two inverse cases, the *c* for [g] in *macus* (that is, Simon Magus, *JM* 39) and the *p* for [b] in *pacipatur* (for *parcebatur*, *DDM* 16), are only explicable if the voicing has become so normal by now that the letter *c* regularly corresponded to the sound [-g-] and *p* to the sound [-b-]. In the genuinely fascinating form *retet* (*DDM* 18) for standard *reddet*, pronounced originally with geminate [dd], the first letter *t* might even be due to a [t]; this suggestion looks strange, yet Walsh has argued that there was a general change of intervocalic [dd] to [t], proposing a number of new etymologies.[6]

The form *tiui* for *tibi* is the only case of confusion between the letters *b* and *u*, due in this case to fricativisation (*DDM* 8); the confusion of these letters is so common

---

[5] J. Linskill, *Saint Léger* (Paris, 1937), p. 157; *Der Altprovenzalische 'Boeci'*, ed. C. Schwarze (Münster, 1963).

[6] T.J. Walsh, 'The etymology of Sp./Port. *aterirse* "to be stiff or numb with cold", *aterecerse* "to become stiff or numb with cold" and Sp. *derretirse* / Port. *derreterse* "to melt, thaw"', in *Essays in Hispanic Linguistics Dedicated to Paul M. Lloyd*, ed. R. Blake *et al.* (Newark, DE, 1999), pp. 223–36.

in other texts that its relative absence here is striking. In view of this, and the paucity of incorrect letters that betray voicing, we can perhaps deduce that although our scribe may not have been concentrating years before on vowel-homework day, he was certainly awake during the consonant-spelling lesson.

There is one written case of the metathesis of *r* that was common in speech: *pretinet* for *pertinet* (*JM* 12); and an *r* has been omitted in *pacipatur* (for *parcebatur*, *DDM* 16).

7. *Degemination.* The use of single consonantal letters in spelling instead of standard geminates, however, is common here. There are twenty-one cases altogether in which one consonantal letter is written where we would expect a standard two, and only one the other way round (*dimmortoos*, *JM* 3). The regular orthographic degemination is explicable phonetically so long as the texts were not written in Italy, for such degemination was normal in speech further west. The most initially surprising example is probably the spelling of the forms of *ille* with one *l*, which happens all five times that this lexical item appears in the *De dies malus* (4, 6, 6, 9, 25), as well as in the only other candidate (*tole* for *tolle*, 22); but not at all in the *Joca monachorum* (*illis* and *illi*, *JM* 8 and 32), although *miliarios* is found there rather than *milli-* (*JM* 22). In fact, the only other written geminate forms to survive in these texts are those of *terra* (*JM* 12, 15); all others have simplified, whether the consonant is voiced or not. There are only six unvoiced candidates for degemination, but all have simplified (e.g. *sopliciom* for *supplicium*, *DDM* 15).

The forms with single *l* rather than *ll*, and the single *n* that often occurs here in forms of *annos*, suggest that the writer is not working in the Iberian peninsula, where, rather than merely degeminating, these two geminates survived later than this and subsequently palatalised (e.g. to Spanish *ellos*, *año*). The palatalised and degeminated development of the double nasal [ɲɲ] (written *gn*), however, as exemplified in *renum*, *renauit*, *conouet* (*JM* 19, 25, 33), *benenote*, *benenetas* and *dinetur* (*DDM* 17, 17, 25), has no obvious geographical significance; this happened everywhere (in the west).

8. *Sibilants.* The original [tj] and [kj] sequences had evolved into an identical sound, probably [tsj] or even already [ts], which explains why scribes were unsure how to spell it; here, as usual, our scribe seems to have opted for the letters *ci*: *iusticiā*, *penetenciam* twice, *reuelacionis*, *duriciam* (*DDM* 6, 16, 17, 18, 18) and *oracionē* (*JM* 11); only *mintiatur* resists this spelling (*DDM* 8), although this letter is not clear and could perhaps be a *c* in any case.

Double sibilants seem to have had the potential to lead to some chaos, in view of the following forms: *exseptis* for *exceptis*, *axsenderit* for *ascenderit* and *sussetauit* for *suscitauit* (*JM* 5, 39, 47), *exelera* for *scelera* and *espectabatur* for *exspectabatur* (*DDM* 15, 16). The first four of these had had an original [k] before a front vowel ([e] or [i]), a combination which regularly assibilated in Romance, leading in these five words to a double sibilant, although in practice the *exs-* of *exspectare* probably never represented a real double sibilant at any time. The resulting sound could thus be spelt as any of *sc*, *xs*, *x* or *ss*.

Word-initially, these combinations ran into another problem. Romance was developing a rule whereby preconsonantal [s] could only be syllable-final, which came to mean that a word could not begin in speech with an [s] plus a consonant (as is still true in Spanish). The problem of how to pronounce such words was usually solved by adding an initial front vowel; there is an echo of this in *espolias* for standard *spolias* (*DDM* 6) and the forms *exelera* for *scelera*, *estate* for *statim* (*DDM* 15) and *iscalam* for *scalam* (*JM* 42). The added vowel is not, however, consistently represented here in writing, and *spolias* is also spelt in the normal way (*DDM* 4). The question of the possible presence or absence of the *ex-* prefix also confuses the picture in verbs in this category, since perhaps *espectabatur* appears instead of *spectabatur* rather than instead of *exspectabatur*, and *espolias* for *exspolias* (which appears here in some manuscripts) rather than for *spolias*; conversely, *spectis* may even represent a form with an unwritten prefix [e-] (*DDM* 10), although the meaning suggests otherwise.

9. *Greek letters.* Other non-standard orthographic details in these texts include the use of the originally Greek letter *k*, in *karo* and *kain* only, rather than *c* (*JM* 8, 5). Generally, when this letter was adopted the reason usually lay in the fact that the letter *c* could be phonetically ambiguous, while *k* always represented [k]. These two words have the *k* followed by *a* representing the vowel [a]; this detail might be geographically significant, for it was only in northern France that [ka-] changed (e.g. French *charnier*, derived from *caro*, while Spanish and Italian have *carne*). On the other hand, we find *carnē* in *DDM* 5. The use of the [k] could imply, therefore, that this scribe is not working in northern France, even though he might know of their phonetic habits. The Greek letter *z* is not in his ken, however; the two occasions that seem to require it, in the word here written *temsauricas* (*DDM* 18) and in the proper name *Lacarus* (*JM* 13), may attest an inability to write *z* rather than anything else, despite Lowe's excitement at its potential phonetic significance, and despite the presence of both words in the Vulgate. Yet *-icare* was no less available as a suffix than was *-izare*, in any case.

Overall, the spelling is not too bad. Some words which were undergoing major phonetic developments, such as *factus*, *filius* and *quomodo*, are even so spelt here in the standard form. This suggests that the written forms of these words may have been taught whole, as single logographic units, on one of the apprentice scribe's better afternoons. Perhaps, in fact, it was precisely such common words, that had suffered considerably from phonetic evolution already by this time, that were given individual logographic attention in class.

## MORPHOLOGY AND SYNTAX

10. *Nominal morphology.* The main development in early Romance nominal morphology concerned the progressive loss of the oblique inflections; that is, the old ablative, dative and genitive endings slowly became less common in speech. Eventually the originally accusative case came to be used instead of all these, with the meaning inherent in the original inflection tending eventually to be expressed (if at all) by a preposition. Thus the genitive cases with possessive meaning were over time replaced by the use of *de* plus the noun in the originally accusative case. But *de* could all along be used with other senses as well, such as 'about' (as in the title of *DDM*, *JM* 34) and 'from' (as in *JM* 6, 8, 45), and these are the only uses of *de* in these texts; the use of *de* is thus apparently not yet possessive, as it would increasingly become in Romance. Burton makes the same point about biblical texts, where *de* is not used possessively.[7] The most obvious example in these texts, of this development of *de* plus accusative but without possessive meaning, concerns the title *De dies malus* ('About the evil days') itself; even though the noun phrase *dies malus* looks to a modern Latinist like a nominative singular, it is here an accusative plural, with the second vowel spelt as *u* rather than the standard *o* of *malos*. Other examples of prepositions taking accusative rather than the standard ablative include *hab elum* rather than *ab illo*, *ab alterum* rather than *ab altero*, *d/ cos* (that is, *de quos*) rather than *de quibus* (*DDM* 9, 13, 25), *in morte̅*, *in terram*, *cu̅ asinam* and *d/ celo̅* (*JM* 11, 12, 26, 45). But this is not always so: the standard ablative is also found after these prepositions, in *in diae* (that is, *in die*, in the quotation from Romans) and *in dia* *ela* (*DDM* 18, 25), *ex do̅*, *d/ sorore sua*, *d/ hominebus*, *in uentre* and *in uentri*, *in alia prouincia*, *in terra* (*JM* 1, 6, 8, 15, 16, 27, 37). The unambiguous ablative in *-bus* even survived without a preposition in *tribus d/ebus et tribus noctebus* (*JM* 15), which is the kind of set phrase that can intelligibly preserve incipient archaisms.

The original oblique form usually still appears in pronouns, however, whose oblique inflections survived much longer in speech than those of nouns (and in some cases still survive in Romance): thus we find *tibi*, *in te ipso*, *in altero* (as well as *ab alterum* mentioned above) (*DDM* 3, 10, 10); *illis*, *uobis* and dative *illi* (*JM* 8, 8, 32). The forms of *alter* seem to be chosen almost at random in *DDM* 10–13, in fact, which suggests that the scribe knew what the available endings were, but could not remember when to write which; and in general, as regards the accusative/ablative confusions after prepositions, this is the conclusion to draw. Not that the scribe sometimes got it right and sometimes got it wrong; but that he had no idea on the whole which to use, although he did know what the available endings were. Choosing almost at random, inevitably he sometimes got it right and sometimes

[7] P. Burton, *The Old Latin Gospels: A Study of their Texts and Language* (Oxford, 2000).

got it wrong, but in each case the spelling distinction corresponded to no audible phonetic difference in speech, or in the sermon, or in reading aloud.

This explains how we can on three occasions find both inflections in the same prepositional phrase; these are *ex maria uergene scam*, where *Maria* and *Vergene* seem to be ablatives but *scam* (that is, *Sanctam*) has the supposedly accusative-marking *m* (*JM* 8); *sene glad/o et fustē* (*JM* 18); and *in co montē* (*JM* 44). This uncertainty explains why instructions concerning when to write a final letter -*m* turned up in treatises on *Orthographia* rather than in the grammars; it was seen as a spelling phenomenon, a problem of when to insert a silent letter or tilde. There are also accusatives used instead of datives: *proximom tuum male facere et tibi bene* (*DDM* 3), where the pronoun's dative form is chosen, *tibi*, but not the dative of the noun and the adjective (it is not *proximo tuo*); and *cum male feceres carnē alterios* (*DDM* 5), with *carnē* rather than *carni*.

There are genitive forms as well as *de* phrases here: accuracy in these is better achieved. Even *alterios* (*DDM* 5) is almost right (for *alterius*); also *oxoris* (for *uxoris*, *JM* 12); *Lot* in the same noun-phrase, *uxoris Lot*, 'Lot's wife', is a morphologically unmarked genitive, as normally happens to Semitic names ending in a consonant. The inflection on *uolocrū* is a notable success (*JM* 30). Yet there is no form here in -*orum* or -*arum*: the phrase *cuncopitores res alienas* (*DDM* 23) noticeably avoids the obvious genitives of *rerum alienarum* in favour of an accusative form only awkwardly construable as the object of the verbal root (*concupiscunt*) of the nominalised agent; and it is thus likely that the second text, which has no title in the manuscript, would not in fact have been entitled with such a splendid genitive as *(Joca) monachorum* (we have left it as such here out of convenience rather than conviction). Genitive singulars survive in set phrases such as *paradysus dī* (for *Dei*, *DDM* 14), *benenote dī* and *benenetas dī*, found in the same biblically based sections as the genitives within *duriciam cordis tuae, in diae ire, iusti iudicium dī* (*DDM* 17–18), *portas parad/si, in uentre citi*, and *uistimenta xp̃i* (*JM* 8, 15–16, 43). We also find *eius* and *cuius* (*JM* 34, 11, 37), but as we have already seen the oblique relative pronoun forms had anyway a longer life than in nouns; *cuius* even survived in Ibero-Romance, e.g. as Spanish *cuyo*, 'whose'.[8]

The functional basis of the accusative/nominative distinction was also slowly breaking down, with originally accusative forms capable of being used as sentence subjects or complements. Nominative forms, on the other hand, rarely appear outside subject position in these texts. This accurately reflects the way that the originally accusative forms came to have all-purpose functions in Romance. In these two texts they are particularly prone to appear as complements, in fact, rather than as subjects, as in *et sunt xxx filius et xxxx filias, Q̃d p̃uincias sū* and *Q̃d linguas sunt* (*JM* 5, 28, 29). In the first of these examples, the originally accusative

[8] J. Aguirre, 'Cujum pecus, anne Latinum?', *Tesserae* 3 (1997), pp. 43–87.

nature of the masculine form seems clear enough (*filius* = *filios*), but the femi-nine form *filias* raises a question; specialists in the history of Italian have suggested that the *-as* inflection may in fact have come to be nominative in Italy before the functional distinction itself broke down. This hypothesis is anyway controversial; although sceptics such as myself are a minority, it still seems inadvisable to draw geographical conclusions from this use of *filias*. There are singular examples of ostensibly accusative subjects too: both *euam* and *baptismo* (missing a tilde) seem to be subjects in *JM* 8. Conversely, *hec* seems once to be used instead of an ap-parently required accusative *hanc* (*DDM* 19). Since Old French Romance (that is, in the north) usually maintained the morphological subject–object distinction, these confusions may be usable as evidence for a textual provenance from further south.

11. *Gender.* The neuter gender eventually fell from use in speech as a morpho-logical category for nouns. But the lexical items concerned often survived, which meant that they needed to be assigned to one of the other two categories. Some-times the choice was not obvious. *Cor*, for example, which appears as a neuter in the Vulgate version of Rom. 2.5 in the phrase 'secundum . . . inpaenitens cor', needs a genitive in this sermon's rephrasing of that text, and *cordis tuae* (*DDM* 18) shows that the scribe took it to be feminine. This is in contrast to later Romance, where the word is regularly masculine (e.g. French *le cœur*, Italian *il cuore*), but a long period of indecision around these centuries is only to be expected. *Corpus*, however, seems to be still neuter in *JM* 8 (which is probably a quotation from an apocryphal source), although it could be either neuter or masculine in *JM* 12; *sepulchrum* (*JM* 16, 37) is probably neuter, being the sentence subject, but the use of ostensible accusative forms as subjects elsewhere means that this conclusion is not secure. The form *miliarios* rather than standard *milliaria* (*JM* 22) shows an example of reassignment of a word to the masculine gender, which is what tended to happen to those neuter nouns whose singular ended in *-um*. *Quit primus* (*JM* 1) offers us an adjective without a neuter form, *primus* being preferred in this subject position rather than the original neuter, *primum*; *quid*, being a pronoun, preserved its neuter form in speech for longer than the adjective did.

The plurals of neuter nouns, however, had usually ended in *-a*; these forms tended to get reanalysed as feminine singulars, and in this way to become separate lexical items from their original singular counterpart. Neuters in *-us* had plurals in *-ra*; Thus *hopera*, in the quotation from Rom. 2.6 (*DDM* 18) was neuter plural (*opera*, plural of *opus*); *milia*, *sidira* for *sidera* (plural of *sidus*) and *uistimenta* for *uestimenta* (*JM* 8, 39, 43) are still clearly plural in meaning. But we can also see attested here a further development; these neuter plurals in *-a* which were reinterpreted as feminine singulars could then acquire new plural forms in *-ae*, and this is what we have here in *genere* (*JM* 30), which can only be the plural of *genera* (which was in turn originally the plural of *genus*) rather than the ablative of *genus* that it resembles.

The plural is also spelt as *genera* (*JM* 31). We see attested here a transitional phase in which both old (*genera*) and very new (*genere*) co-exist as plurals of the neuter noun *genus*, which is the kind of variation that historical sociolinguistics tells us to expect in speech, so it is not surprising to find it attested also in writing.

*Dies* is masculine in the general plural phrase *dies mali* (*dies malos*) and feminine in the singular and specific *dies irae*; but this alternation had been normal Imperial usage.

12. *Imparisyllabicity.* Lowe commented on the three forms *reges*, *precepes* and *caesares* used here instead of their nominative singulars (all in answers, *JM* 11, 20, 23), explaining them as analogically reconstructed forms designed to reduce the psychological awkwardness involved in having a nominative singular form (such as *rex*, *princeps* or *Caesar*) with a syllable fewer than the other forms in the paradigm. This suggestion is probably right, even though each written form here ostensibly looks more like a genitive, and even though there seems to have been no perceived problem elsewhere with the monosyllable *rex* (*JM* 19, 24, in the same section).

13. *Verb morphology.* The verb inflections of Latin lasted better in speech than the nominal ones, and a majority are still there in Romance. Synthetic passives, however, were disappearing gradually from speech. This change was definitely known about, and scribes must have been warned about it in their training, since we can see in many texts over several centuries that keen scribes tended to include unnecessary endings in -*ur* where an active verb might have been preferable in any case. This uncertainty was exacerbated by the presence of deponent verbs, which were commoner in Latin than tends to be realised by the modern Romanist, with several verbs available for use both as deponents and as actives.

Passive infinitives, however, did not survive in speech, with the active infinitive being usable instead (as it is in Romance even now with passive meaning, in some circumstances); thus it is unsurprising to find *ledere* rather than *laedi*, *iud/care* rather than *iudicari* and *dañare* rather than *damnari* (*DDM* 11–13). Yet the standard forms of deponents are still also accessible to the scribe, as in *operares*, *letares*, *mintiatur*, *dinetur* (*DDM* 2, 8, 25), *es natus* and *natus est*, *moriebatur* and *locutos ē* with past meaning (*JM* 3, 6, 8, 26). And some passive forms seem genuinely to be passives in meaning as well, such as *seruetur* (*DDM* 9), *dabitor; est sepultus, factus est, sepolti sunt* and *ucisus ē* with their standard past meaning (*JM* 8, 16, 20, 21, 24, 40, 41, 45); the point here is that in Romance compound verb forms with past participles have the same tense as their auxiliary, so compounds such as *factus est* would thus in Romance be present tenses ('is made' rather than as here, 'was made'). This latter development might in fact be attested in *JM* 47; *erat mortuos* could mean 'had died', in the standard way, but the simple past 'died', as in Romance, may make better sense.

The phrase *quod sequitur* (*DDM* 18) is the kind of phrase in which obsolescent (or 'crepuscular', the description used in Green's acute analysis of the history of these inflections) morphology survives longer than in free active speech.[9] The old passive morphology was replaced to some extent in Romance by extending the use of the syntactically reflexive construction to semantically non-reflexive meanings;[10] the reflexive grammar of the sentence *ne nusmed ipsus in diae ela malis adamus* (*DDM* 25) is an example of the semantically transitional state during this change, because the scribe might still have meant 'lest we add ourselves' but also could well have actually meant 'lest we be added'. *Te ipsum perdes* (*DDM* 5) might have been similarly ambiguous. As in so many other examples of this time, the advent of the new did not mean the immediate loss of the old (in this case, new and old meanings of the reflexive), and there were many centuries in which texts could attest both old and new simultaneously. This is not because the texts were a 'mixture of Latin and Romance', but just because the language of the time was flexible and versatile enough to contain both old and new phenomena, perhaps with differing pragmatic value.

The only other non-standard phenomenon in the verb morphology here seems to be the loss of the present participle in *-ns, -ntis*, at least in a verbal sense, and its replacement in speech by the gerund in [-ndo]; this inflection, with participial meaning, is spelt here as *-ndum*, in *uiuindum* and *psiquendum* (*JM* 10, 19); *redimentes* (*DDM* 20) is in the biblical quotation. The loss of this usage is an argument against Lowe's suggestion that *suspiontam* (*JM* 42) represented *suspicientem* rather than *suspensam*.

Irregular verbs are produced excellently. Forms such as *uis* (*DDM* 8–13), *obtulit, uicit* and *tetigit* (*JM* 7, 10, 15) were to be regularised in speech, but there is no hint of that development here; perhaps the process was not yet far advanced, or perhaps the scribe had been fully awake in that lesson also. The form *tangit* is used for past meaning instead of *tetigit* (*JM* 27), but this probably represents a choice of the wrong tense rather than an alternative form of the past; and the *i* in *spectis* (*DDM* 10) could be a confusion abetted by the choice between *(de)spicis* and *(de)spectas*.

14. *Derivational morphology*. One of the vital areas of linguistic enterprise of the age lay in the lively use of ostensibly unnecessary verbal prefixes. We have already seen how the potential use of the prefix *ex-* can confuse our analysis of the prothetic *e-* before [s] and a consonant, at least in verbs. The scribe of these texts particularly demonstrates a liking for the prefix *de-* (here written *di-* or *dl-*), as can be seen in *dimmortuos, duiholauet* (*JM* 3, 6) and *dlripias* (*DDM* 7), none of whose prefixes are remotely needed or even helpful. Perhaps this co-existence of many verbs

[9] J.N. Green, 'The collapse and replacement of verbal inflection in late Latin/early Romance: how would one know?', in *Latin and the Romance Languages*, ed. Wright, pp. 83–99.

[10] R. Wright, 'La sintaxis reflexiva con semántica no agentiva', in *Actas del I Congreso Nacional de Latín Medieval*, ed. M. Pérez González (León, 1995), pp. 415–32.

with and without a prefix *de-* can also explain the apparent loss of *de-* in *spectis* (*DDM* 10).

As Lowe pointed out, our scribe prefers the prefixes to be transparent; hence *adtendis* rather than *attendis* (*DDM* 7), *cūtemnis* and *cuncopitores* rather than *con-* (*DDM* 17, 23), *inposuit* rather than *im-* (*JM* 32), although, pace Lowe, *inperator* does not really include a prefix *in-* (*JM* 23) despite its etymological link with *paro*. The question of whether such prefixes should be transparent was one which exercised the compilers of works *De Orthographia*, and it seems that this scribe's teacher had been on the side of transparency rather than phonetic transcription.

15. *Syntax*. The word order may not seem 'classical', but even in Imperial times any order of Subject, Verb and Object was possible; and that is still the case here, as it was in much early Romance.[11] The main detail of syntactic interest in these texts is that originally precise subordinating conjunctions (complementisers) can be used for other purposes; *ut* is found after *uis* for example (in *DDM* 8–9), 'you do not wish that one should lie to you', 'you want faith to be kept by him towards you', rather than any kind of accusative or infinitive, or a *quod* clause. In *JM* 22 (*ut eā totam circis*) the force of the *ut* is so imprecise that a translation as equally imprecise as seems justified. The negative of *ut*, though, *ne* (*DDM* 25), keeps the precise meaning of 'purpose' that *ut* appears to have lost. *Ut* did not survive in Romance, perhaps in part precisely because it had lost any clear meaning. As well as *quod*, the words *quoniam*, *quare* and *quomodo* all seem available for use as all-purpose connectives; this is not surprising, and well attested elsewhere.[12] Conversely, the Vulgate's *quoniam* in Eph. 5.16 corresponds to *quod* in *DDM* 20.

16. *Vocabulary*. In addition to several details mentioned above, the following are worth noting: the *absque* of the biblical quotation from Daniel is replaced by *sene* here (*JM* 18), which corresponds to reconstructable early Romance, in which *absque* does not survive generally but *sine* became e.g. Spanish *sin*.[13] The Vulgate's *eius* in Rom. 2.6 corresponds to *sua* in *DDM* 18, which occurs here in some Vulgate manuscripts, and also reflects reconstructable early Romance in that all words for 'his/her' come from *suus* (e.g. Italian *suo*); but *eius* is still there too (*JM* 34). The Vulgate's *ambuletis* in Eph. 5.15 remains here, as *amboletes* (*DDM* 20); the Bible texts are not in general an example of 'Vulgar Latin', as Burton shows, but this is a case in point, attributable here to the Bible rather than to our scribe (this use of *ambulare* is often seen to be the root of French *aller*). The *capit* of *capit*

---

[11] H. Pinkster, 'Evidence for SVO in Latin?', in *Latin and the Romance Languages*, ed. Wright, pp. 69–82.

[12] Herman, *Vulgar Latin*, 6.3, pp. 88–91.

[13] F. Diez, *Etymologisches Wörterbuch der Romanischen Sprachen* (Bonn, 1878), p. 353, registers *asca* from this etymon in Lombardy.

*te Paradisus Dei* (*DDM* 14) appears to be in the transitional semantic stage from 'capture' to 'have room for', which is to go even further later in Spanish *caber* ('to fit in'), rather than being on its way to Italian *capire*, 'understand'; this may be usable as geographical evidence against Italian provenance. *Hunc* seems to be used for *hinc* in *JM* 8, which is an understandable confusion between two similar words both probably falling out of use; *modo* in the same passage was probably reflecting spoken usage (cf. Old Italian *mo'*, also meaning 'now'). The form *semul* (*JM* 13, 14) is an orthographic cross between *simul* ('at the same time') and *semel* ('once'), meaning the same as *semel*; perhaps we could see this form as evidence for a hypothesis that the combined phonetic and semantic similarity of the two words led to sufficient confusion for both words to drop from use, since neither survives in Romance.

In *JM* 44–5 we find *plouet* and *pluit*, meaning the same, 'rains'. *Pluit* was the older form. Both probably existed in Romance (cf. Italian *piove* but French *pleut*), and it is instructive to see both in close proximity here, again attesting neatly (as did *genera* and *genere*) the fact that the language of this time is variable; new features had come in, but the corresponding old features had not necessarily gone.

17. *Dialect geography.* There are a few slight indications mentioned above that the scribe is not working in northern France or in the Iberian or Italian peninsulas. This is negative evidence; the form *quamdius*, found as *quandius* in Romance in southern France *c.* AD 1000 and (apparently) nowhere else, could be positive evidence; and overall, if only by a process of elimination, Burgundy seems on linguistic grounds a reasonable location for the scribe (or scribes) of this text, and thus probably for the scriptorium as well.

18. *Implications of the linguistic analysis.* It is tempting to consider whether the above analysis has implications for an attempt to understand the method of composition or of reading these two texts. We can at least confirm that the scribe was not merely making whimsical and random errors. He was preparing a written version of the early Romance language he actually spoke, but without bothering to polish it up into as formal a register as he did on other occasions. Many written texts would probably have gone through a transitional stage such as the one recorded here, before being eventually corrected and given their final archaic veneer (with the drafts being thrown away). The words *correctus* and *cultus* were in origin the past participles of the verbs *corrigere* and *colere*; that is, in the Romance-speaking areas, 'correct' written Latin was not merely correct but 'corrected' from a more spontaneous original state, and 'cultivated' Latin had been carefully tended to fruition from a vernacular seed. But in the unusual case of these two texts, this comparatively uncultivated version happens to have been made on a fully prepared quire, and thus been preserved for posterity. The evidence is also consistent with the hypothesis that he may have prepared these texts from dictation, rather than

directly from a previous textual version; many of the small details are unlikely to have been in any text being copied.

Most of the non-classical phenomena here could be considered as being actual errors only if we assume that aiming for the archaically correct form was the scribe's intention. But clearly, on these folios that was not what he was doing. Further correction would have been laborious; the usual point of it lay in the fact that the great advantage of following the established standards of spelling, and to a lesser degree of morphology and syntax, lies in the immediate ability of the reader to recognise the words and therefore understand the sense. In the modern English-speaking world it might be easier for us to write 'sox' and 'hy' to represent the words pronounced by everybody as [soks] and [haj], but an intended reader can be more readily trusted to recognise the normal forms, *socks* and *high*. It is worth pointing out that this advantage of standard spelling, even if it includes 'silent' letters, holds for the reader-aloud as well; in these early medieval centuries as in any other, the main task of the *lector* was to recognise the separate individual words, find their entry in his mental lexicon – which includes the word's phonology – and then pronounce them according to his normal phonetics; that is, operating logographically (one word at a time) rather than phonographically (one sound at a time). There is no need to assume that the orthography should be a kind of phonetic script exactly isomorphic with speech, and still less that it actually was; which is fortunate, for otherwise Modern English and seventh-century Romance would have been impossible to read aloud intelligibly. The implication, therefore, of the scribe's insouciance in this matter on these folios seems to be that he is not really intending other people to read them. They are written here for his own benefit. He can read his own writing and understand his own spelling well enough, presumably, and maybe he was the only intended reader.

This may imply that he was going to read this version of the *De dies malus* aloud himself, verbatim, as a sermon; although it also seems quite possible that these were prompt notes, and any actual sermon in practice given on the basis of the text in this manuscript would have been longer than this. It also seems to imply that he may have been intending to read aloud the questions in the *Joca monachorum* himself, perhaps with the answers being included merely in case he forgot them. I see the *Joca* (at least in this incarnation) as being a kind of quiz. *Joca*, of course, are 'games' (including word-play) rather than 'jokes'; the English word 'joke' was borrowed from the Latin word and then subsequently changed its meaning to 'joke', while the Latin word itself persisted with its original meaning, as seen in French *jeux*, Italian *giuochi*, Spanish *juegos*. This title is not there in this manuscript, so we need not necessarily see this version of the quiz as specifically intended for monks (or oblates), although that remains likely in view of the contents (despite their relatively trivial air).

If the scribe of these texts is the same as that of the rest of the manuscript, as is possible, he made more of an effort on the other folios to be 'correct'. Lowe believed that he probably was the same scribe, using a less formal script in the same way as I suggest he was using less formal composition techniques. More correct old-fashioned orthography would make a text easier for somebody else to read, and to read aloud, but correct archaic morphology and syntax might well have made it harder for the Romance-speaking listener to such a reading to understand (whereas the Germanic-speaker, who had learnt Latin as a foreign language, from texts, would probably prefer the archaic alternative); so we may be entitled to deduce that the intended listeners to these texts, when later read aloud, were of Romance native speech. There is no space here to analyse the grammar of the other texts in this manuscript, but it seems initially reasonable to suggest that the main difference between the formal and informal styles is in the spelling; perhaps we can, then, further conclude that the other texts were indeed meant for other people than just the scribe to read aloud, in comparatively formal settings, in exactly the way that our two texts were not.

As to why these texts are here at all, in this form, one could propose the following scenario; a visitor from one monastery to another has copied the Commentary on the Gospels which is the first text in the quire, but has left a large amount of blank space after that, either by accident or design. The visitor then takes advantage of the space, and asks his host to read him the Sermon and the *Joca* at slow dictation speed, which he takes down in a comparatively informal mode and has no time to 'correct' before he has to travel home.[14]

[14] Here we have strayed from philological and linguistic analysis into sociophilological speculation; see my *A Sociophilological Study of Late Latin*, Utrecht Studies in Medieval Literacy 10 (Turnhout, 2003).

# 7

## *The liturgy of the Bobbio Missal**

YITZHAK HEN

For more than three centuries the liturgy of the Bobbio Missal has been classified as Gallican.[1] Even those who insist that the Bobbio Missal is an Irish or a north Italian compilation admit that its liturgy is, to a greater extent, Gallican.[2] But what does 'Gallican' mean? In his, now largely out-of-date, survey of liturgical manuscripts, Klaus Gamber gives the following definition:

The so-called Gallican rite was in use not only in Gaul, but also in large parts of Spain and northern Italy (Gallia Transpadana). It is different from the African-Roman rite, which spread from the seventh and eighth centuries not only in (north) Africa, where at a fairly early stage the Latin liturgical language had developed, but also in central and southern Italy, as well as in parts of Spain and the Balkans.[3]

Such a definition, however, is extremely confusing and misleading. It groups under a single rubric the various liturgical traditions of northern Italy, Merovingian Gaul and Visigothic Spain, assuming that they are all mere derivatives of the Roman rite, and therefore represent a parallel stage in a linear line of liturgical development.[4] However, in the last twenty years there has been an increasing scholarly

---

* This paper was writtten during a sabbatical year at the Netherlands Institute for Advanced Study in the Humanities and Social Sciences (NIAS). I would like to express my gratitude to the rector, staff and fellows of NIAS for providing an ideal environment for research.

[1] The first to classify the liturgy of the Bobbio Missal as Gallican was J. Mabillon, *Museum Italicum seu collectio veterum scriptorum ex bibliothecis Italicis* (Paris, 1687), I.2, pp. 273–7.

[2] See, for example, E. Bishop, *Liturgica historica* (Oxford, 1918), p. 58 n. 3; see also pp. 90–2, 178–9; *CLLA* 220, pp. 167–9. For more details on the debate over the origins of the Bobbio Missal, see above pp. 1–7.

[3] *CLLA* I, p. 153: 'Der sog. gallikanische Ritus war außer in Gallien auch in weiten Gebieten Spaniens sowie in Norditalien (Gallia Traspadana) in Gebrauch. Er is zu unterscheiden vom afrikanisch-römischen Ritus, dessen Verbreitungsgebiet bis zum 7./8. Jh. außer (Nord-) Afrika, wo schon früh die lateinische Liturgiesprache ausgebildet worden ist, Mittel- und Süditalien sowie Teile Spaniens un des Balkans war.'

[4] On the so-called Gallican liturgy, see W.S. Porter, *The Gallican Liturgy*, Studies in Eucharistic Faith and Prayer 4 (London, 1958). For further bibliography, see C. Vogel, *Medieval Liturgy: An Introduction to the Sources*, trans. and rev. W.G. Storey and N.K. Rasmussen (Washington, DC, 1981), pp. 275–7.

interest in issues related to the formation of western liturgy, and modern schol-arship is revealing just how profoundly creative and dynamic were the various sub-divisions of the western rite.[5] It is a commonplace today that each of the branches of western liturgy developed in their own peculiar ways, responding to local needs and preferences, although it is assumed that all of them made ample use of Roman material. Against this background, Gamber's definition of the Gallican rite is untenable anymore, and it was emphatically not the definition Mabillon had in mind when he argued that the liturgy of the Bobbio Missal is Gallican.[6] 'Liturgia Gallicana' for Mabillon and many of his followers simply meant the liturgy of Merovingian Gaul, and that, I would argue, is how the term 'Gallican' should be understood and used. Let us, then, dwell for a moment on the features and characteristics of the Merovingian liturgy, in order to get a better understanding of the liturgy displayed by the Bobbio Missal.

### THE GALLICAN LITURGY

Very little that is certain can be said about the liturgical tradition of late an-tique and early medieval Gaul, mainly because of lack of evidence. But, even from the little evidence that survives in sermons, hagiography, poems and historical narratives (none of which is purely liturgical), the fifth and the sixth centuries in Gaul emerge as a rich and dynamic period of liturgical activity.[7] Fortunately, our understanding of the Merovingian liturgy (especially in the seventh and eighth centuries) does not depend solely on non-liturgical sources. A remarkable series of liturgical manuscripts, such as the *Missale Gothicum*,[8] the *Missale Gallicanum Vetus*,[9] the *Missale Francorum*[10] and the Lectionary of

---

[5] For a general survey of western liturgies, see A.A. King, *Liturgies of the Past* (London, 1959); A.A. King, *Liturgies of the Primatial Sees* (London, 1957); P.-M. Gy, 'History of the liturgy in the west to the council of Trent', in *The Church at Prayer*, ed. A.G. Martimort, trans. M.J. O'Connell, 4 vols. (London, 1986–7), I, pp. 45–61.

[6] See Mabillon, *Museum Italicum*, I.2, pp. 273–4 and 277.

[7] See Y. Hen, *The Royal Patronage of Liturgy in Frankish Gaul to the Death of Charles the Bald (877)*, HBS subsidia 3 (London, 2001), pp. 21–8.

[8] Vatican City, BAV, Reg. lat. 317 (Burgundy, s. viii[in]); *CLA* I.106; *CLLA* 210. For an edition, see *Missale Gothicum*, ed. L.C. Mohlbeg, Rerum Ecclesiasticarum Documenta, series maior 5 (Rome, 1961). See also E. Rose, *Communitas in commemoratione. Liturgisch Latijn en liturgische gedachtenis in het Missale Gothicum (Vat. reg. lat. 317)*, (PhD thesis, Utrecht, 2001).

[9] Vatican City, BAV, Pal. lat. 493 (?Chelles/Faremoutier/Rebais, s. viii[1]); *CLA* I.92–3; *CLLA* 212–14. For an edition, see *Missale Gallicanum Vetus*, ed. L.C. Mohlberg, L. Eizenhöfer and P. Siffrin, Rerum Ecclesiasticarum Documenta, series maior 3 (Rome, 1958).

[10] Vatican City, BAV, Reg. lat. 257 (?Poitiers/Faremoutier/Rebais, s. viii[1]); *CLA* I.103; *CLLA* 410. For an edition, see *Missale Francorum*, ed. L.C. Mohlberg, L. Eizenhöfer and P. Siffrin, Rerum Ecclesiasticarum Documenta, series maior 2 (Rome, 1957).

Luxeuil,[11] bears witness to the prolific liturgical productivity of later Merovingian Francia,[12] and juxtaposed with the information conveyed by Pseudo-Germanus' commentary on the mass,[13] and by other narrative sources, the structure and significance of the Merovingian liturgy begin to emerge.[14]

Yet, paradoxically, delineating the various general characteristics of the Merovingian liturgy is extremely slippery, first and foremost because of its two principal characteristics, that is, diversity and eclecticism. A striking degree of diversity characterised the Merovingian rite, and it is apparent on two different levels of the liturgical practice.[15] On the first level, different feasts for different saints were celebrated at different Merovingian centres, and thus turned the liturgical calendar into a very local one. Moreover, different votive and private masses are listed in each of the liturgical manuscripts we possess, probably in response to local demand and personal inclinations of those who commissioned the books. On the second level are the different prayers and reading passages that were assigned to the masses in the different sacramentaries and lectionaries. These reflect not only a diversity in local custom and usage, but also different ideals and standards on the part of the composers.[16]

The diversity which characterised the Frankish rite was considerably enriched by eclecticism. Merovingian liturgy was constantly under a variety of external influences, most notably Roman, but also Mozarabic (Visigothic), northern and southern Italian and Anglo-Saxon,[17] and consequently many prayers and customs which originated outside Francia were embedded in the Frankish rite. In turn, the Frankish liturgy itself influenced the liturgical development and creativity

[11] Paris, BNF 9427 (Luxeuil, s. vii–viii); *CLA* V.579; *CLLA* 255. For an edition, see *Le Lectionnaire de Luxeuil-Paris, ms. lat. 9427: édition et étude comparative*, ed. P. Salmon, Collectanea Biblica Latina 7 (Rome, 1944).

[12] See Hen, *The Royal Patronage of Liturgy*, pp. 28–33.

[13] Pseudo-Germanus, *Expositio antiquae liturgiae gallicanae*, ed. E.A. Ratcliff, HBS 98 (London, 1971). On this treatise, see Hen, *The Royal Patronage of Liturgy*, pp. 5–7, and see there for further references.

[14] See, for example, Y. Hen, *Culture and Religion in Merovingian Gaul, A.D. 481–751* (Leiden, New York and Cologne, 1995), pp. 43–153; Hen, *The Royal Patronage of Liturgy*, pp. 28–41; P. Bernard, *Du chant romain au chant grégorien* (Paris, 1996), pp. 639–709.

[15] See, for example, Hen, *The Royal Patronage of Liturgy*, pp. 30–3; Hen, 'Unity in diversity: the liturgy of Frankish Gaul before the Carolingians', in *Unity and Diversity in the Church*, ed. R.N. Swanson, Studies in Church History 32 (Oxford, 1996), pp. 19–30; Bernard, *Du chant romain au chant grégorien*, pp. 660–86.

[16] For various examples, see Hen, *The Royal Patronage of Liturgy*, pp. 31–3.

[17] See, for example, Porter, *The Gallican Liturgy*, pp. 19–53; C. Vogel, 'Les échanges liturgiques entre Rome et les pays francs jusqu'à l'époque de Charlemagne', in *Le Chiese nei regni dell'Europa occidentale e i loro rapporti con Roma sino all'800*, Settimane 7 (Spoleto, 1960), pp. 185–295; Y. Hen, 'The liturgy of St Willibrord', *Anglo-Saxon England* 26 (1997), pp. 41–62; Hen, 'Rome, Anglo-Saxon England and the formation of the Frankish liturgy', *Revue Bénédictine* 112 (2002), pp. 301–22.

in Visigothic Spain, Anglo-Saxon England, northern Italy and even Rome.[18] It is, then, not at all surprising to find prayers and practices common to both the Merovingian liturgy and to those liturgies that influenced it or were influenced by it, and it is not always clear in which direction such an influence operated.

Thus, both the diversity and the eclecticism of the Merovingian practice make it almost impossible to delineate clear-cut boundaries between what is 'Gallican' and what is not. Nevertheless, some observations can be made. Apart from diversity and eclecticism, the third major characteristic of the Merovingian liturgy is the language and style of its prayers, which are often described as 'rhetorical and effusive, or at worst long-winded and bombastic in a way which contrasted strongly with Roman sobriety'.[19] The verbosity and peculiar style of Frankish liturgists are best manifested in the so-called episcopal benedictions. Although in Rome short benedictions were often given by the celebrant after communion,[20] elaborate episcopal benedictions *ad populum* were basically a Gallican innovation devised by the Merovingian church.[21] These benedictions were, as Mayr-Harting puts it, 'the perfect expression in worship of Gaulish episcopal might',[22] and unlike the Roman short formulaic and succinct benedictions, they tend to be prolonged with a colourful language, full of images and ideas, and sometimes even opaque theology. No wonder Pope Zacharaias described them as vainglorious, and heartily advised Boniface not to use them.[23] Although at first glance these benedictions seem to be less cultivated and learned than their Roman counterparts, their florid style, with its liking for metaphor and biblical expressions, makes them a unique and most eloquent witness to the liturgical vitality and creativity of Merovingian Gaul.

[18] See, for example, H. Mayr-Harting, *The Coming of Christianity to Anglo-Saxon England* (3rd edn, London, 1991), pp. 174–82; C. Cubitt, *Anglo-Saxon Church Councils c. 650–c. 850* (London and New York, 1995), pp. 127–32; Hen, 'The liturgy of St Willibrord', p. 48; J.M. Pinell, *De liturgiis occidentalibus cum speciali tractatione de liturgia hispanica*, 2 vols. (Rome, 1967); J.M. Pinell, 'Liturgia, A. Liturgia Hispánica', in *Diccionario de Historia Eclesiástica de España*, II (Madrid, 1972), cols. 1303–20; P.C. Díaz, 'Monasticism and liturgy in Visigothic Spain', in *The Visigoths. Studies in Culture and Society*, ed. A. Ferreiro (Leiden, Boston and Cologne, 1999), pp. 169–99, at pp. 191–3.

[19] Mayr-Harting, *The Coming of Christianity*, p. 177.

[20] See J. Jungmann, *The Mass of the Roman Rite: Its Origins and Development (Missarum Sollemnia)*, trans. F.A. Brunner (New York, 1951), pp. 294–7.

[21] For an excellent introduction to the episcopal benedictions, see *The Benedictional of Freising*, ed. R. Amiet, HBS 88 (1974), pp. 1–22. See also E. Dekkers, '"Benedictiones quas faciunt Galli". Qu'a voulu demander saint Boniface?', in *Lateinische Kultur im VIII. Jahrhundert. Traube-Gedenkschrift*, ed. A. Lehner and W. Berschin (Saint-Ottilien, 1989), pp. 41–6; Hen, *Culture and Religion*, pp. 69–70.

[22] Mayr-Harting, *The Coming of Christianity*, p. 179.

[23] Boniface, *Ep.* 87, ed. M. Tangl, *Die Briefe des heiligen Bonifatius und Lullus*, MGH Epistulae selectae 1 (Berlin, 1916), p. 198.

Other Merovingian peculiarities may be found in the liturgical calendar. For example, Rogation days are, as we all know, a special innovation of the Gallican-Merovingian church,[24] and in Merovingian sacramentaries they always appear before Ascension day.[25] Also, the feast of the *Cathedra Petri* was quite widespread in Merovingian Gaul,[26] and in Merovingian sacramentaries it is immediately followed by the mass for the Assumption of the Virgin Mary.[27] To these one can add feasts in honour of typical Merovingian saints, such as Symphorianus and Leodegarius who are commemorated in the *Missale Gothicum*,[28] or Genovefa who is mentioned in the Lectionary of Luxeuil.[29]

Further characteristics can be found in the order of celebrating the mass. For example, it was common in Merovingian Gaul to have three readings of passages from the Bible during the celebration of several feasts – one from the Old Testament Prophets, one from the Gospels and one from the Epistles.[30] Moreover, it was a normal practice in Merovingian Gaul to have the 'kiss of peace' before the eucharistic prayer,[31] and it may well be that the episcopal benediction in Merovingian Gaul was given right after the *Pater Noster* and before communion.[32] Unfortunately, though, these peculiar variations of the Frankish rite are almost impossible to detect in our liturgical manuscripts, since these manuscripts contain in most cases only the texts to be recited by the celebrant during mass (i.e. sacramentaries) or the various biblical readings (i.e. lectionaries).

Lastly, most Merovingian sacramentaries which represent the so-called 'Gallican' rite contain a huge variety of votive and private masses for various occasions, as well

---

[24] See Hen, *Culture and Religion*, pp. 63–4; Hen, *The Royal Patronage of Liturgy*, pp. 18 and 23–4; J. Hill, 'The *Litaniae maiores* and *minores* in Rome, Francia and Anglo-Saxon England: terminology, texts and traditions', *Early Medieval Europe* 9 (2000), pp. 211–46.

[25] See, for example, *Missale Gallicanum Vetus*, cc. 256–66, ed. Mohlberg *et al.*, pp. 55–7; *Missale Gothicum*, cc. 327–42, ed. Mohlberg, pp. 82–6 (ed. Rose, pp. 122–6); *Le Lectionnaire de Luxeuil*, nos. 54–7, ed. Salmon, pp. 137–68.

[26] See, for example, *Missale Gothicum*, cc. 148–57, ed. Mohlberg, pp. 43–5 (ed. Rose, pp. 63–7); *Le Lectionnaire de Luxeuil*, no. 23, ed. Salmon, pp. 66–8. See also P. Salmon, *Le Lectionnaire de Luxeuil. Etude paléographique et liturgique*, Collectanea Biblica Latina 9 (Rome, 1953), p. 41.

[27] In Gaul, the Assumption of the Virgin Mary was celebrated on 18 January.

[28] *Missale Gothicum*, cc. 414–18 and 425–31, ed. Mohlberg, pp. 101–2 and 104–6 (ed. Rose, pp. 147–8 and 153–5) respectively. See also Rose, 'Communitas in commemoratione', pp. 441–4 and 457–61.

[29] *Le Lectionnaire de Luxeuil*, no. 16, ed. Salmon, pp. 23–4.

[30] On the Gallican programme of readings, see Salmon's comments in *Le Lectionnaire de Luxeuil*, pp. lxxxvii–xcii, with his important remark in Salmon, *Le Lectionnaire de Luxeuil. Etude paléographique et liturgique*, pp. 54–7. See also Vogel, *Medieval Liturgy*, pp. 303–4; E. Palazzo, *A History of Liturgical Books from the Beginning to the Thirteenth Century*, trans. M. Beaumont (Collegeville, 1998), pp. 98–9.

[31] See *Expositio antiquae liturgiae gallicanae*, I.22, ed. Ratcliff, pp. 13–14; Gregory of Tours, *Decem libri historiarum*, ed. B. Krusch and W. Levison, MGH SRM I.1 (Hannover, 1951), VI.40, pp. 310–11. See also Hen, *Culture and Religion*, p. 69.

[32] See *Expositio antiquae liturgiae gallicanae*, I.26, ed. Ratcliff, pp. 15–16. See also Hen, *Culture and Religion*, pp. 69–70.

as a considerable selection of masses for the ordination of priests, bishops, monks and nuns.[33]

Having listed all these characteristics of the Merovingian-Gallican rite, some reservations must be made. First, it is crucial to remember that not all the characteristics mentioned above have to be present in a manuscript in order to classify its liturgy as 'Gallican'. Second, it may well be that some of these characteristics are also common to other liturgies, such as the Mozarabic or the northern Italian and, therefore, none of these characteristics on its own is enough to classify a liturgical manuscript as 'Gallican'. Third, differentiating between what is Roman and what is Gallican is not always simple. We know very little about the liturgy celebrated in early medieval Rome,[34] and what we know derives almost exclusively from non-liturgical narrative sources, or from liturgical manuscripts which were copied and used in Merovingian Gaul, such as the Old Gelasian Sacramentary.[35] However, the use of such manuscripts in order to study the Roman liturgy of the sixth, seventh and eighth centuries has rightly been questioned in the past.[36] After all, these manuscripts, although using Roman material abundantly, were produced in Francia for the use of the Frankish church. Bearing these reservations in mind, let us see whether the liturgy of the Bobbio Missal qualifies for the title 'Gallican'.

## THE BOBBIO MISSAL AND THE GALLICAN LITURGY

The liturgical section of Paris, BNF lat. 13246 begins with the so-called Roman *canon missae* (to which I shall return later),[37] and continues immediately with readings and masses for the temporal and the sanctoral cycles. The two cycles are combined into one sequence of masses, which follows the liturgical calendar from Advent, through Easter and Pentecost, up to early November, when the feast of

---

[33] See, for example, *Missale Francorum*, cc. 1–79, ed. Mohlberg *et al.*, pp. 3–21; *Missale Gallicanum Vetus*, cc. 13–16, ed. Mohlberg *et al.*, pp. 6–8; *Liber sacramentorum Romanae aecclesiae ordinis anni circuli (Sacramentarium Gelasianum)*, ed. L.C. Mohlbeg, L. Eizenhöfer and P. Siffrin, Rerum Ecclesiasticarum Documenta, series maior 4 (Rome, 1960), cc. 1313–700, pp. 191–248; *Le Lectionnaire de Luxeuil*, nos. 69–80, ed. Salmon, pp. 197–217.

[34] On the liturgy of Rome, see G.G. Willis, *A History of Early Roman Liturgy to the Death of Pope Gregory the Great*, HBS subsidia 1 (London, 1994); A.A. King, *The Liturgy of the Roman Church* (London, 1957).

[35] For an attempt to reconstruct the supposedly Roman liturgy of the seventh century by using the Old Gelasian Sacramentary, see A. Chavasse, *Le sacramentaire gélasien (Vaticanus Reginensis 316). Sacramentaire presbytérial en usage dans les titres romains au VIIe siècle* (Paris and Tournai, 1957).

[36] See, for example, Chavasse's critics, J. Janini, *Analecta Taraconensia* 31 (1958), pp. 196–8; C. Coebergh, 'Le sacramentaire gélasien ancien', *Archiv für Liturgiewissenschaft* 7 (1961), pp. 45–88; J.D. Thompson, 'The contribution of *Vaticanus Reginensis* 316 to the history of western service books', *Studia Patristica* 13 (1975), pp. 425–9.

[37] See below, pp. 150–2.

St Martin of Tours was celebrated (11 November). It has two masses in honour of the Virgin Mary (*in sollemnitate sanctae Mariae* and *in adsumptione sanctae Mariae*),[38] which immediately follow the mass *in Cathedra sancti Petri*.[39] It also has a mass *in invencione sancte crucis*, a feast whose origins are 'Gallican';[40] and it places the Rogation days just before the mass *in Ascensione Domini*.[41]

The sanctoral cycle of the Bobbio Missal is also revealing. Like most Merovingian sacramentaries, the Bobbio Missal commemorates only a small number of saints days.[42] Twelve masses in honour of specific saints were incorporated into the sanctoral cycle of the Bobbio Missal,[43] and four other masses are dedicated to unspecified martyrs, confessors and virgins.[44] From among the saints which the Bobbio Missal mentions, only Sigismund may be considered as a distinctive Burgundian saint, whose unique appearance in the sanctoral cycle of the Bobbio Missal is extremely significant.[45] The rest are what may be called 'international' saints, whose cults had spread far and wide by the end of the seventh century. Even St Martin of Tours cannot be regarded as a distinctive Gaulish/Frankish saint. By the time the Bobbio Missal was composed, Martin had already appeared in the dazzling mosaic of Sant'Apollinare Nuovo in Ravenna, and had churches dedicated to him in Anglo-Saxon England.[46] Nevertheless, the incorporation of the feasts for St Martin and St Sigismund, as well as the fact that both Martin and Hilary are mentioned in the *memento* of the *canon missae*,[47] gives the sanctoral cycle of the Bobbio Missal a noteworthy 'Gallican' tint.

---

[38] *Bobbio* 122–33, pp. 37–41.    [39] Ibid. 115–21, pp. 35–7.

[40] Ibid. 288–92, pp. 86–8. On this feast, see L. Duchesne, *Origines du culte chrétien. Etude sur la liturgie avant Charlemagne* (5th edn, Paris, 1925), pp. 290–2; A. Bugnini, 'Croce, VII', in *Encyclopedia Cattolica*, IV (Rome, 1950), cols. 960–3; H. Leclercq, 'Croix, invention et exaltation de la vraie', *DACL* III.2 (Paris, 1914), cols. 3131–9.

[41] *Bobbio* 293–9, pp. 88–90 (Rogations) and 300–4, pp. 90–1 (Ascension).

[42] On the sanctoral cycles of Merovingian Gaul, see Hen, *Culture and Religion*, pp. 88–107. The most elaborate sanctoral cycle is that of the *Missale Gothicum*, which includes masses for twenty-seven saints' days; see Rose, 'Communitas in commemoratione', pp. 321–72. For the possible Anglo-Saxon influence on the sanctoral cycle of the *Missale Gothicum*, see Hen, 'Rome, Anglo-Saxon England and the formation of the Frankish liturgy', pp. 301–22.

[43] *Bobbio* 80–6, pp. 27–9 (Stephen); 87–93, pp. 29–30 (Holy Innocents); 94–100, pp. 31–2 (James and John); 115–21, pp. 35–7 (*Cathedra Petri*); 122–8, pp. 37–9 (Mary's Solemnity); 129–33, pp. 39–41 (Mary's Assumption); 313–21, pp. 94–7 (John the Baptist); 322–6, pp. 98–9 (John the Baptist's Passion); 327–33, pp. 99–101 (Peter and Paul); 334–8, pp. 101–2 (Sigismund); 360–7, pp. 107–10 (Martin); and 393–7, pp. 117–18 (Michael).

[44] Ibid. 339–44, pp. 102–4 (*Missa in sanctorum martyrum*); 345–51, pp. 104–6 (*Missa unius martyris*); 352–9, pp. 106–7 (*Missa de uno confessore*); and 368–76, pp. 110–12 (*Missa unius virginis*).

[45] See the contribution of Ian Wood to this volume, below pp. 206–18.

[46] See E. Ewig, 'Der Martinskult im Frühmittelalter', *Archiv für mittelrheinische Kirchengeschichte* 14 (1962), pp. 11–30 (repr. in E. Ewig, *Spätantikes und fränkisches Gallien*, ed. H. Atsma, 2 vols., Beihefte der Francia 3 (Sigmaringen, 1976–9), II, pp. 371–92; W. Levison, *England and the Continent in the Eighth Century* (Oxford, 1946), p. 259.

[47] *Bobbio* 11, p. 10.

The second liturgical part of the Bobbio Missal contains a small selection of votive and private masses for various occasions, and a considerable amount of episcopal benedictions, including benedictions for the consecration of monks and nuns.[48] This section concludes with the so-called *Paenitentiale Bobbiense*, which has some distinctive Merovingian parallels,[49] and with two short *orationes super penitentem*.[50]

As already noted by Mabillon, the diversity of the Frankish rite accounts for the fact that this manuscript is unlike any other liturgical manuscript known to us from the Merovingian period.[51] Yet, many of the Bobbio prayers can be found in other Merovingian sacramentaries, such as the *Missale Gothicum*, the *Missale Gallicanum Vetus*, the *Missale Francorum* and the Old Gelasian Sacramentary.[52] Moreover, following the 'Gallican' practice, the Bobbio Missal assigns three readings to several masses,[53] and the biblical readings assigned to each mass in the Bobbio Missal agree, in most cases, with the passages assigned to the very same feasts in the Lectionary of Luxeuil.[54] The eclecticism of the Frankish liturgy is well attested by the many prayers which, with minor changes and variations, could be traced in the *libelli missarum* of the *Sacramentarium Veronense* and in the Spanish *Liber ordinum* and the *Liber mozarabicus sacramentorum*.[55] However, these must not be taken to imply that the compiler of the Bobbio Missal copied those prayers directly from Roman or Mozarabic texts known to us, as thought by Stevenson with reference to the Bobbio Missal's nuptial blessings.[56] There is no evidence whatsoever to support such a claim, and as Lowe had already noted, 'the appearance of the same form in different texts . . . does not at all necessarily indicate that one has borrowed from the other. It is evidence rather of the use of common matter, already existing and accessible where the earlier text was compiled'.[57]

---

[48] Ibid. 375–576, pp. 112–73.

[49] Ibid. 577, pp. 173–6. On this penitential, see Rob Meens, below pp. 154–67.

[50] *Bobbio* 577–8, pp. 176–7.    [51] Mabillon, *Museum Italicum*, I.2, p. 275.

[52] See Lowe, 'Notes', *passim*.

[53] These masses are *De adventu domini*; *In natale domini*; *In initio quadragesimae*; *In traditione symboli*; *In Parasceue*; *Primo die paschae*; *Missa paschae*; *Missa S. Iohannis Baptistae*; *Missa de uno confessore*; *Missa S. Martini*; *In dedicatione ecclesiae*; and three *Missae dominicalis*.

[54] See Salmon's comparative table in *Le Lectionnaire de Luxeuil*, pp. civ–cxxiii.

[55] See Lowe, 'Notes', *passim*. For editions of these texts, see *Sacramentarium Veronense*, ed. L.C. Mohlbeg, L. Eizenhöfer and P. Siffrin, Rerum Ecclesiasticarum Documenta, series maior 1 (Rome, 1956); *Liber ordinum sacerdotal (Cod. Silos, Arch. monástico 3)*, ed. J. Janini, Studia Silensia 7 (Silos, 1981); *Liber missarum de Toledo y libros místicos*, ed. J. Janini, 2 vols., Instituto de estudios Visigótico-Mozárabes de Toledo, series litúrgica 3–4 (Toledo, 1982–3).

[56] See K. Stevenson, *Nuptial Blessing. A Study of Christian Marriage Rite* (London, 1982), pp. 56–7; and compare Hen, *Culture and Religion*, pp. 133–7.

[57] Lowe, 'Notes', p. 110.

The style and language of the Bobbio Missal point unmistakably to Merovingian Gaul.[58] A brief look at the short benediction for the mass *in natale apostolorum Petri et Pauli* of the *Sacramentarium Veronense* and the Bobbio Missal's *contestatio* for the very same day will clarify how different is the liturgical style of these two sacramentaries.

| *Sacramentarium Veronense* | *The Bobbio Missal* |
|---|---|
| [BENEDICTIO] | CONTESTATIO |
| Vere dignum: qui secundum promissionis tuae ineffabile constitutum apostolicae confessioni[s] superna dispensatione largiris, ut in ueritatis tuae fundamine solidatae nulla mortiferae falsitatis iura praeualeant; et quantaliuet exsistat errantium multitudino, illi sint redemptionis tuae filii et illis aeclesia tota numeretur, qui ab electorum tuorum principali traditione non dissonant: per.[59] | Vere dignum et iustum est · omnipotens deus te gloriosum · in sanctis tuis · te mirabilem · in tuis discipolis · declamare; te enim · uerum deum deprecantes · apostoli · in omnem terram sonum prebuerunt · et in fines · orbis terrae uerbum sancti · certamenis · tradedirunt ex quibus · beatum petrum · in fundamentum · aeclessiae conlocasti · cuius fide · in omnium discipolorum tuorum · gaudio confortasti · Huic gencium magistrum tradedisti · collegam nouissimo <nouissiomo> quidam in curso sed · aequalem · ad premium · Plus enim omnibus laborat in predicacione qui plus · in persecucione presumpserat |
| | Et quem saulum persequentem · nominabat: aeclesia · predicantem paulum appellat · par efficitur · petro · in passione, ut credatur · eius particeps esse in remuneracione; haec tu omnia · domine operaris · qui ad prophetis · demonstratis · ab angelis · adoraris · et ad omnem saeculum apostolorum lumine declararis · et ideo cum angelis et archangelis conlaud ·····[60] |

[58] See also the contributions by Els Rose and by Charles Wright and Roger Wright, above pp. 67–78 and 79–139 respectively.
[59] *Sacramentarium Veronense*, c. 282, ed. Mohlberg *et al.*, p. 37.
[60] *Bobbio* 333, pp. 100–1. I retain the punctuation as given by Lowe's edition.

The Merovingian *contestatio* is not only longer, but also much more vivid and flam-
boyant, ornamented with biblical allusions.[61] This tendency is apparent in many
of the Bobbio Missal's masses. In the *in invencione sancte crucis*,[62] to give just one
more example, the verbosity of our compiler is seen at its best. It reveals him as an
author whose orthography and morphology may have been shaky, but whose grasp
of rhetoric remained strong. His basic vocabulary is indeed relatively unadorned,
with a tendency to metaphor and biblical expressions; but nevertheless his prose
seems to be carefully structured, abounds in the effective use of rhetorical figures
and with a considerable attention to effects of metrics and rhythm. Moreover, the
fondness of Merovingian liturgists for apocryphal texts is also attested by the choice
of three readings, which were falsely ascribed to Jerome, the Epistle to Titus and
the Epistle to the Colossians.[63] Lastly, the names given by the author to the various
prayers of the mass – *collectio, post nomina, ad pacem* and *contestatio* – accord with
the names given to those prayers in other Merovingian sacramentaries, such as the
*Missale Gothicum* or the *Missale Gallicanum Vetus*.[64]

From all the details and characteristics adduced above, it appears that the Bobbio
Missal is indeed an honourable representative of the Frankish rite. Nevertheless,
several scholars in the past expressed some reservations regarding the 'Gallican'
nature of the Bobbio Missal. Louis Duchesne, for example, had written at the end
of the nineteenth century that 'le missel de Bobbio n'est qu'un des plus médiocres
témoins de l'usage gallican',[65] and Cyrille Vogel followed suit, arguing that 'the
Bobbio Missal is a rather poor witness to the Gallican rite because of its mixed
character'.[66] This mixed character, which Vogel defines as 'Romano-Gelasian *formulae*', is apparent in the presence of many Roman prayers throughout the Bobbio
Missal, as well as in the inclusion of the so-called Roman *canon missae* at the very
beginning of the liturgical section. Both the Roman prayers and the Roman *canon*,
according to Duchesne and Vogel, point to the author's heavy reliance on Roman
material, and consequently turn the Bobbio Missal into an unreliable source on
'Gallican' matters. The situation, however, is not as simple and straightforward as
Duchesne and Vogel believed.

---

[61] Compare, for example, the *contestatio*'s 'in omnem terram sonum prebuerunt et in fines orbis
terrae uerbum' with Rom. 10.18; and 'gencium magistrum' with II Tim. 1.11.

[62] *Bobbio* 290–2, pp. 86–8. This mass has no parallel in any of the Merovingian, Roman or Mozarabic
sacramentaries.

[63] These are *Bobbio* 352, 353 and 436, pp. 106 and 129 respectively. On the latter, see M. McNamara,
*The Apocrypha in the Irish Church* (Dublin, 1975), p. 104, no. 90. On the character of *Bobbio* 436, see
R. Busch, 'Die vielen Messen für das Seelenheil. Beobachtungen zum Frömmigkeitsgeschichtlichen
Kontext der "Missa pro uiuis et defunctis" des Bobbio-Missale', *Regulae Benedicti Studia* 19 (1997),
pp. 141–73, at pp. 159–60.

[64] See *Missale Gothicum, passim; Missale Gallicanum Vetus, passim*.

[65] Duchesne, *Origines du culte chrétien*, p. 167.      [66] Vogel, *Medieval Liturgy*, p. 324.

It is true that many prayers which can also be found in the *Sacramentarium Veronense* were incorporated into the Bobbio Missal. The mass *in natale Petri et Pauli* just cited, is an excellent case in point. Four of its *formulae* (that is, the two *collectiones* and the prayers *post nomina* and *ad pacem*) are found in four different masses of the *Sacramentarium Veronense*.[67] They were incorporated with minor changes and variations into a single mass *in natale Petri et Pauli*, and were duly supplemented with a very Gallican *contestatio*.[68] These are the facts; the rest, I am afraid, is a matter of individual interpretation.

If one is convinced that the liturgy of Frankish Gaul is a mere derivative of the Roman rite, and that it represents a stage of chaos and anarchy in the development of western liturgy,[69] then the Bobbio Missal is indeed a hybrid specimen, not at all representative of the so-called 'Gallican' rite. It has too much that is Roman incorporated into its prayers, indeed more than in many of the liturgical manuscripts known to us from Merovingian Gaul. But, if one is willing to accept the view that Merovingian Gaul was a fertile centre of liturgical activity,[70] things might look rather different. The composer of the Bobbio Missal picked and mixed various prayers which he found in his sources, arranged them according to his peculiar needs, changed and altered their language whenever he felt it was necessary and even added new prayers which were most probably composed by Merovingian authors,[71] if not by the compiler himself. Roman prayers, then, were only one sort of bricks used by the compiler of the Bobbio Missal in constructing this remarkable sacramentary, and choosing those Roman prayers was only one part of the creative process. Viewed from that perspective, the Bobbio Missal can clearly be regarded as an extraordinary witness to the vitality and richness of Merovingian liturgy.

The second point, that is, the presence of the Roman *canon missae* in the Bobbio Missal, is a bit more complicated. The liturgical section of the Bobbio Missal begins with the *Missa Romensis cotidiana*,[72] followed immediately by the so-called Roman *canon missae*,[73] which is the western equivalent of the eastern *anaphora*.[74] The

---

[67] *Bobbio* 329–32, p. 100, are to be found also in *Sacramentarium Veronense*, c. 280, ed. Mohlberg *et al.*, p. 37; c. 359, p. 49; c. 364, p. 49; and c. 313, p. 42 respectively.

[68] *Bobbio* 333, pp. 100–1. On this *contestatio*, see above, pp. 148–9.

[69] See, for example, Vogel, *Medieval Liturgy*, pp. 149–50; *Les 'Ordines romani' du haut Moyen Age*, ed. M. Andrieu, 5 vols., Spicilegium Sacrum Lovaniense 11, 23, 24, 28, 29 (Louvain, 1931–61), I, pp. xvii–xx; Bishop, *Liturgica historica*, p. 15.

[70] See, for example, Bernard, *Du chant romain au chant grégorien*, pp. 656–60 and 687–93; Hen, *The Royal Patronage of Liturgy*, pp. 25–41.

[71] This can be deduced from the language, style and content of the prayers.

[72] *Bobbio* 1–8, pp. 8–9.    [73] Ibid. 9–24, pp. 10–14.

[74] On the evolution of the western *canon*, see B. Botte, *Le canon de la messe romaine* (Louvain, 1935); A. Bouley, *From Freedom to Formula. The Evolution of the Eucharistic Prayer from Oral Improvisation to Written Text* (Washington, DC, 1981), especially pp. 159–215; E. Mazza, *The Origins of the Eucharistic Prayer*, trans. R.E. Lane (Collegeville, 1995), pp. 240–82.

*canon* is a succession of short prayers, commonly known by their opening words, which were supposedly recited in each celebration of the mass. It usually follows the dialogue *Sursum corda*,[75] a preface and the *Sanctus*,[76] and it traditionally begins with the words *Te igitur*. While a wide range of different *anaphorae* existed in the liturgy of the east, it was assumed by scholars that a single *canon* evolved in the west. This assumption, however, is based on extremely shaky ground. We know from various references in the writings of Jerome, Augustine and other late antique and early medieval authors that a certain *canon* for the celebration of the mass was followed in Rome already by the end of the fourth century.[77] Yet, we do not know exactly what this *canon* included. There is no full description of it in any of the sources, and none of them, not even Pope Innocent I's letter to Decentius of Gubbio or Ambrose of Milan's *De sacramentis*,[78] alludes to the fact that a single *canon* for celebrating the mass exists, and should be followed by all Christians. The first written versions of this so-called Roman *canon* were copied in Merovingian Gaul,[79] and its earliest complete version is none other than the *canon* of the Bobbio Missal.[80] The fact that similar versions of the *canon* were also incorporated into the Old Gelasian Sacramentary, the eighth-century Gelasian sacramentaries and the various versions of the Gregorian sacramentary[81] is insufficient to prove the Roman origins of this *canon missae*, whose first written versions were all copied in Francia.[82]

---

[75] The *Sursum corda* is missing from the Bobbio version of the *canon*.     [76] *Bobbio* 8, p. 9.

[77] See the various notes and commentary in Botte, *Le canon de la messe romaine*.

[78] See Innocent I, *Ep.* 25, PL 20, cols. 551–2; Ambrose of Milan, *De sacramentis. De mysteriis*, ed. and trans. J. Schmitz, Fontes Christiani 3 (Freiburg, 1990).

[79] See *Missale Francorum*, cc. 156–69, ed. Mohlberg *et al.*, pp. 31–3; *Sacramentarium Gelasianum*, cc. 1242–72, ed. Mohlberg *et al.*, pp. 183–7. It may well be that the *Missale Gothicum* also had such a *canon*, but all that survives is the first prayer of the *Missa cotidiana Rominsis*; see *Missale Gothicum*, c. 543, ed. Mohlberg, p. 122 (ed. Rose, p. 177). On the probable Roman canon of the Munich palimpsest Sacramentary, see A. Dold and L. Eizenhöfer, *Das irische Palimpsestsakramentar im Clm 14429 der Staatsbibliothek München*, Texte und Arbeiten 53–4 (Beuron, 1964), pp. 105*–6*. The so-called *canon missae* also appears in Dublin, Royal Irish Academy D.II.3 (the Stowe Missal) (?Tallaght; s. viii[ex]); *CLA* II. 268; *CLLA* 101; see *The Stowe Missal*, ed. G.F. Warner, HBS 31–2 (London, 1906–15), pp. 10–19.

[80] *Bobbio* 9–24, pp. 10–14.

[81] For a comprehensive edition of the *canon missae*, see *Canon missae*, ed. E. Moeller, I.M. Clément and B. Coppieters 't Wallant, Corpus orationum 10 [= CCSL 161]' (Turnhout, 1997).

[82] One has to bear in mind that both the Old Gelasian Sacramentary and the eighth-century Gelasian sacramentaries, although using Roman material, are basically Frankish compilations; see Hen, *The Royal Patronage of Liturgy*, pp. 29–32 and 57–61. As for the Gregorian sacramentaries, it is not improbable that the *canon missae* was introduced to them only in Francia. The earliest copy of a Gregorian sacramentary, the so-called *Hadrianum* (Cambrai, BM 164) is dated to 811/812, more than two decades after the initial arrival of the *Hadrianum* at the court of Charlemagne. Alternatively, the *canon* may have been introduced to the Gregorian sacramentary in Rome, under Frankish influence.

Moreover, there is no real basis for the claim that in the west a single, uniform way of celebrating the Eucharist existed, nor that a standard text was available. A quick look at the Bobbio Missal will prove this point. After the prayer for the *consummatio missae*, which concludes the so-called Roman *canon*, the compiler of the Bobbio Missal copied another unique 'Gallican' *canon*, which does not appear in any other sacramentary.[83] This *canon*, it appears, is an alternative *canon*, composed by someone familiar with the Frankish way of celebrating mass, who was also acquainted with some Gallican liturgical books or *libelli*.[84] Such an addition could only imply that no uniformity was at stake, and it clearly points to the distinctive local 'Gallican' character of the Bobbio Missal.

### THE USE OF THE BOBBIO MISSAL

Before concluding, one has to consider briefly the general type of this extraordinary liturgical manuscript. Was it designed for use in an episcopal church, a parochial one or a monastic community? The palaeographical and codicological features of the Bobbio Missal were enough for E.A. Lowe to conclude that 'what we have before us is the work of a private individual – a cleric who made a copy of the service book of which he stood in need, and which, to judge from its size, he probably carried about with him in his travels'.[85] I agree with Lowe's conclusion and I think we can provide it with some logistical support.

Following some observations made by N.K. Rasmussen,[86] I have elsewhere suggested possible criteria according to which one can detect the presbyteral destination of a liturgical handbook, and let me repeat these in brief.[87] First, the modest material aspects and the simple layout of the manuscripts. Second, the liturgical content of the volume and the fact that it combines several different types of liturgical books, such as a sacramentary and a lectionary, in one volume. And last, the inclusion of some canonical material, appended to the liturgical prayers. All these characteristics point to the probable presbyteral destination of the volume in question, and the Bobbio Missal seems to conform with all three criteria.

---

[83] *Bobbio* 25–33, pp. 14–16.   [84] See Lowe, 'Notes', pp. 113–16.

[85] Lowe, 'Palaeography', pp. 67–8.

[86] N.K. Rasmussen, 'Célébration épiscopale et célébration presbytériale: un essai de typologie', in *Segni et riti nella chiesa altomedievale occidentale*, Settimane 33 (Spoleto, 1987), pp. 581–603.

[87] See Y. Hen, 'A liturgical handbook for a use of a rural priest (Brussels, BR 10127–10144)', in *Organising the Written Word: Scripts, Manuscripts and Texts*, ed. M. Mostert, Utrecht Studies in Medieval Literacy 2 (Turnhout, in press).

Judging from the script and the manuscript layout, it is well justified to describe the Bobbio Missal as a *vade mecum* of a Merovingian clergyman. This impression gets further support whenever the Bobbio Missal is compared with the Merovingian *de luxe* liturgical manuscripts, such as the *Missale Gothicum* or the Old Gelasian Sacramentary. Moreover, the core of the Bobbio Missal is a unique combination of a lectionary and a sacramentary, to which some canonical material was added.[88] To these, our compiler appended several quires, which contain a plethora of miscellaneous material, such as a short selection from Pseudo-Theophilus' commentary on the Gospel of Matthew,[89] the Pseudo-Augustinian sermon entitled *De dies malus*,[90] the so-called *Joca monachorum*,[91] several incantation formulae,[92] instructions on how to celebrate a mass,[93] an Ordinal of Christ[94] and some computistical material.[95] It seems, therefore, safe to conclude that the Bobbio Missal is indeed a *vade mecum* of a bishop or even a priest, who offered liturgical services to secular, clerical[96] and monastic communities.[97] The liturgy of the Bobbio Missal, with its unique and practical selection of prayers and benedictions, supports this conclusion. A sacramentary like the Bobbio Missal would have been inadequate for the liturgical celebration in a Merovingian episcopal church.

---

[88] Such as a penitential; see *Bobbio* 577, pp. 173–6.

[89] *Bobbio*, pp. 1–4. On this text, see Y. Hen, 'The uses of the Bible and the perception of kingship in Merovingian Gaul', *Early Medieval Europe* 7 (1998), pp. 277–90, especially p. 280; Y. Hen, 'A Merovingian commentary on the four Gospels (CPL 1001)', *Revue des Etudes Augustiniennes* 49 (2003), pp. 167–87.

[90] *Bobbio*, pp. 4–5. On this sermon, see *Opera homiletica*, ed. J. Machielsen, I, Clavis Patristica Pseudoepigraphorum Medii Aevi 1A (Turnhout, 1990), no. 3314; and see the contribution by Charles Wright and Roger Wright to this volume.

[91] *Bobbio*, pp. 5–7. On the *Joca monachorum*, see Charles Wright and Roger Wright, above, pp. 79–139.

[92] *Bobbio* 497, p. 153.      [93] Ibid. 581, pp. 177–8.

[94] Ibid. 582, p. 178. On this Ordinal of Christ, see R. Reynolds, *The Ordinals of Christ from their Origins to the Twelfth Century*, Beiträge zur Geschichte und Quellenkunde des Mittelalters 7 (Berlin and New York, 1978), especially p. 58.

[95] *Bobbio* 548, p. 179.

[96] I follow here the argument put forward by Rob Meens, see below, pp. 154–67.

[97] The fact that this priest offered pastoral services to a community of nuns as well is suggested by the various benedictions for the consecration of nuns, virgins, abbesses and widows. See *Bobbio* 546–9, pp. 166–7.

# 8

## Reforming the clergy: a context for the use of the Bobbio penitential*

ROB MEENS

The Bobbio Missal is a unique document which allows us to recreate the ordinary functions of a priest in the Merovingian period. Its unique character, however, makes it, unfortunately, impossible to assess its representativeness. Are we dealing with a peculiar collection of texts, or does it represent a whole group of pastoral manuscripts from this period, which have not survived until the present day? From the later eighth and the ninth centuries we have some manuscripts of a pastoral character which can be compared to the Bobbio Missal, but from the Merovingian period they seem to be totally lacking.[1]

As André Wilmart has already observed, the Bobbio Missal allows a priest to perform all the necessary sacerdotal tasks.[2] Such priestly tasks apparently consisted of saying mass on Sundays and feast days, of baptising at Easter (nos. 234–54), taking care of the sick and the dying through prayers and liturgical anointment (nos. 377–83, 528–39) or blessing the matrimonial bed of a newly wed couple (nos. 550–2).[3] The priest would further bless a boy at the rite of his first shaving, the *barbatoria* (no. 555), or a well to liberate it from diabolical temptations and

---

* Research for this chapter has been supported by the Netherlands Organisation for Scientific Research (NWO).

[1] D. Bullough, 'The Carolingian liturgical experience', in *Continuity and Change in Christian Worship*, ed. R.N. Swanson, Studies in Church History 35 (Woodbridge, 1999), pp. 29–64, esp. p. 48; Y. Hen, 'Knowledge of canon law among rural priests: the evidence of two Carolingian manuscripts from around 800', *Journal of Theological Studies* 50 (1999), pp. 117–34; Y. Hen, 'Educating the clergy: canon law and liturgy in a Carolingian handbook from the time of Charles the Bald', in *De Sion exibit lex et verbum domini de Hierusalem. Essays on Medieval Law, Liturgy, and Literature in Honour of Amnon Linder*, ed. Y. Hen (Turnhout, 2001), pp. 43–58.

[2] Wilmart, 'Notice', p. 38: 'c'est à dire une collection de textes liturgiques, riche et variée, brève et maniable, permettant de subvenir aisément aux besoins ordinaires du culte'.

[3] For the liturgy of the sick and the dying in this period, see F. Paxton, *Christianizing Death. The Creation of a Ritual Process in Early Medieval Europe* (Ithaca and London, 1990); Merovingian marriage is discussed in Y. Hen, *Culture and Religion in Merovingian Gaul, A.D. 481–751* (Leiden, New York and Cologne, 1995), pp. 122–37.

clean it from some form of pollution (no. 556).[4] He could bless a vessel into which
something unclean had fallen (no. 557), but he could also simply bless apples
(no. 560). The book further contains evening and morning prayers (nos. 563–73),
exorcism formulae (nos. 540–4) and liturgical ordinations for the consecration of
nuns or an abbess (nos. 546 and 548). The *Joca monachorum* and other catechetical
material included in the manuscript might have been meant to instruct the priest,
but could also have served as source material for preaching.[5] The manuscript
furthermore contains a penitential, instructing a priest on how to hear confession
and on the proper penances to be imposed for a multitude of sins.[6] Prayers to
be said for the penitent, which immediately follow this handbook for a confessor
(nos. 578–9), were probably meant to be used in the liturgical setting of hearing
confession. Two more prayers of this sort were later added to the manuscript,
showing that the practice of hearing confession mattered to the user of the Missal
(nos. 585 and 586). In the votive masses, furthermore, the remission of sins is
a central theme, and recent research has emphasised the distinctiveness of the
Bobbio Missal since it contains the earliest specimens of such masses in the context
of tariffed penance.[7]

### CONFESSION IN THE BOBBIO MISSAL

It is on the priestly task of hearing confession that I will focus, because this aspect
seems to be of particular importance for the compilers and users of the Missal, but
also provides a clue for the question of who was using the Missal as a whole, thereby
illuminating the cultural context of its compilation. Indeed, if the manuscript of
the Missal can be dated to perhaps as early as the end of the seventh century, as is
argued here by Rosamond McKitterick, then it is not only the earliest witness to
several masses in which remission of sins holds a central place, but also the earliest

[4] On the *barbatoria*, see Hen, *Culture and Religion*, pp. 137–43. On the impurity of wells, see
R. Meens, 'Pollution in the early Middle Ages: the case of the food regulations in penitentials', *Early
Medieval Europe* 4 (1995), pp. 3–19, esp. pp. 17–18.
[5] For the *Joca monachorum*, see M. Bayless, 'The *Collectanea* and medieval dialogues and riddles',
in *Collectanea Pseudo-Bedae*, ed. M. Bayless and M. Lapidge, Scriptores Latini Hiberniae 14 (Dublin,
1998), pp. 13–24, at pp. 13–14, and Charles Wright and Roger Wright, above, pp. 79–139.
[6] For an introduction to these texts, see C. Vogel, *Les 'Libri Paenitentiales'*, Typologie des Sources
du Moyen Age Occidental 27 (Turnhout, 1978), and the 'Mise à jour' of this volume by A. Frantzen
(Turnhout, 1985); R. Kottje, 'Bußbücher', *Lexikon des Mittelalters*, II (Munich and Zurich, 1983), cols.
1118–22; I discuss new ideas challenging the older views of the history of penance and confession, in
'The frequency and nature of early medieval penance', in *Handling Sin: Confession in the Middle Ages*,
ed. P. Biller and A.J. Minnis, York Studies in Medieval Theology 2 (Woodbridge, 1998), pp. 35–61.
[7] A. Angenendt, 'Missa specialis. Zugleich ein Beitrag zur Entstehung der Privatmessen',
*Frühmittelalterliche Studien* 17 (1983), pp. 153–221, at pp. 182–3.

extant manuscript containing a penitential handbook, being somewhat earlier than the Copenhagen manuscript of the *Excarpsus Cummeani*.[8]

The Bobbio Missal contains not only prayers for the rite of hearing confession, but its votive masses regularly stress the remission of sins as one of the principal aims of prayers and the gifts of the faithful.[9] Alms offered at the altar were means to obtain remission of sin. As such they frequently appear in lists of commutations appended to penitential texts which provide alternatives for the fasts regularly prescribed in penitential rules. The mass for the living and the dead (nos. 438–440) is also closely related to the concept of tariffed penance.[10] The liturgical reading prescribed for this mass, moreover, looks much more like a sermon than a liturgical reading. In fact, it is the only reading which, although its title refers to the letter of Paul to the Colossians, is not based on a biblical text. It comprises a combination of excerpts from the Old Testament combined with material from apocryphal traditions, visionary and sermon literature and stresses man's sinfulness 'per singolus dies peccatum super peccatum facemus' and the need to lead a good life and give alms to extinguish his sins.[11] It mentions the sins of perjury, theft, adultery, giving false witness and accepting bribes, topics which are frequently discussed in penitential literature. This text, therefore, seems to be an extremely early example of a sermon preached to the laity by 'a simple parish priest' addressing the topic of Christian morals and the necessity to do penance.

A similar text, known as *De dies malus*, was later added to the Bobbio Missal. This text also discusses proper Christian conduct and particular vices, and exhorts the audience to do penance because 'the days are not evil for those who repent'.[12] The fact that it concerns a later addition to the original manuscript underlines the importance of hearing confession for the user of the Bobbio Missal. Another text added later to the core of the manuscript addresses the triad 'thought, word and deed' (no. 583), which according to Patrick Sims-Williams in this early period is a typical Irish phenomenon.[13] It discusses three ways which can lead a man to eternal damnation or to heavenly salvation: bad thoughts, wrong words and vile deeds on

---

[8] For which see R. Meens, 'The oldest manuscript witness of the *Collectio canonum Hibernensis*', *Peritia* 14 (2000), pp. 1–19.

[9] See, for example, *Bobbio* 428, p. 127: 'oblacionem dignanter accipias et in eius humilitatem intendas, peccata dileas, oracionem accipias'; see Angenendt, 'Missa specialis', p. 181.

[10] R. Busch, 'Die vielen Messen für das Seelenheil. Beobachtungen zum frömmigkeitsgeschichtlichen Kontext der "Missa pro uiuis et defunctis" des Bobbio-Missale', *Regulae Benedicti Studia* 19 (1997), pp. 141–73.

[11] *Bobbio* 436, p. 130: 'et elimosina qui extingit omni peccata'; see Busch, 'Die vielen Messen', pp. 159–60.

[12] See Charles Wright and Roger Wright, above, p. 101; *De dies malus* 22: 'non sunt dies mali ad penetentes'.

[13] P. Sims-Williams, 'Thought, word and deed: an Irish triad', *Ériu* 29 (1978), pp. 78–111, at p. 87; the Bobbio text is clearly related to the one in Zurich, Zentralbibliothek, Rheinau 140, discussed by Sims-Williams, 'Thought, word and deed', pp. 86–7.

the one hand, and holy thoughts, good words and their fulfilment in deeds on the other. Through the example of the six sins of Adam the text explains the major vices and as such it can be regarded as a short catechetical treatise on sins, a text that might have been useful in preaching, again stressing the importance of sins in the Missal as a whole.

### SINNING CLERICS?

Recent research has stressed that the votive masses and the mass for the living and the dead in the Bobbio Missal have to be interpreted in the light of the system of tariffed penance, introduced in Francia by Irish monks, of whom Columbanus was the most influential.[14] It would appear that penance was of particular importance for the compiler of the Bobbio Missal, as well as for its later users. Let us now look in some more detail at the *Paenitentiale Bobbiense*, the handbook for a confessor included in our manuscript. This text forms part of a group of penitentials, which are based upon the penitential attributed to the Irish *peregrinus* Columbanus, enriched by some conciliar material.[15] This group of texts, known as the 'simple Frankish penitentials', or the *paenitentialia simplicia*, consists of eight texts, which are known in only one or two manuscript copies. The synoptic edition which has lately been published by Raymund Kottje clearly shows their close affinity.[16] They all have a body of some forty canons in common, treating offences like murder, sexual licence, theft, forms of divination and the like, roughly in the same order.

The Bobbio penitential, just like the other texts from this group, begins with the case of homicide. The canon reads as follows: 'When a cleric has committed murder and killed his neighbour, he has to do penance for ten years in exile, after these let him be restored to his native land and let him give satisfaction to the relatives of the person he killed.' Then the text goes on to discuss the case in which someone has 'fallen to the depth of ruin and begotten a child'. Although the text does not specify that we are dealing with a clerical offence here, the content makes it obvious that it is aimed at someone leading a celibate life. The following canons dealing with homosexual relations, perjury, theft and various forms of superstitions and divination are similarly formulated in a general way, so as to leave the question open whether the perpetrator of the sin is a cleric or a layman. The eleventh canon,

---

[14] Angenendt, 'Missa specialis'; Busch, 'Die vielen Messen'.

[15] For the penitential attributed to Columbanus, see T. Charles-Edwards, 'The penitential of Columbanus', in *Columbanus. Studies on the Latin Writings*, ed. M. Lapidge, Studies in Celtic History 17 (Woodbridge, 1997), pp. 217–39.

[16] *Paenitentialia minora Franciae et Italiae saeculi VIII–IX*, ed. R. Kottje, L. Körntgen and U. Spengler-Reffgen, CCSL 156 (Turnhout, 1994), pp. 1–60.

dealing with a cleric or someone with a higher order resuming sexual relations with his wife, again clearly aims at members of the clerical order. There follow a number of sexual offences and, strangely enough in this context, the case of a violation of a grave, again formulated in a neutral way.[17] The following two sentences concerning the desecration of the Eucharist and the case of infanticide are unquestionably addressed to members of the clerical order. The cases of weather magic, self-mutilation, usury and burglary are again formulated in an unspecific way, while the next sentence concerns clerics shedding blood. The subsequent canon censuring the use of the so-called *sortes sanctorum*, if this form of divination really consisted of randomly opening a sacred book and interpreting the textual passage thus found, presupposes some kind of literacy among its practitioners.[18] After another unspecifically formulated canon addressing the problem of people making or fulfilling vows near springs and trees, or in other sacred places outside the church, the next canon censures clerics who return to the world and take a wife. The following canon treats the sin of falsehood (probably deceit in writing or in the use of weights) in a neutral manner, but the succeeding canon again specifically addresses clerics, this time censuring sexual relations with animals. In the ensuing sentences, treating such diverse topics as the celebration of the New Year, abortion, causing mental illness through the invocation of demons, sexual assault on (consecrated) virgins and widows, leading someone in captivity or burning down someone else's house, it remains unclear whether clerics or lay people are being addressed, although the canon penalising a woman for having had an abortion seems to be aimed at a lay audience. The last canon of the main body of the 'simple Frankish penitentials' about the neglect or mishandling of church property again suggests a clerical audience. From the canons that the Bobbio penitential has in common with the other 'simple Frankish penitentials', therefore, some are specifically addressed to members of the clergy, while the rest are formulated in a general way, so that they may refer to clerical misbehaviour as well as such behaviour by the laity.

---

[17] For the different contexts in which the violation of a grave may occur, see R. Künzel, 'Paganisme, syncrétisme et culture religieuse populaire au Haut Moyen Age', *Annales ESC* 47 (1992), pp. 1055–69, at p. 1061.

[18] On the *Sortes sanctorum*, see V. Flint, *The Rise of Magic in Early Medieval Europe* (Oxford, 1991), pp. 222–5, and M. Mostert, 'La magie de l'écrit dans le Haut Moyen Age. Quelques réflexions générales', in *Haut Moyen-Age. Culture, éducation et société. Etudes offertes à Pierre Riché*, ed. M. Sot (La Garenne and Colombes, 1990), pp. 273–81; M. Mostert, 'De magie van het geschreven woord', in *De betovering van het middeleeuwse christendom. Studies over ritueel en magie in de Middeleeuwen*, ed. M. Mostert and A. Demyttenaere (Hilversum, 1995), pp. 61–100, at p. 91; different interpretations are offered by D. Harmening, *Superstitio. Ueberlieferungs- und theoriegeschichtliche Untersuchungen zur kirchlich-theologischen Aberglaubensliteratur des Mittelalters* (Berlin, 1979), pp. 198–204, and W. Klingshirn, 'Defining the *Sortes sanctorum*: Gibbon, Du Cange, and early Christian lot divination', *Journal of Early Christian Studies* 10 (2002), pp. 77–130. Only Harmening's interpretation does not require a literate practitioner of this form of divination.

To this common stock of canons the *Bobbiense* adds a batch of ten canons which are almost totally related to the sexual purity of the priest and his handling of the Eucharist. These canons, treating a topic that was of particular interest to clerics in the Frankish kingdoms during the eighth and ninth centuries, derive from the *Paenitentiale Ambrosianum*, a sixth-century penitential from the Irish or British church, that was the underlying source of the more influential penitential of Cummean.[19] It was mostly through the latter that these canons concerning clerical purity and neglect of the Eucharist came to be known on the Continent.[20] In the Bobbio penitential, however, they derive from the older *Paenitentiale Ambrosianum*, a text that was also used, directly or indirectly, in three other texts of the 'simple Frankish penitentials'.[21] These sentences first treat the problem of nocturnal pollutions and the ways to atone for such an impurity according to the gravity of the situation in which it occurred. The following canons treat negligent priestly behaviour towards the Eucharist. These sentences carefully describe the ways in which a priest has to take precautions to prevent the defilement of the Eucharist, which could occur, for example, through mice nibbling from it or when it fell to the ground. The penitential also prescribes a penance for a priest stumbling over the Lord's Prayer. The last two sentences deal with someone who communicates unknowingly (*inconscius*) or because of a lack of knowledge (*per ignorantiam*), apparently in a condition in which taking part in the Eucharist was not allowed. The context here suggests that these sentences were also applied to priests, possibly communicating in a state of impurity, although they could also concern lay people communicating in such a condition.

The canons of the Bobbio penitential seem, therefore, mainly to be concerned with clerical behaviour. All canons which are specifically addressed to a particular group are aimed at the clergy, while only a single canon is clearly related to the behaviour of lay people.[22] As for the other canons it remains unclear whether they refer to clerics or a lay audience. This squares with the fact that most sentences adopted from the penitential of Columbanus derive from the first twelve sentences of the so-called B-part, which were devoted to the sins of clerics. Only a few stem from the part of Columbanus' penitential meant to be used for the laity. We can, therefore, conclude that a great part of the sentences of the Bobbio penitential were aimed at disciplining clerical conduct.

---

[19] For the *Paenitentiale Ambrosianum*, see L. Körntgen, *Studien zu den Quellen der frühmittelalterlichen Bußbücher*, Quellen und Forschungen zum Recht im Mittelalter 7 (Sigmaringen, 1993), pp. 7–86; some reservations regarding Körntgen's views are aired by Charles-Edwards, 'The penitential of Columbanus', p. 218 n. 4.

[20] R. Meens, *Het tripartite boeteboek. Overlevering en betekenis van vroegmiddeleeuwse biechtvoorschriften (met editie en vertaling van vier 'tripartita')* (Hilversum, 1994), pp. 286–7.

[21] On the *Paenitentiale Parisiense simplex*, the *Paenitentiale Oxoniense I* and the *Paenitentiale Sangallense simplex*, see Körntgen, *Studien zu den Quellen*, pp. 76–7.

[22] The canon on abortion, *Bobbio 32*.

## THE 'SIMPLE FRANKISH PENITENTIALS' AND
### BURGUNDIAN REFORM MOVEMENTS

If we look at the sources used in the main body of the 'simple Frankish penitentials' then we can see that in addition to the penitential of Columbanus, the *Lex Romana Visigothorum* and conciliar legislation were also used. The most recent council to be cited is the council of Auxerre (585–92).[23] The canon on perjury enacted under duress has a parallel in the penitential of Theodore of Canterbury.[24] If this canon really stems from a collection of Theodorian sentences, the 'simple Frankish penitentials' cannot have been composed before the beginning of the eighth century, the earliest possible date for the compilations of the Theodorian collections.[25] Although the earliest extant manuscripts with these Theodorian collections date from the eighth century, they were already quoted in the Irish collection of canon law, the *Collectio Hibernensis* and the penitential known as the *Excarpsus Cummeani*, both texts written in the first quarter of the eighth century.[26] It seems rather unlikely though that a compiler of a penitential would only use a single canon from the rich collection of penitential rulings going under the name of Theodore. Although the formulation of the offence is very similar, we can observe a major difference in the penance assigned to it in Theodore's work and in the 'simple Frankish penitentials'. The forty days assigned to this offence by Theodore stand in marked contrast to the three years in the Bobbio penitential and the other 'simple Frankish penitentials'. The *Bobbiense* is, therefore, closer to the much more austere position on perjury that we find in Irish penitential texts.[27] It seems, therefore, more likely that what we have here is not an adoption of a Theodorian sentence, but rather from another,

---

[23] For the date of this council, traditionally dated to the years 561–605, see H. Atsma, 'Klöster und Mönchtum im Bistum Auxerre bis zum Ende des 6. Jahrhunderts', *Francia* 11 (1983), pp. 1–96, at pp. 6–9; O. Pontal, *Histoire des conciles mérovingiens* (Paris, 1989), pp. 192–3, proposes to date the council in the year 585 or shortly thereafter, supposing that Bishop Aunacharius wanted to disseminate the decisions of the council of Mâcon of the year 585 to his own clerics immediately after it had come together.

[24] *Paenitentiale Bobbiense*, c. 7 (Burg. 6); cf. *Paenitentiale Theodori* U I,6,2, ed. P.W. Finsterwalder, *Die Canones Theodori Cantuariensis und ihre Überlieferungsformen* (Weimar, 1929), p. 297. In the Frankish penitentials the penance is, however, much higher: three years instead of the forty days prescribed by Theodore.

[25] R. Kottje, 'Paenitentiale Theodori', in *Handwörterbuch zur deutschen Rechtsgeschichte*, III (Berlin, 1984), cols. 1413–16; Charles-Edwards, 'The penitential of Theodore', pp. 141–74.

[26] For the date of the *Collectio Hibernensis*, see B. Jaski, 'Cú Chuimne, Ruben and the compilation of the "Collectio Canonum Hibernensis"', *Peritia* 14 (2000), pp. 51–69, at pp. 52–3, and L. Davies, 'Isidorian texts and the "Hibernensis"', *Peritia* 11 (1997), pp. 207–49, at pp. 215–16; for the date of the *Excarpsus Cummeani*, see Meens, *Tripartite boeteboek*, p. 46.

[27] See the Penitential of Finnian, c. 22 and Cummean III, c. 8, ed. L. Bieler, *The Irish Penitentials, with an Appendix by D.A. Binchy*, Scriptores Latini Hiberniae 5 (Dublin, 1963), p. 118; on these differences, see Meens, *Tripartite boeteboek*, pp. 294–5.

possibly Insular, source, upon which Theodore also drew, mitigating the harsh penance as he also did in other cases.

If this is correct and the canon on perjury does not derive from Theodore's penitential, then we can see in the main body of the 'simple Frankish penitentials' a collection of penitential rulings from the beginning of the seventh century, combining two reform movements in the Merovingian church. The Columbanian sentences represent the stimulus to penitential practice and the monastic life that was the result of the arrival of Columbanus in Burgundy, while the conciliar decisions represent the ecclesiastical reforms propagated in Burgundy at the end of the sixth century.[28] The council of Auxerre, the latest text to be used in the 'simple Frankish penitentials', should be seen as part of a wider reform movement within the Merovingian church.[29] This movement was supported by King Guntram, whose cooperation with the bishops earned him the praise of Gregory of Tours.[30] The historical significance of Guntram's cooperation with the bishops has been highlighted by interpreting it not only as symbiosis of royal military power with the civil traditions of a romanised Gaul, but also as a prelude to the Carolingian reforms of the late eighth and early ninth centuries.[31] Guntram's reform

[28] The impact of Columbanus' activities has been downplayed by A. Dierkens, 'Prolégomènes à une histoire des relations culturelles entre les îles britanniques et le continent pendant le Haut Moyen Age. La diffusion du monachisme dit colombanien ou iro-franc dans quelques monastères de la région parisienne au VIIe siècle et la politique religieuse de la reine Bathilde', in *La Neustrie. Les pays au nord de la Loire de 650 à 850*, ed. H. Atsma, 2 vols., Beihefte der Francia 16 (Sigmaringen, 1989), II, pp. 371–94. See, however, M. Richter, *Ireland and her Neighbours in the Seventh Century* (Dublin, 1999), p. 26, and T. Charles-Edwards, *Early Christian Ireland* (Cambridge, 2000), pp. 344–90, for a more positive evaluation of Columbanian monasticism.

[29] For the analysis of the synod of Auxerre and its background, I have profited from A. Gaastra, 'Kerkelijke vernieuwing in het Merovingische koninkrijk: Een studie naar de inhoud en achtergronden van de synode van Auxerre (585–592)' (MA thesis, Utrecht, 2000). An article by Gaastra based upon his thesis is forthcoming.

[30] For Gregory's praise of Guntram, see M. Heinzelmann, *Gregor von Tours (538–594) 'Zehn Bücher Geschichte'. Historiographie und Gesellschaftskonzept im 6. Jahrhundert* (Darmstadt, 1994), pp. 49–65, who, however, sees an opposition between the ecclesiological views of Guntram and Gregory on the one hand and the Burgundian episcopate on the other. For a possible background to such a distinction, see E. Magnou-Nortier, 'Existe-t-il une géographie des courants de pensée dans le clergé de Gaule au VIe siècle?', in *Grégoire de Tours et l'espace gaulois. Actes du congrès international, Tours, 3–5 Novembre 1994*, ed. N. Gauthier and H. Galinié (Tours, 1997), pp. 139–57. Both views seem, however, a bit too schematic, for I find it hard to reconcile Guntram's cooperation with the bishops from Burgundy and Neustria with such crucial differences regarding the role of the king and bishops, as expounded by Heinzelmann. A. Breukelaar, *Historiography and Episcopal Authority in Sixth-Century Gaul: The Histories of Gregory of Tours Interpreted in their Historical Context*, Forschungen zur Kirchen- und Dogmengeschichte 57 (Göttingen, 1994), pp. 238–40, sees a development in Gregory's assessment of Guntram, which might explain the differences. For a nuanced view of Gregory's appreciation of Guntram, see M. Reydellet, *La royauté dans la littérature latine de Sidoine Apollinaire à Isidore de Séville*, Bibliothèques des Ecoles françaises d'Athènes et de Rome 243 (Rome, 1981), pp. 381–4 and 420–35.

[31] G. Tabacco, 'Re Gontrano e i suoi vescovi nella Gallia di Gregorio di Tours', *Rivista Storica Italiana* 103 (1991), pp. 327–54, at pp. 352–3.

efforts had their centre in Burgundy, where the two councils of Mâcon (581/3 and 585) assembled by the king and presided over by the metropolitan bishop of Lyons, Priscus, initiated the reform. Guntram's subsequent effort to call together an all Frankish council to discuss moral failings with bishops from Burgundy, Neustria and Austrasia failed because the bishops of Austrasia were unwilling to take part in such a meeting.[32] These councils of Mâcon are among the latest texts incorporated into the extremely influential collection of canon law emanating from this movement: the *Collectio Vetus Gallica*.[33] This canon law collection, argued by Hubert Mordek to have been compiled in Lyons at the end of the sixth or the beginning of the seventh century, was itself also a manifestation of this Burgundian reform movement.[34] Possibly it was Priscus himself who took the initiative in compiling this collection, although his successor Etherius (586–602) is a more plausible candidate for its authorship.[35] By issuing an edict in the year 585 Guntram confirmed the decisions of the second Council of Mâcon, while the synod of Auxerre in its turn seems to refer to Guntram's edict.[36] To this burst of legislative activity in the Burgundian region at the close of the sixth century, the redaction of the Martyrology of Pseudo-Jerome could be added, which took place at exactly this period.[37] In this text, in which the names and dates of martyrs and holy bishops are recorded, Guntram himself was included, thus showing the close affinity between this king and the reforming circles.[38]

---

[32] Heinzelmann, *Gregor von Tours*, p. 64.

[33] H. Mordek, *Kirchenrecht und Reform im Frankenreich. Die Collectio Vetus Gallica, die älteste systematische Kanonessammlung des fränkischen Gallien. Studien und Edition*, Beiträge zur Geschichte und Quellenkunde des Mittelalters 1 (Berlin and New York 1975), pp. 70–3; for the influence of this collection of canon law, see pp. 97–207.

[34] Ibid., p. 75: 'die Lyoner Metropoliten versuchen, durch Einberufung mehrerer Synoden eine Reform der fränkischen Kirche zumindest in ihrem Gebiet in die Wege zu leiten'.

[35] Ibid., pp. 79–82.

[36] Council of Auxerre, c. 44: 'insuper et multa, quam gloriosissimus domnus rex praecepto suo instituit', ed. C. de Clercq, *Concilia Galliae A. 511–A. 695*, CCSL 148A (Turnhout, 1963); cf. I. Woll, *Untersuchungen zu Überlieferung und Eigenart der merowingischen Kapitularien*, Freiburger Beiträge zur mittelalterlichen Geschichte 6 (Frankfurt and Berlin, 1994), pp. 230–8, and Ian Wood, *The Merovingian Kingdoms, 450–751* (London and New York, 1994), pp. 104–8.

[37] See J. Dubois, *Les Martyrologes du Moyen Age Latin*, Typologie des Sources du Moyen Age Occidental 26 (Turnhout, 1978), pp. 33–5; for the fervent debate on the origin of this text between Krusch and Duchesne, see B. Krusch, 'Zum Martyrologium Hieronymianum', *Neues Archiv* 20 (1895), pp. 437–40; B. Krusch, 'Zur Afralegende und zum Martyrologium Hieronymianum. Eine Entgegnung', *Neues Archiv* 24 (1899), pp. 289–337; L. Duchesne, 'A propos du martyrologe Hiéronymien', *Analecta Bollandiana* 17 (1898), pp. 421–47; L. Duchesne, 'Un dernier mot sur le martyrologe Hiéronymien', *Analecta Bollandiana* 20 (1901), pp. 241–5; cf. J. Chapman, 'A propos des martyrologes', *Revue Bénédictine* 20 (1903), pp. 285–313.

[38] On 28 March, the Martyrology reads: 'Cavillono depositio domni Gunthramni regis bene pausati'. See *Martyrologium Hieronymianum*, ed. J.B. de Rossi and L. Duchesne, AASS, Nov. II.1 (Brussels, 1894), p. 37, and ed. H. Quentin, AASS, Nov. II.2 (Brussels, 1931), p. 165. Gregory of Tours demonstrates his firm belief in the miracle working *virtus* of the king in chapter IX.21 of the *Libri historiarum*, ed. B. Krusch and W. Levison, MGH SRM I.1 (Hannover, 1951), pp. 441–2; cf. Heinzelmann, *Gregor*

Taken together these texts clearly indicate the existence at the end of the sixth century of a concerted effort on the part of King Guntram, the metropolitan bishops of Lyons and the Burgundian episcopate as such to reform the clergy and the moral life of the laity. The synod of Auxerre is a clear example of this reform movement, since it is the first known instance of a bishop legislating for the clergy of his bishopric.[39] Bishop Aunacharius of Auxerre, who convened this synod, used it to communicate the decisions of the second council of Mâcon to his clergy. It might be that Auxerre is just a lucky case in which the decisions of a local synod have been preserved, whereas in other cases they have not, but it has recently been suggested that precisely those diocesan synods of which we have a written record might be the outcome of 'reforming aspirations'.[40] In any case, the canons of the synod of Auxerre can be seen as forerunners of the later Carolingian episcopal capitularies and this may explain why this text was still disseminated in the Carolingian period, when, in some manuscripts at least, it seemed to function as an episcopal capitulary, providing basic instruction for the clergy.[41] One of the main aims of this synod seems to have been to set apart the clergy from the laity, but it also tried to improve the moral life of the laity.[42]

If we regard the Burgundian legislative activity at the end of the sixth century as a concerted attempt to improve the moral life of the clergy and the laity, then the traditional view of the Irish monk Columbanus who entered Gaul around the year 590 and found the country in a desolate state, where 'through the number of external enemies and the negligence of the bishops the strength of the Christian religion had been almost extinguished' stands in need of revision.[43] In Burgundy, in particular, the bishops demonstrated their willingness to improve the religious life of their flocks, and Columbanus arrived with his band of Irish monks right

---

*von Tours*, p. 65, and Breukelaar, *Historiography and Episcopal Authority*, p. 240: 'the bishop of Tours came close to canonising his king [scil. Guntram]'. Paul the Deacon speaks about Guntram as 'rex pacificus et omni bonitate conspicuus' and relates a miraculous vision of the king, *Historia Langobardorum* III.34, ed. G. Waitz, MGH Scriptores rerum Langobardicarum (Hannover, 1878), pp. 112–13.

[39] Pontal, *Histoire des conciles mérovingiens*, p. 192.

[40] S. Hamilton, *The Practice of Penance, 900–1050* (Woodbridge, 2001), p. 55: 'But the proceedings of those synods which left a record should be treated with caution; they may not be representative of universal norms but rather of the reforming aspirations of that particular assembly.'

[41] See, for example, in Copenhagen, Kongelige Bibliotek, Ny. Kgl. S. 58 8o (s. viii[1], N. France), and Oxford, Bodleian Library, Bodley 572 (s. ix[1/3], N. France); on the Copenhagen manuscript, see Meens, 'The oldest manuscript witness of the *Collectio canonum Hibernensis*'; on the Oxford manuscript, see F.B. Asbach, *Das Poenitentiale Remense und der sogen. Excarpsus Cummeani: Überlieferung, Quellen und Entwicklung zweier kontinentaler Bußbücher aus der 1. Hälfte des 8. Jahrhunderts* (Regensburg, 1975), pp. 28–30.

[42] Gaastra, 'Kerkelijke vernieuwing'.

[43] This traditional view owed much to this statement of Columbanus' biographer Jonas of Bobbio, *Vita Columbani*, I.5; cf. I.N. Wood, 'The *Vita Columbani* and Merovingian Hagiography', *Peritia* 1 (1982), pp. 63–80, and C. Stancliffe, 'Jonas' Life of Columbanus and his disciples', in *Studies in Irish Hagiography*, ed. J. Carey, M. Herbert and P. Ó Riain (Dublin, 1999), pp. 189–220.

after this burst of canonical activity. Columbanus might have been welcomed by the reform-minded Guntram, although Jonas of Orléans does not tell us so.[44] Columbanus' activities should perhaps be seen as a counteroffensive of Brunhild and her circle, trying to outbalance the reforms of Guntram after his death. The Irish abbot was clearly a charismatic personality and during his career several kings extended him a warm welcome. Theuderic and Brunhild seem to have favoured him as their 'personal' saint, strengthening their royal house. Possibly their support of Columbanus was a reaction to the beginnings of a cult of Guntram.

One should not, however, rule out the possibility that Columbanus' activities should be regarded as a follow-up to the earlier religious reforms. This at least is suggested by the 'simple Frankish penitentials', which, as observed above, combine sentences from the penitential of Columbanus with those emanating from Merovingian conciliar and canonical legislation. The fact that early manuscripts of the Martyrology of Pseudo-Jerome include not only the name of Guntram but also that of Columbanus, points in the same direction.[45] The manuscript tradition of the *Collectio Vetus Gallica* and that of the council of Auxerre also imply some form of fusion of Iro-Frankish monasticism and the Burgundian reform movement, since both of these texts are found in codices containing canonical texts of an Insular nature.[46]

The 'simple Frankish penitentials', therefore, seem to reflect a fusion of Columbanian concerns for the proper form of religious life with Merovingian efforts going in the same direction. It is unclear when exactly such a fusion had taken place. Possibly it was already a feature of Columbanian monasticism during the saint's lifetime, but a more plausible period for such a blending to take place is in the generation after the saint's death, when his successors were trying to accommodate the Columbanian peculiarities to Merovingian ecclesiastical practice.[47]

[44] I.N. Wood, 'Jonas, the Merovingians, and Pope Honorius: *Diplomata* and the *Vita Columbani*', in *After Rome's Fall. Narrators and Sources of Early Medieval History. Essays Presented to Walter Goffart*, ed. A.C. Murray (Toronto, Buffalo and London 1998), pp. 99–120, at pp. 106 and 111.

[45] Pseudo-Jerome, *Martyrologium*, 23 Nov.: 'Italia monasterio Bobio depositio sancti Columbani abbatis', ed. De Rossi and Duchesne, p. 146; ed. Quentin, p. 615.

[46] For the *Vetus Gallica*, see Mordek, *Kirchenrecht*, pp. 268–301; this combination with Insular traditions seems, however, to be the result of the editorial work done at the monastery of Corbie, see ibid., pp. 86–92, and R. Meens, 'The uses of the Old Testament in early medieval canon law. The Collectio Vetus Gallica and the Collectio Hibernensis', in *The Uses of the Past in Early Medieval Europe*, ed. Y. Hen and M. Innes (Cambridge, 1999), pp. 67–77, at pp. 75–6; for the council of Auxerre, see the manuscripts in Copenhagen and Oxford cited above, n. 41.

[47] The latter possibility is advanced by Stancliffe, 'Jonas' Life', pp. 214–15, although if one accepts, as I do, Diem's view of what constitutes a monastic rule – not a written text, but the teachings of the founder or abbot – then it is equally possible that such a fussion had already taken place during Columbanus' life. I do not believe that opposition to Columbanus on specific points necessarily implies that cooperation was impossible in all respects, see A. Diem, 'Keusch und rein. Eine Untersuchung zu den Ursprüngen des frühmittelalterlichen Klosterwesens und seine Quellen' (PhD thesis, Utrecht, 2000), and A. Diem, 'Was bedeutet Regula Columbani?', in *Integration und Herrschaft. Ethnische*

## CLERICAL PURITY

The last part of the Bobbio penitential, deriving its material from the *Paenitentiale Ambrosianum*, is almost exclusively concerned with the purity of the priest. For Columbanian monks, as has been recently demonstrated, bodily purity was of crucial importance because the holiness of the monastery and the subsequent power of prayer depended mainly on the bodily purity maintained by the monastic community.[48] The Bobbio penitential, however, just like the other penitentials of this group, was not primarily interested in the bodily purity of monks or nuns, for it did not adopt sentences from the monastic part of Columbanus' penitential, but mainly from the part devoted to clerics. It seems, therefore, to have been particularly concerned with the moral status and the bodily purity of clerics. Apparently the clerical status also required a particular kind of purity, allowing access to holy places and bolstering the effectivity of prayer. The purity stressed in the Bobbio penitential, exemplified by its last part, concerns mass and the Eucharist in particular, thereby emphasising sacerdotal functions. We have already observed that the synod of Auxerre and other synods related to the Burgundian reform movement had a strong interest in distinguishing the priests from the laity. This distinction seems to have been strengthened by the Columbanian interest in ritual purity, so that in this case again we can note a fusion of Columbanian interests and those of the Burgundian reform movement, with the help of a text of an Insular background. The earliest texts which show knowledge of the *Paenitentiale Ambrosianum*, the source of the last part of the Bobbio Missal, are all, apart from the sixth-century Irish penitential of Cummean, related to the Columbanian tradition: the *Regula coenobialis* of Columbanus might already have used this text, while it is further utilised in three 'simple Frankish penitentials', which all draw upon Columbanus' confessional handbook. So the use of this exceptional source strengthens the relationship between the Bobbio penitential and Columbanian monasticism.[49]

## CLERICAL COMMUNITIES

We may therefore conclude that one of the main aims of the penitential was the moral conduct of the clergy, particularly of priests.[50] The Missal contains a *Missa quomodo sacerdus pro se orare debit*, the earliest example of a mass in which

*Identitäten und soziale Organisation im Frühmittelalter*, ed. M. Diesenberger and W. Pohl (Vienna, 2002), pp. 63–89.

[48] Diem, *Keusch und rein*.

[49] Körntgen, *Studien zu den Quellen*, pp. 44–7 and 76–80.

[50] Ibid., p. 78.

the priest asks for the pardon of his sins (nos. 407–11), also a text, therefore, concerned with the purity of the priest.[51] This mass was intended to be performed by the priest himself for his own salvation, but it seems unlikely that the canons in the penitential were intended to be used for the priest's own sake only. The most likely setting for the use of the Bobbio penitential, therefore, seems to be that of a priest who regularly heard confession of other clerics. How may we imagine such a practice? Did he travel around, hearing confession, saying mass, baptising, burying, blessing and performing other pastoral functions? The fact that the Missal contains a *Missa in domo cuiuslibet* demonstrates that the book was meant to be carried around, and the same can be concluded from the *oratio in domo* (no. 545) and the liturgical *ordines* for the consecration of nuns and an abbess (nos. 546 and 548). Several blessings also imply that the book was carried around. But why then this stress on sinning clerics? Did the owner of the Bobbio Missal visit other priests to hear their confession, or did he live in a clerical community of some sort and did the text serve to regulate life within the community as well? The combination of these two possibilities seems to me most probable, i.e. that the book served a clerical community, which provided a number of liturgical functions for a widespread community, while at the same time it was used to keep up discipline within the community by stressing the need for clerics to be pure of heart and body, and additionally providing the opportunity to clean themselves of the impurity of sin. Such a use of this manuscript within a clerical community might also explain the presence of two or more near-contemporary hands that we find in the manuscript.[52]

If we assume that the canons of the Bobbio penitential mainly deal with forms of clerical misconduct, they permit us to sketch an extremely unflattering picture of these clerics. They are sexually depraved, violent members of the local community, playing a key role in all kinds of magical rituals – rituals which we find so often condemned in ecclesiastical legislation – neglecting the host and stumbling over their prayers. This surely is too negative a view of the Merovingian clergy, since the penitential, as has been argued here, is part of a reform movement, and reform movements normally paint a dark background in order for their renewal to shine more brightly. Instead, we could say that the Bobbio penitential is a manifestation of a movement which was very much concerned with the moral life of the clergy. It demonstrates the aims of the Burgundian reform movement which, though showing some interest in the religious life of the laity, mainly tried to confront the failings of members of the clergy, while at the same time providing them with the means to atone for their sins. This possibility for clerics to do penance and thereby

[51] See Angenendt, 'Missa specialis', p. 184.
[52] Rosamond McKitterick (above, pp. 19–52, especially p. 50) allows for some more chronological scope than Lowe did, but her views would also square with production and use of the text in a clerical community.

regain their ritual purity which enabled them to say mass in a manner that would please God seems to have been a new feature of Columbanian monasticism, a feature which was warmly welcomed in the Merovingian world, as the eight surviving 'simple Frankish penitentials' seem to imply. If we assume that these texts were meant to be used by individual priests or by clerics living together in some sort of community, we may infer that there must have existed more texts like this, since manuscripts owned by individual priests or in communities without much institutional stability stood in much greater danger of disappearing from the historical record than those kept in monastic libraries. The existence of the group of 'simple Frankish penitentials', although most of these texts are known from manuscripts dating from around the middle of the eighth to the tenth century, implies that more texts of this kind must have circulated than have come down to us. The use made of these texts in the tripartite penitentials, texts whose sources comprise the Irish penitential of Cummean, a Theodorian tradition of penitential canons and the simple Frankish ones, leads to the same conclusion.

On the basis of this analysis of the Bobbio penitential, Lowe's somewhat romantic view of the Bobbio Missal as the book owned by an old individual priest in a remote village in which he gathered outdated text for his personal use, therefore, seems tenuous. It seems more likely that the book was a product of a clerical community in which the ideals of the Burgundian reform movement of the close of the sixth century were combined with Columbanian ideas about the purity of monks, clerics and priests. The Bobbio Missal shows that around the year 700 such ideals were still very much alive.

# 9

## Doctrinal and theological themes in the prayers of the Bobbio Missal

LOUISE P.M. BATSTONE

The purpose of this chapter is to enable us to see more distinctly which theological themes dominate the fixed and variable prayers of the Bobbio Missal, and with what consistency and in what circumstances they are used (i.e. for which feasts). This enables us to identify any theological peculiarities in the Bobbio Missal which may or may not be present in other Merovingian sacramentaries, indicating important doctrinal themes that are distinctive to the particular region of Gaul and period for which the sacramentary was produced and might thereby be termed 'local theology', incomplete a term as that inherently is. It is impossible to ascertain with exacting accuracy which prayers in the Missal we have were original compositions and which were copied verbatim from another source (or sources), as we lack the original sources. It is, thereby, difficult to suggest whether our composer should be designated simply as a compiler of pre-existent materials, or a *de novo* composer. It is clear to me, taking into account both the large number of prayers in the Bobbio Missal which are related to prayers in other Frankish missals and the living nature of the liturgical traditions that this compiler has used, that he (or possibly she) was both. It is true that many liturgical books were 'inherited'. It is true that the Merovingians were proud of their particular liturgical traditions. However, it is also true that they were not averse to manipulating those very traditions to suit the needs of their individual churches, both spiritual and political. I believe, therefore, that it is possible to say that the use of particular fixed prayers and the compilation and composition of variable prefaces and collects suggest to us what the compiler/composer of the contents of the Bobbio Missal responded to in the particular situation of the local church or churches that the sacramentary served. The variable prayers, as original compilations or compositions, are potentially most revealing of the theology of the local church both in the period immediately following the composition of the Missal, and historically in the traditions of the church for which it was produced. These prayers may also betray, in their theological formation, some information that might help us in reconstructing the process of the compilation of the Missal.

This chapter does not attempt anything like a full theological analysis of each theological theme or each prayer of the Bobbio Missal, which would be well beyond its scope. Rather, the aim is to highlight the principal doctrinal assertions of the Bobbio Missal, and assess what that tells us about the teaching of the Christian church that was being transmitted to the audience for which the sacramentary was produced. In this regard, the theology of the Missal may be suggestive of the political and religious circumstances surrounding the community for which it was compiled and thereby indicate the period and location of the Missal's (and where the compiler is copying pre-existent texts, its exemplars') composition.

## THE MASS-SETS OF THE BOBBIO MISSAL

The first prayer of the Merovingian mass for which we have evidence from the Bobbio Missal is the fixed prayer known as the *Aius*, since the Bobbio Missal gives, amongst its collection of *orationes ad missam,* two prayers, *Post Aius.*[1]

The *Aius* would appear to indicate the *Trisagion* rather than the *Sanctus*. It is possible that the *Trisagion* was a very primitive hymn in early Roman liturgy, identical to that used in the Byzantine rite, preserved in the liturgy described by the Bobbio Missal.[2] The *Trisagion* first appears to have arrived in Gaul following the *Trisagion* rites of the fifth century. There are other witnesses to the use of the *Trisagion*, or at least awareness of it, in south-east Gaul from the late fifth until well into the seventh century, allowing this region to be regarded as a plausible place of origin for the Missal, or at least the use of a south-east Gallican source by the Missal's compiler.[3]

However, the use of the *Trisagion* in Gaul has a different theological purpose from its use in the Byzantine rite. Unlike the original Byzantine usage, in the Bobbio Missal it is not related to the Eucharist. That it is used like the *Sanctus* also suggests that the original influence for its use in the liturgy of Gaul came

---

[1] *Bobbio* 25 and 32, pp. 14–15. The *Dicitur post Aios* occurs twice in the *orationes ad missam* indicating that this prayer was in ordinary use in the liturgy of the churches using the Bobbio Missal. It was sung twice, not only at the start of mass, but also before the Gospel. M. Ferrotin, in his *Liber Mozarabicus sacramentorum et les manuscrits mozarabes,* 2 vols. (Paris, 1912), cols. 740, 745, 756, 760 and 763, attests its use in Spain although in a different form and it is not repeated before the Gospel.

[2] It is certainly described in the Greek liturgy of St Hippolytus of Rome.

[3] Avitus, *Ep.* 3 (to King Gundobad), ed. R. Peiper, MGH AA VI.2 (Berlin, 1883), pp. 22–9. Avitus of Vienne (who was commissioned by King Gundobad to write a treatise on the *Trisagion*), while speaking of it as a prayer foreign to the liturgy known by him, none the less condemns attempts to make it Christological in its address by the adding of 'who is crucified for us' before the 'have mercy on us'. See also *Vita Gaucerici episcopi Camaracensis,* c. 8, ed. B. Krusch, MGH SRM III, pp. 649–58, at pp. 654–5, refers to the singing of the *Trisagion* at the start of the liturgy. It is possible that this suggests either the more widespread use of the *Trisagion*, or the use of a south-east Gallican exemplar of the liturgy by the author of this *vita.*

from Rome rather than the east, and that there was probably confusion between the *Trisagion* and what was meant by the term *(ter)Sanctus*.[4] The Bobbio's use of the *Trisagion* appears to be making a clear statement about the Trinitarian faith of the community at the commencement of the liturgical celebration. This is quite different from its use in eastern rites where it is a chant invoking the action of the Trinity in the Eucharistic prayer. In its Gallican context, its use is clearly anti-Arian. This Gallican adaptation of a prayer, I believe, lends support to the conclusions of Wood and McKitterick, who argue for the south-east Gallican origin of the Missal based on both textual and manuscript evidence,[5] for which there will be further evidence as we examine the other prayers of the liturgy in this chapter.

The distinctive way in which this prayer is used in the Bobbio Missal is further highlighted if we observe that the *Trisagion* hymn in the Bobbio Missal appears to have replaced the more typical Gallican usage of the *Gloria in excelsis*.[6] The *Gloria* is used in all the other Frankish sacramentaries as the opening hymn of the Synaxis. The *Gloria* is also present in the Bobbio Missal and was clearly used in the celebration of some of the masses.[7] The fact that the *Aius* is mentioned only by name, however, and that the *Gloria* is written out in full, appears to indicate that in the church or churches using the Bobbio Missal, the *Aius* was known by heart and that the *Gloria* was less familiar. The use of the *Trisagion* in south-east Gaul may be explained by the particular historical or present need in this region for more explicit Trinitarian teaching in short, concise prayers. This may reflect a background of theological dissent concerning the Trinitarian teaching of the church in this region, or perhaps the desire of the compiler/composer to reaffirm the doctrine of the Trinity to preserve orthodox Catholicism in the face of potential threat from foreign rulers. The *Gloria*, while also Trinitarian inasmuch as it praises God the Father and the Son for their work of redemption, only mentions the Holy Spirit in its closing formulae and is more a hymn dedicated to the praise of God. It is less repetitive and considerably longer, which would have presumably made it more difficult to memorise. The need for Trinitarian instruction gains some support from the strong Trinitarian affirmations explicit in the prayers for such masses as that for the Advent of the Lord,[8] which tells us that God in Trinity is praised by the

---

[4] There has been considerable confusion over whether *Sanctus* designated the actual *Sanctus* or the *Trisagion*.

[5] I refer the reader to the contributions of Ian Wood and Rosamond McKitterick in this volume.

[6] The *Expositio* I:3 tells us that the *Aius* (apparently the Trisagion from what the author describes) was chanted before the *Prophetia*. Avitus of Vienne appears to know of it, but as a prayer that is foreign to him; *Ep.* III to King Gundobad, in PL 59, col. 211. There is also a reference to the *Trisagion* in the *Vita Gaucericus*, written at the turn of the seventh century, although it is not referred to in the context of the Eucharist.

[7] *Bobbio* 26, p. 14.      [8] Ibid. 496, p. 153: 'Te in personis trinum unum deum'.

multitude of angels.[9] The virtues of that union are also explained.[10] The Bobbio
Missal also uses frequent references to God as the God of Abraham, the God of Isaac
and the God of Jacob to refer to the Trinitarian nature of God.[11] This distinctive
use of the *Trisagion* in the Bobbio Missal seems to suggest a relationship between
the Missal, or at least its sources, and the religio-political situation of the south-east
region of Gaul in the sixth century and affirms the desire of the compiler/composer
to preserve this distinctive tradition of his community.

The two variable *Post Aius* prayers pick up the theme of the prayer of God as
Holy and the plea for His mercy. They act as closing formulae to the fixed prayer.
The first praises God for His omnipotence and fatherhood, having answered the
plea to show His mercy to mankind, He came down from Heaven (described as
'the most excellent, glorious and divine Jerusalem') and by His most Holy Blood,
saved and redeemed man. Here there is no reference to the resurrection, but to
the Incarnation and 'blood' by which man was saved. Neither is there any explicit
mention of the cross. Certainly the attributes of God and the coeternity of the Son
are emphasised, and the language used to describe Heaven can only be described
as a clear use of Old Testament typology which will be discussed more extensively
below. The second *Post Aius* collect refers to God as the Judge and asks Him to
have pity on mankind expressing hope in His mercy that man may not die for his
sins but be brought to life. Both prayers maintain the focus of the *Aius* itself on
man's need for God's mercy, and God's initiative in the economy of redemption
and salvation. In this regard the variable collects can be described as anti-Pelagian.

The next prayer of the Synaxis that we are told about in the Bobbio Missal is the
*Prophetia*, also known as the canticle of Zechariah.[12] It is referred to by the *Collectio
post prophetiam* in seven mass-sets of the Bobbio Missal.[13] The significance of the

[9] Ibid. 63, p. 23: 'Presta unita et indivisa trinetas deus quem celorum multiplex et ineffabiles numerum quem omnium angelorum.'
[10] Ibid. 488, p. 148: 'Una divinitas et trina cuius spiritu omnia nunciantur, una divinitas et trina maiestas, natura inseparabiles, persona individua deus unus et solus unitas triplex incomp[reh]ensa . . . qui unum insubstancialiter trinum personaliter nominamus credemus confitemur.'
[11] Ibid. 451, p. 134, Missa dominicalis.   [12] Luke 1.68–79: 'Benedictus dominus Deus Israel'.
[13] These are the masses for the Advent of the Lord, for the feasts of St John the Baptist and the selection of four Sunday mass-sets. This can be compared to the presence of only one mass of the *Missale Gothicum*, Vatican City, BAV, Reg. lat. 317 (?Luxeuil, early s.viii), ed. L.C. Mohlberg, Rerum Ecclesiasticarum Documenta, series maior 5 (Rome, 1961), no. IV, pp. 5–8; six masses in the *Missale Gallicanum Vetus*, Vatican City, BAV, Pal. lat. 493 (?Chelles, s.viii^in), ed. L.C. Mohlberg, Rerum Ecclesiasticarum Documenta, series maior 3 (Rome, 1958); three masses of the *Missale Francorum*, Vatican City, BAV, Reg. lat. 257 (?Poitiers, s.viii^in), ed. L.C. Mohlberg, Rerum Ecclesiasticarum Documenta, series maior 2 (Rome, 1957); and two mass-sets in the masses of Mone, Karlsruhe, Badische Landesbibliothek Aug. 253 (Reichenau, 760–80), ed. L.C. Mohlberg, Rerum Ecclesiasticarum Documenta, series maior 3 (Rome, 1958), nos. 6 and 7, pp. 86–91. Gregory of Tours' *Libri Historiarum* VIII.7 attests the regular use of the *Prophetia* on Sundays and tells us that the bishop sang it. It was introduced into the 'Roman' liturgy by the fifth century and into the Gallican at least by the sixth.

*Prophetia*, according to the author of the later *Expositio liturgiae antiquae gallicanae*, is that it was sung in honour of St John the Baptist.[14] Despite this, the *Prophetia* does not appear to have been used for any of St John the Baptist's feasts in the *Missale Gothicum* or Mone masses. However, the *Gallicanum Vetus* and the Bobbio Missal both use it for the feasts of John the Baptist, although not exclusively so. Its wide and continued usage is certainly supported by the fact that it is nowhere written out in full, leaving us to assume that it was perhaps known by heart.

The following variable collect was usually either a paraphrase of the most significant verses of the preceding chant or an allusion to the feast. Its position was similar to that of the Byzantine liturgies, these sacramentaries also imitating the eastern practice referred to by Cassian of Marseilles, of placing collects after each preface.[15] The theological association between baptism and resurrection on the Last Day is apparent in the *Collectio post prophetiam* for both the Bobbio Missal and the *Missale Gallicanum Vetus*. In contrast to the Pauline theme of baptism into the death of Christ, epitomised by the *Missale Gothicum*,[16] the *Collectio post prophetiam* in the Bobbio Missal associates resurrection and baptism. In this association, original sin is annihilated by baptism into the resurrection of Jesus, rather than baptism into the death of Jesus, demonstrating either little awareness, or little appreciation, of a Pauline theology of the cross.

Following the variable collect, the Bobbio Missal goes on to prescribe the triple lections that demonstrate its conjunctive use as a lectionary and indicate its pastoral function.[17] After the readings, the Bobbio Missal tells us that there was a *Collectio [oratio] post benedictione*.[18] This indicates that the next fixed prayer or hymn was the *Benedicite*, so called because of the frequent repetition of the benediction.[19] The hymn describes the litanic prayer of Shadrach, Meshach and Abed'Nego recorded in

E. Griffe, 'Aux origines de la liturgie Gallicane', *Bulletin de littérature ecclésiastique* 52 (1951), pp. 17–43, at p. 27. For a discussion of the origins of the other Gallican sacramentaries see Y. Hen, *The Royal Patronage of Liturgy in Frankish Gaul to the death of Charles the Bald (877)*, HBS subsidia 3 (London, 2001).

[14] Pseudo-Germanus, *Expositio antiquae liturgiae gallicanae*, ed. E.A. Ratcliff, HBS 98 (London, 1971), I.6, p. 5: 'Canticum autem Zachariae pontificis in honorem sancti Johannis Baptistae cantatur.'

[15] All the Frankish missals follow this pattern of placing a collect after a psalmody of the office. For example, the *Missale Gothicum* mass IX (for the vigil of Epiphany) provides six prefaces separated by six collects. Cassian's *Institutiones* II.V testifies that this was the regular practice 'per omnem orientem' as well as in his own monastery at Marseilles, and it is also noted in the Jerusalem liturgy by the pilgrim Egeria. See *Itinerarium Egeriae*, ed A. Franceschini and R. Weber, CCSL 175 (Turnhout, 1965), pp. 37–90.

[16] For example, see the *praefatio missae* of the *Missa clausum paschae* in the *Missale Gothicum*, ed. Mohlberg, p. 79.

[17] For the agreement in the system of lections see *Le Lectionnaire de Luxeuil: Paris, ms. lat. 9427: édition et étude comparative*, ed. P. Salmon, Collectanea Biblica Latina 7 (Rome, 1944).

[18] PL 72, col. 458; *Bobbio 33 (Orationes ad missam)*, p. 16.

[19] L. Duchesne, *Christian Worship: Its Origin and Evolution: A Study of the Latin Liturgy up to the Time of Charlemagne*, trans. from the 3rd French edn M.L. McClure (London, 1903), p. 196.

Dan. 3.51–90. A prayer of this kind also occurs in the Old Gelasian Sacramentary after *Benedictus es* on Ember Saturdays. The use of this hymn in the Old Gelasian Sacramentary, supposedly produced in the Paris region for the bishop either of Paris or of Meaux,[20] even in its restriction to ember Saturdays, witnesses the continued use of this hymn in or around Paris into the eighth century. Its longevity is also witnessed in the *Expositio* where we are told that it was sung as a figure or symbol of the saints of old who lived in the shadow of darkness awaiting the coming of the Lord. This regular use of the *Benedicite* as a fixed prayer at every mass in the Bobbio Missal appears to have been an enduring feature of the liturgy in south-east Gaul, a feature which was apparently dying out in the regular liturgies of the Paris and Langres regions.

The theological emphasis of the *Benedicite* is clearly upon the confession of the salvation promised by God to His people, and on the assurance that no matter how great human adversity, God carries out His promises to those who are faithful to Him. It might suggest that the use of the *Benedicite* in the Bobbio Missal and the Old Gelasian Sacramentary may indicate a period of persecution or a period of particular hardship when encouragement in the Christian faith was needed and the promise of God's fidelity to those who were suffering was emphasised in the regions for which these sacramentaries, or their exemplars, were produced. Again, the fact that this litanic hymn/prayer was not written out in full would perhaps suggest that it may have been learnt and memorised by those who recited it.

The first prayer of the mass of the Faithful mentioned in the Bobbio Missal was the variable bidding-prayer termed *Praefatio missae* and its connected *Collectio* which followed the offertory in the order of mass. Sometimes it is termed *Secreta* in the Old Gelasian Sacramentary and this is also seen in some masses in the Bobbio Missal.[21] Whereas the other Frankish sacramentaries frequently use this preface to recount a condensed version of the redemption history of mankind, in the Bobbio Missal this short bidding-prayer is addressed to the faithful. It exhorts the people to pray that they might receive grace from 'the mystery of the day', which is presumably a reference to the celebration of the Eucharist. This asserts that the Eucharist was the means of receiving Grace. The invocatory collect, which was addressed to God, was preceded by the rubric *Collectio sequitur* and focused most commonly on the petition for God to prepare the faithful by purification to

[20] On the origin of this missal see Y. Hen, *Culture and Religion in Merovingian Gaul, A.D. 481–751* (Leiden, New York and Cologne, 1995), pp. 44–5 and 59–60; and R. McKitterick, 'Nuns' scriptoria in England and Francia in the eighth century', *Francia* 19 (1992), pp. 1–35 (repr. in R. McKitterick, *Books, Scribes and Learning in the Frankish Kingdoms, 6th–9th Centuries* (Aldershot, 1994), ch. 7).

[21] Masses in the Bobbio Missal that term the collect as *Secreta* are those for the Assumption of the Virgin Mary, the first Lenten mass, the Invention of the Cross, Ascension, St John the Baptist's Passion, St Sigismund, for saints and martyrs, St Michael, three *missa votiva*, one mass for the dead, *missa in domo cuiuslibet* and three *missa cottidiana dominicalis*. See further discussion in J.A. Jungmann, 'Praefatio und stiller Kanon', *Zeitschrift für katholische Theologie* 53 (1929), pp. 66–94 and 247–71.

receive the 'mysteries'. Only in the Christmas vigil mass do we find clear reference to redemption as it related to the feast. Here, the collect refers to Jesus' birth of the Virgin and His role in creation *ex nihilo* with the Father.[22] The theological combination of exhortation and invocation clearly follows that of the 'Roman' rite, or the so-called Verona Sacramentary.[23]

The rest of the variable prayers provided for each mass-set in the Bobbio Missal are the *Collectio post nomina*, *Collectio ad pacem* and the *contestatio*. The *Collectio post nomina* indicates that the names of the living and the dead were read from the diptychs at each mass. If the Bobbio Missal was a portable combined sacramentary and lectionary for a priest to use while touring the churches in his parish, then presumably the names of those read from the diptychs changed according to the church and audience of the mass. This reading of names is none the less significant for the establishment of the doctrine of the communion of saints, both living and dead.[24] All the Frankish sacramentaries relate their *Post nomina* collects to the feast of the day. They are usually short prayers and praise particular attributes of God, relating these to the feast being celebrated. For example, the *Post nomina* for the Christmas vigil in the Bobbio Missal affirms the Virgin birth of Jesus as announced by the Archangel Gabriel. This was, the prayer explains, so that man might have faith.[25] The *Collectio post nomina* for the first day of Easter says that the Paschal sacrifice was a 'good work', which enabled grace and piety to be received.[26] It is interesting that the offering of the sacrifice at this early stage was to be seen, at

---

[22] The *Collectio* appears to have been the counterpart to the *Super oblata* or *Secreta* in the Roman rite, known from the so-called Verona Sacramentary (Verona, Biblioteca Capitolare LXXXV (80)). For an edition of this libelli collection see L. Mohlberg, Rerum Ecclesiasticarum Documenta, series maior I (Rome, 1956). For extensive notes and discussion see D.M. Hope, *The Leonine Sacramentary* (London, 1971).

[23] A.A. King, *Liturgies of the Past* (London, 1959), p. 168; Duchesne, *Christian Worship*, p. 207.

[24] On the recitation of the names and its relation to the *Liber vitae* see M. McLaughlin, *Consorting with Saints: Prayers for the Dead in Early Medieval France* (Ithaca, 1994); A. von Euw, *Liber viventium Fabariensis. Das Karolingische Memorialbuch von Pfäfers in seiner Liturgie-und Kunstgeschichtlichen Bedeutung*, Studia Fabariensia. Beiträge zur Pfäferser Klostergeschichte 1 (Bern and Stuttgart, 1989); L. Koep, *Das himmlische Buch in Antike und Christentum. Eine religionsgeschichtliche Untersuchung zu altchristliche bildersprache*, Theophaneia Beiträge zur Religions- und Kirchengeschichte des Altertums 8 (Bonn, 1952). For more detailed information on the *Liber vitae* in Gaul in the early Middle Ages, see K. Schmid, 'Probleme der Erschliessung des Salzburger Verbrüderungsbuches', in *Frühes Mönchtum in Salzburg*, ed. E. Zwink, Salzburg Diskussionen 4 (Salzburg, 1983), pp. 175–95; K. Schmid, 'Das ältere und das neuentdeckte jüngere St. Galler Verbrüderungsbuch', in *Subsidia Sangallensia*, I, ed. M. Borgolte, D. Geuenich and K. Schmid (St Gallen, 1986), pp. 15–38; *Der Liber Vitae der Abtei Corvey*, ed. K. Schmid and J. Wollasch, 2 vols., Veröffentlichungen der historischen Kommission für Westfalen 40 (Westfälische Gedenkbücher und Nekrologien 2.1–2) (Wiesbaden, 1983–9); O.G. Oexle, 'Memoria und Memorialüberlieferung im früheren Mittelalter', *Frühmittelalterliche Studien* 10 (1976), pp. 70–95, at pp. 82–7. S.D. Keynes gives a good overview of *Libri vitae* in his introduction to his edition of the *Liber vitae of the New Minster and Hyde Abbey in Winchester*, Early English Manuscripts in Facsimile 26 (Copenhagen, 1996).

[25] *Bobbio* 68, p. 24.    [26] Ibid. 267, p. 80.

least by the compiler of this text, as a good work of man. This concept was not something that was discussed until the central and late Middle Ages. It is also particularly anti-Pelagian in that Grace and piety are expressly seen as having their source not in man but rather in God, as does the offering of the sacrifice itself. God then is seen as the source of the good work and also of the corresponding spiritual Graces that good works accrue. This theology, pertinent to the Pelagian debate, again appears to reinforce the attribution of this Missal or its sources to south-east Gaul. The *Collectio post nomina* for Christmas in the Bobbio Missal expresses the humility of Jesus that was necessary for the exaltation of man.[27] Since pride condemned man, humility would redeem him. Here there is a clear theology of the relationship between condemnation and redemption, Adam and Jesus. The role of redemption appears to have to undo what Adam did through Jesus' virtue overcoming Adam's sin.

The separation of the *pax* from the offertory by the recitation of the names is a characteristic of all the Frankish sacramentaries, as distinct from the Roman prayers contained in the Verona Sacramentary and the later Roman liturgy of the *Ordines*. Roman liturgy presented the *pax* as the seal of the Eucharistic prayer, the seal of the sacrament of Christian unity, which is the oblation.[28] Pope Innocent I (401–17) in his letter to Decentius of Gubbio voicing complaints about the liturgical diversity of the church in the west, said that the *pax* was not to be exchanged *ante confecta mysteria*.[29] Innocent located the *pax* before communion,[30] but after the offertory, theologically framing the *pax* within the unity of the Eucharist. The Frankish sacramentaries place the *pax* before the offertory as a preliminary act by which the unity of the people was established before the Eucharistic offering was made. The Eucharist depended upon this fraternal peace for authentic communion, according to Jesus' command in Matt. 5.23–5. If Innocent's letter can be seen as a witness to the Gallican practice of the fifth century, then the Frankish sacramentaries of the eighth century show a remarkable continuity of Gallican practice, perhaps demonstrating the reluctance of the Frankish church to move a prayer in an instance when such a movement was not in accordance with Frankish theological perception of that prayer, and did not serve the needs of the Frankish church.

The *Collectio ad pacem* prayers in the Bobbio Missal provide us with some particularly interesting information about Frankish theology of the Eucharist and the economy of salvation. The *Item missa in adventum Domini* calls the Eucharistic host the everlasting immolation that operates God's salvation for man through the sacred institution of the mysteries (of the Eucharist).[31] The *Collectio ad pacem* in

[27] Ibid. 77, p. 27.    [28] King, *Liturgies of the Past*, p. 171.
[29] Innocent I, *Ep.* 25.1, PL 20, col. 553.
[30] As did Justin Martyr, *L'Apologie de saint Justin, philosophe et martyr*, ed. and trans. C. Munier (Freiburg, 1994).
[31] *Bobbio* 60, p. 22.

the Sunday mass I parallels the end of the *Pater Noster* where God is called 'all powerful and eternal God who has delivered man from evil and from the adversary so that men might adore him with pure hearts'.[32] God has then saved man. Man responds to and receives that salvation through the celebration of the Eucharist. The Eucharistic celebration is clearly a sacrificial act. This sacrificial theme is common to all the Frankish sacramentaries.

The *canon* of the Gallican mass, as exemplified by all the Frankish sacramentaries, consists of five principal prayers.[33] These are the variable prayer of the *Contestatio* or the *Praefatio missae* which corresponds to the Roman variable preface. The Bobbio Missal provides a different *Contestatio* for each mass-set. Then comes the invariable *Sanctus*, the variable *Post Sanctus*, of which the only example in the Bobbio Missal is contained in the *Canon actionis* at the start of the Missal, the invariable *Secreta* proper (which was an amalgamation of biblical texts of the Institution Narrative)[34] and the variable *Post Secreta*, which drew from the narrative for its discursive prayer. The *Post Secreta* is also only present in a single example in the Bobbio Missal.

The variable Eucharistic prayer in the Bobbio Missal, as in most of the other Frankish missals, is termed *Contestatio* and was equivalent to the Roman preface. It opened in the same way taking up the last line of the *Sursum Corda* with 'Truly it is meet and right'.[35] There was a different *Contestatio* for each mass of the church year and it was related to the feast or ordinary of time to be celebrated. The Bobbio Missal provides seventy-six *Contestationes* for the sixty-two masses. Some of these are paraphrases of the sermons of Augustine, Maximus the Confessor and Ambrose.[36] It is significant that we see patristic sermons incorporated into the prayers of the liturgy. Many monasteries were active in the production of patristic texts, especially sermons[37] and liturgical manuscripts, at least from the

---

[32] Ibid. 452, p. 135.

[33] I refer the reader to Yitzhak Hen's contribution in this volume where the *canon* of the mass is also discussed.

[34] The *Secreta* is frequently omitted in the sacramentaries for the masses of each day. It is usually present in perhaps the first mass in the sacramentary and introduced only with the opening formula for the masses thereafter. It was perhaps known by heart.

[35] 'Vere dignum et iustum est.'

[36] For example *Bobbio* 77, p. 27, for the mass of Christmas and *Bobbio* 93, p. 30, for the mass of the Holy Innocents.

[37] Chelles is just one example of a late Merovingian and early Carolingian female monastery that produced and commissioned manuscripts. It was responsible for producing Cologne, Dombibliothek 63, 65, 67, 97 of Augustine's *Enarrationes in Psalmos* (*CLA* VIII.1152) and Cologne, Historisches Archiv Kasten B. 155 (*CLA* VIII.1170) of Augustine on Psalms 96:10–12, and also possibly produced Vatican City, BAV, Reg. lat. 316 (*CLA* I.105), the Old Gelasian Sacramentary, and also possibly London, British Library Add. 24143 (*CLA* II.170), Gregory the Great's *Moralia in Iob* and Oxford, Bodleian Library Laud. Misc. 126 (*CLA* II.252), Augustine's *De Trinitate*. For this activity see McKitterick, 'Nuns' scriptoria'. How many of the literary parallels that can be identified between patristic texts and the liturgical prayers could be ascribed to the creative hands of the nuns or monks producing the manuscripts is a fascinating question that unfortunately cannot be explored here.

eighth century. That this sacramentary suggests the use of and paraphrasing of sermons as prayers for the liturgy raises three important issues that cannot be understated. First, the composer of these prayers used by the compiler of the Bobbio Missal knew his patristic theology very well and had access to a library (a monastic library?) which he used either to compose these prayers as original compositions based upon his patristic sources, or to avail himself of a variety of existing prayers of which at least some were composed using sermons as models.[38] Secondly, it bears witness to the process of creative liturgical composition, a process in which the centre producing this manuscript was possibly involved. Thirdly, it demonstrates the continuity of thought between sermon theology and liturgical theology, and the desire to reproduce patristic sermon theology in liturgical prayers as a prominent, recognisable (as the sermons were also preached) and effective method of instruction of the congregation.[39] In addition to these three points, those *Contestationes* that are the object of such paraphrasing, especially with regard to the sermons of Maximus, would have been composed later than the sixth-century context of many of the prayers. Whereas Augustine's sermons enjoyed undisputed popularity throughout the late Roman and Merovingian periods and manuscript evidence demonstrates wide diffusion of his sermons throughout every region of Merovingian Gaul, the same cannot be said of Maximus the Confessor. Maximus' sermons, from the evidence of surviving manuscripts and manuscript lists, do not appear to have been widely available in Gaul until the second half of the seventh and early eighth centuries,[40] suggesting that a number of the prayers of the Bobbio Missal which make use of his sermons are in fact recent and perhaps original compositions.[41]

---

[38] One makes the assumption here that the prayers used the sermons as models and not vice versa. If the reverse were true, then some of these prayers have remained remarkably pure in their replication of whole sections of sermons and are of extremely ancient origin.

[39] On the subject of these sermons and prayers being understood purely in terms of their language I refer the reader to L.P.M. Batstone, 'Doctrine and liturgy in Merovingian Gaul c.481–c.751' (PhD thesis, Cambridge, 2000), pp. 26–32. See also Hen, *Culture and Religion*, pp. 21–3.

[40] Aside from their use as liturgical sermons, sermons were also important for devotional purposes and they were used to supply the readings for the Divine office. They therefore shaped the theological perceptions of the clergy and religious without as well as within the liturgy of the mass. The library holdings of Merovingian Gaul, and the late Merovingian homiliaries, provide incontestable evidence of the popularity and consistent use during the Merovingian period of the sermons of Augustine, Jerome, Leo the Great and Gregory the Great. Gallo-Roman sermon authors were Faustus of Riez and Avitus of Vienne. The only surviving sermon material we have that was composed during the Merovingian period is that of Caesarius of Arles and Eligius of Noyon. I have carried out an extensive survey of the manuscript tradition of patristic holdings of a number of Merovingian monastic scriptoria, but the scope of this chapter prevents its inclusion. My PhD thesis provides maps showing the distribution of surviving manuscripts of patristic sermons that were copied and distributed in Merovingian Gaul.

[41] It is also possible that Maximus' sermons were influenced by particular liturgical prayers, the source for which was also available to the compiler of these *Contestationes*. This, however, seems less likely to me. There is no manuscript evidence for the circulation of foreign liturgical manuscripts in Gaul during the Merovingian period. There is, however, voluminous evidence for the widespread and

Other than in the *Missale Francorum*, the *Contestatio* has mostly lost its original theme of thanksgiving. The *Contestatio* generally takes up the praise to God, extolling His virtues and the desire of the community to follow His will and be united with Him for ever in Heaven. God is praised and received in anticipation as Lord and as Father, creator and redeemer, and the dependence of man upon His Grace for perseverance in the faith is also asserted. The *Contestationes* of saints' feasts in all the Frankish sacramentaries are very particular in their line of theological development and are clearly later compositions than those *Contestationes* which have retained their original theme of thanksgiving. It is typical of all the *Contestationes* for the feast of a saint in the Merovingian sacramentaries that the life of the saint be retold in brief. There is distinct emphasis on their holy deeds and virtues, and how these virtues associate them with God and put them in a powerful intercessory position. This indicates that as the cult of the saints within the liturgy developed, the original thanksgiving for creation–fall–redemption theme of the *Contestationes* was replaced by a new focus on the saint whose virtuous life epitomised the redeemed state described in the earlier prayers. We see a clear development along consistent theological lines. Particular *Contestationes* with this focus for saints' feasts are numerous throughout all the sacramentaries[42] and therefore demonstrate a particular aspect of Gallican theology whose development we see translated into the liturgical life of the church.

The *Contestatio* of the Sunday mass I in the Bobbio Missal reiterates the sacrificial theme of the *Collectio ad pacem* from the mass of the Advent of the Lord. It calls Jesus the Host of praise, immolated at mass to give thanks to God.[43] Christ is presented as the priest and victim of the Paschal sacrifice. The gifts are very clearly and literally identified with Christ. The cross itself is what offers, in the Eucharist, the possibility of eternal life. There is no mention of the resurrection. The reason that Christ took the form of flesh to save man from his sins and death, explains the Bobbio *Missa quomodo sacerdus pro se orare debet*, was due to God's love for man that sought to reconcile him with Himself.[44] The *Contestatio* for the *Missa quadraginsimalis I* tells the congregation that the Eucharist was the living and true bread of eternal substance that had fed Moses. This bread had the power to heal.[45] The Paschal immolation, explains the *Contestatio* for the Easter vigil, is none other than Christ Himself, the true Lamb who takes away the sins of

---

popular activity surrounding the copying and sharing of sermon collections. See Batstone, 'Doctrine and liturgy', ch. 2 and conclusion.

[42] For example, the *Contestatio* of the mass for St Martin's feast in the Irish Palimpsest Sacramentary, fol. 37r–v, in A. Dold and L. Eizenhöfer, *Das irische Palimpsestsakramentar im Clm 14429 der Staatsbibliothek München*, Texte und Arbeiten 53–4 (Beuron, 1964), pp. 149–50; the feast of St Felix and the feast of St Marcellus in the Old Gelasian Sacramentary, ed. Mohlberg, p. 130; the sixth mass of Mone, ed. Mohlberg, p. 87, and the feast of St Stephen in the *Missale Gothicum*, ed. Mohlberg, p. 10.

[43] *Bobbio* 453, p. 135.      [44] Ibid. 411, p. 122.      [45] Ibid. 134, p. 42.

the world and destroyed death.[46] This prayer bears a remarkable resemblance to the *Agnus Dei* of the Roman mass. While the sacrificial themes in relation to the Eucharist are powerful, the associations between the sacrifice of Christ on the cross and redemption in the prayers are absent in the *Item Contestatio dominicalis* [490], where Jesus is explicitly called the Victor. It continues praising God for the immortality won by baptism in Christ and its triumph over the devil and the world. There is the theme of triumph here, but of eternal life won by baptism rather than of the cross.[47] One wonders if two different sources have been used here by the compiler of the sacramentary that might account for the lack of theological consistency: one older source that lacks a theology of the cross and one more recent, perhaps composed by the compiler of the Bobbio, that has a clearer perception of the role of the cross and the sacrifice of the Eucharist in the economy of salvation. Certainly the sacrificial language used of the Eucharist and the cross is charged with Old Testament language that was used in Jewish Temple worship, which is consistent with the language elsewhere in the Missal.[48]

One should not ignore the notable use of the New Testament to contextualise the Old Testament ritual themes in the texts of the Bobbio Missal. This is exemplified in the juxtaposition of Adam and Eve and Mary and Jesus which also occurs in the *Missale Gothicum*. The Bobbio Missal does not, however, present such a highly charged view of Mary as could be said of the *Missale Gothicum*. The Bobbio Missal confines itself to affirming Mary's perpetual virginity, and asserts that from her Jesus took flesh, because as the flesh had caused man to be lost to death, so by the flesh man was to be freed.[49] Her role here is restricted to providing the flesh for Jesus who would then redeem mankind. What is significant here, as in the Old Gelasian Sacramentary and the *Missale Gothicum*, is the relationship between Adam, Eve and the fall on the one hand and Jesus, Mary and redemption on the other. What has 'gone wrong' with mankind in the Old Testament has been 'fixed' in the New. From this stems the Bobbio Missal's Mariology.

Old Testament ritual themes are again prominent in the *Post Sanctus*. The *Post Sanctus* developed the Trinitarian theme of the *Sanctus*[50] with more specifically christological data cast in a form not so much of praise, but of *anamnesis*. The *Sanctus* provided the Christian church with the counterpart to the election and

---

[46] Ibid. 261, p. 77.     [47] Ibid. 490, p. 150.

[48] These examples include references to the church as the Temple, Jesus as the sacrificial Lamb and receiving the Eucharist becomes the sign of entering into the New Covenant with God as the new people of Israel, just as the participation of the Jews in the sacrifice in the Temple was the renewal of the Old Covenant that God had made with the Israelites. This language of Temple ritual is used throughout the Bobbio Missal in the context of Christianity representing the New Israel.

[49] *Bobbio* 70 and 128, pp. 24 and 39.

[50] L. Chavoutier, 'Un libellus pseudo-ambrosien sur le Saint-Esprit', *Sacris Erudiri* (1960), pp. 136–92; B.J. Moreton, 'The significance of the Sanctus in the Anaphoral prayer', *Studia Patristica* 107 (1970), pp. 396–401.

redemption of Israel, which in the second and third benedictions of the *Shema* follow the *Qedusha*.[51] The *Post Sanctus* attaches this election and redemption of the New Israel to the sacrifice of the Lamb. It usually began with the words 'Truly holy, truly blessed Son are you, Our Lord Jesus Christ',[52] linking up the *Contestatio* with the *Sanctus* and the prayers of consecration. Usually, the *Post Sanctus* prayer was short, leading straight into the Institution Narrative and followed on into the fixed prayer of the Institution Narrative.

The Institution Narrative of the *Secreta* of the *Missa Romensis cotidiana* of the Bobbio Missal is identical to the *Incipit canon actionis* of the *Missale Francorum*.[53] While the conflations of this text are not an attempt to harmonise the Synoptic narratives, the narrative as a whole is a gospel narrative based on Matt. 26.26–8. The text of I Cor. 11.25 has also made a distinct contribution to the narrative, filling in the gap between the two parts of the liturgical narrative and supplying the material for recasting the Dominical words over the chalice. The command *hoc facite in meam commemorationem* was an element of the Institution Narrative of the second century.[54] What is prescribed and asserted by the Lord in Matthew's Gospel is confirmed and handed down by Paul in I Cor. 11, and is therefore an apostolic and authoritative witness to, and commentary upon, the Matthean narrative. The word *memoria* is deemed to be the synonym of *anamnesis*. The *memoria Christi* was the liturgical action of sacrifice and communion instituted by Christ Himself, and not merely a recollection of Him in a *carmen* or *oratio*.

The reference to the hands of the Lord *in sanctas ac venerabiles manus suas* recalls the devout oratorical usage found in the Greek church copied by Rome. The same may be said of the phrase *ad Te Deum patrem omnipotentem* which also finds parallels in the Greek liturgy, and was similarly imitated by Rome. The words *sanctus sanguis* are characteristic of Irish expression.[55] The phrase *eleuatis oculis in caelum* recalls Jesus' action at the feeding of the five thousand, the type of the Eucharist and His

---

[51] The *Qedusha* of Isa. 6.3 is found in three places in the synagogue service: the *Shema* at the beginning, the *Amidah*, and after the reading of the *Torah*. The first benediction glorifies the God of Abraham, Isaac and Jacob, the second benediction glorifies the God who sustains the living and the dead. The third is 'We will sanctify thy name in the world as they sanctify it in the highest heavens' to which the *Qedusha* is attached, 'And they called unto one another and said, "Holy, Holy, Holy is the Lord of hosts, the whole earth is full of his glory." Those beside them said, "Blessed be the glory of the Lord from his place."' Isa. 6.3; Ezek. 3.2; Moreton, 'The significance of the Sanctus', p. 396. S.C. Reif, *Judaism and Hebrew Prayer. New Perspectives on Jewish Liturgical History* (Cambridge, 1993).

[52] 'Vere sanctus, vere benedictus Filius tuus, Dominus noster Iesus Christus.'

[53] And almost identical to that in the Old Gelasian Sacramentary, pp. 234–6.

[54] See Justin Martyr, '*L'Apologie*', 66.3. Irenaeus alludes to it at the end of his reference to the institution, *Adversus haereses*, IV.17.5.

[55] See the 'liturgical note' of E. Bishop in *The Book of Cerne*, ed. A.B. Kuypers (Cambridge, 1902), pp. 247–8 and 282 n. 1.

final discourse in John 17.1. It also appears in the Syrian liturgy of St James and St Mark.[56]

To the *novi testamenti* the words *et aeterni* are added. This is found in the Old Latin pre-Vulgate version of the Bible. They constitute a significant doctrinal addition borrowed from Heb. 13.20–1. Together with the words *mysterium fidei* from I Tim. 3.9, they heighten the doctrinal importance of the Eucharistic cup. Not only is the cup the cup of the blood of Christ, but drinking from that cup draws the faithful into the eternal covenant established by Christ on the cross. It also ratifies that covenant between God and mankind, in the same way that Old Testament covenants were ratified by splashing the blood of the victim on the people.[57] The eternity of the sacrifice of Christ is emphasised, as is the Eucharist as the exclusive celebration of that sacrifice. The sacredness of the Eucharist is also heightened with the clarification as to what it meant to receive the body and blood of the Lord. There is no clue as to how early these additions entered into the liturgy, but they are clear in the Roman, Gallican and eastern narratives. They can only be descended from manuscripts dating from the pre-Vulgate age, as the biblical witness to the Institution Narratives used is the Old Latin version of Matt. 26.26–8 and I Cor. 11.

The final important addition was of the *pro vobis* before the *[et] pro multis effunditur*. This text was presumably borrowed from Luke 22.20 and was also present in the Institution Narrative known to Augustine of Hippo,[58] and might be another example of Augustinian theology in the prayers of the Merovingian mass. It clearly attempts to address the present congregation and emphasise their inclusion in the sacrifice, thereby making the celebration a personal participation in the mystery.

The *Secreta* of the Bobbio Missal is a graphic and impressive presentation of Jesus' institution of the Eucharist *pridie quam pateretur*. The additions have doctrinally heightened and clarified the narrative without losing its directness. It seems fair to say that this example of a Gallican Institution Narrative belongs to a common liturgical tradition with that of the Verona Sacramentary, for which the careful preservation of the scriptural form and character of the narrative was held to be vital. This desire for the correct celebration of the Eucharist is a particular feature of the Merovingian sacramentaries, including the Bobbio Missal, and is more particularly evinced by the use of the words *Legitima Eucharistia* in the *anaphora*. This is particularly idiosyncratic and is a central concept in the Eucharistic theology and

---

[56] The Syrian liturgy follows Matt. 14.9, Mark 6.41 and Luke 9.16.

[57] This is mirrored closely in the mass for the consecration of a church in the Old Gelasian Sacramentary.

[58] *Sermo* 216.3.

euchology of the Frankish sacramentaries.[59] These words occur in seven *Post Secreta* prayers in the Frankish sacramentaries, and although numerous *Post Secreta* prayers in the Frankish sacramentaries do not use the actual words *Legitima Eucharistia*, they none the less espouse the same Eucharistic theology characterised by the precision and intensity of the narrative drama. There is in these other *Post Secreta* prayers the same emphasis on the need to observe faithfully the instituted command of Christ.[60] There appears to have been a distinct desire that the Eucharistic offering be 'legitimate', but this is linked not to the naming of the Holy Spirit as part of the Trinity, but rather to the earlier statement, 'therefore, keeping these commands'. The desire for the Eucharist to be legitimate or lawful, more often than not coupled with an invocation of the Trinity, not just of the Holy Spirit, was clearly a later insertion into the prayer, and was of great significance. There are other similar adjectives used to describe the Eucharist, including *pura* and *vera* and less commonly *et verus sanguis*. This is clear in the *Missale Francorum*[61] and the Bobbio Missal in which the Eucharistic elements are called 'A pure host, a holy host, an immaculate host, holy bread of eternal life and cup of eternal salvation.'[62]

What makes the *Eucharistia legitima* is that it be celebrated, as the *Sacrificium vetus* was, in the correct manner prescribed by the law of the Lord. The *Eucharistia* is the Passion of Christ that He offered at the Last Supper and completed on the cross, and which He ordained to be continued in the Eucharist instituted by Him at the Last Supper. The Last Supper, the Passion and the mass are therefore inseparable, and Christ is Himself the *sacerdos* of the liturgy. If the Passion of Christ is to be reproduced in church, it must be a careful imitation of Jesus' procedure at

---

[59] The term *Legitima Eucharistia* can be found in two of the African fathers, Tertullian (in his liturgy of the hours at terces, sextes and nones): see Tertullian, *De oratione* 25, PL 1, cols. 1300–1: 'Exceptis utique legitimis orationibus, quae sine ulla admonitione debentur ingressu lucis et noctis'; J. Pinell, 'El número sagrado de las horas del oficio', in *Miscellanea Liturgica Card. G.Lecaro*, II (Rome, Paris, Tournai and New York, 1967), pp. 887–934 esp. pp. 911–13; J. Pinell, 'Legitima Eucharistia: cuestiones sobre la anamnesis y la epiclesis en el antiguo rito gallicano', in *Mélanges liturgiques offerts au R.P. Dom B. Botte* (Louvain, 1972), pp. 445–461, at p. 446. Cyprian refers to the Eucharist much more clearly in his Ep. 63, 17, 14, 10 and 19. He tries to demonstrate the need to use the chalice in the Eucharistic celebration and this furnishes him with the opportunity to present a theology on the sacramental tradition of the gospel. See Pinell, 'Legitima Eucharistia: cuestiones', p. 446. A fragment of a *Post Secreta* from a Frankish mass for Christmas Eve has substituted *Legitima Eucharistia* for the original *verum corpus*. The corrector – who may or may not have been the scribe – neglected to remove the corresponding *verus sanguis* and the resulting: 'That through the mystery of your [God the Father's] operation, they become for us a legitimate Eucharist and the true blood of your Son', is clumsy (Cambridge, Gonville and Caius College 153).

[60] Pinell, 'Legitima Eucharistia: cuestiones', p. 449.

[61] *Missale Francorum* ('Incipit canon cctionis'), ed. Mohlberg, p. 32.

[62] 'Hostiam puram, hostiam sanctam, hostiam inmaculatam, panem sanctum vitae aeternae et calicem salutis perpetuae . . . et quod tibi obtulit summus sacerdos tuus Melchisadek, sanctum sacrificium. Inmaculatam hostiam.' The Old Gelasian Sacramentary ('Incipit canon actionis'), ed. Mohlberg, p. 185, and the *Missale Gothicum* ('Ordo missae in circumcisione domini nostri Iesu Christi'), ed. Mohlberg, p. 18, use similar expressions.

•

the institution. The function of the Institution Narrative in making the Eucharist *legitima* is not merely to revive the memory of the important historic event, or to provide a reason for the celebration of the Eucharist, as the eastern narratives do, but rather to make the significant historic event continuously present and operative. By its adherence to the institution of Christ, the Church's Eucharistic action becomes the very same action of Christ at the Last Supper, completed on the cross. Perhaps this desire for the correct and lawful accomplishment of the Eucharistic sacrifice in the liturgy is reflected to some degree by the Merovingians' particular interest in the copying and distribution of canon law codes.[63] Interestingly enough from a theological viewpoint, the commemoration of the Passion does not appear to be the reception of the Eucharist itself, but rather the correct performance of the consecration rite. It was the Institution Narrative that brought about the consecration, not an *epiclesis*. It is hard to find clear evidence of an *epiclesis* anywhere in the Gallican liturgy, including the Bobbio Missal, with the exception of the rite of church consecration.[64]

## CONCLUSION

This assessment of the basic themes of the prayers of the Bobbio Missal enables us to highlight several aspects of the theology expressed in the texts of the Bobbio Missal and their relation to that of other Frankish sacramentaries. How far one can say that these prayers represent 'Gallican' theology or 'local' theology is not wholly ascertainable given the fragmentary nature of our sources.

The Bobbio Missal's use of the *Aius* rather than the *Gloria* suggests that in the region and period of its composition, there was either a powerful tradition of or a specific present need for Trinitarian, or perhaps anti-Arian, instruction. Even the variable prayers throughout the Bobbio Missal assert the action of God in Trinity and the indivisibility of the persons of the Trinity in nature. Their equality, and that of their gifts and virtues, is also asserted. The concern with anti-Arian theology might perhaps have been more pertinent to the south-east Gaul which had been under Arian Gothic rule. The Eucharistic prayers are notable as the Trinity rather than the Holy Spirit is invoked at the consecration. The variable *Post Aius* prayers pick up the themes of the Trinity and are also clearly anti-Pelagian in their particular emphasis on man's need of God's Grace.

---

[63] On this subject see R. McKitterick, 'Knowledge of canon law in the Frankish kingdoms before 789: the manuscript evidence', *Journal of Theological Studies* 36 (1985), pp. 97–117, and Hen, *The Royal Patronage of Liturgy*, pp. 28–33.

[64] The rite of church consecration in the Bobbio Missal is particularly distinctive and the constraints of this chapter preclude proper exploration of it here. Suffice to say that it does include an invocatory *epiclesis* for the consecration of the church but not in the context of the Eucharistic consecration.

Throughout Gaul, the *prophetia* was in use. The following *collectio* in all the sacramentaries takes up the theme of the need of God's Grace and are all clearly anti-Pelagian in their emphasis. This might suggest that the prayers of the liturgy of Gaul were asserting the orthodoxy of the Gallic church following the fifth-century controversy over the so-called semi-Pelagian debate. The continued prominence of these anti-Arian and anti-Pelagian themes demonstrates both the power of doctrinal tradition within the local church and the continued need to reaffirm those doctrines of the church in the region and period for which this Missal was produced. Clearly the compiler of the Bobbio Missal has made use of an exemplar here.

The Bobbio Missal's description of the people's offering of the Eucharist as a good work of man, the grace for which was attributable to God, is quite distinct theologically when compared to the other Frankish mass books.[65] God sanctifies and completes the offering man makes in good faith and piety. The Bobbio Missal's contents' preoccupation with anti-Pelagian theological themes possibly indicates a novel and original aspect of the theology of this local community. This consistent use of prayers with a particular south-east Gallican perspective by the compiler of the Bobbio Missal leads one to conclude that the Missal was indeed intended for a community in this region.

The use of the *Benedicite* in the Bobbio Missal but not in the other Frankish sacramentaries indicates that the theme of confessing faith in times of persecution, based on Dan. 3.51–90, was in fairly wide, but declining, use across Gaul. This might be because the immediate occasions for confession of faith and consequent martyrdom were rapidly declining by the sixth century and thereafter, even as a part of the tradition of the church, the prayer was losing its relevance. This theme was therefore gradually succeeded by one which stressed the blessed state of the saints, with a shift of emphasis away from martyrdom towards virtuous living in imitation of the saints. This literary activity within the liturgy may possibly be associated with the literary activity concerning the lives of the saints so prominent in the seventh and eighth centuries. This theological development is evident particularly in the *Contestationes* for saints' feasts. On feast days, the references to the redemptive act of Christ is replaced with reflections on the redeemed state of the saints, their virtues, the fruits they bore in this life and their heroic death and sojourn in paradise. In this redeemed state lies both the power of the saints to intercede on behalf of the faithful for temporal favours, and the promise of eternal blessedness for those who imitate them. Inherent in this is the threat of judgement for those who do not. The theological development of the cult of the saints clearly led to an innovative

[65] This is in contrast to the *Missale Gallicanum Vetus* where the Eucharist is clearly described as God's gift to mankind, and this is the overriding attitude of all the other sacramentaries, although it is only clearly stated in the *Missale Gallicanum Vetus*.

corresponding liturgical development. This may indicate that the *Contestationes* for saints' feasts were original compositions.

The texts of the Bobbio Missal are also particularly revealing of the creative process of the liturgy and its response to local needs in the way their compiler actively either selected some recently composed prayers which paraphrased a number of sermons of the Fathers, or perhaps even composed them himself. This paraphrasing can be seen in a number of the prayers of the Missal but a clear example is the Mariology of the Bobbio Missal where the theological juxtaposition of Mary and Eve, Jesus and Adam clearly derives from the sermons of Leo the Great.

There is, as one would expect, a clear association between the Eucharist and the cross in all the sacramentaries of various geographical and chronological origins. It might be possible therefore to suggest that this unequivocal theological association is an aspect of truly Gallican theology. The Bobbio Missal however, lacks a clear theology of the cross and looks more to the resurrection for redemptive themes, despite the sacrificial language used of the Eucharist. That the compiler/composer appears to be trying to remedy this in some of the prayers would possibly indicate a local, and possibly very early, aspect of theology particular to the Bobbio Missal. The connection between the Eucharist and eternal life appears in all the sacramentaries without exception.

The Bobbio Missal is loaded with the language and themes reminiscent of Jewish Temple worship in the Old Testament which are to be found throughout the Missal. The Bobbio Missal relates the Eucharist to the manna fed to the Israelites in the desert. Only the Eucharist is eternal food, and the manna was not. The church is the Temple and the priest is 'a priest forever, like Melchisedech of old'. Jesus is the Lamb of God and each mass includes the Roman *Agnus Dei*. These associations probably derive from their Eucharistic sacrificial associations and the Eucharist is referred to explicitly as a holocaust. The idea of the cross as the significant event of redemption might not have been consistent across Gaul or within the Bobbio Missal itself, but the themes of Eucharistic sacrifice and the access it gave to redemption certainly were.

A concern for the legitimacy and purity of the Eucharist also appears to be another particular aspect of 'Gallican' theology. The concern for lawfulness and the correctness of liturgical procedure to ensure the validity of the Eucharist might be linked to the Merovingians' interest in legality and discipline, stretching from the emphasis on the imitation of the virtues of the saints, through to their assiduous collection of and copying of canon law codes. In this case, as a literary endeavour reflecting genuinely Gallican concerns, the liturgy is an excellent example.

Roman influences, or influences that can be said to be Roman inasmuch as they relate to the Verona Sacramentary and the eighth-century Roman *Ordines*, can be seen in the Bobbio Missal, especially in the naming of the *Praefatio Missae* as the *Secreta*. The Bobbio Missal uses the Roman *Agnus Dei*.[66] This may demonstrate simply that the liturgy of Gaul was continually developing throughout the Merovingian period and reflects the influence of Roman prayer traditions.

It is clear that the liturgy itself was a very significant teacher of the doctrine of the church and its discipline to the laity, although this is difficult to demonstrate definitively from such a brief assessment of the theological and doctrinal themes of the prayers of the Bobbio Missal.[67] In all the prayers of the Bobbio Missal we see clear doctrinal assertions and easily memorised doctrinal formulae. The diversity that existed in the liturgical traditions of local churches and the church more widely was a feature of the liturgy that was both accepted and expected. Gaul's Catholic church was a champion of local traditions and responded keenly to local situations. This has left us with a rich supply of living liturgical compositions that were continually adapting to the local needs of the Merovingian world, of which the Bobbio Missal is a particularly important and fascinating example.

[66] The *Missale Gallicanum Vetus* includes the *Agnus Dei* as a collect for the fourth Sunday after Easter, but it is the only other source that does, to the best of my knowledge.

[67] While Els Rose's chapter in this volume has suggested that it is hard to get at the meaning of some of the prayers of the Bobbio Missal, and the *Missale Gothicum* is a useful tool in enabling us to accomplish this, she has concentrated on a small number of prayers whose Latin appears to be corrupt.

# IO

# *The* Missa pro principe *in the Bobbio Missal*\*

MARY GARRISON

> Some kings were conquered in the terrifying crash of battle and others emerged
> victorious according to what Columba asked of God by the power of prayer.[1]

The *Missa pro principe* in the Bobbio Missal is a fascinating and enigmatic composition. Its usefulness as historical evidence suffers particularly acutely from the
uncertainties surrounding the date and provenance of the manuscript in which it
is transmitted, and yet, as will be shown, any progress towards dating and localis-
ing the whole manuscript will not necessarily resolve the difficulties raised by the
*Missa pro principe*. The discussion that follows therefore offers more questions than
answers – in the hope that there is some value in making explicit assumptions that
are often implicit, and something to be gained by translating the text and setting
its exempla alongside those of its analogues.

The direction to pray for kings and those in high stations can be found in Paul's
first letter to Timothy.[2] The assumption that such prayers were part of the Christian
liturgy from the earliest times, even during periods of persecution, and even before
the conversion of Constantine can be corroborated from scattered testimonies.[3]
Thereafter, the evidence for the practice in both east and west becomes slightly less
sparse, but is still fragmentary in the extreme.[4] In the early medieval west, royal
injunctions to pray for a king are well attested and their importance corroborated

---

* I thank Yitzhak Hen for patience, assistance and discussion, and Els Rose, Meta Niederkorn and
Irene van Renswoude for discussion of various points.

[1] Adomnán of Iona, *Life of St Columba*, trans. R. Sharpe (Harmondsworth, 1995), I.1, p. 110;
A.O. Anderson and M.O. Anderson, *Adomnán's Life of Columba*, revised by M.O. Anderson (Oxford,
1991), p. 14.

[2] 1 Tim. 2.2: 'pro regibus et omnibus qui in sublimitate sunt'.

[3] For discussion, see L. Biehl, *Das liturgische Gebet für Kaiser und Reich: Ein Beitrag zur Geschichte
des Verhältnisses von Kirche und Staat*, Görres-Gesellschaft zur Pflege der Wissenschaft im Katholiken
Deutschland 75 (Paderborn, 1937), pp. 30–5.

[4] Ibid., pp. 36ff.

both by a few colourful anecdotes about figures who refused to do so[5] and by dramatic assertions of the efficacy of such prayers.[6] Accordingly prayers within the mass for kings, and eventually masses for kings, and then prayers and masses for their victories,[7] and for armies going into battle, must once have been extremely commonplace despite their poor representation in the extant liturgical manuscripts and fragments.[8]

To clarify the relationship between those biblically enjoined prayers for those in authority incorporated into the liturgy, on the one hand, and on the other, the various extant masses for rulers, for their armies and especially for their hoped-for victories is a task outside the scope of this discussion and points to the first of many uncertainties raised by this category of liturgical evidence. When, where and by whom masses for a king's victories might have been construed as fulfilling the injunction of 1 Tim. 2.2 is an interesting question. That they could be is undeniable, for only a powerful king could bring peace and 1 Tim. 2.2 states that the prayers for those in high station are to be made 'that we may lead a quiet and a peaceable life'. But it is not to be assumed that every liturgical form concerned with royal victory was understood in relation to that command.

As in the study of all liturgical evidence, prayers for rulers present acute challenges of method and interpretation. None the less, and despite some enduring uncertainties about date, origin and context, the extant texts have been adduced chiefly to illuminate a range of topics which includes emerging concepts of church

---

[5] On Columba and Theudebert, see M. McCormick, *Eternal Victory: Triumphal Rulership in Late Antiquity, Byzantium and the Early Medieval West* (Cambridge, 1986), p. 344 n. 68 (Jonas, *Vita Columbani*, I.28 ed. B. Krusch, MGH SRM IV (Hannover, 1902), pp. 218–19). On the accusations in 781 against Potho of San Vincenzo, who was charged with having avoided reciting the usual psalm for Charlemagne and with having spoken disrespectfully of him, see *Codex Carolinus, Ep.* 67, ed. W. Gundlach, MGH Epistolae III [= Epistolae Merowingici et Karolini Aevi I] (Berlin, 1892), pp. 594–7; E. Ewig, 'La prière pour le roi et le royaume dans les privilèges épiscopaux de l'époque mérovingienne', in *Mélanges offerts à Jean Dauvillier* (Toulouse, 1979), pp. 255–67; *Concilium Aschheimense*, c. 1, MGH Concilia Aevi Karolini II.1, ed. A. Werminghoff (Hannover, 1906) p. 57; Avitus of Vienne, *Ep.* 85, ed. R. Peiper, MGH AA VI.2 (Berlin, 1883), p. 95.

[6] For example, see Adomnán of Iona, *Life of St Columba*, I.1 (regarding Oswald's victory over Cadwallon, after Columba's death), ed. Anderson and Anderson, p. 14; and the *Annals of Ulster*, s.a. 561 (for the Uí Néills' victory at Cúl Drebene thanks to Columba's prayers), ed. and trans. S. MacAirt and G. MacNiocall, *The Annals of Ulster* (to AD 1131) (Dublin 1983), pp. 80–1. For translation and discussion of the incident in the life of Columba, see Adomnán of Iona, *Life of St Columba*, trans. Sharpe, p. 110, with notes on p. 250.

[7] On liturgical contexts for prayers for the ruler, see Biehl, *Das liturgische Gebet*, pp. 48–70, and on prayers for the ruler as especially characteristic of Good Friday and the Saturday before Easter, see ibid., pp. 83–6.

[8] For example, on the hypothesis that the Reichenau palimpsest prayer for a king's victory (Karlsruhe, Badische Landesbibliothek, Aug. 253, fol. 16r) was part of a widely diffused Frankish collection, see *Das Palimpsestsakramentar im Codex Augiensis CXII: Ein Messbuch ältester Struktur aus dem Alpengebiet mit Anhang: Zwei altfränkische Gebete aus Codex Aug. CCLIII*, ed. A. Dold and A. Baumstark (Beuron, 1925), p. 34.

and state, the christianisation of kingship and the development of the ceremonial of 'triumphal rulership'.[9] Merely to assemble and survey the evidence raises questions about the development of the liturgy in post-Roman polities.[10] To what extent can the liturgy be expected to reflect changes of regime? What would be the appropriate way to pray for 'kings and all those in high stations' in the kingdom of a barbarian ruler who believed that he was in fact a subordinate of an eastern Roman emperor, or in that of one who did not? If liturgical books tend to inertia and conservatism, then what historical circumstances foster innovation, whether in the manuscripts or in the conduct of the liturgy itself? As Tellenbach demonstrated, prayers for the Roman emperor and Empire were recopied for many centuries after they ceased to be politically relevant in the west and 'corrections', such as the substitution of 'Christian' for 'Roman' in relevant contexts, were slow to take root. The liturgy (or liturgical manuscripts at any rate) did not always walk in step with political developments.[11] Hence the necessity to trace changes across the corpus of evidence as a whole.[12] Yet because a liturgical manuscript could be a formulary from which offices might be celebrated *mutatis mutandis*, or could even merely an *aide mémoire* for the celebrant, we are not entitled to assume that archaic or inapposite forms attested in the extant manuscripts were in use; thus the relationship between text and practice is uncertain. This uncertainty in turn raises the question of how (or even whether) the extant evidence can be used as *historical* evidence. The problem points to some of the difficulties of interpreting these exceedingly challenging sources. Yet uncertainties about audience and origin notwithstanding, royal masses, prayers and blessings are full of interest for the historian, for the light they can shed on a wide range of topics related to kingship as well as what they might show about the concerns of different liturgical communities.[13] Finally,

---

[9] G. Tellenbach, 'Römischer und christlicher Reichsgedanke in der Liturgie des frühen Mittelalters', in G. Tellenbach, *Ausgewählte Abhandlungen und Aufsätze*, II (Stutttgart, 1988), pp. 343–410 (originally published in 1934/5); E. Ewig, 'Zum christlichen Königsgedanken im Frühmittelalter', E. Ewig, *Spätantikes und Fränkisches Gallien*, ed. H. Atsma, 2 vols., Beihefte der Francia 1 (Munich 1976), I, pp. 3–71 (originally published in 1956); McCormick, *Eternal Victory*.

[10] Tellenbach's exemplary marshalling of the evidence in the appendix to his article is particularly valuable in this regard, despite that fact that newer editions of many of the relevant liturgical manuscripts are now available: see Tellenbach, 'Römischer und christlicher Reichsgedanke', pp. 385–410. Many of the relevant eighth-century texts have also been conveniently printed by R.A. Jackson in his *Ordines Coronationis Franciae: Texts and Ordines for the Coronation of Frankish and French Kings and Queens in the Middle Ages* (Philadelphia, 1995), although the attempt to conflate manuscript texts into *ordines* which may never have existed independently means that a reader must study the apparatus with care.

[11] Tellenbach, 'Römischer und christlicher Reichsgedanke', *passim*; see, for example, pp. 356, 359 and 372.

[12] Ibid., p. 357. Y. Hen, *The Royal Patronage of Liturgy in Frankish Gaul to the Death of Charles the Bald (877)*, HBS subsidia 3 (London, 2001).

[13] Y. Hen, 'The uses of the Bible and the perception of kingship in Merovingian Gaul', *Early Medieval Europe* 7 (1998), pp. 277–90.

certain royal blessings were later incorporated into coronation *ordines* which have benefited from more scholarly attention than the royal blessings which are in some cases their raw materials.[14]

To turn from the issue of prayers for rulers in general, and the broad trends associated with their evolution, performance and preservation to a single example invites one to address, or to attempt to address, questions about date, context and provenance. But precisely because of the features of liturgical texts discussed above, it is unreasonable to expect any particular mass for a ruler to mirror precisely the political circumstances of its manuscript context – if that can even be determined with certainty. By the same token, an early medieval mass for a ruler cannot necessarily be expected to provide straightforward evidence which could be used to date or localise the manuscript in which it appears.

The prayers comprising what Mabillon entitled the *Missa pro principe* in the Bobbio Missal have no parallel in any other early medieval liturgical manuscript. The mass implores God's help so that the ruler will be ever victorious and reign prosperously. The ruler's army is mentioned. The wish is expressed that God ensure that anyone who tries to oppose the ruler's authority will collapse at his feet. The emphasis on victory and the inclusion of the army could suggest that the Bobbio *missa* is a votive mass for a special occasion, perhaps to be said before battle, but one must also consider whether it, or parts of it, could have been used during the customary Good Friday and Holy Saturday prayers for rulers. The text is not only utterly distinct from other extant masses for kings, but also stands apart from the rest of the manuscript in which it occurs, for the leaves containing the *Missa pro principe*, fols. 251–4, clearly constitute a separate gathering appended to the manuscript.[15] The later addition of these leaves implies that some agent in the commissioning, production or later use and transmission of the manuscript regarded the *Missa pro principe* as essential, perhaps to rectify a lacuna (assuming that the codex at the time of the addition had no subsequently lost leaves or quires containing analogous material). The circumstances that might have provoked the decision to add the material invite speculation. Why should a compiler or user of the miscellany suddenly have wished to make good the lack of masses for rulers? A change in his role and responsibilities? The transfer of the compilation to an individual or community who needed such a rite? A change in royal policy or regime? Or simply the recognition that an important rite, whether or not available in the sources he had first laid under consideration, had been omitted? It is tempting to juxtapose the addition of the Bobbio *Missa pro principe* to the addition, somewhere in Francia,

[14] Jackson, *Ordines Coronationis Franciae*; see also many of the articles collected in J.L. Nelson, *Politics and Ritual in Early Medieval Europe* (London, 1986).
[15] For palaeographical and codicological discussion, see McKitterick, above, pp. 19–52; Lowe, 'Palaeography'.

of the earliest extant Frankish *laudes regiae* to the Bavarian Mondsee psalter. In both manuscripts, royal liturgical formulae are later additions.[16] It is interesting to note that there is also a third manuscript to which royal liturgical material has been added, although in this case, the addition was made to a section where masses for a king were already present: the Sacramentary of Echternach.[17] Here the additions, including a *Missa pro rege canenda*, were made on a small flyleaf inserted in the middle of one of the *Missae pro regibus*. Whereas the circumstances which led to the addition of the Frankish *laudes* in the Mondsee psalter can be plausibly reconstructed, this is not the case for the Bobbio Missal or the Sacramentary of Echternach. Beyond the obvious fact that the compiler clearly wished to include the material, one can only speculate: were masses for kings especially likely to circulate in individual transmission outside liturgical manuscripts, only to be incorporated later? Or did their perceived importance mean that they were especially likely to be added to extant codices, in contrast to other liturgical forms which may have circulated on loose leaves or quires, outside of codices? The arguments about the relative date of the hand which added these leaves are subject to the micropalaeographical uncertainties, including those which result from the problem of 'the age of the scribe', and can therefore offer little help in recovering intentions.[18] In short, all three examples of added royal liturgical material might be thought to demonstrate their users' or compilers' regard for the importance of masses for kings as well as perhaps the *ad hoc* status of such forms.

Other explanations for the insertion of the Bobbio *Missa pro principe* and the simultaneous additions are also possible. It has been conjectured that the occurrence of (an otherwise unparalleled) *contestatio* similar to the (otherwise unparalleled) one which concludes the Bobbio *Missa pro principe* spurred the scribe of the inserted leaves which contain the *Missa pro principe* to his work.[19] If so, the reason that the added leaves were ruled to allow more lines per page than the book they were to join also invites consideration, especially since the added palimpsest leaves were not in

---

[16] The *laudes* are presumed to have been added to the psalter after it had been brought to Francia by a member of Tassilo's family. *Die Glossen des Psalters von Mondsee (vor 788), Montpellier, Faculté de Médecine MS 409*, ed. F. Unterkircher, Spicilegium Friburgense 20 (Fribourg, 1974), p. 511; E. Kantorowicz, *Laudes Regiae: A Study in Liturgical Acclamations and Mediaeval Ruler Worship* (Berkeley, 1958), pp. 33–7. For discussion and further secondary literature, see M. Garrison, 'The Franks as the New Israel? Education for an identity from Pippin to Charlemagne', in *The Uses of the Past in the Early Middle Ages*, ed. Y. Hen and M. Innes (Cambridge, 2000), pp. 114–61, at pp. 140–2.

[17] See *The Sacramentary of Echternach*, ed. Y. Hen, HBS 110 (London, 1997), pp. 403–4, where the text on the leaf inserted between fols. 223 and 225 is printed in the apparatus and includes a *missa pro rege canenda*; on the date of the manuscript (895 × 898), see ibid., p. 20.

[18] On the imprecision of 'micropalaeography', see J.P. Gumbert, 'Writing and dating: some general remarks', *Scriptorium* 54 (2000), pp. 5–8, at p. 6; on the hand of the added *Missa pro principe*, see McKitterick, above, pp. 33–5; Lowe, 'Palaeography', pp. 71–3.

[19] Wilmart, 'Notice', p. 9.

fact completely filled by the *missa* or the material which follows it. Did the scribe intend to add more texts to fill the new leaves, perhaps to replicate the lineation of his exemplar precisely? Was he simply not very adept at estimating the space required? Was the exemplar in a different script, thus entailing more complex arithmetic (or letter counting) to estimate the space needed? Or is the blank space insignificant? While it is tantalising to speculate about precise motivations which might have led someone to add the leaves, to rule them, and to insert the texts found there, it is more prudent to avoid unfalsifiable assertions about the reason for the insertion of the leaves.

One is on more certain ground in characterising the *Missa pro principe*. It uses Old Testament exempla liberally to evoke an image of kingship redolent of the war-like world of a society that lives by pillage and gift, reminiscent, perhaps, of the characterisations of Germanic peoples by Tacitus and Gregory of Tours. The text is (as far as I know) the only mass for a king to mention booty so explicitly or to amplify its biblical exempla so fully.[20] Thus the benedictions in the mass beseech God to offer the same kind of divine aid as He granted to various figures in the Old Testament: Abraham with his 318 servants defeating the five kings with their armies laid low, achieving victory miraculously, rejoicing to have rescued his nephew Lot and brought back booty, blessed by Melchisedech and blessed by God; Moses fighting the Amalechites; Joshua as Moses' helper; Joshua at the walls of Jericho, as a warrior not yet a leader; David, not the law-giver, king or psalmist, but the shepherd-boy fighting Goliath . . . and so forth.

All of the Bobbio *Missa pro principe* prayers are uttered for 'our ruler' and many also for the army. All but one of the exempla are from the history of Israel at the time before Israel had kings. Victory is overwhelmingly emphasised: there is no mention of any royal virtues.[21] Nor are there prayers for justice or just government. Here God is evoked as the sole possessor of *sapientia* and is said to have ordered the world so that nothing would exist in peace without kings and princes: without them, justice could not flourish nor wickedness wither. This affirmation about royal and princely power as the guarantor of justice seems odd when preceded by the story of Abraham the warrior. (Where, one might ask, is Solomon?) The implication is that rulers maintain justice by their God-given might rather than their virtues. And yet the emphasis on victory is not inconsistent with the notion that royal and princely power is ordained by God, since strong kings and their victories could ensure peace for the church. Of course the cultural and political importance of victory for an early medieval ruler was incalculable: the spoils of victory enabled leaders to reward their followers and make gifts to churches. Victory both required

[20] A translation is provided in Appendix I.
[21] Contrast, for example, the cardinal virtues wished for King Zwentibold in *The Sacramentary of Echternach*, cc. 2094–106, ed. Hen, pp. 404–7.

and gave proof of might and courage; more important, it both depended on and demonstrated divine approval.

To use the Bobbio *Missa pro principe* as historical evidence one might begin by practising a version of biblical form-criticism on it, attempting to extrapolate from its distinctive choices and emphases to a possible *Sitz im Leben*. Such an approach, however, has severe weaknesses when applied to liturgical texts, for liturgical compositions could have a very long afterlife in contexts utterly unlike those in which they were developed. Thus, as mentioned above, references to the Roman Empire's struggles with barbarians persisted for centuries after the end of the western empire.[22] References to the sceptres of the Mercians, Northumbrians and Saxons appear in the coronation blessings for King Charles V of France (1365). However, such blatant anachronisms were apparently irrelevant to participants in the rituals since meaningful social and symbolic communication could transcend the words of the rite.[23]

If one were nonetheless to attempt to characterise the cultural context in which the Bobbio *Missa pro principe* was composed one might surmise that it arose in the post-Roman world, in a monastery (hence the address to *fratres*) in an exceedingly war-like polity, one where pillage and gift were fundamental, where the ruler was designated *princeps*. This does not take us very far, however, for *princeps* may be a designation for a very wide range of supreme rulers: it can be used of emperors, it can be used as a royal or ducal epithet, it can designate the Arnulfing mayors of the palace, or refer to a duke who was a local top man; it is attested for Visigoths, Alamans, Burgundians, Bavarians, Franks and Lombards.[24] In short, the word *princeps* can neither point to, nor exclude, any particular group. The frequency of the word in the Vulgate alone could explain its adoption in a liturgical text. In short, in a composition as heavy with scriptural reminiscences as the Bobbio *Missa pro principe* it would be misguided to use the word as a clue to the *intitulatio* of the ruler for whom the composition was first composed.

One could cavil about almost any hypothetical place of origin. For example, the Old Testament heroes cited in the prayers were invariably fighting against pagans. Does this entitle us to assume that the *missa* was composed for a king fighting heathens or heretics? The possibility is attractive, but unconvincing. First, and obviously, it is hard to imagine how any extensive series of Old Testament heroes could be assembled where the foes were *not* gentiles. Second, the exempla do not

[22] Tellenbach, 'Römischer und christlicher Reichsgedanke, p. 357.

[23] J. Nelson, 'Ritual and reality in the early Medieval *Ordines*', in Nelson, *Politics and Rituals*, pp. 329–39 at p. 333.

[24] J.F. Niermeyer and C. van Kieft, *Mediae Latinitatis Lexicon Minus* (Leiden, 1976); C. Du Cange, *Glossarium Mediae et Infimae Latinitatis*, VI (Paris, 1883–7), s.v. *princeps*; *Lexikon des Mittelalters*, VII (Munich, 1995), s.v. *princeps*. H. Wolfram, *Intitulatio I: Lateinische Königs und Fürstentitel bis zum Ende des 8. Jahrhunderts* (Vienna, 1967), p. 148, on *princeps* as a designation of the non-royal Arnulfing mayors of the palace.

emphasise the gentile status of the enemies, but rather their defeat by heroes with divine assistance. It is clear only that the *missa* applies to a polity with a single ruler, not two, but even in this case it would be easy to imagine the composition being emended as it was celebrated.

Other chapters in this volume will have suggested that Burgundy is a plausible context for the Bobbio Missal, but a plausible context is not a necessary context, nor the sole possible one. The *missa* itself has also reasonably been assumed to be Merovingian (which would not necessarily have any bearing on the locale of the compiler's activity), although an Italo-Lombard origin for the codex has also been suggested.[25] If the *missa*-text is indeed very early (from the late fifth or early sixth century, as those who support a Burgundian origin might contend) then we need to consider the significance of the fact that it was available and presumably used for centuries afterwards. What would the implications of such a *Nachleben* be for developing notions of kingship or for the liturgy? Do various chronological contexts need to be considered? In this connection it may be useful to recall the problems raised by the dating of the Anglo-Saxon poem *Beowulf*.[26] The poem refers to a sixth-century Frankish king (Hygelac, who makes an appearance as Chlochiliacus in Gregory of Tours' *Decem libri historiarum*).[27] It has linguistic pointers to the seventh century. It survives in a manuscript made after AD 1000. For a story which was transmitted, transformed, read, performed and of course copied over such a long expanse of time it is necessary to ask how or even whether putative dates of origin inform our understanding. What does 'origin' mean in such a context? How does the significance of the poem as historical evidence change in relation to various alleged contexts of creation, performance and reception? While the text of the Bobbio *Missa pro principe* would not have been subject to the recompositions of a poem derived from an oral tradition, the problems of interpreting any composition where a unique manuscript captures a mere snapshot in a long-lasting and multifarious existence, a single moment in complex process of performance and transmission, are analogous. Merely to assert a particular origin for *Beowulf* or for the Bobbio *Missa pro principe* does not begin to shed light on their cultural significance until subsequent transmission and reception are added to the picture. Origins are only beginnings: longevity and subsequent reception are no less a part of the meaning of the artifact.[28]

---

[25] McCormick, *Eternal Victory*, pp. 345–6; Ewig, 'Zum christlichen Königsgedanken im Frühmittelalter', p. 20: 'gallo-fränkische oder italo-lombardische'.

[26] K. Kiernan, *Beowulf and the Beowulf Manuscript* (New Jersey, 1984); C. Chase, *The Dating of Beowulf* (Toronto, 1981); M. Lapidge, 'The Archetype of Beowulf', *Anglo-Saxon England* 29 (2000), pp. 5–42.

[27] Gregory of Tours, *Decem libri historiarum*, III.3, ed. B. Krusch and W. Levison, MGH SRM I.1 (Hannover, 1951), p. 99.

[28] Compare Nelson, 'Ritual and reality', pp. 333–9.

One might seek to place the Bobbio *Missa pro principe* into other contexts besides chronology. One could ask about its status and place in the liturgy. Is it to be a votive mass? A mass for a particular occasion, either liturgical or political? Is the participation of the king and his army presumed? The manuscript gives no clue to the precise liturgical context of the *missa*; while the address to *fratres* clearly implies a monastic audience, the possibility that the *princeps* and perhaps also his troops might be present cannot be excluded.

One might also seek to place the *Missa pro principe* in the context of the development of rituals, attitudes and practices associated with what Michael McCormick has called 'triumphal rulership', the emergence of a Christian theology of victorious kingship. McCormick has demonstrated that Frankish victory celebrations were at first indebted to the Byzantine liturgy as well as the Roman liturgy.[29] The ceremonies were initially devised and conducted at the instigation of local elites.[30] By the early eighth century, according to his study, the appropriate texts were being codified and prayers for victorious Merovingians were sometimes derived from older formulae. By the end of the century, however, the impetus for the development would change. Royal initiatives for the liturgy of war become visible in the activities of the Carolingians in the late eighth century.[31] Carolingian aspirations towards what was believed to be a romanisation of the liturgy did not stamp out the liturgy of war, but gave it a new form of expression: hence, for example, the mass for troops going into battle in the Sacramentary of Gellone, where the army is in the foreground and the king mentioned almost as an afterthought.[32]

McCormick writes, after summarising an early eighth-century fragment of evidence from Reichenau and the Bobbio Missal:

such texts assure us that . . . despite the silence of other sectors of evidence, attempts to insure and magnify the king's victory did not completely cease in the last centuries of Merovingian dominion. Victory remained an essential trait of rulership even for puppet kings who no longer led their people to war. New ecclesiastical measures designed to provide victory were devised in circumstances which escape us.[33]

And yet, the Bobbio *Missa pro principe* is by not so much *magnifying* the ruler's victory as evoking God's awesome power to ensure victory against mighty odds; it implies the ruler's extreme need for divine assistance. But surely there is more to learn from the text than this, and surely liturgical conservatism or inertia could explain the survival of a text no longer relevant?

---

[29] McCormick, *Eternal Victory*, pp. 344 and 347.   [30] Ibid., pp. 344 and 346.

[31] Ibid., p. 347; see now Hen, *The Royal Patronage of Liturgy*, especially pp. 42–95.

[32] McCormick's characterisation, *Eternal Victory*, p. 346; J.L. Nelson, 'Kingship and empire', in *The Cambridge History of Medieval Political Thought c. 350–1450*, ed. J.H. Burns (Cambridge, 1988), pp. 211–51, at p. 215. *Liber sacramentorum Gellonensis*, 2750–7, ed. A. Dumas, CCSL 159–159A (Turnhout, 1981), pp. 431–3.

[33] McCormick, *Eternal Victory*, pp. 345–6.

Eugen Ewig, in contrast, ventured an association between this text and Charles Martel, and saw the text as representing the thought-world of the late seventh or early eighth century.[34] Both McCormick and Ewig, then, assimilated the Bobbio *Missa pro principe* into a long-term pattern of development – liturgical for McCormick, the christianisation of kingship for Ewig. There is an undeniable elegance to such an approach whichever long-term trend one chooses, but also, and especially in the case of a text where both the original context and manuscript context are so little known, the danger of a procrustean bed. What if the *Missa pro principe* was transmitted and performed long after the date of its original composition and in other territories? Or if it is not Frankish? Again, what is its significance as historical evidence if, as Yitzhak Hen has pointed out, liturgical texts for kings may offer a view of kingship destined for a particular group and perhaps at odds with the views expressed in other genres?[35]

The significance of the Bobbio *Missa pro principe* therefore needs to be evaluated not just in a teleological scheme, but through comparison with masses for kings in other liturgical books and through a more patient analysis of the biblical exempla. A close reading of the text itself in order to consider what message about God, kingship and victory it would have communicated to the celebrant and others should accompany such a consideration. To this end, a translation is appended to this article.

How can the Bobbio *Missa pro principe* be characterised in relation to other masses for rulers? To start, a fundamental demarcation can be drawn between those masses for kings which use Old Testament exempla and those which do not. It will be convenient to begin by listing the three liturgical books whose royal prayers do not include Old Testament exempla:

1. The *Missale Francorum* (Vatican City, BAV, Reg. lat. 257; s. viii[1]) once kept at Saint-Denis. Prayers for the king might have been lifted from the Roman liturgy and 'Franks' substituted for 'Romans'.[36]
2. The Old Gelasian Sacramentary, as represented by Vatican City, BAV, Reg. lat. 316 + Paris, BNF lat. 7193, fols. 41–56, perhaps a Frankish version of a Roman book, copied at Chelles in the middle of the eighth century. Here the masses for kings have not been brought into line with contemporary circumstances and mention Romans and the Roman Empire throughout.[37]

---

[34] Ewig, 'Zum christlichen Königsgedanken', pp. 20 and 42.

[35] Hen, 'The uses of the Bible and the perception of kingship'.

[36] *Missale Francorum*, ed. L.C. Mohlbeg, L. Eizenhöfer and P. Siffrin, Rerum Ecclesiasticarum Documenta, series maior 2 (Rome, 1957), no. 13, 'orationes et preces pro regibus', pp. 20–1. C. Vogel, *Medieval Liturgy. An Introduction to the Sources*, trans. and rev. W.G. Storey and N.K. Rasmussen (Washington, DC, 1986), pp. 41 and 108; Hen, *The Royal Patronage of Liturgy*, p. 29.

[37] *Liber sacramentorum Romanae aecclesiae ordinis anni circuli (Sacramentarium Gelasianum)*, ed. L.C. Mohlbeg, L. Eizenhöfer and P. Siffrin, Rerum Ecclesiasticarum Documenta, series maior 4 (Rome, 1960), nos. LVII, LXIIII, LX, LXI and LXII, pp. 214–18; Vogel, *Medieval Liturgy*, pp. 31 and 64–70; Hen, *The Royal Patronage of Liturgy*, p. 29.

3. The Sacramentary of Echternach (Paris, BNF lat. 9433), copied under King Zwentibold of Lotharingia (895 × 898). It also entirely lacks Old Testament exempla in its prayers for kings, although a prayer does ask that the king have wisdom.[38] There are verbal parallels with other sacramentaries, the Gelasian, Gellone and Angoulême. References to Romans and the Roman Empire are not present and thus can be presumed to have been removed either in the making of the sacramentary or in the copying of its forebears.

In contrast, the five liturgical manuscripts which do include Old Testament exempla in their prayers for kings are:

1. The Reichenau fragment (Karlsruhe, Badische Landesbibliothek, Aug. 253), of perhaps the first half of the eighth century.[39]
2. The Frankish Gelasian Sacramentaries:[40]
   (a) The Sacramentary of Gellone (Paris, BNF lat. 12048)? Meaux, 790 × 810.[41]
   (b) The Sacramentary of Angoulême (Paris, BNF lat. 860) perhaps associated with the Frankish court in Aquitaine, *c.* 800.[42]
   (c) The Sacramentary of Autun (Berlin, Staatsbibliothek, Phillipps 105) Autun, s. ix$^{1/2}$.[43]
3. The Bobbio Missal.

The contrast between the two groups is particularly remarkable because there are instances of parallel phrases which do not entail parallelism of the Testament exempla. (An example would be the phrases shared by Echternach, on the one hand, and the Gelasian, Gellone and Angoulême Sacramentaries, on the other.)[44] What

---

[38] *The Sacramentary of Echternach*, ed. Hen, cc. 2089, 2094, 2098, 2102 at pp. 403–7.

[39] Vogel, *Medieval Liturgy*, pp. 57 (sixth century) and 108 (seventh century); for the text, see Dold and Baumstark, *Das Palimpsestsakramentar im Codex Augiensis CXII*, ed. Dold and Baumstark, pp. 36–7, text I; Hen, *The Royal Patronage of Liturgy*, p. 29. Hereafter, this and all texts under consideration will be cited according to the edition here specified in abbreviated form according to their conventional place names. Note also that each sacramentary's exempla are given separately and do not conflate the exempla of those prayers deemed equivalent in collation tables.

[40] On which see Vogel, *Medieval Liturgy*, pp. 70–8; Hen, *The Royal Patronage of Liturgy*, pp. 57–61.

[41] *Sacramentorum Gellonensis*, ed. Dumas, cc. 2091, 2092, 2093, 2094, pp. 296–8, and compare c. 2750, p. 431 (a mass for an army setting out to battle). The texts from the Gellone and Angoulême Sacramentaries plus those in a ninth-century Freising are also available in *Ordines Coronationis Franciae*, ed. Jackson, pp. 51–68.

[42] *Liber Sacramentorum Engolismensis*, ed. P. Saint-Roch, CCSL 159C (Turnhout, 1987), cc. 2307, 2311, 2317, pp. 358–61. Note that this codex is distinctive in including masses for kings both with and without Old Testament exempla. I enumerate it among the sacramentaries with Old Testament exempla in their royal masses because the masses with Old Testament exempla are, in relation to the Old Gelasian Sacramentary (and Roman books), the apparent innovation that invites explanation.

[43] *Liber sacramentorum Augustodunensis*, ed. O. Heiming, CCSL 159B (Turnhout, 1984), cc. 1642–3, pp. 201–2.

[44] See *The Sacramentary of Echternach*, ed. Hen, p. 506, collation tables for 2089–97.

links the manuscripts in the second group? While proximity of origin might seem to link Gellone, Angoulême and Autun, Bobbio cannot necessarily be associated with them. I leave aside the implications of this contrast for hypotheses about the genesis, composition and interrelationships of the texts and turn to the simplest conclusion: that we are dealing with two distinct worlds of liturgical composition. On the one hand, there is a liturgical style in which prayers are made directly to God with minimal elaboration about His past accomplishments. Such prayers were originally transmitted with references to Romans or the Roman Empire. These prayers, conveniently assembled by Tellenbach, have been thought to have originated in the liturgy of the Roman Empire and to have filtered northwards at various times.[45] On the other, there is a mode of prayer in which biblical exempla are used; though they may be used in connection with kings, they function chiefly to affirm that the God who is addressed is the same one who accomplished feats for Israel in the past and to hope that He will accomplish similar feats on behalf of those who are praying to him and their king. The two types of prayers and masses are almost utterly distinct: hence Old Testament benedictions are almost entirely absent from those masses which mention the Romans or the Roman Empire or substitutions for them and vice versa (with one or two exiguous exceptions; one should also note that there are two liturgical manuscripts, Autun and Angoulême, which include both types of masses for kings). The distinctness of the two modes supports the hypothesis of different origins: the Roman/Frankish prayers are derived from forms current in the Roman liturgy, usually Western, but occasionally Eastern, whereas the forms which employ Old Testament comparisons might be presumed to have originated elsewhere and most likely by polygenesis, in a number of centres, where and when the concept of *imperium* was less relevant.[46] A table listing the various Old Testament comparisons used in the relevant masses for kings (see Appendix II) reveals affiliations which may point to some shared schemes of exempla that would predate the extant manuscript witnesses.

The Bobbio exempla consistently evoke victories won against great odds by faith rather than, for example, the royal virtues of wisdom or righteousness. Thus Moses appears as a victor rather than a law-giver; Joshua not as a king but as a warrior, Moses' helper; David, again, not as the king or psalmist but rather as the boy-shepherd who is able to prevail against Goliath because he comes 'in the name of the Lord'; Abraham, as a victor who obtained the blessing of Melchisedek and thus his inheritance by righteousness rather than law.

[45] Tellenbach, 'Römischer und christlicher Reichsgedanke', pp. 392–410.
[46] It is intriguing to note that the eighth-century flourishing of this mode of liturgical composition (for royal masses at least) seems to coincide with the creation of monuments whose decorative programmes juxtapose easily recognisable biblical figures: the great stone crosses of Northumbria, Scotland and Ireland.

The comparison tables reveal how far the Bobbio text stands apart from the masses for kings found in other sacramentaries. Yet there are tantalising similarities between the exempla used in the Bobbio *Missa pro principe* and those used by an Insular writer named Clemens Peregrinus in a letter to Tassilo written in the early 770s, perhaps 772. Not only is the sequence of exempla very similar, but the two rosters of exempla are linked by a common error found in none of the other sacramentaries which use the example in question. Both Clemens and the Bobbio Missal mention five kings instead of four in connection with Abraham's victory (cf. Gen. 14.14).[47] The conclusions that can be drawn from these similarities are limited but have implications for both Clemens and the Bobbio *Missa pro principe*. Although the Bobbio composition is unique, vulgar Latin spellings and the accompanying syntactical confusion combined with the substitution of *ill.* for the name of the ruler indicate that it was not freshly composed for the leaves where it occurs, but, rather, that it must descend, perhaps at many removes, from an exemplar which might reasonably be assumed to have had other descendants as well. The exempla in the letter of Clemens to Tassilo would appear to reflect familiarity with a text which descends from a composition similar to the Bobbio *Missa pro principe*'s source, as if Clemens were not choosing his exempla from scratch, but consulting or recalling an extant liturgical composition. Such a process, and the reference to a liturgical source, would be consonant with what can be inferred about Clemens' method of composition in the letter, his intentions and the occasion for which the letter might have been composed.[48] The language of his letter to Tassilo is evocative not only of the liturgy but also of the tradition of private prayer found in the prayer books circulated on the Continent by Insular missionaries. One hypothesis, therefore, is that a descendant of the archetype of the Bobbio *Missa pro principe* reached Bavaria in a devotional or liturgical compilation where it was available to Clemens. A corollary of this hypothesis is that a Frankish or continental origin for the *missa* should not be too hastily assumed. While it is true that there are no extant examples of early Insular masses for kings, examples of the close alliance of victorious Insular kings and churchmen invite one to consider what form the liturgical practices associated with them might have taken. At least one saint was remembered as able to ensure victory by his prayers.[49]

The possible importance of the seventh-century Irish exegetical text *de mirabilibus sacrae scripturae* for the exempla also needs to be considered. Clemens'

---

[47] A misreading of the very confusing accounts of the battles in Gen. 14.14 is possible, as is an erroneous reminiscence of another Old Testament passage, Josh. 10.5, about the five kings of the Amorrhites who made war against Gabaon and were defeated by Joshua.

[48] A more extensive study than M. Garrison, 'Letters to a king and biblical exempla: the examples of Cathuulf and Clemens Peregrinus', *Early Medieval Europe* 7 (1998), pp. 305–28, is in preparation by Mary Garrison and Anton Scharer.

[49] See the epigraph to this chapter.

letter, as Anton Scharer has observed, shares its Old Testament exempla with those biblical battle-*mirabilia* expounded in the Irish Augustine's tract *De mirabilibus sacrae scripturae.*[50] Many of the exempla shared by Bobbio and Clemens are cited as heroes of faith in Paul's letter to the Hebrews.[51] It is also notable that their victories attracted the attention of the *De mirabilibus* author as examples of unexpected victories which required explanation if the Irish Augustine were to succeed in his goal of demonstrating that miraculous events in the Bible were based on special cases of the operation of natural principles established by God, rather than on the suspension of those principles.

The similarities in Clemens' sequence of exempla and those of the Bobbio Missal's *Missa pro principe* exempla would not be worth noting if it were not for the fact that the Bobbio *missa* is so utterly distinct from the extant comparanda. These similarities raise the possibility that the Bobbio *missa* represents the sole extant version of a liturgical form which circulated more widely, and not exclusively in Francia, and which was available to an Insular peregrinus in eighth-century Bavaria. It is too easy to assume that Old Testament comparisons and the Old Testament ideology of rulership which would become so important in ninth-century (and later) thought about royal power were inevitable developments. But the prior and wide diffusion of masses for kings *without* Old Testament exempla reveals the use of such exempla to be a new direction which required inspiration, patrons, composers, audiences and liturgical occasions. Whatever its place of origin and use, the Bobbio *Missa pro principe* is a remarkable early witness to that process.

[50] A. Scharer, 'Duke Tassilo of Bavaria and the origins of the Rupertus Cross', in *Belief and Culture in the Middle Ages: Studies Presented to Henry Mayr-Harting*, ed. R. Gameson and H. Leyser (Oxford, 2001), pp. 69–75, at p. 74; for the text of *De mirabilibus*, see PL 35, col. 2192. M. Lapidge and R. Sharpe, *A Bibliography of Celtic-Latin Literature 400–1200* (Dublin, 1985), no. 291; B. Löfstedt, 'Notes on the Latin of the *De Mirabilibus sacrae scripturae* of Augustinus Hibernicus', in *The Scriptures and Early Medieval Ireland*, ed. T. O' Loughlin, Instrumenta Patristica XXXI (Turnhout, 1999), pp. 145–50.
[51] See Hebr. 11, *passim* and 11.32, the list of those who 'by faith conquered kingdoms, wrought justice, obtained promises and stopped the mouth of lions'.

APPENDIX I

# THE *MISSA PRO PRINCIPE*[52]

There is no completely satisfactory approach to adopt in attempting a translation of a text with the difficulties and peculiarities of the *Missa pro principe*. Besides the usual orthographic, phonetic and syntactic characteristics of vulgar Latin, there are places in the *Missa pro principe* where the language is corrupt beyond sense (for example, *hos* in the collect, virtually untranslatable unless one follows the editors in emending it to the proper name *Hur*); other difficulties may result from the omission of words or from the addition of extra words or phrases imperfectly integrated into the syntax. To force a coherent and grammatical translation from the text would therefore be a distortion. Similarly, to remedy all its difficulties by emendation and conjecture, even when there *are* solutions to be found, would create an entirely misleading impression of the Bobbio *Missa pro principe*. While I have smoothed out some difficulties (for example translating participles as finite verbs where necessary), I have allowed some of the awkwardness and even nonsense to stand. Certain necessary corrections are inserted in square brackets; to read the text ignoring the bracketed solutions will give the best indication of the garbled quality of the original. To be sure, some obvious errors might easily have been corrected by the celebrant: *innumeros* for *numeros* for example. But others which defy easy resolution surely will not have been. In view of all of these considerations, and bearing in mind our ignorance of contemporary expectations, the biblical exempla take on even greater importance as fixed and familiar points of reference, recognisable allusions able to evoke both God's nature, by reference to His past assistance for figures named, and the hopes for the ruler on whose behalf the mass was performed.

[MASS FOR THE RULER]

Dearest brothers, with one mind let us entreat the King of Kings, even the Omnipotent Lord, God of all rulers, by whose command and power all kingdoms of the earth subsist with holy restraint, that he may guard our ruler continually with just the kind of assistance with which [Gen. 14.14] he once saved Abraham, (who) with his three hundred and eighteen servants was bringing back the victory from

[52] For discussion of the language of the Bobbio Missal, see the contributions of Els Rose and Charles Wright and Roger Wright, above, pp. 67–78 and 79–139 respectively. The translation that follows is from *Bobbio* 492–6, pp. 151–3.

the five kings, with their ranks laid low, they rejoicing, he brought back the booty and[53] his nephew (*sic*) Lot and his [Lot's] property [Gen. 14.16] to [his] place. Thus may He who [made] Melchisedek and Abraham to reign prosperously in the world, make live, preserve, watch over, our ruler, unharmed,[54] ever a victor against all adversaries.[55] Through the Lord.

## [COLLECTIO]

God, Omnipotent Lord, who through incalculable wisdom so disposed the world that without kings and rulers no epochs of the world should exist in peace, so that with the justice of good men flourishing, all things subjected to the evil of wicked men should wither away, wherefore O Lord as suppliants we beseech you, with minds devoted to you; on this day we shall pour forth prayers for your faithful servant, our ruler X and for his entire army: thus O Lord by your right hand may you command your powers ever to be present against all adversaries for him, a victor with triumphs. Just as once you helped Moses while he was struggling against his enemies [Exod. 17.12], those [Hur][56] supported his arms until dusk, he raising his eyes to the heavens, soon, with you helping O Lord he smote and laid low his enemies unto death. Just so, depending on the Lord, we ask that in such a way our ruler be continuously supported in all matters by your aid; may he prosper blessedly through numbers[57] years (*sic!*) in his kingdom through the Lord.

## [POST NOMINA]

O Lord, Ruler, who exists and died; as you will have wished, merciful, persist in your will, hear our prayers. As we are assisted by the collected names of the saints on account of their merits, and may these sacrifices which we offer to you both avail the living for their salvation and be of aid to the dead, for their peace, for truly with these gifts offered, may our ruler and his entire army continuously and in all matters obtain divine support, with us praying. And just as formerly Joshua, [Josh. 6] when he had gone with the trumpets seven times around the

---

[53] For *ut* read *et*.     [54] *inleso*, apparently ablative for accusative.

[55] The four verbs in asyndeton (*uiuificit psaluit tueatur conseruit*) are problematic, as is the lack of a finite verb for *rignare*. Note that Mabillon read *saluum* for *psaluit*. The four verbs seem to reflect a process of growth by accretion, as if alternative verbs were incorporated into the text at some stage, perhaps after the phrase *Ita principem nostrum uiuificet* received the interpolation *semper victorem contra cunctos adversarius*. To remedy the lack of a verb in the last clause, one could conjecture *fecit*.

[56] Lowe and Legg's suggested emendation for *hos*. Unemended, the passage can hardly be made to make sense.

[57] The editors assume that *numeros* is an error for *innumeros*.

wall of Jericho, with the walls tumbling down, had the victory over the city, thus omnipotent Lord God, praying we ask that if perchance any (foes) will have tried to go against the dominion of our ruler they may wither quickly at his feet, laid low, grant omnipotent God.

[AD PACEM]

Mediator of heaven and earth omnipotent God Jesus Christ who loves the pacified and peaceful hearts of men, as suppliants we beseech you that that peace [which] must be maintained which you left to your apostles, enduring ceaselessly may it flourish in our hearts and just as the strong hand of David once, with Goliath smitten[58] made peace (1 Reg. 17) in the people of Saul, so may our ruler, with you helping, with nations on all sides conquered, shine peacefully in his rule, prosperously for countless years.

[CONTESTATIO (FRAGMENTARY)]

Right and fitting, Omnipotent Lord God is the praises of our voices, if it is right for the choirs of angels to . . . although they in the celestial realms to you, One God in three persons, in Godhead[s],[59] praising together without cease . . . but our earthly exile, walled in by dust, is able [to utter] at least a very few things about your ineffable works.

[58] Corrupt. The text reads *fortis manu purio*. The editors cite Mabillon's reading in the apparatus: *forti manu spurio*.
[59] The *s* is partially erased.

APPENDIX II

# COMPARATIVE TABLE

| Reichenau[1] | Gellone[2] | Gellone[3] | Autun[4] | Autun[5] | Angoulême[6] | Bobbio[7] | Clemens Peregrinus[8] | De Mirabilibus Sacrae Scripturae[9] | Hebrews 11 |
|---|---|---|---|---|---|---|---|---|---|
| Franks | Franks | Franks | | Romani | Franks | ? | Bavarians | | Abel |
| Israel from Egypt | Abraham (sanctified) / Abraham chosen | Israel from Egypt | Moses / Red Sea | I. Daviticum | Israel from Egypt | Abraham with 318 servants and 5 kings | Abraham and 5 kings | | Enoch Noah Abraham (Isaac, Jacob) |
| Patriarchs sanctified | Moses (with army) / Moses (Red Sea) | David and Goliath | Iesaue in agro | Solomon | Moses, Aaron, Egypt | Moses holding the arm against the Amalechites | Moses | Jesus *filius Nun* (Exod. 17.11–13) victory over Amalechites while Moses holds his arms aloft | Sara Abraham Isaac, Jacob and Esau Jacob Joseph |
| II Macc. 1.24 | Elias (in desert) / Joshua (in the field) and Joshua son of Nun | Gideon *cum trecentis* | Iesu Naue *in proelio* | Abraham and 4 kings | Joshua at Jericho | Joshua at Jericho | Joshua slaying of King Seon of Amorrhites and Og of Basaan (Josh. 12.2, 4, 8) | (Israel / Moses) victory over Sehon king of Amorrhites and Og king of Basaan (Num. 21.24, 33 and 22.5) | Moses Jericho Rahab . . . Gideon, Barac, Samson, Jephtha, David, Samuel, prophets |
| | Samuel (in temple) // | | Samuel *crinitum in templo* | Manna in Egypt | David and Goliath | David and Goliath | David and Goliath | The 31 kings slain by Joshua and children of Israel (Josh. 12.7 and 12.34) | |
| | Aaron in tabernacle, Heliseus in river, Hezekiah, Zachariah, Joshua, Gideon, Peter, Paul, Isaac, Jacob / David as psalmist | | David / Solomon | | | | | Gideon and 300 defeat Midianites (Jud. 7) | |
| verbatim | *sicut* and *quam* | *sicut* or nothing | | | | *quondam* | | Jephta over Ammonites (Jud. 11) Samson and lion, and foxes, slays 1,000 with ass's jawbone, pulls down prison (Jud. 14.6; 15.4, 5; 15.15; 16.3) | |

Israelites defeat Benjaminites (Jud. 20)

Jonathan's victory against Philistines (I Kings 14.13)

David and Goliath (I Kings 14.13)

David spares Saul (I Kings 24.8; 26.10–11)

David's victory against Philistines, including killing 80 in one blow (sic: it was Jesbaham) (II Kings 5. 20; 23.8)

Abishai killed 300 (II Kings 23.18)

David refuses water obtained at peril (II Kings 23.16–17)

Banaias son of Joiada slays three lions (II Kings 23.20)

David against Philistines (II Kings 21.15ff)

David's army (II Kings 18.6–7)

1 *Das Palimpsestsakramentar im Codex Augiensis CXII*, ed. Dold and Baumstark, p. 37.
2 *Liber Sacramentorum Gellonensis*, cc. 2091–2, ed. Dumas, pp. 296–7: the regal benedictions. The exempla from the two royal benedictions are amalgamated in this column. In every case, the first name is the exempla from c. 2091, the second from c. 2092 and the two are divided by a slash. However, when the two exempla are identical, the name from 2092 will not be repeated and there will be a double slash.
3 Ibid., cc. 2750–7, ed. Dumas, pp. 431–3: 'missa in profectionem hostium eontibus in proheliom'.
4 *Liber Sacramentorum Augustodunensis*, c. 1642, ed. Heiming, p. 201.
5 Ibid., c. 1643, ed. Heiming, p. 202.
6 *Liber Sacramentorum Engolismensis*, cc. 2307–10, ed. Saint-Roch, pp. 358–61.
7 *Bobbio* 492–6, pp. 151–3.
8 For Clemens' letter's original manuscript context, see B. Bischoff, *Salzburger Formelbücher und Briefe aus Tassilonischer und Karolingischer Zeit*, Bayerische Akademie der Wissenschaften Philosophisch-Historische Klasse 4 (Munich, 1973), and for the text, see MGH Epistolae IV (Berlin, 1895), pp. 496–7. For discussion, see Garrison, 'Letters to a king'.
9 *De Mirabilibus Sacrae Scripturae*, c. xxiv: 'De bellis praecipuis quae Domini auxilio peracta sunt', PL 35, cols. 2192–3.

## II

# *Liturgy in the Rhône valley and the Bobbio Missal*

IAN N. WOOD

The origin of the Bobbio Missal and its contents have exercised the minds of liturgical scholars for generations. One reason for this is that it appears to be a compendium of various liturgical texts, not all of which can have originated in the same milieu. One need only set the blessings for consecrating nuns (nos. 546–8) alongside the frequent invocations of *fratres* to see that this is a collection made from more than one source. Moreover, despite the fact that some of the texts are certainly appropriate to a monastic setting, the Missal is usually held to have been intended for a priest.[1] Textual, as opposed to palaeographical and codicological, evidence can point to the possible origin of certain individual prayers and masses – but since a high proportion of the prayers can be paralleled in various Gallican and Ambrosian missals, the texts which may possibly be localisable are relatively few.[2] One such is the *contestatio* which seems to emanate from the burnt city of *Landoglado* (491), which, alas, cannot be identified. Another might be the mass to be celebrated in a church of Saints Peter and Paul on their feast day (no. 329), but the dedication is so general as not to be of much use in identifying the church for which the mass was originally composed.

Of all the masses in the Missal which might reasonably be linked to a specific site, the most interesting is the *Missa sancti Sigismundi* (nos. 334–8). It has long been recognised that this mass must in some way derive from the monastery of Agaune, where the martyred Burgundian king was buried. Indeed the mass has been central to studies of the cult of the king[3] – yet it may be that there is a little more to be said about the text, and its connections with Agaune, which may have been underemphasised in part because the mass is also to be found in the

---

[1] The classic statement is that of Lowe, 'Palaeography', pp. 105–6.
[2] The parallels are listed by Lowe, 'Notes', pp. 107–47.
[3] F. Paxton, 'Power and the power to heal. The cult of St Sigismund of Burgundy', *Early Medieval Europe* 2 (1993), pp. 95–110, with references to previous work.

Sacramentary of Angoulême as well as the Ambrosian *Liber Sacramentorum* from Bergamo.[4]

The main body of my argument will begin by revisiting the Sigismund mass, before turning to the question of whether there are further indications of possible links with Agaune in the texts of the Bobbio Missal. However, since it is clear that the masses and prayers of the Bobbio Missal come from more than one place, I will move on to consider other liturgical evidence relating to the Rhône valley, notably to Avitus of Vienne's sermons, with their evidence for church dedication[5] and to the initiation of the Rogation processions by his predecessor Mamertus. This will, I hope, serve to shed light on some of the riches of the evidence relating to liturgy in the Rhône valley in the fifth and sixth centuries, that is before the Bobbio Missal, or indeed any of the surviving Frankish missals, a number of which have Burgundian connections,[6] were put down on parchment.

The central Rhône valley was the scene of interesting liturgical innovation in the fifth and sixth centuries, and it is as well to set out some of the key points of that innovation before embarking on a more detailed consideration of individual masses of the Bobbio Missal. Following an earthquake which came near to destroying much of Vienne, at some point before 473 Bishop Mamertus introduced a series of penitential prayers and processions into the ecclesiastical calendar of his cathedral city, to be held on the three days before Ascension.[7] There had been Rogations before, but these were unusual in that they were to be an annual expression of penance by the community of Vienne, and not an *ad hoc* set of prayers for rain or fine weather, as had been the case with previous rogational litanies.[8] The new practices spread quickly, and were introduced by Sidonius Apollinaris to Clermont in 473, hence the *terminus ante quem* for Mamertus' action. One may wonder to what extent the popularity of the Rogations was underpinned by the uncertainties of the period – not just those associated with natural disaster, but also those caused by the establishment and expansion of the new barbarian kingdoms of the Burgundians and Visigoths. Natural disaster, in this case the plagues of the 540s, would, however, return as a factor, and another set of Rogations was

---

[4] Lowe, 'Notes', p. 135.

[5] The significance of these sermons for the history of late antique architecture is discussed in I.N. Wood, 'The audience of architecture in post-Roman Gaul', in *The Anglo-Saxon Church*, ed. L.A.S. Butler and R.K. Morris (London, 1986), pp. 74–9.

[6] Y. Hen, *Culture and Religion in Merovingian Gaul, A.D. 481–751* (Leiden, New York and Cologne, 1995), pp. 44–6.

[7] J. Hill, 'The *Litaniae maiores* and *minores* in Rome, Francia and Anglo-Saxon England: terminology, texts and traditions', *Early Medieval Europe* 9 (2000), pp. 211–46. See the commentary on Avitus of Vienne, *Hom.* 6 in D. Shanzer and I.N. Wood, *Avitus of Vienne, Prose Works* (Liverpool, 2002), pp. 381–8.

[8] Sidonius Apollinaris, *Ep.* V.14, ed. A. Loyen (Paris, 1970).

introduced in Clermont, when Bishop Gallus instituted a penitential pilgrimage from his cathedral city to the cult site of Brioude, some sixty kilometres distant.[9] Vienne may have been the centre of further innovations in penitential practice in the middle of the sixth century, when Theudarius, a pupil of Caesarius of Arles, is said to have been appointed intercessor for the city, but unfortunately the evidence for the office and the appointment comes from the ninth century and could be suspect.[10]

Apart from these penitential traditions, the most important liturgical innovations of the period may be associated with the Burgundian royal court.[11] The Burgundians had been settled in Sapaudia, in the vicinity of Geneva, since the 440s – from which region they spread out to dominate the lower Rhône and Saône valleys.[12] Their most able king, Gundobad, served as *magister militum* to the emperors Olybrius and Glycerius, before returning to his people in 473. Having served at the heart of the western empire he was among the most romanised of all the Germanic kings, and despite his formal attachment to Arianism his court and his Catholic episcopate seem to have developed a liturgy which included prayers for the ruler.[13] His son, Sigismund, abandoned his father's religion, becoming a Catholic, perhaps around 500.[14] He was to have a yet more remarkable religious profile than his father.[15] As sub-king, based in Geneva, he founded the monastery of Agaune in 515, where a peculiar liturgy, known to modern historians as the *laus perennis*, which involved uninterrupted liturgical performance, was developed. Although it was once thought that this liturgy was derived from Byzantium, it is likely that local influences were at least as strong in creating what seems to have been a novel

---

[9] Gregory of Tours, *Decem libri historiarum*, IV.5, ed. B. Krusch and W. Levison, MGH SRM I.1 (Hannover, 1951), pp. 138–9; Gregory, *Liber vitae Patrum* VI.6, ed. B. Krusch, MGH SRM I.2 (Hannover, 1885), pp. 234–5.

[10] Ado, *Vita Theudarii*, cc. 13–15, ed. B. Krusch, MGH SRM III (Hannover, 1896), pp. 529–30; I.N. Wood, 'A prelude to Columbanus: the monastic achievement in the Burgundian territories', in *Columbanus and Merovingian Monasticism*, ed. H.B. Clarke and M. Brennan, BAR International Series 113 (Oxford, 1981), pp. 3–32, at p. 9; F. Prinz, *Frühes Mönchtum im Frankenreich. Kultur und gesellschaft in Gallien, den Rheinlanden und Bayern am Beispiel der monastischen Entwiklung (4. bis 8. Jahrhundert)* (Munich, 1965), pp. 83–4.

[11] This might be read as a rider to the comments of Y. Hen, *The Royal Patronage of Liturgy in Frankish Gaul to the Death of Charles the Bald (877)*, HBS subsidia 3 (London, 2000), pp. 21–8.

[12] The most recent discussion of the Burgundian kingdom is that of J. Favrod, *Histoire politique du royaume burgonde (443–534)* (Lausanne, 1997).

[13] Avitus of Vienne, *Ep.* 85, ed. R. Peiper, MGH AA VI.2 (Berlin, 1883), p. 95. M. McCormick, *Eternal Victory. Triumphal Rulership in Late Antiquity, Byzantium and the Early Medieval West* (Cambridge, 1986), p. 267 n. 37, states that Avitus of Vienne, *Ep.* 85 'indicates that the Catholic liturgy of Burgundy included prayers for the king on, I should think, the Vigil of Easter'. Other occasions during the Easter festival are just as likely.

[14] For the event and the chronology see the discussion in Shanzer and Wood, *Avitus of Vienne, Prose Works*, pp. 220–24 (on Avitus of Vienne, *Ep.* 8).

[15] For one aspect of this see I.N. Wood, 'Incest, law and the Bible in sixth-century Gaul', *Early Medieval Europe* 7 (1998), pp. 291–303.

practice for the west.[16] Apart from the evidence for Agaune, which is of obvious importance for any consideration of the Bobbio Missal, there are other indications of liturgical practice, or perhaps ideology which impinged on liturgy, associated with the royal Burgundian court, notably to do with the ideal of the *rex pacificus*, which will concern us a good deal. With regard to this issue most of what I will offer amounts to little more than suggestions and suspicions – yet it may be that these suspicions are worth airing.

I begin by stating what is startlingly obvious. The Burgundian king Sigismund, who ruled from 516 to 522, had a very special significance for the compiler of the Bobbio Missal. Leaving aside the biblical cults of Christ, the Virgin, the Apostles, John the Baptist, Stephen and Michael, the Missal contains only two masses for named saints: Martin (360–7) and Sigismund. The *Missa sancti Sigismundi* appears directly before a more general *Missa sanctorum martyrum* and *Missa unius martyris*, while that for Martin follows a general *Missa de uno confessore*. This suggests that for the compiler of the texts of the Bobbio Missal Sigismund was almost a type martyr, while Martin was a type confessor. Both, for some reason, deserved individualised masses, while the rank and file of martyrs and confessors could be covered by standard formulae. Given this remarkable highlighting of these two individual saints, it is reasonable to conclude that the masses of Sigismund and Martin were of particular importance to whoever compiled the Missal. One might add that Gregory of Tours follows his chapter on Sigismund in the *Liber in gloria martyrum* with one on the Theban legion,[17] the martyred regiment led by St Maurice, whose bones were preserved at Agaune, and indeed whose cult prompted the foundation of the monastery. The two chapters parallel the arrangement in the Bobbio Missal, where the *Missa sancti Sigismundi* is followed by the *Missa sanctorum martyrum*. It is striking that Gregory places Sigismund – the more recent and arguably less worthy saint – before the long-revered Theban legion. This juxtaposition further highlights the importance of Sigismund for the compiler of the Bobbio Missal texts, which include no mass specifically dedicated to St Maurice and his companions, although the *Missale Gothicum* includes exactly such a mass.[18] The absence of a liturgy expressly dedicated to the Theban legion in the Bobbio Missal, it might be

---

[16] The most substantial recent study of the liturgy of Agaune is B. Rosenwein, 'Perennial prayer at Agaune', in *Monks, Nuns, Saints and Outcasts. Religion in Medieval Society. Essays in Honour of Lester K. Little*, ed. S. Farmer and B. Rosenwein (Ithaca, 2000), pp. 37–56, who challenges the use of the term *laus perennis*. On the other hand the term has become established, and the notion of a ceaseless liturgy could be referred to by the phrase *ad praesens psalmisonum solemne* in Avitus of Vienne, *Hom.* 25. See the comments on the homily in Shanzer and Wood, *Avitus of Vienne, Prose Works*, pp. 377–81.

[17] Gregory of Tours, *Liber in gloria martyrum*, cc. 74–5, ed. B. Krusch, MGH SRM I.2 (Hannover, 1885), pp. 87–8.

[18] *Missale Gothicum* 62 (= 419–23). See the edition by E. Rose, 'Communitas in commemoratione. Liturgisch Latijn en liturgische gedachtenis in het Missale Gothicum (Vat. reg. lat. 317)' (PhD thesis, Utrecht, 2001), with the commentary on pp. 447–53.

noted, makes it unlikely that the compilation was made at Agaune, however much it borrowed texts from that monastery. At the same time, the fact that masses for the two major cults of Agaune circulated in Francia could be an indication that the house was an influential centre of liturgical composition.

The *Missa sancti Sigismundi* is worth extended consideration. It is specifically a mass asking for the cure of individuals suffering from quartan fever (336–7). The mass seems to take place in the vicinity of the martyr's relics: *Nunc ergo dono maiestatis tuae agnuscimus reliquiae esse homeni pacifico* ('Now therefore we acknowledge by the gift of your majesty that the relics are those of a peaceful man'). The direct reference to relics would seem to indicate that we are dealing with a mass which was in origin celebrated at Agaune. Despite the crucial epithet of *homo pacificus*, Sigismund himself is seen as having been granted martyrdom *inter bellorum tumultos non examinacione persecutoris* ('among the tumults of war, not at the examination of a persecutor') – a description that is not quite accurate, in that the king did not die in war, but was instead dragged out of the eremitical retreat to which he had retired, and was only subsequently killed on the orders of Chlodomer. God is asked to show through the miracles of the dead martyr what He had already shown in the faith of the living Sigismund, and to cure the *frigora tempestatis* and the *ardor febrium*.

It must be said that the three short prayers of the mass of Sigismund contained in the Bobbio Missal are not very informative about the cult of the king. They do not allude to events which would certainly have been well known at Agaune: Sigismund's foundation of the monastery in 515 or his entry into his foundation in 522. Of course prayers would not have been the place to deal with such history, which would have been covered, as far as was appropriate, in the reading of a *Passio*. The surviving *Passio* of the martyr significantly ignores the fact that Sigismund was ever Arian and that he murdered his son, which seems to have been his reason for retiring to Agaune. Whether this text was itself used at Agaune has, however, been questioned, and it has been suggested that the hagiographer was a pilgrim to the monastery.[19] In any case the prayers of the Missal could reasonably limit themselves to a comment on the king's *fides*, which might have been understood by those in the know as a reference to his conversion from Arianism, and his martyrdom.

Although there would have been no need for greater detail in a liturgical text, it is worth noting the contrast between the impression given by the Missal and that offered by Gregory of Tours in his account of the mass.[20] Gregory presents

[19] J.M. Theurillat, *L'Abbaye de Saint-Maurice d'Agaune, des origines à la réforme canoniale 515–830* (Sion, 1954), pp. 82–4. Paxton, 'Power and the power to heal', p. 108, assumes there was no early *vita*. It would be surprising, however, if there were no reading for the festival.

[20] Gregory of Tours, *Liber in gloria Martyrum*, c. 74, ed. Krusch, p. 87, but compare Gregory of Tours, *Libri historiarum*, III.5, ed. Krusch and Levison, pp. 100–1. R. Folz, 'Zur Frage der heiligen Könige: Heiligkeit und Nachleben in der Geschichte des Burgundischen Königtums', *Deutsches Archiv*

the king as an object lesson in penitence. He details the murder of the king's son Sigistrix, Sigismund's penance at the shrine of the Theban legion, his foundation of a monastery, which performed the liturgy of the *laus perennis*, and the subsequent killing of the king and his sons by Chlodomer. Gregory, incidentally, is wrong to place the monastic foundation after the murder. The bishop of Tours then goes on to state that Sigismund's body was returned to Agaune, and continues:

This event indicates that he was received into the company of the saints. For whenever people suffering from chills (*frigoritici*) piously celebrate a mass in his honour and make an offering to God for the king's repose, immediately their tremors cease (*compressis tremoribus*), their fevers disappear (*restinctis febribus*), and they are restored to earlier health.

The curious compact in which the sufferer prays for the repose of the penitent king, and in return receives a cure, is worth more attention than it has received from scholars.[21] Sigismund's sanctity is not, it seems, to be taken for granted: the king still needs the prayers of pilgrims. This element of a *quid pro quo*, however, is not stated in the mass, and need not detain us now – although it should be noted that a penitential reading of Sigismund's claim to sanctity fits well with the concerns of Mamertus in founding the Rogations. It may also have been precisely this fallibility which made Sigismund a more attractive cult figure than the austere Theban legion.

What I wish to concentrate on is the question of how the liturgy of Agaune, as opposed to the impression of that liturgy conveyed by Gregory, presented Sigismund in the sixth and seventh centuries. I want to pause in particular on two points in the mass: on the king as a *rex pacificus* whose sanctity was conferred among the tumults of war – a paradox not noted by Gregory, and one that depended, as we have seen, on a rather loose reading of Sigismund's retirement to Agaune, his betrayal to invading Franks and his subsequent murder; and on the cure of quartan fever. These two points may shed some light on the influences which lay behind the royal cult, and on one of the reasons for its popularity.

To take the issue of cure first. Historians have not, I think, paid enough attention to the precise type of fever involved.[22] Another mass for the sick is to be found in the Bobbio Missal (377–83), but it does not limit itself to any one specific disease. Oddly enough, misplaced in the middle of a *Missa pro principe* (492–8) (to which I shall return), there is a set of *devotiones sive imprecationes* (497) (the heading is editorial) which refer, among other diseases, to *frioreteca* and quartan and tertian fevers. This brings us rather closer to the basic group of fevers with which

14 (1958), pp. 317–44, draws the various traditions relating to Sigismund together (pp. 321–7), whereas they arguably belong to different and separate traditions.

[21] But see Folz, 'Zur Frage der heiligen Könige', p. 325.

[22] Paxton, 'Power and the power to heal', provides a different approach to the whole question of the cures at Agaune, although he does, to my mind rightly, emphasise the situation of the monastery (p. 104). He does not, however, consider the exact nature of the disease.

Sigismund seems to be associated: Gregory of Tours speaks of chills, while the *Passio sancti Sigismundi* speaks of tremors and fevers, and specifies the quartan. This is very similar to the specifications of the mass, which refers to *frigora tempestatis* and the *ardor febrium* in the *contestatio*, but mentions only the *typum quartani* in its first two prayers. One point that historians have failed to note is that tertian and quartan fever are two variants of one very specific disease: malaria.

Malaria is not an obvious disease of the upper Rhône valley, with its fast-flowing, cold river. Yet it may give us a clue as to the specifically medicinal development of the cult of Sigismund. While it is not associated with the upper Rhône, malaria is a disease which was in all probability rampant in the low-lying plain of the Po,[23] as well as – though less importantly for the present argument – the Rhône delta. For travellers returning to Francia from Italy, through either the Great St Bernard or the Simplon Passes, the monastery of Agaune would have been an obvious stopping point after the labours of the mountains. A cult specifically dedicated to the cure of a disease which could easily be contracted on the other side of the Alps would have been especially welcome to those re-entering the Frankish world.

Whoever compiled the text of the Bobbio Missal certainly had an interest in travellers, since the collection includes a *Missa pro iter agentibus* (400–4). While most of this mass is to be found in other liturgical books,[24] the *ad pacem* (403) has no exact parallels. Interestingly it is a prayer offered for the man *qui in longa terrarum spacia detenitur*, and God is asked to return *eum ad domicilium suum saluum et incolumem*. Concern for travellers may well have been a recurrent issue for the monks of Agaune, based as they were on one of the main routes through the Alps. On the other hand this prayer would best have been offered at the man's home, by his relatives.

But to return to Sigismund and the interest shown in him by the compiler of the Bobbio Missal: although only one mass refers to the king by name, it is worth asking if there are other masses which one might link with him or his cult. I have already noted the *Missa pro principe* (492–8), and the fact that a set of prayers for the sick, including those suffering from malaria, is intruded into it. One might wonder if the intrusion reflects an awareness by the compiler of the fact that the mass for Sigismund specifically dealt with the cure of malaria sufferers. If so, could the *Missa pro principe*, most of whose text is uniquely witnessed by the Bobbio Missal,[25] or the ideas contained within it, be linked in any way with the Burgundian king?

---

[23] Perhaps malaria should be envisaged as being one among the *diversis febribus* of Gregory of Tours, *Libri historiarum*, III.32, ed. Krusch and Levison, p. 128.

[24] Lowe, 'Notes', p. 138.

[25] Ibid., pp. 143–4. Although the mass is 'written by a different hand on inserted leaves', Lowe's comments suggest that it was copied for insertion into the rest of the compilation. However, as pointed out by Rosamond McKitterick (above, pp. 33–5) the *Missa pro principe* may have been produced elsewhere.

Again we are in the world of speculation, but it is worth noting that the *ad pacem* of this mass is concerned to emphasise the notion of peace. God loves the *pacifica corda hominum*. He is asked for peace, as David achieved peace in striking Goliath. The hope is that the *princeps* will live long *pacifece*. Two uses of *pax* and two uses of *pacificus/pacefice* in seven lines is striking. So too is the parallel with the epithet of *rex pacificus* in the *Missa sancti Sigismundi*. The two words *rex* and *pacificus* are not commonly associated in the sixth century. Is it possible that *pax* was in some ways specifically championed by Burgundian royalty? Here it is perhaps significant that Gundobad, Sigismund's father, issued a set of coins bearing the legend *Pax et Abundantia*.[26] The phrase should also be read as having religious overtones: Avitus of Vienne juxtaposed the two concepts in one of his dedication homilies preached before the king and his son, and he was presumably understood to be referring to the coin legend.[27] The coin legend is certainly to be taken very seriously – and Gundobad's interest in the subject of peace is attested elsewhere, featuring prominently in one of the theological exchanges he had with Avitus.[28] Peace was something which must have increasingly concerned both Gundobad and Sigismund, as their kingdom found itself squeezed by the Franks on the one hand and the Ostrogoths on the other. Indeed, one might wonder whether the references to peace on the coinage, in Avitus' exchange with the king and in his homilies, reflect a growing desire to avoid potentially destructive military confrontation. Peace was something that the Burgundians made much of, on occasion, and the emphasis to be found on *pax* in the Bobbio Missal may perhaps reflect a particular concern of the Burgundian royal house – a piece of political ideology which then crept into the liturgy of the Rhône valley.

The other concern of the *Missa pro principe* is war: indeed the hope is that the king will defeat his enemies before returning to establish peace. Masses for kings setting out for war are not unknown,[29] although the mass preserved in the Bobbio Missal is not the same as any equivalent liturgy preserved elsewhere. The few surviving texts are enough to suggest that already by the early sixth century the kings of the successor states, perhaps copying imperial precedent, lived in a world where major formal actions were marked by liturgy. Interestingly

---

[26] P. Grierson and M. Blackburn, *Medieval European Coinage*, I: *The Early Middle Ages (5th–10th centuries)* (Cambridge, 1986), p. 76.

[27] Avitus of Vienne, *Hom.* 24: 'haec populorum abundantia contigat in turribus, sicque ei fiat pax in virtute'. For a more recent edition of this homily, with translation and commentary, see C. Perrat and A. Audin, 'Alcimi Ecdicii viennensis episcopi homilia dicta in dedicatione superioris basilicae', in *Studi in Onore di Aristide Calderini e Roberto Paribeni*, II (Milan, 1957), pp. 433–51.

[28] Avitus of Vienne, *Ep.* 20, ed. Peiper, p. 53. See also the commentary in Shanzer and Wood, *Avitus of Vienne, Prose Works*, pp. 154–5.

[29] McCormick, *Eternal Victory*, pp. 238–40, 283, 305–6, 308–11, 342–62; Hen, *The Royal Patronage of Liturgy*, pp. 39–41; Y. Hen, 'The uses of the Bible and the perception of kingship in Merovingian Gaul', *Early Medieval Europe* 7 (1998), pp. 286–9.

Avitus of Vienne offers prayers for Sigismund's fortune in war in three letters addressed to the king.[30] It is certainly possible that the Bobbio Missal's *Missa pro principe* reflects a liturgy developed in the Burgundian kingdom. If so, it would be entirely to be expected that such a mass would be celebrated at Agaune, Sigismund's foundation, a place doubtless well aware of the royal ideology of near-by Geneva and more-distant Lyons, and ultimately the martyr's resting place. Even if the mass is not Burgundian in origin, it may present us with an indication of the type of liturgical background out of which the image of Sigismund as a *rex pacificus*, sanctified *inter bellorum tumultos*, might have developed. The *Missa pro principe* may explain the presentation of Sigismund in the Bobbio Missal as a man of peace rather than as the penitent of Gregory of Tours' account of the mass: we may be dealing with a memory of royal propaganda dating to the king's lifetime.

If there is a case for arguing that the *Missa pro principe* echoes ideas current in the Burgundian kingdom, it is worth asking if there are any other indications of influences from the courts of Gundobad and Sigismund in the Bobbio Missal. There is another mass in the Missal, the third of the *Missae dominicales* (465–71), in which peace features remarkably heavily. Here the word *pax* appears thirteen times in eleven lines – the concentration is remarkable, and certainly seems to indicate that the mass in question originated in a context in which the notion of peace was of particular significance. This mass, again only known from one manuscript, the Bobbio Missal, attracted the particular attention of Mabillon, who dated it to the period in which the Franks were penetrating Gaul or the Lombards Italy; Neale and Forbes dated it later on the grounds that it prays for the conversion of barbarian *gentes*.[31] The conversion of *gentes*, however, does not necessitate a late date: Avitus is remarkable for encouraging Clovis to convert still pagan *gentes*,[32] and in any case the whole context of the acceptance of Catholicism by both Burgundians and Franks would provide an appropriate context for the phrase *gentis barbaras ad invocacionem nomenis tui convertere*. It would not be impossible to see this *Missa dominicalis* as belonging to the same context as the *Missa pro principe* – but there is nothing further to prove or disprove the conjecture.

A fuller case for origins in the Rhône valley in the time of Avitus might be made for a mass included in the Bobbio Missal with totally other concerns: that for the dedication of a church (nos. 384–92). Here the Old Testament *lectio* concerns Jacob's pillow (Gen. 28.10–22). Interestingly Avitus' dedication Homily on

---

[30] Avitus of Vienne, *Epp.* 45, 91, 92, ed. Peiper, pp. 79 and 99. On these letters see McCormick, *Eternal Victory*, p. 267, and the commentary in Shanzer and Wood, *Avitus of Vienne, Prose Works*, pp. 233–5 and 238–41.

[31] Lowe, 'Notes', p. 142.  [32] Avitus of Vienne, *Ep.* 46, ed. Peiper, p. 75.

a Church of St Michael, arguably that founded in Lyons by Gundobad's Queen Caretena, begins with an allusion to the same passage in Genesis.[33] It is perfectly likely that Avitus made the reference because the reading prescribed by the Bobbio Missal was used at the Lyons dedication ceremony. The argument of the homily itself makes no other use of the biblical story, and an allusion to a liturgical reading would explain its presence. If the connection is accepted, it could take on a particular significance if the homily of Avitus really did concern a monastic church founded by Caretena, Sigismund's mother – again there would be a connection with the Burgundian royal family.

The connection between Avitus' Lyons homily and the lection in the *Missa in dedicatione ecclesiae* in the Bobbio Missal could well be an indication that the Missal includes texts used in the Burgundian kingdom, and indeed used in very high status contexts therein. On the other hand, if that is the case, there are some notable lacunae in the Missal's texts. Of all the dedication homilies of Avitus to have survived, admittedly many of them as fragments, only the homily for the church of St Michael seems to indicate a direct connection with the dedication mass preserved in the Bobbio Missal – though that may reflect the licence given to a metropolitan bishop and recognised theologian whose sermons might stray far from the readings prescribed by the liturgy. On the other hand, were the compiler of the Bobbio Missal to have been working largely from a liturgical collection from Agaune, one might have hoped to find some verbal connection with Avitus' homily for the dedication of the monastery.[34] The absence of such a connection adds to the point suggested earlier, on grounds of the lack of any reference to the Theban legion, that the influence of Agaune on the Missal, while present, is limited. At the same time the precise point that there is nothing in the manuscript reflecting the peculiar monastic liturgy of Agaune itself, the *laus perennis*,[35] could be explained away by the fact that a liturgy dependent on squadrons of monks performing without interruption would have been useless to anyone outside a

---

[33] Avitus of Vienne, *Hom.* 17. This traditional identification is denied by J.-F. Reynaud, *Lyon (Rhône) aux premiers temps chrétiens: basiliques et nécropoles*, Guides archéologiques de la France (Paris, 1986), p. 131. Unfortunately Reynaud seems to have been unaware of the Life of Marcellus of Die, which mentions the queen's foundation of a church of St Michael in Lyons: *Vita Marcelli*, c. 9, ed. F. Dolbeau, 'La Vie en prose de Saint Marcel, évêque de Die', *Francia* 11 (1983), pp. 97–130. The traditional identification is upheld by Favrod, *Histoire politique du royaume burgonde*, pp. 368–71, although it must be said that there is no indication in Avitus' homily that he is celebrating a royal foundation. Moreover, Favrod's insistence on the rarity of dedications to St Michael in the west is overstated, and it is not impossible that there was more than one church dedicated to the archangel in the Burgundian kingdom. On Caretena see also G. Kampers, 'Caretena – Königin und Asketin', *Francia* 27 (2000), pp. 1–32.

[34] Avitus of Vienne, *Hom.* 25, ed. Peiper, pp. 145–6.

[35] Rosenwein, 'Perennial prayer at Agaune'; on *Hom.* 25, see the comments of Shanzer and Wood, *Avitus of Vienne, Prose Works*, pp. 377–81.

monastery following that particular practice. As already stated, most studies of the Missal have accepted that it appears to be a priest's mass book, and not for use in a monastic community.

Thus far I have concentrated on possible indications of connections between the texts in the Bobbio Missal and the known religious culture of the Rhône valley, especially in the days of Gundobad and Sigismund. I wish now to turn to a liturgical practice instigated in the Rhône valley, which is also recorded in the Missal – but only in such a way as to suggest that the liturgy in the manuscript differed significantly from that practised in Vienne and Lyons: Rogation. As we have seen, the Rogations, which were three days of prayer leading up to Ascension, were instituted by Bishop Mamertus of Vienne in the third quarter of the fifth century.[36] They quickly spread throughout Gaul. The tale of their institution is told both by Avitus[37] and also by his older relative Sidonius Apollinaris.[38] The prayers of the Rogations were essentially penitential litanies, intended to avert catastrophe: a recreation of the penance of the Ninevites. Sidonius explains clearly what was different between the old Rogation ceremonies and those instituted by Mamertus.[39] In a letter to his friend Aper, he points out that all could join in the Mamertan Rogations, while the previous ceremonies, which had been intended specifically to pray either for rain or sunshine, did not please the potter and the gardener at the same time. Despite this, it is precisely these old Rogations which seem to be invoked by the *Missa in Litaniis* in the Bobbio Missal (293–9). Here the *contestatio* (299) specifically asks for rain, despite the fact that, placed as the mass is, directly before that for Ascension (300–4), the Rogations of the Bobbio Missal appear to have been celebrated on the same days of the year as those instituted by Mamertus. We, therefore, have Rogations practised at the time of year envisaged by the bishop of Vienne, but responding to older concerns to do with the weather rather than the more general repentance of the new rite.

Avitus' homily on Rogation seems to have been included in his homiliary, and not, unlike his homilies for specific occasions, in his letter collection.[40] The homiliary is preserved only as fragments, largely in works by Florus of Lyons. It is striking that there is no apparent link between any of what appear to be surviving fragments of the homiliary and the relevant masses in the Bobbio Missal. Indeed, it is striking how few of the feasts and liturgical ceremonies known to have been dealt with by Avitus appear in the Missal. There are fragments of sermons by Avitus for the *Dies Natalis Calicis*, presumably Maundy Thursday, Good Friday, Easter

[36] Hill, 'The *Litaniae maiores* and *minores*'.
[37] Avitus of Vienne, *Hom.* 6, trans. Shanzer and Wood, *Avitus of Vienne, Prose Works*, pp. 381–8.
[38] Sidonius Apollinaris, *Ep.* VII.1.    [39] Sidonius Apollinaris, *Ep.* V.14.2.
[40] I.N. Wood, 'Letters and letter-collections from antiquity to the early Middle Ages: the prose works of Avitus of Vienne', in *The Culture of Christendom*, ed. M.A. Meyer (London, 1993), pp. 29–43.

Day and the first and sixth days of Easter, the three days of Rogations, Ascension, Pentecost, the Creed and the consecration of bishops.[41] Of these feasts the Bobbio Missal includes only masses for Maundy Thursday, Good Friday, Easter Day and the first day of Easter, one day of Rogation, Ascension and the *Traditio Symboli*. The implication is of a different set of priorities in the two liturgical calendars. Moreover, the absence of any reference in these Avitus fragments to the lections prescribed in the Bobbio Missal suggests that the liturgy followed by the bishop generally used a different set of readings. This may imply that for the most part the masses contained in the Missal differed from those normally celebrated in the middle Rhône valley – despite the evidence that some influence from that region is probable. One may guess that none of the lost masses of Sidonius Apollinaris is to be found in the Bobbio Missal.

The homily on the dedication of St Michael's, which I have suggested may refer to a mass contained in the Missal, is, by contrast, an occasional piece, and as such is likely to have been preserved along with the bishop's letters. The strongest indication of a link between the Missal and Avitus' sermons, therefore, comes from a work which could well have been preached before Sigismund's mother, and which would thus be associated, once more, with the royal court.

If these observations carry any weight a number of points follow. First, the case for seeing the Rhône valley as a centre of liturgical experiment in the sixth century is strengthened. That innovations in liturgy did take place in the region is known from Mamertus' Rogations and also from Sigismund's institution of the *laus perennis* at Agaune, even if rumours of Byzantine practice were of some importance in this latter case. Just to the west of the Rhône valley one might also note the rather different Rogations instituted by Gallus in Clermont, which involved a pilgrimage from Clermont to Brioude. In addition to the evidence for the practice of Rogation and for the *laus perennis* at Agaune, the homilies of Avitus of Vienne shed some further light on the liturgy of the middle Rhône, particularly with regard to church dedication. Correlation of the evidence of Avitus' writings and of the Bobbio Missal texts may also allow us to infer a certain amount of court influence, particularly with regard to the ideology of the *rex pacificus*, on liturgical developments of the period. It seems possible that concern with peace apparent in certain texts of the Bobbio Missal reflects the ideology of the courts of Gundobad and Sigismund, filtered, in the case of the *Missa sancti Sigismundi*, through the cult of the martyred king.

I conclude by reiterating a point already made at the start of this chapter: that the masses and prayers of the Bobbio Missal are taken from more than one place. I certainly have no wish to claim that the Missal is largely that of Agaune, or more

---

[41] Avitus of Vienne, *Hom.* 1–12, 16.

broadly of the Burgundian kingdom. On the other hand I hope to have suggested that there may be some traces of the liturgical world of Avitus of Vienne and more particularly of the Burgundian king Sigismund in the Bobbio Missal. The *Missa sancti Sigismundi* seems to me to lie at the end of a tradition which had its origins in the kingdom of Burgundy, where, perhaps surprisingly for a barbarian *regnum*, peace was a central point of propaganda.

# 12

## Conclusion

YITZHAK HEN AND ROB MEENS

The manuscript commonly known as the Bobbio Missal is now in the Bibliothèque Nationale de France in Paris, where it bears the shelfmark MS lat. 13246. It was copied, as suggested by McKitterick, perhaps as early as the later seventh century in south-eastern Gaul, conceivably in or around the city of Vienne. It contains a unique combination of a lectionary and a sacramentary, to which some canonical material was added, such as a penitential. At some later stage, most probably during the first half of the eighth century, several other quires were added to the original codex. These quires contain a plethora of miscellaneous material, such as a *Missa pro principe*, an abridged version of Pseudo-Theophilus' commentary on selected passages from the four Gospels, a sermon entitled *De dies malus*, the so-called *Joca monachorum*, several incantation formulae, instructions on how to celebrate a mass, an Ordinal of Christ and some computistical material.

It is clear from the various essays in the present volume that the Bobbio Missal is not an arbitrary gathering of unrelated prayers and texts. It is rather a careful compilation – a unique entity – that can profitably be studied as a reflection of the local, as well as the cultural and historical, circumstances that produced it and the text layers that lie behind it. As some of the chapters, notably those of McKitterick, Hen and Meens, have argued, the original manuscript was primarily intended as a *vade mecum* for a Merovingian priest. This priest, it appears, could have belonged to a community of clerics (which may even have been a monastery) who shared pastoral responsibilities, and offered liturgical services to the lay inhabitants of the region, as well as to monks and nuns.

The scriptorium in which the original codex was prepared may not have been so out of the way as Lowe believed. McKitterick's palaeographical analysis and Mostert's discussion of the punctuation indicate that the Bobbio Missal was produced in a centre where written tradition in book production and use of documents for legal purposes remained strong. Although the palimpsest leaves discussed by Ganz suggest that it was not a major writing centre, where fresh parchment was available in abundance, it was none the less a centre of learning, where some patristic works, such as a rare copy of Ambrose's commentary on Luke, were preserved. Moreover, the handwriting of the added quires clearly reflects palaeographical developments which were well underway in Francia during the first half of the eighth century, and the content of these quires points to a plethora of canonical and non-canonical material that was available to the compiler.

The copying of Paris, BNF lat. 13246 should not be confused with the initial composition of the various prayers and treatises included in the codex. As pointed out by several contributors the masses and prayers of the Bobbio Missal were taken from more than one source. Wood makes a forceful case for this view, by suggesting that some of the prayers in the Bobbio Missal originated in the liturgical world of Avitus of Vienne, and contain traces of the Burgundian liturgy of Agaune at the time of King Sigismund. Garrison, on the other hand, draws attention to similarities between several ideological undertones of the *Missa pro principe* and mid-eighth-century Bavarian circles. And Meens clearly illustrates how the Burgundian reform movement of the late sixth century together with some Columbanian ideas regarding the purity of monks, had quite an influence on the compiler's decisions and choice of texts. These, however, must not be taken to imply that the texts of the Bobbio Missal are a random pick and mix of older material available to their compiler. It appears that a great amount of consideration and careful thought were invested in choosing the various prayers and texts. The liturgical content of the volume enables one to stand on safer ground when characterising the Bobbio Missal as a *vade mecum* of a priest, for it contains the most crucial aids that a priest might need in order to execute his pastoral duties: a selection of prayers and reading passages for the major feasts, a *canon missae* to guide him in celebrating the mass and a penitential to assist him in administering penance. Moreover, a whole range of canonical material to instruct him on doctrinal matters was added to the original codex, and thus turned it into a more useful tool for an itinerant priest.

Yet the ingenuity and creativity of the compiler is revealed not only in the choice of texts. It is highly possible, as suggested by Hen, that some of the liturgy was composed especially for this prayer book or its exemplar, and thus reflects liturgical tendencies and peculiarities characteristic of south-eastern Gaul at the turn of the seventh century or the beginning of the eighth. Furthermore, theological and doctrinal themes, which undoubtedly preoccupied the minds of bishops and clerics in Merovingian Gaul, are also reflected in several prayers of the Bobbio Missal, and thus, as argued by Batstone, may have turned the liturgy itself into a means of propagating doctrinal and theological messages to the laity. Finally, the linguistic analyses by Rose and by Wright and Wright, reveal how profoundly dynamic and multi-layered was the Latin of the composers/compilers of the texts of both the original volume and the material appended to it.

The overall picture of the Bobbio Missal which emerges from the various chapters in this book is indeed of a composite collection of texts, carefully chosen by a cleric (or a group of clerics) for pastoral purposes. It is, one must admit, rather different from Lowe's 'romantic' impression of the shaky old cleric who hurriedly crowded into his tattered missal whatever he could find, without giving it much thought. Lowe's views of the Bobbio Missal should be understood against a double background. First, the Bobbio Missal is unique and entirely different from all the other liturgical manuscripts known to us from Merovingian Gaul, not only in its form, but also in its content.[1] Unlike the lavishly produced volumes, such as the Old Gelasian Sacramentary, the *Missale Gothicum* or the Lectionary of Luxeuil, the Bobbio Missal is very small and modest. Moreover, it was not intended for use in a large ecclesiastical institution, and it contains many non-liturgical texts, 'much more than properly belonged there' according to Lowe.[2] Indeed, when compared with the splendid Merovingian sacramentaries of the late seventh and eighth century, the Bobbio Missal seems poor and unpretentious. But should these Merovingian sacramentaries be the yardstick by which the Bobbio Missal is to be measured? Being the sole codex of its kind, it is impossible to gauge how widespread the production of similar *vade mecum* volumes was in late Merovingian Francia. A true comparison will be possible only after a careful re-examination of the liturgical manuscripts and fragments from the Merovingian and the early Carolingian period is completed.

Second, Lowe was a man of his generation, and that generation had a rather limited view of Merovingian culture and society. The period between the fifth and the eighth century, unjustly and anachronistically known as the 'Dark Ages', had traditionally been seen – at least since the time of Petrarch – as a period of stagnation, if not decline, in cultural activity. The reasons for that image are complex. In part, the Merovingians had fared badly because of the *damnatio memoriae* to which they were subjected by their successors, namely the Carolingians. Yet, it was also because Merovingian society and culture have been too often examined through the prism of classical culture or patristic theology, which, important and illuminating as it is, does not enlighten us about the cultural or religious situation of early medieval Francia.

Luckily research has moved forward, and scholars are becoming more and more aware of the limitations of such a comparison, which encompasses the bias and shortcomings of Renaissance and Humanistic thought. Modern scholarship is increasingly revealing how profoundly dynamic and creative the Merovingian period

---

[1] On these manuscripts, see Y. Hen, *Culture and Religion in Merovingian Gaul, A.D. 481–751* (Leiden, New York and Cologne, 1995), pp. 43–60; Y. Hen, *The Royal Patronage of Liturgy in Frankish Gaul to the Death of Charles the Bald (877)*, HBS subsidia 3 (London, 2001), pp. 28–33, and see the references cited there.

[2] Lowe, 'Palaeography', p. 106.

was,[3] and subsequently a greater degree of continuity and creativity is now widely acknowledged by historians, archaeologists and literary critics. We hope that the various essays collected in this volume have managed to demonstrate, each in its own particular field of interest, that far from representing an age of obscurity and decline, the Bobbio Missal is one of the most eloquent witnesses to the vitality and creativity of Merovingian culture.

[3] See, for example, P.J. Geary, *Before France and Germany. The Creation and Transformation of the Merovingian World* (New York and Oxford, 1988); E. James, *The Franks* (Oxford, 1988); I.N. Wood, *The Merovingian Kingdoms, 450–751* (London and New York, 1994); *Die Franken Wegbereiter Europas*, ed. A. Wieczorek *et al.*, 2 vols. (Mainz, 1996); *The World of Gregory of Tours*, ed. K. Mitchell and I.N. Wood (Leiden, Boston and Cologne, 2002).

# Index of manuscripts

# General index

9 780521 126915